Don't Start Me Talking

Interviews with Contemporary Poets

Edited by

TIM ALLEN & ANDREW DUNCAN

Interviews conducted by: Tim Allen, Andrew Duncan,
Steve Pereira, M.P. Ryan and R.F. Walker

SALT

CAMBRIDGE

PUBLISHED BY SALT PUBLISHING
PO Box 937, Great Wilbraham PDO, Cambridge CB1 5JX United Kingdom

First published 2006

Printed and bound in the United Kingdom by Lightning Source

Typeset in Swift 9.5 / 13

ISBN-13 978 1 84471 079 9 paperback
ISBN-10 1 84471 079 3 paperback

Salt Publishing Ltd gratefully acknowledges
the financial assistance of Arts Council England

1 3 5 7 9 8 6 4 2

Don't Start Me Talking

TIM ALLEN lives in Plymouth, he is the editor of *Terrible Work* a major online poetry reviews magazine. Allen is the author of two pamphlets, *Texts For A Holy Saturday* (Phlebas 1996) and *The Cruising Duct* (Maquette 1998) and his poetry has been featured in mags such as *First Offense*, *Oasis* and *Shearsman*. His essays have appeared in *Binary Myths* (Stride) and *Eratica* magazine.

ANDREW DUNCAN studied as a mediaevalist and started writing in punk fanzines. He has been publishing poetry since the late 70s, including *In a German Hotel*, *Anxiety Before Entering a Room*, *Sound Surface*, *Surveillance and Compliance*, and most recently *The Imaginary in Geometry*. He was one of the editors of *Angel Exhaust* and has translated much modern German poetry.

To David Herd and Robert Potts — visionary editors for a new sight

Contents

Introduction

Words are an archaic system, full of ambiguity. Modern poetry, rather consistently, strives to follow and enhance this ambiguity. Each line opens a number of pathways. Different readers follow different pathways. Their choice then predisposes them to certain responses to succeeding lines. Readers diverge—without failing, without breaking the rules, without missing the impact or the point. Where the evidence you collect always proves your initial suppositions right, you can, instead, move through the poetry to a world of your own. Permissiveness and suggestibility go together. Suggestive verbal patterns allow free interpretation and increase diversity. This landscape of conjecture, rapid leaps of intuition, self-reference, and shifting values, is the inside of the poems as well as the outside they swim through. Everyone follows the path which suits them.

In the 1970s, there was a great increase in the complexity of English poetry. Several dozen modern-style, ambiguous poets created a burst of unique trajectories—a real landscape to sustain the freedom designed at the start. This left much of the audience behind, and prose commentary was desirable. Prynne was against explaining anything (and in favour of resistance and difficulty), while Mottram when taking over *Poetry Review* got rid of the reviews and began just listing published works. This evacuation of the mediating space, of prose and instruction, by the leaders of the scene, possibly influenced everyone else away from explaining things. The brain produces this rich suggestibility—if it is held back by fatigue, or by rage and resentment, it will fail to respond to the words and lines at all. That is, the reader collaborates in the production of the text-response. The poem is inaudible until the reader creates it. It has much less sensory existence than music or painting—which may be why the institutions have not accepted modernity in poetry in the way they have, for example, in the visual arts. A number of conservative critics specialise in destructive un-readings of artistic texts. There is modern poetry, and writing which presents itself as the theory of modern literature, but the latter does not account for the former by any applicable standards. For whatever reasons, reviewing did not flourish in the underground scene. The series of interviews which Mottram carried out at the National Poetry Centre (which were published at the time in *Poetry Information*) were gleaming exceptions. It may in fact be that reading modern poetry in large quantities is the only effective preparation for reading any single text of modern poetry. The nucleus of prose explaining modern British poetry is, along with issues of *Spanner* magazine, certain interviews—read and re-read by the interested. Some which have become modern classics are ones with Roy Fisher, Peter Riley, and Ken Smith. We began to collect interviews with poets in September 2003.

The scene needs a Fable in which a great innovator is scorned by the fogey-ogres for many years and then wins all the prizes, as part of a needed argument against the fogey-ogres. This fable has outlived the status and shared values which it relies on. There is a pressure on the poetic 'underground' to form stable scales of value in order to show unity in verbal struggles against the mainstream. This may blur the structural inconsistency and nonconformism within the scene. There is a problem, evidently, in saying 'all aesthetic values are uncertain and sociologically conditioned' and, simultaneously, 'our sector is aesthetically superior and this is a fact we all agree on'. There is some kind of consensus about the importance of Raworth, Allen Fisher, and Prynne. But this is very different from the kind of consensus which existed at earlier stages of society—or the kind which features in the fantasies of acclaim of adolescent poets. No-one is bound by it. The institutions have yet to accept the innovators of the 1960s, or unclench the prizes for them.

Someone did a count and found over 2000 new books of poetry being published in a year. This suggests maybe 20,000 in a ten-year period. You have to decide not to read most of these. The key decisions are all made on the basis of no evidence. Of course this makes poets miserable. There is a traffic in reputation which lets you decide what not to read—and which is based on superficial stylistic signs, not on deep reliable knowledge. Poets develop stylistic assets in the hope that they will be recognised as owning those assets, that these assets will form a reputation in the world for them, that a group will use those assets to form its selective consumption choices. All of this is chancy, unreliable.

Theory fails to be useful as theory if it fails various tests. For example, it may be explanations about poetry being written in around 1914, which is masquerading as a theory of modern poetry. Or, it may ignore all salient questions. Or, it may address texts which are of very faint interest. Or, it may be one-dimensional, focussing on one factor, over which it feels a kind of ownership, while obscuring the fact that poetic attention is many-dimensional and a poet has to manage a many-dimensional array of stimuli. Or, it may deal with planes of existence which are not really literary and which have little to say about whether a text is good or bad, or what helps us to understand it. Or, it may provide an explanation of something which is not happening in any really existing poems.

There are now thousands of poets writing. We didn't interview all of them. The selection process was not especially robust. Quite probably, hundreds of poets would have given interesting interviews. It would be pleasant to say that 'folks, there are another 90 interviews on the way, so don't worry about the gaps', but the usual material problems of exhaustion, satiation, etc. inhibit this. The selection procedure is probably worth discussing briefly. We drew up a short list because we knew there would only be room for 25–30 interviews. The names on the list were based on intuition, partiality, decades of alternating pleasure and frustration, pre-rational all-over washes of feeling. Where there were recent and readily available interviews, we moved on. For example, a whole book of Allen Fisher interviews is announced (from Salt Publishing). Some poets, though, were excluded on qualitative grounds. We didn't want to read texts which were close to application forms, fliers for gigs, book jackets, and other publicity material. It seemed possible to interview some mainstream poets, for contrast, but looking at published interviews made it seem that some people who write conventionally can't even articulate their prejudices in a cogent way. Theory can be bureaucratic. Granting bodies set criteria in search of accountability. They make these criteria public, to achieve fairness. Grant-seeking professional poets register the criteria and compose their work to fulfil them. They spend many days a year filling in grant application forms, matching their work to the criteria. Eventually—and increasingly since 1974 or so—composing the work came to be an extension of filling in the forms, and the criteria became the generative nucleus of the work. We have chosen not to interview such poets. We believe that it would be better to publish the grant application forms. Such people do not have conversations, they practice networking and do validation. This was one of the tests. Another was the willingness to talk in serious terms, rather than to deflect all questions in favour of giggling inanity. Another was the ability to articulate thought processes. In the upshot, we were talking to a tiny area of conscious innovators.

Some kind of theoretical background has been supplied by M. P. Ryan's classic doctoral thesis on *Career Patterns in Contemporary Poetry*. 'The system which produces, disseminates, and evaluates poems can be seen as a loose network or sets of networks characterised by both co-operation and competition. Historically, it must not be conceived as a stable system in which each state evolves from the preceding state, but as [. . .] an interaction of adaptive and fluctuating forces[.]' (p.394) Further, 'the condition of poetry resembles Kuhn's description of science in a 'pre-paradigmatic period': insecurity, random selection from a wide range of models, continual debate over methods, and a proliferation of theories 'with the incompleteness of logical contact that consistently characterises paradigm debates'.' (p.403) Ryan is not implying that a state with a shared paradigm of values is on its way. This is a most unlikely outcome. The remark about *a wide range of models* means that poets, and readers, have no shared standard of values. The implication for a poet is that their ascribed 'value' shoots up and down in size as they pass from one room to another, or even as they cross one room. One faction of people thinks they're great—another faction thinks they're mediocre, grandiose, or out of date. The discontinuity exists at the level of microsocial space. Poets have in fact to impose a solidity on the fleeting vapours of beauty and opinion in order to retain psychological and linguistic cohesion. They wish—I suspect—for a book they've written to have a stable value, and to retain that value still 20 years later. They want to achieve status. That is, they wish for the shimmering multiplicity of values to stop when it reaches their door.

There is an unambiguous winner from the collapse of norms and genre conventions: the individual. Free will, arbitrary and unimpaired, has accumulated rights to air, sea, and underground, its rivals set aside by enactment. A landscape has been emptied for the individual to fill with constructions, as bold and highly organised as they can manage. The quality of language is that air gives way in whichever way you push it. For the onlooker, everything has become symptomatic: the limits of the work show the limits of the poet's energy, as the secret core of fatigue, creativity, hope, is blown up and ruthlessly externalised in a totalized readability. Performance implies competition and assets. In an earlier period, and probably outside England, the poet used a language associated with the court or local nobility, and recorded the deeds and feelings and possessions of those people. The poem acquired a value from real social power. In an individualist society, the stress of the poem is all loaded on the individual; the reader makes up the values (of the style and feelings of the poem) freely and arbitrarily. The contemporary poet cannot make do with original variations on inherited norms, but has to make up and learn the procedures by which the poem is generated. The choice of procedures is arbitrary—but can be good or bad. The poem is self-referential—a circularity which, used as a unit structure, may be as robust as Flemish bond in bricks. The poem is 'validated' by tests—which readers impose and which are themselves circular and self-referential.

We asked poets to give close and prolonged attention to their own texts. Attention is a pure good. What brings states of high attention, is successful as art without further ado. It is perverse to try and prove that someone's attention was misdirected. No, reading something is misdirected because of the states of inattention, somnolence, blur, which it induced. There is a circularity in the situation where someone perceives something vividly because they are in a high attentional state, and are in a highly attentive state because they perceive a cognitive object or set vividly. I believe this circle is at the core of poetry, and there is nothing to be gained by tearing it open and spilling its contents. Social cueing is central to these heightened states—humans copy the eagerness of other humans. The poet is someone with unusual control of the subliminal cues which set off emotional states. Identification, belonging, attention, and boundaries are related concepts, in an area subject to *skill*.

One of the features of the poetry scene is a dual optic. Readers behave differently towards poets (and their utterances) depending on whether they regard the poet as part of their in-group or not. Complicity is close to the circularity we have just noted. Grounds for criticising the intense identification of a reader with a poet are weak. The goal of poetry is to achieve complicity—shared attention to real or symbolic objects. It is unrealistic to aim for a unified optic which simultaneously is with the poet and not-with them. We believe more in the existence of finite optics, and of borders between them as fascinating transit zones. Conflict is traditionally a source of lyric poetry. There are reasons for thinking that good poems are found where two frames of perception meet. What a problem must ensue when we come to talk about the experience afterwards. This sharing may simply fail to work.

Poets may ask themselves technical questions, but the main question for them is 'how can I make this poem wonderful?', and the more answers they find, the more often they ask the question. The question for the interview is then 'why *is* your poetry so wonderful'. This turns on powerful inhibitions, and many of the poets fall dumb at this point. The interview has to find a path of indirect questions which may allow the poet to speak.

Marion Milner's wonderful book *On Not Being Able to Paint* talks about the drawings she made (while unable to *paint*) and gives the stories she wrote down to explain the drawings: 'that yellow cliff on the left with its curious lines like hieroglyphic writing, it makes me think of Cleopatra's needle [. . .] in the bulge of the cliff, is a shape like [. . .] the flint heart in that fairy tale[.]' It turns out the milling equipment is there to break down the cliff, as the substance of rational authority, and turn it into a drink which she swallows. This kind of simultaneous interpretation points away from the usefulness of theory: there is no general story which fits every poem, rather art is a breakout into an uncoded universe where meaning is free and is generated by the processes of consciousness at every step, in a resistless flow. The objects are not the same as the meanings, and the poem may point to something larger than itself.

Some of the information found in the interviews adds to the poems, or to the images found inside them, like Milner's stories. The words go together to exclude some possibilities, but do not cut the meanings down to a single one. This loss of constraint may bear a structural relationship to the excess load of constraint characterising the poem at other levels of organisation: a line of verse has to pass various tests to be properly poetic. Perhaps the soaring release of the semantic level is hidden behind this constraint, which protects it.

A key failing of certain poets is perhaps their belief that introducing objects ties down and stabilises the poem, the irrefutability of the objects making the poem itself irrefutable (and authentic): whereas the meaning of objects is freely assigned and constantly re-assigned. Objects are common in symbolic discourse because they can be *assigned* meanings. Human beings give time to their objects because they are pliable to human purposes. Then, a cliff is something you can drink.

Readers may actually resent the idea that a poem does not unwrap itself ready for consumption. They could object to poet interviews, for this reason. Perhaps the stories the poets provide are better than the stories which other people, for whatever reasons, tell about them.

The topic of procedures appears in several interviews. This is something little understood by poets under 40. There seems to have been a division of assets, whereby the conceptual set of ideas have been cherished and made central by visual artists, but have disappeared from the collective memory of poetry. But without a grasp of the procedural approach it is impossible to understand poets like Andrew Crozier and Allen Fisher. Searching for autobiographical situations which would explain the configuration of poems like *Place Book I* can lead to the creation of mountains of conjectural and wrong interpretations.

I have to say that the jackets of books are systematically unreliable. This wouldn't matter if there were decent reviews too. As things stand, the blurb texts make the landscape even more treacherous—pitted with lies, disinformation, disbelief, pseudo-events. If you tell the truth (about a wonderful book) it *sounds like* the lies on book jackets; familiar and used up.

Rigour is the vehicle which takes the poet to an unheard of and transformed landscape. But the poet has to transcend themselves—suspending this internal rigour in order to admire, accurately, other sets of procedures.

Because diversity causes incomprehension, cultural managers have wanted to eliminate diversity. The most authoritative and institutionalised critics have striven to eliminate everything except one central, crushed tradition of 'Englishness' 'common sense' 'littleness' 'irony'. Having rooted out ambiguity, they then wonder where the poetry has gone to. The lack of consensus is why we have to go back to primary witnesses—interviews where poets speak for themselves.

Peter Ryan's framework, then, gives us a context in which it would be quite undesirable to look for convergent patterns in the interviews. Something we could have researched—but didn't, for reasons you now know—was whether this divergence and scatter have increased since 1976–8, when Ryan was doing his research. My belief is that it has. I certainly don't anticipate that the balkanized environment which Eric Homberger complained of, around that time, is going to turn back into an empire—that the scattered shells are going to re-form into one heavenly dome. No, no, my message is 'learn Serbo-Croat'.

It is difficult to go through the experience of your 'size' shooting up and down all the time. What we call paranoia would be a quite common response. That is, someone is paranoid in a limited context, not about the whole of life. *Scurra* is a kind of minstrel, a performer of poetry. Maybe the scurrilous is a vital function of poets. The terrible truth is that, if you record a thousand scurrilous stories about the scene, a lot of truth is in them, and material you don't get from any other angle. I really enjoy those stories. Rowlandson and Hogarth are not simply distorting reality—their gaze pierces right to the core. Breton's description (in the incomplete *Third Surrealist Manifesto*) of Dali as 'Avida Dollars' is a brilliant moment, a proof that the surreal is more real than the real. But there are convincing reasons for not putting these tales into print. High quality information must come first. Scurrility provokes damaging loyalty contests in which groups polarise and form gangs. They turn cruelty into the most admired act, the one most often recalled in gossip and anecdote.

Ryan does not say why the phenomena he discusses should be seen as a system. Would this not suggest something where the parts relate to each other and are somehow different from what is happening outside them? It may be better to think of an ocean of speech, mutating and self-generating, of which some parts are written down and classified as poetry. This speech ocean would be like photography. A camera gives someone the power to record snatches of the visible but does not lock them into a system of 'photographic art'. Most of the innovations in 20th century poetry have been aimed at making the medium quicker and easier to use—like cameras. There are so many gates which the medium has gone through to exit into a wide and boundless plain; and so few rectifiers, where individuals pass through and become more like each other. Does it really make sense to discuss 'poetry' separately from speech in general, from its subject matter, from the speech networks the poets are listening and speaking inside? Does it make sense to put, say, Allen Fisher, Peter Redgrove, and Robert Crawford into one category, as if there were some poem-base which they are all writing variations on?

Ryan's thesis has interviews with poets born roughly 1905 to 1942, and a restricted description of the present book is, interviews with poets born 1936 to 1973. Although there are 'clusters of ideas in the air and informing cultural decisions', and these are temporary, we are wary of leaping from that to saying that everyone going through a formative phase in 1980 went through the same cluster of ideas. Given that poets hang out in small groups, it is worth looking for possible similarities based on closeness in space; and the interviews go into the scenes in particular towns in some detail.

TIM ALLEN INTERVIEWED BY ANDREW DUNCAN

Get the Lute, Go Up the Soak

from Sea ExChange

Come and sea what I'm doing

Kingdom of the shoreline—bountiful and solemn

Between high and low watermark my solemn and seductive

kingdom delicately scrapes

Cramp (severe), title (clichéd), grit (untrue)

Amphibian syntax flows, looks up

Your dream was of a scruffy shambles (a realism made of

newspaper)

Zimmerman was a zephyr and the zephyr was zebra meat

A California populated by fire extinguishers where fridges suffer

multiple strokes

Deluxe algae gesticulating at quarrelling Red-Cross and St John's

Ambulance camps

An underneath *a* egg an even larger ego makes do—mesmeric

and sober

Endurance swimmer's digits in splints of sprinting dust—well,

the logistics of dust

A body in a sack is the only subject in this kingdom

Smell the tower of scrambled egg and rank towels from a

different downstairs

Left Althusser on the seawall then went home to study an

alternative edge

Stiff neat and a morsel dissimilar I mothballed myself while

hallucinogenic wars raged

I've a garden a yard a garage a drive a pond a lake a sea a hard-

standing but no house

The beaches in this garden are an isomorphic commonwealth

From the ledge of silver lining a wreck watches what I'm doing

on the ledge of golden braid

Out of my own reach I sack my own adjectival city (mutinous

wistful rags)

Ages ago in the ancient of days when ridiculous creatures

attacked each other's beds

Animals and their friends—wings abstract and eyes hefty

Patience of minutes and hours then sudden storm of dishonesty

After-dinner speech and maggots

Clouds of livestock rise darken and piss things down—on us

Rude realm of frozen white rum mistaken for vodka-in-a-basket

DUNCAN This is poetry quite heavy on procedures, and I think it would
be helpful to be as explicit as possible. Can you tell us about these
procedures?

ALLEN Andrew, that is probably one of the most difficult questions you could possibly have opened with because for me a procedure is a way of witnessing control, it is not a question of having any real control yourself and that turns the 'explicit' into a secret, secret even to me. On the surface however, among the multiplicity of possible procedures, I choose one, and the realisation of that, the pausing between one poem and the next, is enough to move me away from any notion of the naturally spontaneous as a pre-determined frame and move towards the idea that a more programme-orientated poetic procedure could shape the frame in which the spontaneous could breathe and come to life. But it was never that self-conscious, and there's the problem. I always was instinctively procedural, the difference was that as a young poet I fantasised an authorial power over what I was writing but when I got older it amused me greatly to discover such a gap between what I thought I was doing and what actually appeared on the page. Ironically, it was that realisation that exerted a small, yet highly significant, degree of control and that came in the form of arbitrary, yet clearly defined, procedures. Now, 99% of what I write fits into one procedural frame or another. For example in my *Settings* sequence I lay out a set of rules which included writing roughly a half-page of A4 in prose paragraphs which would each contain some philosophic (Pataphysic if you like) question/s written down as a quite obvious and careless verbalisation. These would be 'set' against other things, real things, unreal things, meanings, unmeanings. The aim was to entertain myself and feel good by producing a block of word-art that looked like every other block of word-art. They look like prose poems, probably smell like them too, but I don't consider them as such because if they are prose poems then they are bad prose poems, and I happen to think they are quite wonderful.

DUNCAN I think the publication record may be a bit incomplete. Can you talk us through your work as written? Give us a guide?

ALLEN Publication record? That's a laugh. A spineless little book appeared in '95, *Texts For A Holy Saturday*, published by Phlebas, the same imprint that published people like Martin Hibbert and A.C. Evans, and *The Cruising Duct*, published by Andy Brown's Maquette in '98, before he went mainstream. Otherwise it is just a flurry—blizzard if

I'm counting—of magazine appearances through the mid 90s. The only things I've had published recently have been on poetry webzines: Ethan Paquin's *Slope* (USA), Rupert Loydell's *Stride*, David Bircumshaw's *Chide's Alphabet* and John Mingay's *Raunchland* site etc. The vast bulk of my work remains unpublished in any form, quite simply because, apart from that flurry I mentioned, I do not send my work out. It is not so simple to explain why that is though. Back in the 70s I began submitting to magazines but I only chose the biggies, *London Magazine* etc., and the few exotic avant garde names I discovered, an important one being *Alembic*, edited by a young man just off the plane from Gibraltar called Ken Edwards. I got a very encouraging response from Ken who directed me to some of the more proto-surrealist mags but I never followed through. One of the problems was that at the time I was writing very little, doodling with concrete stuff, writing a haiku a month etc, in addition to which all my energy was going into schools' football and teaching long division. Through my teens I had written reams but when I hit my 20s it came to a stop and didn't start again properly until around 1980 when I reached my 30s. I then wrote a lot but I had absolutely no interest at the time in seeking publication; that always seemed to be something for the future or something that wasn't really my concern. But when I started having things published in magazines in the 90s I thought it was great. I was getting published in things like *Memes*, *Ramraid Extraordinaire*, *10th Muse*, *First Offence* etc. but after a while the thrill wore off, and many of those magazines closed down too. By the late 90s I had become thoroughly unimpressed by the majority of little magazines around, all dominated by the domestic realism of the New Poetic, and I lost my enthusiasm again. The only ones my work occasionally appeared in then were *Oasis* and *Shearsman*. Ian Robinson was very enthusiastic about my work and wanted to publish a collection of my prose poems but I didn't get them organised. Then he was going to publish *Sea ExChange* but the poem became too big. Then he died. He was a lovely man and he did so much for poets and poetry—very sad.

DUNCAN I appreciate this may tend to pack everything safely back inside a biographical narrative, but I'm curious to know how you got to this realm, certainly rather far away from most English poetry of the day. How did you get there?

ALLEN I got there principally through an early obsession with surrealism and a consequent love of modern French poetry in translation. This was tempered later by ancient Chinese and American postmodernism. I always loved the strange, the surprising. Rimbaud was to blame. I think around 1966 I bought the Penguin Rimbaud and Alvarez' *The New Poetry* within weeks of each other and there was no contest. I was doomed. This is not to say that I was not impressed by Hughes, Plath and co., I certainly was, still am, but nothing they wrote got to me in the same way as Rimbaud (or Oliver Bernard actually) writing, 'On the slope of the bank, angels turn their robes of wool in pastures of steel and emerald.' There were many reasons for that of course, conditioners: catholic childhood, the Isle of Portland where I was brought up, my rebellious Irish mother, red in hair and politics. Before that my imagination had been focussed by science fiction, or what we were calling Speculative Fiction back then; I used to send short stories to Michael Moorcock's *New Worlds* and get lovely chatty rejection letters from him saying that I was basically writing poems, not stories. So around that time, I was a 16 year old working in W.H. Smiths in Weymouth, I made two 'bad' choices as a writer, I moved away from S.F. into poetry and in poetry I was swept away from the fast mainstream into the nutrient rich but isolated dark pools of foreign modernism. And basically I stuck with it, because I had found something that matched my inner life.

DUNCAN Don't think the name Zimmerman is there by accident (at start of *Sea ExChange*). Let me cite 'Yeah heavy and a bottle of bread' ('Call zoot get a mute and go and catch a trout'.) Am I right to think of Blonde on Blonde, the Basement Tapes, and that whole free-association period around 1966–8?

   Sea ExChange seems quite close to oral procedures—autonomous phrases which could be made up by musicians in an improvised exchange, for example. Each line is lavishly unpredictable with respect to the previous one, but also there is some kind of flow of mood. Maybe we could shed light on it by discussing the opposite kind of poetry, where each line is locked to the previous one in a situation, and the situation is locked in place by a whole notion of social realism and conventions of behaviour, a kind of closed circuit of increasing predictability.

ALLEN First, you are right, Zimmerman is not there by accident; the entire poem, the poem as it was before it was written if you like, is 'concerned' with one of Dylan's songs. I say 'concerned' but it isn't really the right word, I haven't got the right word for it. And yes, that free-association period of his was very important for me, big entertainment . . . I was going to say 'and big influence' but that would not be right either, there was too much of a parallel to be influenced. What I was though was curious, not about where it was coming from, I understood that, I was curious to know where it was going, in the sense of its poetry—what sort of a poetry could actually be developed from that etc? I remember reading an article by Lee Harwood back in the mid 70s in which he talked about the redundancy of still writing surrealist poetry in the manner of the 1930s, about how he was looking for new ways to carry on such projects. I agreed strongly and in Lee's own work and Raworth's and Ashbery's I experienced such examples for the first time. I realised I was not alone, I had cousins, but nevertheless I had to find my own way and *Sea ExChange*, written some 20 years later, was the culmination of that going alone. So, as you pointed out earlier, I ended up writing a very different poetry to that being written in Britain today, the distance between something like *Sea ExChange* and the stuff that wins T.S. Eliot prizes cannot be exaggerated. Yet, ironically, there was a time in the mid 80s when I was actually writing some things that were not too far removed from what the early Northern School were up to, so I think I understand, even appreciate it to an extent. Whether such poetry is, as you call it, the opposite of what I do, I am not sure. Can there be an opposite of such things? Even when you say that 'each line is locked to the previous one in a situation' I wonder, because in a sense so are mine, but not 'locked' in the same way of course. However, when you say that in such poetry, 'the situation is locked in place by a whole notion of social realism and conventions of behaviour, a kind of closed circuit of increasing predictability' I have to agree, though I think there is a problem with the term social realism. The trouble is, I do not think there is anything inherently wrong in a poem being 'locked in place by a whole notion', whatever the notion is of, and neither do I find anything inherently wrong in a closed circuit. My problem with such poetry is more to do with the predictability itself, and what I see as a bad faith within the poetic, resulting in either a flawed finished product or a paltry one. From my point of view the flaw is more to do with the ideology of transparency that lurks behind the material than with the mechanics of the material itself. I actually consider modern British mainstream poetry to be the anomaly, stunted growth etc—what I write is normal, as obvious to me as cheese.

DUNCAN What poetry are you working on at the moment?

ALLEN Recently I've been working on a new sequence, provisionally titled *The Failure of Myth*, in which I find myself dealing with the politics of popular music along with the philosophical problem posed by our co-existence with animals. However, those subjects are not there for their own sake—though everything is for its own sake in a sense, that's where its concrete value lives—but they are there as things that give access to my on-going critique of cool human value, cool in the sense of *birth of the cool* etc. I never approach anything directly—I'm a crab. But I'm also still trying to complete/fine-tune a number of long poems I've been working on for the last decade. They are all problematic for one reason or another, for example there is a poem called *Glitches and Quicksand* which arose out of my negative engagement with post-modernism, especially regarding political anger and the impossibility of redressing injustice—Ben Watson read a huge chunk out on his Resonance FM programme—I was really chuffed. Its structure is similar to *Sea ExChange* in that it uses discrete lines but unlike *Sea ExChange* it uses quasi repetition: the same basic packet of words is exhausted by shuffling them into every possible order, whereas in *Sea ExChange* the opposite happens, the same image is constantly shuffled into fresh words—which is where your earlier comment about jazz is relevant.

DUNCAN Because the home of language is inside social networks, I'm curious to find out about social networks around poetry. We may have heard a little too much about the groups in London and Cambridge. We'll get on to 'distance' networks in a minute. But, can you talk about the Plymouth scene? There seems to be a lot going on down there.

ALLEN Coincidence, that's all. I came to live and work in Plymouth as a Primary School teacher, Norman Jope was born and brought up here and Steve Spence arrived at some point etc. People do things and then things start to happen. The difference in this case was that although on the outside the things we did were no different to any other provincial grouping—poetry circle, discussions, performances in local hall, magazines—, on the inside we were all coming from somewhere else; our tastes and enthusiasms were not staple fare. We all had working-class backgrounds, were obsessed with poetry, never had academic jobs, took our writing very seriously, none of us considered it a hobby for example, and we all had a healthy disrespect for the cut and colour of Andrew Motion's ironed jeans.

There are other circumstances though which gave our mini social group an edge; Plymouth is not a cultural city, it is predominantly working class and its history is tied up with the Navy and defence, so it is essentially a 'conservative' working-class city. It therefore does not have a large enough liberal-minded middle-class to sustain, with any strength, the kinds of literary groups which would act as on-going filterers of current establishment poetic fashions, values and concerns. Its middle class is large enough to support a theatre and numerous drama and music groups, but poetry is a minority sport here as everywhere else, so when Kenny Knight and myself took over the reins of the only poetry group in town, the Swarthmore Poets, in 1990, we had a bit of a fight on our hands but nothing too dramatic, as, to put it simply, mainstreamers with any gumption were too thin on the ground. The other factor is the West Country itself, both with regard to its idiosyncrasies and its distance from London and the North. Distances are psychological as well as geographical, they tend to make people think they are different even when they aren't: whatever was happening in London tended to happen here five years after and the whole movement of poetry through the 90s was centred on the North anyway, even further away. The west country is rural, for a long time now it has acted as a magnet for a certain mind-set wanting to move out of the smoke so its scattered literati are more inclined to be New Age sympathisers with a bent towards the mystical than they are to be street-wise rappers or theoretical avants—most of this is thin coating but such thin coating does its job, people act out roles, and in the end it comes down to numbers. So in a place like Plymouth, an urban island in all this, we actually get a very good mix of different poetries without any being dominant. In some places that can lead to bland neutrality but one of the things our organisations have fostered here, first through the Poetry Exchange and now with The Language Club, is a kind of hard-edged eclectic dynamic that tends to dramatise and have fun with difference; similar, though less confrontational, to what I did with *Terrible Work* on a larger scale.

DUNCAN Can you shed light on the history of poetry in the south-west? What was happening down there in the 60s, or the 70s?

ALLEN I have no idea about the 60s. I know that in the early 70s things started happening in Bridport, Dorset, around Elsa Corbluth—they published a poem by my mate David. At some point *Westwords* appeared, edited from Plymouth by David Woolley and, more importantly, *South West Review*, which at different times was edited by Owen Davis and Ken Smith, before Smith hit it relatively big time. *South West Review* was published from Exeter and had Arts Council funding. It provided a good sampling of that eclectic mix I mentioned above but at the time I perceived it as middle class mild artiness smeared with the quirky, which is very unfair I know, especially as it was probably the first place I read work by the likes of Maggie O'Sullivan. To be honest I didn't take much notice. Looking back now I can see why such magazines lacked focus, it was because there wasn't one, the thing was too diffuse. In the late 80s and 90s the main New Age focus was centred around Gloucestershire with Jay Ramsay and in the east of the region a lot of magazines appeared around a kind of artificial 'south' thing but talking about that will lead us into the messy issues around Andy Jordan's 'archetypical poetry' scam and 'Charles Mintern'. Today there is relative richness: Shearsman, Stride, etruscan. There are other scenes of course: Harry Chambers with his mainstream publishing enclave, Peterloo, but we might as well be at different ends of the country for all the contact we've had. Then there's *Acumen* magazine, but again, contact is minimal—Patricia Oxley said my work was on a different planet. The Apples and Snakes performance crew have set up shop here recently too, so there is some energy, though I think of it as electricity going through a dummy. And there's Dartington ... ummm, where you put a promising young writer in at one end and get something strange, shiny and unusable out the other. Hey, don't print that ... some people don't have a sense of humour.

DUNCAN *Terrible Work* struck me as a very broad-spectrum magazine in which, rather evidently, your receptive capability was many miles broader than your active predilections as a poet. The 'lines of division' are much on people's minds just now, and will predetermine, for one thing, the way this book is received and even the way most people will choose not to read it. How did you and Steve Spence bring this off with *Terrible Work*, and how do you feel about polarisation?

ALLEN *Terrible Work*'s 'broad-spectrum' was relative, there were plenty of people around who considered it anything but broad-spectrum, but yes, from my perspective it was certainly eclectic, and purposely so. From the beginning I did not want it to be an avant garde ghetto. I was dismayed by what I saw at the time as the closed-shop attitude of the British avant garde which was in danger of dying out through excessive in-breeding. Young poets especially were almost entirely ignorant of it and excluded from it and yet they were actually looking for alternative models and tracks which could give them the confidence to fend off the influence of the Northern School on one hand and the starry-eyed neo-platonists on the other. There was a lot of wasted energy too, in young poets reinventing the wheel by doing things which they thought were radical and original but were in fact staple modernist old-hat. The atomisation of the British poetry scene went very deep yet there was no hint of it in most of the commentaries and even those who were in a position to know didn't seem to care, as long as their corner was doing OK. I include most academics in that by the way. So I wanted *Terrible Work* to expose these gaps both in its choice of material and in its reviewing. I wanted to find out what was going on out there and bring it into the magazine: S.F. poetry came in, Redgrovian stuff, the best (I hope) of what the new-agers were up to, the more quirky edge of the Northern School, the more extreme end of the bed-sit depressives, the more politically aware and/or lexically adventurous of the urban bards, neglected hippy rants, rave generation ecstasies, unabashed lyrical poets struggling with the post-modern condition and even mainstream poems that I thought worked—*Terrible Work* gave Sophie Hannah one of her first ever platforms. And of course there was the material that, within this clash, was beginning to shine and stand out above the rest, let's use those quaint terms, 'linguistically innovative' and 'post-language'. Looking back now I can see we were gradually sloughing off some tendencies and concentrating on others but even by the final issue in 2000 the scope was unusual for a magazine considered, by then, to be experimental. I think *Terrible Work* did manage to pull-off what it intended, but at a price, and part of that price was paid by it ceasing to exist in its hard-copy poetry publishing form.

As for what I feel about polarisation, I'm all for it, as long as people can see the poles and have the occasional twirl around them. Is that too flippant? What I want is openness, honesty; we cannot solve the problems of atomisation by putting up the barricades or pretending to play happy federal families. I have found myself out on a limb as far as these things are concerned as most poetry people are either too happy to keep within their home territory, either aggressively or benignly, or they act-out a false homogeneity, especially out of career considerations. I want debate, not patronisation.

DUNCAN I suspect if I knew more about recent American poetry I would find your poetry easier to assimilate. As this is probably the key issue in infrastructure just now, can you talk to us about 'distance networks'? How did you discover the modern poetry which means most to you? Where do you buy this kind of thing? Do you publish in American magazines?

ALLEN Due to preoccupation with my family and job I lost touch with the more interesting things being written in the late 70s and 80s and because of that I missed out on the L=A=N=G=U=A=G=E explosion in the US. I was aware of the new British things to an extent, had read some Prynne and Doug Oliver for example; I was impressed and curious to know more but not exactly galvanised— when your head is full of Henri Michaux and Li Ho even the Cambridge School can seem a little tame. Then in 1990 an anthology edited by Andrei Codrescu dropped into my hands, *American Poetry Since 1970* (4 Walls 8 Windows, New York 1989). I found it fascinating, there wasn't a page that didn't thrill. It documented brilliantly the slide from late Beat through the later-New York School into Talk poetry and L=A=N=G=U=A=G=E. As I mentioned earlier, I wrote almost continually through the 80s, note books that look like jigsaws made of ink, but I had actually come to a formal impasse and was consciously casting around for clues. The effect of reading the American work was immediate and profound. I discovered poets who were doing similar things to myself but with such confidence and with such a high rate of aesthetic success, and they had been doing it for well over a decade. One of the striking differences was the self-consciousness and reflexivity of the poetry and within seconds of reading some of it I had answers to questions that had been niggling for ages. Much of that was to do with issues of reference and non-reference, though I didn't pay much attention to the theoretics because it was obvious what was going on in the work itself. It also helped me to sort out questions of form, even something as basic as the line break. And on the more philosophic side for the first time I was encountering what seemed like a genuine materialist poetics in the English language. So that was how I 'discovered the modern poetry' that means most to me, my list begins with Hejinian and Silliman and then goes on and on.

Three other things happened at the same time. Firstly my understanding of cultural theory matured; I had been reading continental philosophers for years—I read Barthes and Althusser in the early 70s for example—but suddenly it was all coming together and I was joining up the dots. I was also in the process of having a serious work-related breakdown, which finally happened in '93, forcing me out of my 9to5 profession. Thirdly, by that point I was also using a computer to write, which shifted notions of composition. And of course you cannot edit a magazine without networking, so I was already making long-distance contacts with Europe and the States and the floodgates opened. Scarcity was replaced by glut, a situation that was compounded some seven years later by e-mail and my introduction to the web. From the beginning I was astonished by the amount of work being published in America; I shouldn't have been, after all it's a big place, but it was overwhelming and a strict regime of filtering had to take place. Also, an old inferiority complex was reignited and the only hard-copy American magazine my work appeared in, to my knowledge, was *Lost and Found Times*, and that was a request from the editor. I never submitted anything, but then, I never got around to submitting anything to *Angel Exhaust* this side of the water either. My ambition has always been healthily tempered by the fact that I'm a lazy sod.

Long-distance networks have, in my opinion, changed the nature of the British avant scene, there is a sense in which it has saved it, but at cost. The cross-fertilisation between like-minded poet/academic/critics in universities in Britain and North America has rejuvenated innovation here, it has given many poets a sense of belonging to a larger group, and they no longer feel such a cornered minority. Compared with mainstream inclined poets/academics the numbers are tiny but long-distance networks have actually done very little to influence the insularity of the British mainstream; major current North American poets have not caught on here, if anything the influence seems to have gone the other way, a poet such as the very popular Billy Collins in the US appears to me to have been heavily influenced by English models. Ironically though it is Ashbery who appears alongside Bukowski on our Waterstones shelves.

Bibliography

Texts For A Holy Saturday (Phlebas, 1995).
The Cruising Duct (Maquette, 1998).

EDITOR
Terrible Work magazine 1993–2000 (with Steve Spence and Alexis
     Kirke).
Terrible Work On-line in 2002.

INTERVIEWED
Andy Brown (Ed.), *Binary Myths 1: Conversations with Contemporary
     Poets & Poet-Editors* (Exeter: Stride Publications, 1998—
     reprinted as *Binary Myths 1&2* 2004).

ELISABETH BLETSOE INTERVIEWED BY TIM ALLEN

Homoeopathic Provings
of the Cygnus Remedy

extract from Rainbarrows

deep as the North star,
I can be neither familiar nor close

margravine of desert parishes;
places become crop-mark and
                                soil-shadow,
the lazarus-rattle of dried heather
as the wind slitters off from the Purbecks

adumbratio
I am veiled in a churchyard,
masqued at tide-times, a chimæra
vitrified at the window, eclipsed
by 'disastrous twilight'

soul of all metals I am, but
'in a raw state' dreaming
the black stone of the self;
an idea seeking form as when,
above pondwater,
the ectoplasm of a projected leap
waits for a frog to flow into it

a few ounces of gorse flowers
and several parts each
    gravel, sand, clay
spread by glacial drift
    gravel-caps
plateaux separated by
slope-clays, loam-clenched fistfuls of
      shrub-tree
    cremation burials
an internal grit of crushed flint,
fragment of flanged bowl with
    painted wavilinear bands:
my stride devours the vell of the heath where
splinters of history continually discharge
at the surface of the present
    impatient   tracing the viper's keel,
slough of a lizard caught in rootwire
    a perfect replicant
Belovéd exorcist, what shall we call
this place of our rencounter?
                ('Bruaria?')
where we have never been is real

ALLEN Elisabeth, it is now over ten years since the publication of *The Regardians*, still a remarkable group of poems, and back then they were remarkable as much for the difference between what you were into, when compared with the majority of the country's poets. How do they read to you, now, and could you begin by saying something about their genesis?

BLETSOE When I finish a piece of work I tend to disassociate myself from it and move on to the next project, so now it feels like someone else wrote *The Regardians*. Of course in hindsight I wish I could have expressed myself better, but at the time I felt I achieved what I wanted for my own satisfaction. As to its genesis, obviously whatever is in my head at the moment informs my work and at that time I was studying 16th and 17th Century history, looking at works of art, literature and music as historical documents, and I was engaged with the decline of magic, religious symbolism, eschatological arguments, concepts of hell, 'Paradise Lost' and radical groups such as the Quakers and Diggers; the idea simply coalesced, with strands being pulled out from Rilke, Milton, Blake and Wenders.

ALLEN It always seemed to me, and still does, that the drive behind your work was the desire to understand symbols, utilise their power in order to produce a poetry rich with psychological resonance. Is that true? It is certainly not a poetry that speaks through any realistic reference or straightforward transfer between belief and artefact. Could you say more about these issues as they relate to *The Regardians.*

BLETSOE I was brought up on myth, fairy tale and folklore and I am fascinated by medieval codes, signs and sigils. I believe the idea is true for me, that symbols bypass the intellect and act directly on the soul. Every word, object and act has a significance that plays out in the unconscious and allows the world to burst with different levels of meaning. I'd like to think all my poetry, not just *The Regardians*, reflects that layering, the effort to grasp the meaning beyond meaning. It's fine if readers don't perceive the poems in the way I did when I wrote them, as they will bring their own archetypes and personal symbolism. I would also hope the rhythm and sound of the language I use is strong enough to stand by itself. The angels represented psychological states, turning points in my own development, feelings associated with different seasons. Angels were the most appropriate symbol I could find for the condition of being *overwhelmed*. I used them also to put across some political anxieties at the time; elements of racism and neo-fascism erupting in Cardiff in the early nineties, concerns about urban pollution and decay, general nihilism and seemingly random acts of violence. I use quite a lot of quotes in my work, this also being a different kind of symbol as the significance resides in where I've pulled them from; thus adding another level. It was interesting for me to discover that whole medieval teaching texts for initiates were composed entirely of quotes from other documents, creating an entirely new work but also leading the reader to seek further in past and current literature. Nothing should be taken at face value. There's also a sense of play in this.

ALLEN You have just described an emotionally intense yet systematically broad poetic. How did that develop? For instance I have no idea of the kind of thing you wrote before *The Regardians*. You mentioned the Quakers—your family background was Quaker wasn't it? So could you tell me more about the early work and how it changed? And were you changed by writing?

BLETSOE. I am not a birthright Quaker, but became a member of the Society of Friends as a direct consequence of the first Gulf War. The kind of work I wrote before *The Regardians* was what is now known as *Portraits of the Artist's Sister*, most of which I wrote in my late teenage years. I only write when obsessed/possessed by something; at that time it was Munch's paintings and Norwegian art generally. I wrote most of those poems close together, then for the purposes of the book I wrote a few more about a decade later, which was difficult as my style had changed with *The Regardians,* but I had to deliberately 'regress' for the sake of continuity. I was unable to write longer poems for a time, but while exploring haiku, tanka, renga etc I exploited the idea of stringing them together and developing them so that I could write beyond a short piece, which is far more satisfying to me. I like texts that can be grouped together so they can reflect and rebound from each other: they can be separate but create another whole. I think the process of being immersed in something then struggling to articulate ideas about it will change you subtly, just as you are changed in yourself by reading any text. I have long periods of not writing followed by a burst of activity— there's a line somewhere in *The Regardians*, in 'The Oary Man' about 'secret works being wrought underground', that refers on some level to nature in winter and radical movements under persecution, and also to the process of creativity. It still remains secret, even to me, somewhere in my unconscious.

ALLEN I'll return to the *Portraits* book later, but now I want to pick up on your mentioning your 'long periods of not writing followed by a burst of activity'. It is true to say, isn't it, that such periods for you are unusually long? Could you tell me more about this? What 'secret works' are currently 'being wrought underground'?

BLETSOE I'm not sure precisely what would be 'unusual', although I admit to not being especially prolific. Rilke went through a period of not writing that lasted 10 years before he produced *The Duino Elegies* though the quality of this work would suggest he'd probably been unconsciously processing and re-processing it during this time. My current project is a collection of texts connected to the landscape/ mythology of Dorset; originally it was driven by a great sense of homesickness, but now I actually live there, in a very isolated part, I strangely feel less compulsion to write about it. The work is ongoing, however; I'm absorbed in what I hope will be quite an interesting piece at present. It combines the folkloric concept of the separable soul with imagery from the homoeo-pathic provings of the Cygnus remedy; the setting is the swan herd at Abbotsbury and The Fleet.

ALLEN To be unfazed by these elapses of time between books must speak of a sound self-confidence, a confidence that stamps your work both on the page and in performance, yet your work is so passion-ate, and indeed, deals with passion itself. Most people's idea of a passionate writer is one who writes frequently and impelled, so what are your thoughts on this? Was it different when you were writing the poems that became *Portraits of the Artist's Sister*? Was it easier when you were focussing on the average-sized poem? I've just read 'Ashes' again, a poem I have heard you perform with relish a number of times and again I am struck by the precision which crafts such highly charged material.

BLETSOE Perhaps I have many other areas of my life to be passionate about that draw me away from writing! Any 'passion' evident in the work is no doubt a direct result of being withheld and then set free after some time. I wouldn't say I was 'unfazed' by the time-lapse but I have learned to accept that this is how it happens for me; I might be more so if I was bothered by ideas about reputa-tion, output, etc. I don't like to force my writing; maybe I should discipline myself and be more committed to my craft, but I think it would emerge dead on the page. I do write under bursts of compulsion but I can't tie the length of a poem to a time-factor— the shorter poems were far less spontaneous and hence far less satisfying to me than the more complex ones. In retrospect I would not have published the Munch texts. The poem to which you refer, however, took half an hour to write with no revisions before I was due to give a reading as I was somewhat lacking in material. I was influenced by the performance group I was in at the time (Cabaret 246) to deliver short bouncy poems to engage audience attention, but then I came to realise that audiences were perfectly capable of appreciating longer, more serious pieces and that 'performance' poetry could be so much more than people generally believe. I think you are reading in the self-confidence, as this is only a mask, which many performers assume, on a persona that is quite split off from the rest of me.

ALLEN Yes, but I wasn't only referring to the confidence of performance, which I realise can function as a mask, I was also referring to the work on the page, but then, perhaps that is a type of mask too. Is there actually any 'you' in the poems then, in the sense, say, of the speaking subject of mainstream verse? For example I was going to ask how much you identify with the women characters in *Portraits* but you then said, 'In retrospect I would not have published the Munch texts', which I find quite extraordinary. And how does this use of characters, as in the Munch texts, relate to your later work on the Hardy characters? Aren't the processes basically the same, even if the later work is far more layered and dense?

BLETSOE Even though I write as 'I' in many poems there is very little 'me' in them, except in so far as any writer's experience, knowledge and environment inform their imagination and the kind of language they use. Even a poem like 'Puberty', which has been taken as directly autobiographical, is an amalgam of typical difficulties in adolescence; it speaks for me but also for many others undergoing that kind of trauma. I used my research into Munch's letters and diaries, and events surrounding the provenance of the paintings to form ideas of how these women might have felt and what they would be saying. The process was basically the same for the three Hardy characters; I used a close reading of the novels and visits to the associated area to provide each nuance of emotion in the poems; I did build on them but there is little there that didn't spring from the original text. Except in 'Cross-in-Hand'. The italicised prose-pieces are my observations and feelings about the landscape as I attempted to replicate Tess' walk when she went to seek help from Angel's family. I think I speak most directly as myself in *The Regardians* or *Pharmacopoeia*. In the new work, however, 'I' is male and only half-human, in fact he also wears a mask.

ALLEN I thought all males were only half-human, except me of course, just as I thought all females were half-animal, at least. Tell me about this new creature of yours then.

BLETSOE I was referring to the Ooser, a figure in folklore that appears to be peculiar to Dorset, having a man's body and a bull's head. Half devil, half fertility figure, most villages had someone representative of the Ooser who wore a stylised mask. In his guise as the Christmas Bull, he and his 'keeper' would visit houses during the festive season demanding hospitality; if refused, mischief would be perpetrated! The last Ooser, or at least the mask, existed in Melbury Osmond not far from where I live. He gradually faded away, marginalized and demonised. I wanted to explore issues of alienation, so I'm trying to give him a voice, setting it in 'abandoned' landscapes like Tyneham and Portland. I'm basing it on a theme in early English poetry: the unreconciled contrast between the *wraecca* (wretch, stranger, wanderer, unhappy man) and the *cynn*, or communal unit. My introduction to the Ooser is the 'reconstructed coffin-text' (published in *Terrible Work*) where I attempted to condense world bull-mythology into a short poem.

ALLEN On various counts that description would closely align your poetic to the aims of the New Apocalypse, wouldn't it? And, bearing in mind what you have already said regarding archetypes, do you have any current opinions on the attempts in the early 90s, by Andy Jordan and Norman Jope, to forge some kind of unified front regarding this? As far as I recall you instinctively resisted, why? And of course not long after that Jordan said the whole thing had been a scam anyway which shows that your instinct was correct (though I still think it was only a retrospective scam). I suppose this leads naturally to asking you about any possible current poets or writers who you think are working on similar lines to yourself.

BLETSOE I knew both these writers' work, of course, but I wasn't aware of any unified front. I tend to keep myself deliberately ignorant of current trends and am not really involved in the poetry 'scene'. This is because I want to remain as uninfluenced and apolitical (in terms of poetry politics) as possible. I think I remember being called 'New Age' once but my interests in folklore, history, psychology, botany etc go further back than the emergence of that lifestyle choice label and are mainly a product of my upbringing and education. If people wish to pigeonhole me, then that's OK, but I don't really align myself to any movement. Basically I see myself as a landscape poet, but I try to give a different twist on it by adding multiple layers of myth and symbolism. Chris Torrance's *Citrinas* and Iain Sinclair's *Lud Heat* were the two contemporary works that initially inspired me to write; though our styles are vastly different, there is that 'spirit of place'/psychogeography element in common.

ALLEN I can see the connection with Torrance and Sinclair and I think I understand what you mean by landscape, but could you ground this a little for me, especially with regard to *The Regardians* and its landscape, which I take to be Cardiff, and the Dorset of your Hardy poems. Could you indulge me a bit too with some more information on the influence of Torrance; readers of this will probably be fairly familiar with Sinclair but Chris is unknown to many now; the brutal dismissal he got from John Wilkinson in that review of *Tempers of Hazard* didn't help.

BLETSOE Yes, *The Regardians* was set in Cardiff, more specifically around Bute Park and the streets of the Canton district. 'Rainbarrows' was located around the actual Rainbarrows near Hardy's Cottage on one of the last remnants of 'Egdon Heath'; 'Cross-in-Hand' refers to the mysterious pillar on Batcombe Down and 'Maiden Castle' is set in Dorchester. The Hardy poems are to be included in the 'Ooser' MS along with 'Landscape from a Dream' (Kimmeridge), 'The White Room' (Tyneham House) and 'Gawain's Journey' (Lillington Hill near Sherborne). Sometimes I like to bring in references to artists who were also associated with, or near, that locality; the last three works were partly inspired by a Paul Nash painting, the memoirs of Lilian Bond and a piece of music by Harrison Birtwistle respectively. *Pharmacopoeia* is full of the botany to be found in the Coleridgean landscape of the Quantocks. The resonance with the landscape always emerges first as an anchor, then I gradually feel my way into a narrative that fits.

With regard to Chris Torrance, many writers in South Wales owe him a great debt, due to his long-running creative writing class of over 20 years at Cardiff University and also to his enthusiasm in encouraging the best from people. I was never actually a student of his, but he created several opportunities for me to read my work publicly and offered me tremendous support. I have always loved the exquisite natural observations in his work and his sense of humour, besides, I simply enjoy the details of his isolated and sometimes effortful life in a remote valley. He has painstakingly recorded the myth, history, geology, climate, flora and fauna of his locality. Chris is one of the least affected writers I know. No matter how humble someone's attempts at writing were, he showed them respect and his comments were always constructive. He never speaks negatively of others, a pretty rare quality these days.

ALLEN You mentioned *Pharmacopoeia*, which we haven't talked about yet. Coincidentally I was at a book fair a few days ago and I sold a couple *Pharmacopoeias* I had left and people were asking me about you: 'What's happened to Elisabeth Bletsoe?', 'Where is she?', 'When is she going to get something else published?' etc. You have an audience waiting out there. Anyway, *Pharmacopoeia* . . . ?

BLETSOE Well, we've already touched on the issue of gaps in my output. I have been performing, done a little radio work, my latest works have been published in the States and my partner (Ian Taylor) has translated some of my works into Spanish for publication in Buenos Aires. I am two thirds into my latest MS, which will be far more substantial than any other works to date, but I am heavily involved in academic study, which I find tends to divert my attention. It's nice to know people are interested, though.

As for *Pharmacopoeia*, someone who knew of my background in medical herbalism suggested I wrote about plants. Flowers, of course, are rich in symbolism and mythology, and the language of botany is extraordinarily beautiful. The key to the poem is the Grigson quote: 'we cannot emotionally separate a flower from the place or conditions we find it in'. I decided to root it all in an emotional landscape as well as the physical one of the Quantocks, to add an extra dimension and allow the seemingly small separate sections to flow together into a story. I do enjoy reading it aloud as it often has quite an effect on the listener; I read it to one group and a very straight, shy Irish woman was smiling behind her hand until the end when she burst out laughing and said 'Oh, that's really filthy!'—apparently starchy botanical terminology can be subverted into something quite erotic.

ALLEN The pieces in *Pharmacopoeia* are, without exception, lyrically dense, yet they have a textured lightness and easy momentum. Could you say something about how they achieve this? The very short lines, the in-at-the-deep-end openers, the emphatic endings, all give me hints of an answer. And if anyone ever asks me for an example of baroque minimalism, I point them in the direction of *Pharmacopoeia*.

BLETSOE I imagine that would be the influence of haiku; their brevity and impacted meanings are ideal for describing flower-structures.

ALLEN Yes, except that haiku are not lyrical, not in that western sense of the word anyhow. Perhaps this is a good point to return to significant 'names'; you mentioned Rilke and Wenders and I remember a conversation long ago when you talked about how impressed you were with Jack Spicer.

BLETSOE I do admire Spicer as a great poet of disillusioned love and that in his work 'everything echoes'. I wouldn't consider he had a great deal of influence on me, however, as I came across him after I wrote *The Regardians*. The poets I remember studying (and liking) at school were Frost, Edward Thomas and Donne, later Marvell and Milton. It's very hard to single out names and works, but William Carlos Williams' *Paterson* had a great impact on me, also Lee Harwood's *Crossing The Frozen River*, a volume I used to carry about with me everywhere: it's stuffed full of train tickets. I enjoy the gutsiness of many American writers—Barbara Mor's *a song a song for tralala* stood out for me more recently—they seem to be able to mangle language without rendering it bloodless. Nowadays I don't tend to read so much poetry, more prose: Alan Moore, Ramsay Campbell, Robert Holdstock and Flannery O'Connor. I like horror that is so well-written it transcends the genre, but I also admit to a lot of pulpy trash; Ian said once that seeing me read was like watching an obese person wolfing junk food.

ALLEN What feelings do you experience when your own poetry is being discussed? Do you find yourself saying things such as 'yes, that's it', and 'no, that's not it'? Has anyone, in your opinion, written a good piece on your work, one that perhaps made you understand what you were doing a little better, illuminated some corner? And has anyone got it completely wrong? Or is interpretation open? I would just like to add that in my experience however much we hold to the ideal of 'open interpretation', when it comes down it we instinctively bristle at an interpretation we think is off-mark.

BLETSOE I do feel a little squeamish reading about my work, although I really haven't come across that many reviews. Damian Furniss wrote a balanced appraisal, which can be found on his 'Tower of Silence' website (http://www.dhfurniss.eurobell.co.uk/essgardens.htm). I am reluctant to read them in case I become subtly influenced, whether they be positive or negative—there is a danger that one could be tempted to fossilise in the same style and become a self-parody, or, on the other hand, to force a change that might not be true to oneself. I really do write to please myself first so I wouldn't care if everyone hated it—but at the same time, I wouldn't want to know about it. If someone releases their work into the public domain, they should expect it to have a life of its own, whatever they might have originally intended.

ALLEN What is it like living with another writer? Most poets I know have partners who, if they are artists, tend not to be poets. And isn't Ian (Ian Taylor) a very different writer to you in some respects?

BLETSOE In my experience, many men I meet, writers or otherwise, seem quite threatened by women's creativity. I've come across those who would have been far happier if I'd become silent or who were jealous and destructively critical. Ian, however, is very secure in his own talent; he shows me a genuine respect and would never begrudge me any success. He has translated quite a lot of my work into Spanish, a very arduous task! I could find Ian's prolific output intimidating but we explore very different areas. Ian tends to write novels now and is somewhat removed from the poetry scene. We are both at transitional stages in our lives at the moment and this tends to take the edge off our creativity slightly but we've always been supportive of each other.

ALLEN Didn't I see your name on the bill for the forthcoming Cambridge bash?

BLETSOE Yes, I believe you did. I'm particularly looking forward to hearing the reading of work by Jaime Saenz. And the whole event, I hope, will start me on some new trails of thought.

Bibliography

The Regardians (Nether Stowey, Somerset: Odyssey Poets Press, 1993).

Portraits of the Artist's Sister (Nether Stowey, Somerset: Odyssey Poets Press, 1994).

Pharmacopoeia (Nether Stowey: Odyssey Poets and Plymouth: Terrible Work Press, 1999).

ANTHOLOGIES

J. Ramsay (ed), *Earth Ascending: An Anthology of Living Poetry* (Stride Publications, 1997).

L. Sail and K. Crossley-Holland (eds), *The New Exeter Book of Riddles* (London: Enitharmon Press, 1999).

EDITOR

'Odyssey' issue no 20, *Unanchored in Ecumenopolis*, (1996).

SEAN BONNEY INTERVIEWED BY TIM ALLEN

On the Brink of the Articulate

from Filter OD

and soon asylum seekers will

sit in spit in box;

no land to speak of,

as all cities are curdled,

spat through algebraic memory, oblique

and polite. fatwa on numbers

(who walk in greater circles)

but cities require danger as

all else is too smooth

like a faked baby neutralised

with nails : Branson as interpreter.

Richard Branson as mass memory.

Richard as mouth that says

run it like a firm

is no distortion, job seekers

are his forgetting, his grip

damp with worms (meal brass).

recognise the friendly bacteria as

they do not wear ties

and grin in unison in

high alert, wear chemical suits

and join hands to keep

us out, sick bells. competition

is simple : get the best

seekers find the hidden seroxat

under black stones, botox stubble.

insert transients in cellular matter.

insert into property prices a

green dye, watch its progress -

vascular level—roast with garlic,

toss northern terraces to damp

sand, control information and grind

their stones and scatter the

value of land multiplies as

rumours of heritage coagulate like

sucking clams. look, a picture.

put a gate on it.

breathe in good film dust,

fantasy asbestos. reel in information,

interpret the A–Z, any city

as satellite pincer movement, the

implications are that barren. we

recommend hibernation as first investment:

rich people are growing on

shredded voices gather gas underground

& Branson says make adventure

was meant to be great

but well is kinda dull

frames in specific parameters. eat

nice television. nice exterior. eat

gas, normality is jagged universe :

take the next throat and

split, roast them, nice wierdos.

this is the new hotel:

we have stripped the tenants,

removed them, increased heritage matrix

(mass memory with running electricity).

the commune an aching sore,

a need, to rub amber,

to flash, to yearn counterclockwise

and plug. shut up. flesh.

we are all on pills

and torture. we'll take anything.

the hotel is red disk,

birth muscle . . . . .

ALLEN Sean, it has been a long time since I published you in *Terrible Work*. I still look upon your material back then as one of the highlights of the magazine. Then we lost contact, I rejected a piece and wrote back saying how your work had changed and I wasn't sure of its new direction. I called it 'hard boiled' then you wrote back expressing a degree of hurt and we had no more contact until I discovered you were living in London, involved with Writers Forum etc and that your writing had moved further along your own highly individual track. Could you begin by uncovering some of that 'track' for me?

BONNEY Those poems are from so long ago now that it's difficult to even think about them. No disrespect to your magazine—or anyone else who published them at the time—but I'm no longer interested in talking about them. I see them as apprentice pieces, at best. I certainly wouldn't want anyone taking them as representative of what I'm doing now. The poems that I still consider valid were written after my move to London, or just before that. Things changed when I came across a whole body of poetry that I simply hadn't been aware of before.

I count my serious writing as beginning when I moved down to London. Prior to that, the most important thing was reading Maggie O'Sullivan's 'pre-text' in *Conductors of Chaos*, which spun me around, and forced me into an intensive period of reading contemporary writing—the 'British Poetry Revival' and everything that came after. Also, around this time the *Poems for the Millennium* anthology came out, which again opened my eyes very wide. So I moved to London, started going to Writers Forum, attending SubVoicive readings, as well as going to places like the Klinker. Suddenly I found myself in a community, befriending poets that I could respect, and look up to, and learn from (which continues). And so the way in which I understood the possibilities of writing was transformed. But that meant starting again. It was a year zero experience, in which the earlier work was only valid in the sense that it had enabled me to get where I was, at that point.

ALLEN You seem to be making a wholesale rejection of your early work. I can understand this with regards to your *Marijuana in the Breadbin* perhaps, but not with the material in *now that all the popstars are dead*. That was published by Kerry Sowerby's Damnation press, wasn't it, in '96, and it contained things which still impress and thrill me, 'Becky Rebecca' and 'Earthman' etc. I remember reading

'Becky Rebecca' for the first time in an issue of *Memes* and I knew it was special. What was going on within that was highly original and very effective, for me anyhow.

BONNEY I'm not rejecting it. I'm just not interested in it. It's too long ago.

ALLEN OK, so what is the connection between what was going on in the early work and what is happening in your work now? They are connected, surely? Is one a failure and one a success or are they different animals?

BONNEY It's not really a question of failure or success—its just that the poems you're talking about are all over ten years old, and don't have any relevance to what I'm trying to do now, which is the attempt to make a new form of political poetry, basically. Obviously, there's some small connection, because I wrote them, but that's about it. A lot has happened between then and now, and most of those early poems just seem bad to me now. Maybe the things I'm writing now will seem bad in another ten years, I don't know. It's not that unusual, is it, for a poet to be ambivalent towards their early work?

ALLEN No, certainly not unusual, though I can think of cases where a bit more ambivalence towards early work would not come amiss. However, I think of it more in terms of crucial breaks, sea changes in life that highlight differences between pre-break material and post-break. I think such highlights can have an illusory quality that tends to focus on difference and not on likeness. Just as most poets find it very difficult to read objectively the work of another poet who, at that point, is doing something other, so we find it difficult to look objectively upon the work of earlier incarnations of ourselves. Highly relevant to this, when I first read some of your new work I recognised it immediately as being by Sean Bonney.

BONNEY Well, perhaps. If I ever get to be old I might look on them differently, but I think they're far too sloppy, derivative, and for the most part plain crap, and I don't particularly want to encourage people to seek them out. Obviously, if you've read the older things, they're still by me. But the things I'm writing now—that is, the things I'm interested in talking about, are different in that they're a conscious attempt to make something new—to create a negative poetics—within a contemporary and historic context. With the old things I was just feeling my way, and the only things I'd read were the Beats and the Surrealists.

It's interesting what you mentioned earlier, my 'individual' track, because I think my writing really started to improve when I started working within a wider community, by which I mean sharing the work on a social level, face to face, unlike before when it was much more of a solitary thing—I mean, it still *is* solitary, but now there are friends and poets whose work I respect, who I know will probably see what I'm writing at some point, and that makes it more real, somehow—makes it matter. But 'individual'—obviously any poet worth their salt *is*. The difference is that I feel an affinity with contemporaries, peers. And there's other poets outside of that immediate social group who I feel a strong affinity with—Peter Manson and Keston Sutherland, for instance—and we all sound nothing like each other.

ALLEN I wanted to understand the nature of your poetic break because, to be frank, it is quite unusual for someone who wrote in your 90s manner to appear in the next decade talking of feeling 'a strong affinity with Peter Manson and Keston Sutherland'. In fact it's not just unusual, it's almost unheard of.

BONNEY I did say that we all sound nothing like each other. I wasn't proposing a group, or anything like that. I was talking about community, about the effect on your writing of knowing that people you like and even admire will be reading it, that's all.

ALLEN OK, but before we move on I think it might be helpful, for readers of this interview who have never read your 90s poetry, to have an inkling of what strange stuff it was: on the one hand it was expansively surreal, hallucinatory and high-energy and on the other it was raw, emotional and incantatory. It was heavy with anger and love. The question I asked myself at the time was not 'where the hell does all that come from?', but, 'how does he manage to control it, make it work?' and 'why is this ecstasy generation lad with an enthusiasm for scribbling down his off-the-wall visions'—a not unusual combination, I generally got at least one such submission every day for 5 years—'able to succeed where thousands of others fail miserably?'. I think there is a connection between that fact and your move into the metropolitan innovative community.

BONNEY I didn't know what I was doing with those early things, they were primarily about me and whatever I thought I was when I was tripping out of my head. These days, and this is what's important, I don't write about myself. So *Notes on Heresy*, for example, takes as a jumping off point the anonymous Tom o'Bedlam lyric, the writings of people like Abiezer Coppe, and thinking about the whole 'counter-tradition'. Or the new *Poisons, their Antidotes*, which is an attempt at writing protest poems that are not journalistic, not obvious—but rather giving a shape to the rage and despair that I feel right now. So that's the difference, I think—it's no longer a kid scribbling down his 'visions'. I'm using whatever skill I have to put things across, that I think need to be. I mean, it's not as if I'm that much of a different person—I'll still take whatever drugs are put in front of me, I just don't think what I feel like when I'm on them is an interesting thing to write about. And to be honest, I don't think any of my 90s poetry is worth reading.

ALLEN Yes, that move away from the personal voice would put you on a different road even if nothing else happened. The 'anger' and 'rage' you mention is very important re this. Do you think you are essentially an emotional writer who is presently engaging with unemotional strategies? I ask because the attempt to write this 'anger' and 'rage' in unjournalistic and unobvious ways fascinates me. So tell me more about the sources of this anger and more about how you deal with it in *Poisons, their Antidotes*.

BONNEY I don't think I'm engaging with 'unemotional strategies' at all. The things I do are very emotional, and so are the things I like. I find all this suspicion of the emotional quite dubious, actually.
    The anger sources in the new book are pretty obvious, in that it's about Iraq, the war, and the gang of religious fundamentalists who are trying to take over the world. It's pretty clear we're living through a period of dire emergency, and everything's at stake. But even before Bush came to power that was true—capitalism is a system of violence on all levels, an irrational, metaphysical system

masquerading as the only possible rational truth. Everyone I know is going crazy from it.

The main problem I face now is how to deal with that as a poet. I wasn't consciously trying to write anti-war poems, it just happened—they just happened, Baghdad was suddenly in them. And I felt strange about that, and I worried if maybe I was capitalizing on other people's misery, and profiting from it in some kind of creepy way. There are of course all sorts of problems with writing political poetry. There are, of course, degrees of complicity. I've always considered everything I do to be political, to be my contribution to the anti-capitalist movement, but I think this is the first time I've been that explicit.

And also, I think what interests me about anger, and using it, is that you're writing right on the brink of the articulate. And *sometimes* you slip right over. And sometimes that's where it gets interesting. If you're lucky—otherwise it can just turn out to be a right bloody mess.

But it's not just anger, it's an exploration of an extreme state—liminal. I'm interested in the moments when things change, like at the time I was writing the *Poisons* poems, then that moment announces itself usually through anger. And it couldn't do otherwise, with respect to what was going on in terms of current events. The writing has to be informed by what's going on. And so, in a sense, the poems in *Poisons* are only arbitrarily anti-war poems. 'The Management Consultant has Gone to Lunch' is made out of fear, I'd say. But again, it's an emotional position where things begin to transform through tension. It interests me. I'm interested, in writing, to be on that precise spot where sense begins to break down. Or to change into something else, go into non-sense. 90% of the solar system is invisible. We've got the same DNA as lettuce, more or less.

ALLEN You're right, 'unemotional strategies' is misleading. What I meant to do was distinguish between the emotion and the strategy used to project it. I have seen examples of intense emotion completely watered down by a failure to find the right form or conduit, turning something very real into a hollow cliché. This is what makes your work different, and your intention to use your emotion, your lack of fear of it, it seems to me, is unusual. It is certainly counter to more than one strand of 'received wisdom,' the 'suspicion of the emotional' is prevalent in both certain main-stream and certain avant circles, for reasons that have themselves become clichés. It is quite interesting when you refer to the use of anger in writing as taking it to 'the brink of the articulate'. That is strategy. As you said, that's where things begin to happen, where the unexpected occurs and you 'slip right over' . . . But what is it that you slip into and how do you engender that 'luck' that can stop it from getting in 'a right bloody mess'?

I would also like to ask this: is there any qualitative difference between using the 'personal voice' of your earlier work, in which, as you said, there was an assumption that a reader would be inter-ested in what was going on in your head, with using a projected voice where it could be said there is an assumption that the reader would be interested in your political opinions? Don't both, in the end, depend upon your skill, your relationship with language?

BONNEY I guess so. The difference with the earlier things would be simply that now I do have a relationship with language, I think. I think about what I'm doing. The poems have to be doing some-thing else than just projecting my political opinions—leaflets are better for propaganda purposes than poems.

But I'll try and give an example of what might be a dry strategy being used emotionally; in the long poem that concludes the book there's a section which is a cut-up of the speech that Blair gave on the day of the huge march, February 15th. You know, when he tried to turn the rationale for the war into one of human rights, which as far as I know, he hadn't been using up to that point (I may be wrong, I'm not a great reader of Blair's speeches). But he was essentially accusing the protestors of having blood on their, albeit well intentioned, hands. Classic strategy of false rhetoric, accuse your critics of your own crimes. Anyway, my response was to take a razor to his speech, to make a cut-up—but I think I differed from the classic Burroughsian technique, in that I wasn't interested in making another text out of Blair's words, but of leav-ing the sliced words hanging there. So what I got was a sound poem of, I hope, a high level of intensity (and also something *funny* as well. All this anger has a humorous edge, otherwise it'd be unbearable), in which all the words were Blair's—apart from a bit of Villon that happened to be open on my desk as I was typing. I think Burroughs said something to the effect that if you slice a politician's words, then what they are really saying comes through. Well, as far as I'm concerned Blair really was saying 'I amanathematic ath moneygents wi't tongue lict f vice ho : pril : pitch a ming spa' and so on. Certainly made a lot more sense, in any case. I got a lot of personal satisfaction from using the razor that day, it felt very violent as I was doing it, and it was also funny.

Now what happened when I took this poem into performance was, to me, quite astonishing and, to an extent, quite frightening. I've done it a few times now, and so maybe its edge has been slightly blunted, for me at least, but the combination of the extreme level of control necessary to read it out properly—which you should be able to see quite clearly if you look at it—combined with the energy and rage that it aroused within my own perform-ing body led to a level of tension that was such I felt I was in danger of actually blacking out, all the while keeping up a level of concentration that was sending me into a trance. Also, just to exac-erbate the situation, I was standing on a table at the back of the room bawling the thing down a megaphone, while two very good improvising saxophonists were playing on the stage.

Control is the key in these very emotional performances, other-wise it'd just be shit. Control and absolutely letting go at the same time. I have to be very careful when I'm doing things like this, because I'm epileptic, and I'm often in danger of inducing a fit when I get to certain heights. Luckily, I've never had a full seizure on stage—though I came pretty damn close once, when I was performing from the *Notes on Heresy* book. There's a section in there based on a woman who was burned as a witch in the seven-teenth century, and I made the text by combining something I'd written where I tried to imagine myself into her voice, and then included notes from my walks around London. Again, it's a demanding piece to read, and there was one time when I was in the preliminary stages of a full fit as I was reading—I wasn't in my body, floating all around the room—I scared the shit out of myself.

ALLEN Let's go with the performance line for a moment, as it is obvi-ously important. Is it a case of writing something for the page, which you then turn into something different by performing, or is performance on your mind when writing it in the first place? And could you tell me about any other performers who have impressed you, perhaps made you want to get up there and do it.

BONNEY Like anyone who's worked with Bob Cobbing, I know that anything's performable, and on any level. I think I've performed just about everything I've written at one point or another, and when writing I kind of assume it will be performed, though that's not necessarily what's on my mind at the time of writing. I pay a lot of attention to the physical look of the page, and a lot of my pieces are visually constructed, with words superimposed on top of each other, and breaking up. In that sense, the page itself is a performance, as any reader who looks at it will take a different track through it. And when I read the things in public, they'll be different each time also, as I have to decide what route through the text I will take, instantaneously.

I think I can distinguish between several types of performance that I do, all of which are important to me. The most frequent, the most usual, is obviously the 'poetry reading', when you stand in front of a band of enthusiasts and just read. The audience pay attention, they're interested in hearing 'poetry'. And then there's clubs that I read at, where the focus of the audience is more obviously on music, they're not necessarily there to hear poetry, and that's a different thing, it's slightly more edgy in that it's a little harder to keep their attention, or to get them to listen to you at all, and it's great fun, it's very satisfying (plus you get to hear all sorts of great music for free). Though, of course, there's a different type of edge to a traditional poetry reading, because there your audience will obviously be very knowledgeable about writing, and so you've got to be bloody good.

And then there's some other things I've been involved in—I'm not sure I'd call them readings, or performances at all, but maybe events or situations, where the energy and sense of communal activity generated is what's important, rather than any individual artistic contribution. So, for example, there was an event at a theatre in North London a few months back, with lots of improvisers, and a handful of poets, and everybody was supposed to dip in and out of this long seamless thing. And in addition, participation from the audience, intervention, was also invited. Now that all sounds very idealistic and utopian, but what actually happened was total fucking chaos, in that the only audience members who did intervene were a bunch of hippies out of their heads on acid and special brew (I've got nothing against that, mind you), who yelled all the way through. I really enjoyed yelling my poems to what seemed like a wall of hippy screams. So that's another type of performance, where I was involved in creating a certain level of energy, and didn't give a fuck whether or not anybody could actually hear what I was saying. You know, I enjoy confrontation, and I like to be excited, and to excite. I kind of have a watchword, an old Guy Debord quote, that 'boredom is counter-revolutionary'.

Then there are other, much more intimate things, reading to a group of friends round the flat, which happens spontaneously sometimes. Or when I'm messing about in my sketchbooks and notebooks and read whatever I've just done to whoever happens to be around. It's all performance, really. Or rather, none of it's performance, it's all just things that you do. Everything should be done in public. I think all of this should be going on in the street, really.

ALLEN I like that a lot Sean, the openness to performance as something fluid and organic, responding to location and ambience without any angst for purity. Thinking of performance can bring us back around to Maggie O'Sullivan, who you mentioned earlier, as the presence in *Conductors of Chaos* that got to you so much. Was 'Birth Palette' the first time you had read her, and what was it about the work that struck you so much? For myself, hearing Maggie for the first time was a real eye opener and it changed the way I read her on the page, boosted my response.

BONNEY It was 'pre-text' that got me. It's very hard to say just how, other than it seemed very familiar to me, solved certain problems I was having about where to go in poetry. Though it's strange that when I first read it, I heard it as a very fierce thing—I was probably suffering some kind of testosterone overload at the time. Nowadays, when I read her work, I hear her voice, at times, but still also sometimes the way in which I first imagined it. Both readings are valid, I think.

I see Maggie as central in contemporary manifestations of a *real* British poetry tradition, if we can revert into dodgy concepts of 'countries' for a second. A tradition that includes, among many others, Barry MacSweeney, Bunting, Blake, Shelley, Clare, Abiezer Coppe. It's ridiculous that the 'movement' poets and their successors have managed to propagate this lie that British poetry is tidy little things about middle class boys yearning for their au pairs.

Though I don't really think in terms of 'mainstream' and 'avant-garde'.

I think what I was trying to get at before, when you were asking about my earlier work, is relevant here. It is—and this is always going to be a problem for younger writers until it's sorted out—the simple fact of a completely disappeared generation. When I was 16 I read the Morrison / Motion anthology to find out what was going on in British writing, and was so bored I didn't even bother looking for any for about ten years. You need to have a context to write in, even if simply for the fact of hating it.

ALLEN But do you think there is a connection between radical politics and radical poetics? I mean, would you write the way you do if you were happy with the government, etc? I suppose I am asking you if there is a direct link between your content and form. Many avant commentators tend to forget that Maggie O'Sullivan's work, for example, is very much the way it is, or has developed, because of her anger, and the same could be said for Geraldine Monk.

BONNEY There's no necessary connection. Certainly there was little, if any, communication between 'avant' groups in London and, say, the anti-war movement. But as writing is a social act, in the same way as buying baked beans, or drugs, or doing anything is, then if you have those politics then they're going to be an element of the writing. For me, my content, my starting point, is usually the frustrations and bitterness of living here, inside this system, so it's unavoidable. It's there to a greater or lesser extent in most of the contemporary writing that I value. If I was happy with the government—or whatever—it'd be a different social situation, and so the writing would be different. There's no more reason that people involved in radical poetics—any advanced activity—should be involved in radical politics than people who work in Waterstones should be. And the dogmas of L=A=N=G=U=A=G=E etc., that to break syntax was to subvert capitalist reality, have turned out to be false.

Radical poetics and radical politics need each other. Issues of communication and meaning, and how the individual receives this, would be an important analysis for the left. And social analysis. All the left groups that I've come into contact with—from the SWP to the anarchists—are uniformly screwed when it comes to culture. Anything even remotely difficult or obscure gets routinely denounced as elitist—the 'message' (for chrissake) is focused on, rather than the energy or excitement. I really hate that—you might as well just write a leaflet. That Raworth on a good night can be as mindblowing as a sweaty night jumping about to a punk band (showing my age here) is a revolutionary fact, as far as I'm concerned.

Everything that we write is socially determined—hence the anger in my work, or Maggie, or Geraldine's (tho obviously I can't speak for them). I think if we were living in some kind of socialist utopia my writing would still be about energy, I wouldn't suddenly start writing couplets about flowers, or something. If you look at the work of Bob Cobbing, or at *Finnegan's Wake,* then I think what you have, in its exploration of the very edges of writing, is essentially a statement of possibilities, which in itself *is* revolutionary. I mean, the soft suppression of radical writing in this country—over 100 years of it—is political. If you mess with language you mess with how people see and understand the world. Simon Armitage probably thinks he's a nice liberal, but as far as I'm concerned he's an apologist for corporate reality.

ALLEN Could you tell me something about the agit prop sheets *quic lude* that you put out with Jeff Hilson, and the latest mag you're editing, *cul-de-qui.* Where does the title come from? And tell me something about Jeff, what other collaborations have you done?

BONNEY We put out *quic lude* a couple of times, while the attack on Iraq was at its height. It was just something to give out at demos, and actions; an attempt to provide a forum for anti-war writings— poems, information, whatever. I'm quite proud of it, because it gets quite vicious at times, comes close to capturing what it felt like to me at that particular time.

It was also seen by us as a supplement to *cul-de-qui* (the title's an anagram), because it takes us so long to get an issue out. We're slowly putting issue two together now (well, it'd better be out by the time this gets read!). It's going to be another huge issue, and it's looking good. The first issue quite deliberately carries no reviews, or critical writings—and even the names of the various artists are only on the contents page—so that the work has to stand by itself. The whole becomes a single thing, rather than just a rag-bag collection of disparate materials. The name, by the way, started as a joke—we were wondering which was Mottram's arse in Yoko Ono's famous film—but after a while it stuck. It's got a nice sound.

Jeff and I have been friends for a few years—both started going to Writers Forum at the same time, tho we don't go quite so much now. I think his two volumes of *Stretchers* are magnificent; anyone who can tell us of 'the theory that Simon and Garfunkel are moths' is a friend for life.

ALLEN In *Poisons, Their Antidotes* you use the motif of the sparrow. I experience the recurrence of the sparrows through the sequence as an embodiment of antidote, antidote to the poison of imperialist and capitalist politics. The sparrows seem to be a way of keeping a handle on notions of innocent reality as opposed to the evil abstractions of the prime minister and president. A sparrow is a common bird too, distinctly unexotic, so it also implies a moral judgement against excess and power. Or am I reading it wrong? And what are the other 'antidotes'? Is the very creation and construction of the poem itself an antidote?

BONNEY I'm not sure about that. I don't see it in those terms. The sparrows are in no sense 'innocent', or 'pure'. Tin sparrows, in 'Management Consultant'—at the end the 'assuaged birds / roar'

In any case I don't hold with notions of an 'innocent' reality versus an 'evil' capitalism. My opposition to capitalism isn't based on morality. The birds in the poems, including the sparrows, are more ambiguous than that. There's 'tin sparrows' in there. And at the end of the book the birds are attacking, and roaring, and the whole thing begins with the poem 'sleep of the town disturbed by birds'—a title nicked from an old Bryan Wynter painting, in which they're totally sinister.

But they're not antidotes. If they were they wouldn't be very effective—getting nailed to the table and injected. In fact, I'm not sure where the antidotes are, in the book. The title could be saying that they've all been corrupted, anyway. Or maybe the poems are the poisons—I think that's more likely, actually. I don't think it says who is poisoning who.

ALLEN Poem as poisonous substance? That's poem as a changing agency, a pill made of words, something to turn the world inside-out etc.

BONNEY Something to turn the world upside down, yeh. Real poetry has that power, or should try for it. The poetry that interests me has. Difficulty, the intensity of concentration, leads to a physical response to the work. That's why poetry interests me more than—though not to the exclusion of—other forms.

ALLEN So in that sense, a sense that goes back to Rimbaud, I can understand why you would say your objections to capitalism are not to do with morality, if it wasn't for the poetry I don't think I would understand that. I would still say that your work is mostly concerned with celebrating energy, the 'life force' and because of that you have a much more demanding job on your hands than many other poets. Where do you see this heading, or is that irrelevant?

BONNEY Well, first off my objection to capitalism is *rational*. I genuinely believe that the capitalist system has led to insanity; how else can you explain the continued destruction of the environment, mass paranoia and denial, ridiculous wars. And I'm not pretending that I'm not a part of it—I live in this society. A moral judgement would imply separation from the horror—I immerse myself in it, try and look at things as they really are. Take the poem 'nine' in the Poisons book—that's a true account of the build-up to war. There's no pleading in there, no recourse to moral argument. It's made out of fear, anger, and also a sense of complicity.

So, I don't really think of my work as a celebration of energy. It simply is energetic; when I write, I get myself into a state of high intensity, and just write, fast. And then the long process of editing. What I hope I've done with these poisons poems is let rip with unspoken things. Once the bombing started, a horrible silence descended. A state of denial. We were told we were liberators, not aggressors. The fucking thing disgusts me. Maybe I'm the stinking gob that screams in the middle of the two minute silence, I dunno. But I don't think that means I've got a more difficult job than any other poet; this is simply my work, what I do, and I can't do it any other way. I'm too far into it to worry whether anyone likes it, or whether it conforms to any literary protocol. I guess this is what all poets—or the people that *I* recognise as poets do. We do our work, and it is demanding, it's scary, it can feel like it's driving you mad at times, but you just do it.

As to where it's going, I'm not sure. I've got work in progress, as they say. I'm not sure about it yet—it's quite bleak.

ALLEN Thinking about that 'rational' Sean. In some ways what the American right are doing is 'rational' from their perspective, realpolitik taken to its logical conclusion, going for it and taking as much as they can now, while they are in the ascendance. But can I pick up on two things you said that relate to this, you referred to 'things as they really are' and to 'a true account'. Isn't such certainty rather odd, especially when compared with many poets who we might call post-modernists, poets for whom everything is an area of uncertainty and undecidability. Isn't there a contradiction in expressing such political certainty when the poetry you write depends so much upon the uncertainty of what it will discover?

BONNEY As close as I can get to things as they are, I mean. Which I suppose implies the attempt to avoid as much as possible my subjective intentions getting in the way of the poem, while at the same time taking, and keeping, position.

I guess the 'rational' depends on whether you think humanity is inherently self-destructive or not. If not, then capital's inability to do anything about global warming, for instance, is irrational. The attack on Iraq—as it was pitched, at least—was also highly irrational. Or rather, was pitched rationally, via an irrational ability to look at the facts.. But if Bush really does think, as has been suggested, that we're in the 'last days', then it's a different story.

Anyway, I'm not a postmodernist, and never have been. It's an academic category, used to give a radical flavour to conformist thought. If you think that everything is an 'area of uncertainty and undecidability' then you can't do anything. This doesn't mean that I think there's some great abstraction called 'truth' floating around. But I believe there are certain facts that writing should take account of—if only to acknowledge that they are there—like for example the fact that Jeffrey Archer lives round the corner from where I'm sitting now, in a penthouse the size of a small village, while there's loads of homeless people shivering outside the entrance to Vauxhall tube station; that's wrong, that's unjust, and that's a fact. Now I'm aware that you could give me an argument here about my assumptions regarding 'justice' and so on, but I'd just say that they were arguments in defence of capital. I'm a dogmatic little bastard, basically.

There *is* a contradiction there, between a poetics that relies on contingency, to a large extent, and political certainties. But that's OK. I like contradictions, I like conflict and argument, as I said. The tensions between radical poetics and politics have been going on for decades.

ALLEN Come on Sean, I might play devil's advocate here sometimes, but I don't think I would take it as far as giving an argument in defence of Capital, I share your politics. Something else I share with you is the early influence of beat poetry and surrealism — they were big influences weren't they?

BONNEY About ten years ago, they were . . .

ALLEN Or maybe the beats were an 'influence' whereas surrealism was something 'in' you, or 'induced' in you, perhaps. I mention this because I still find them to be strong elements in your current work. Let's deal with the Beats first, your line breaks still remind me of Corso. I remember you sitting at a bench on a damp Glastonbury morning with a clutch of books in your hand (included Prévert and Diane Di Prima) in preparation for a workshop. What is your view of the Beats now? For myself, I still adore Kerouac's writing but I can no longer read Ginsberg without irritation.

BONNEY Well I certainly feel closer to certain strands of Surrealism — Péret, say, or early Aragon.

I have quite a strained relationship with the Beats. They meant a lot to me when I was younger — I remember being very taken with Ginsberg's line 'go fuck yourself with your atom bomb'. And I've been re-reading them over the summer, as I'm teaching a course on them at the moment. Very strange, to return to something after all that time.

On the whole, I've been enjoying re-reading Kerouac, looking closely at the relationship of his sentence structures to jazz — but so much of it is really sentimental. 'Mexico City Blues' would be better without all that semi-digested Buddhism. It gets very preachy, and that's also a problem with Ginsberg. Once he gets really involved with religion then the work loses its power—the rage goes, and suddenly it's like he's trying to sell you something. He gets too involved with being 'Allen Ginsberg'. But I really like some of his things from the early sixties—'Television Was a Baby Crawling to that Deathchamber', for instance, and the psychedelic poems, when he's really trying to investigate extreme states of mind. But it's not really writing that I would read these days out of choice. I see it as entry level stuff—you start off there, and go on to other things.

ALLEN I agree that Kerouac is sentimental, or at least comes across as such on our terms, maybe not his. I wrote something once about his writing fitting that typical American sentimental-macho dualism, but I love how he dealt so straight with that. But let's move on to surrealism. You mentioned Péret. Péret was special to me too, a huge influence at a certain stage, from the moment I first read him the sparks flew. I also, still, have so much respect for the man and his life that every time I read his disgust-fuelled metamorphic poems I imagine the poverty and the steely idealism behind their fury. Hard for us now, don't you think, to understand such dedication and focus. The only leading surrealist to be basically working-class, the one who stayed most loyal to Breton, the one for whom the 'politics of surrealism' was never a contradiction in terms.

BONNEY Well, there's a really ludic sense in Péret, and a viciousness, that's not there in Breton, say, or even Artaud. The combination of anger and humour really appeals. That's also what I like in the early Aragon things.

But my interest in Surrealism is as a part of the European art / anti-art dialectic; Dada, Cobra, Lettrisme, etc. There was an element of that, at times, in Writers Forum. Surrealism was misrepresented in the UK—if you think about the Tate exhibition a couple of years ago, it's something that continues. Essentially a political movement, recast as a semi-sophisticated version of *Men Only* magazine. Though I take a dim view of those who claim to be Surrealists today.

I don't think it's hard to understand such dedication and focus. As I said earlier, I consider my work to be part of the anti-capitalist movement—and I make the necessary sacrifices. You know, I'm a well educated white male, I could go and make a lot of money working for a merchant bank, or something. But I'm not going to.

Select Bibliography

From the Book of Living and Dying (London: Writers Forum, 1999).
Astrophil and Stella (London: Writers Forum, 1999).
The Rose (London: Hard Eye Ball, 2000).
The Domestic Poem (London: Canary Woof, 2001).
Notes on Heresy (London: Writers Forum, 2002).
Poisons, Their Antidotes (Hay-on-Wye: West House Books, 2003).
Big Dog (Cambridge: Barque Press, 2005).
Blade Pitch Control Unit (Cambridge: Salt Publishing, 2005).

DAVID CHALONER INTERVIEWED BY ANDREW DUNCAN

Lime Crushing-Houses

DUNCAN I thought I'd start formally by asking you about *Void Heaven*.

CHALONER *Void Heaven* is ongoing. It was written probably 5 or 6 years
ago. So it's existed for a long time. I began it as a response to a need
to expand my own creativity into other areas. I had met an archi-
tect and designer in Taipei, a lovely guy called Li Wei-Min, and Wei-
Min's girlfriend at the time was a dancer with the company called
Cloud Gate Dance Theatre, who are, as a dance company, extraor-
dinary. They have been to Sadler's Wells, although I only got to
know of them when I was in Taiwan. Their dance practice if you
like comes out of eastern physical movements and sport, you
know, all those things like Tai Ch'i. Deeply religious and concen-
trated movements of the body, transferred into a musical setting.
And second to that I knew a guy, an American, who had a friend in
England who ran a television company in Taipei, and this televi-
sion company had done some work with the choreographer for the
Cloud Gate Dance Theatre. And I was so intrigued by what they did
and how they did it, I hadn't done any words specifically for them,
I thought, I'm gonna show this guy the work. And it was then
thinking about those possibilities, with a piece of work I'd been
writing anyway, but not placed, but knew I was going to create
something for it, other than a page, as it were. and I talked with
the choreographer, I'll check his name in a moment, he has a
name like Wei-Min, You know Chinese names are backwards, Li is
the surname and Wei-Min is his first name. I'll check that in a

minute. The choreographer is a really extraordinary guy, and he comes out of an American dance tradition, you know, Merce Cunningham, Twyla Tharp, and so on, and then had returned very much into his eastern culture and the heritage of that. And to an extent the political context of Taiwan, and China, and Taiwanese wanting their independence from mainland China, and there are a couple of other poems I've got recently which refer to when I was there, the conflict, as it were that invisible conflict, between mainland China and Taiwan. So all that was going on at the time I was traveling there a lot, and I was also struggling with a dry patch. I don't know when . . . there was a . . . there are quite large gaps between my books. *Delight's Wreckage* and *Trans*, the book before that, had lots of time between them. I'd had lots of hard times anyway in terms of work and non-work, the recession, seeing the end of my own design business, and periods in therapy, quite rigorous therapy. So I'd got to this kind of creative dead-end, as it were, and thinking about *Void Heaven* really freed me up. So the idea was it became a narrative for movement. And the first thing I thought about, it was a narrative that would generate movement. So I started on that. I had various ideas about music. I'm not a musician. Previous to this I'd made a recording with a friend, just using a tape-recorder, the radio, as in transistor radio, you know, BBC World Service after midnight, or after 1 o'clock in fact. I'd done various things with narrative and sound, and I'd also used a little electronic Casio keyboard, and constructed this rather bizarre tape. Which now resides I think somewhere in Worthing. The guy I was working with on that, a lovely guy, another designer who wrote, sang, and played in a band called The Chrysanthemums, they're still around somewhere. And I sent him the tape because we were going to do an EP together. But the EP was going to be the same lyrics treated in four entirely different ways. This was the plan. So he said, OK, do a couple of takes on this. Which I did. All of this was happening at the same time as a means to free myself up a little bit. I was talking to a friend one day, a guy called Malcolm Garrett, who famously is professor of New Media at the Royal College of Art, but who now lives and works in Toronto, he is a designer who'd done a lot of record album sleeves. He'd called himself various things in the past. He was a mate of Peter Saville, who worked for Factory Records. Malcolm did lots of stuff right into sort of mainstream pop, and he knew Heaven-17, and he said to me one day, You'd better have a word with Martyn Ware. And instantly picked up his phone, dialled Martyn. Within minutes I was talking to Martyn Ware. We arranged to meet. And all of this coincided with the time when Vince Clarke, of Yazoo and Erasure, had kind of not finished, but their sort of popular career was less active, and they were looking for other things to do. And Martyn had this fantastic interest, not amazingly, but intriguingly, in art and architecture and installation and light and sound. And Vince had a similar feeling, coming from his side, of synthesizers and so on. So I met the two of them, we had a long chat. It was like being interviewed. It was rather bizarre, being interviewed by those two. We recorded what I had got then of *Void Heaven* in its seven parts. Recorded it first, tried it in Martyn's studio in Primrose Hill, then went down to Surrey, where Vince lived then, with this superb studio in his garden, with a basement sound room, absolutely soundproof studio, and put it onto DAT, and that is now on DAT. And the next stage is to begin the process of editing and manipulating. Manipulating as in, I was interested in what electronics can do to the sound of the voice, and where you could take that, and how you could make the words, and I didn't think of it then any more as poem, but take the text into other areas. I'd also started to fiddle around with a little Camcorder, I was in South America, I'd taken my camcorder with me. I was taken to Rosario, up the River Plate I think it is, between Argentina and Uruguay. I went to Rosario to do a talk to some students. Art students, design students. And I was fortunate enough, again, to be in the back of a car that was part of the Embassy fleet, so I just sat there in the back with my camera and filmed out of the window. On the highway. Because the land was flat, I guess it was probably pampas or something. There were distant trains in the landscape, just chugging through the brush, and I just held my camera on them, and got some footage. I didn't quite know what it was going to be, but I kept it. And then the weekend after that, I was still in Argentina, and I went up to the Iguaçu Falls, which is a huge waterfall, on the border of Brazil and Argentina, and Paraguay, which is where 'The Mission' was filmed. De Niro. And that was stunning. We flew up. It takes about an hour to fly up there. This little aeroplane. And then I got a rickety old cab, down to a rather bizarre hotel, I think it might even be a Holiday Inn, in the jungle, but it's built long and low. It's all been tidied. It sounds grand but it's all been tidied up for people going to visit. The nice thing was there was nobody around. It was the beginning of September. And I wandered out in the evening, on my own with my camera, and just wandered through the jungle, filming. This plume of steam rising from the jungle, which of course is the spray from the falls. I then wandered, as I said there seemed to be nobody around, and of course the footpaths, it wasn't crashing through the jungle with a machete, but nobody around gave me a sense of that wilderness. So I just walked through the jungle filming the tributaries of the falls. I found myself peering down into a gulf. And the following morning I was out at 5.30, filming again, got some little creatures wandering around, cavies, what are they, little hamsters, guinea pigs. I don't think of them as rodents, because they're neat, they just come out and look at you, and chew and chomp, away, and disappear. And butterflies the colours of which I'd never seen before. Brilliant red, and orange. And extraordinary birds. And I went into the jungle and I found this weird little railway, which apparently was very new. And I got on the railway and there were two back-packers way back and we chugged through the jungle and came to a point where there were a couple of huts and the inevitable stuff—post-cards for your family and so on. And from there took a bus to another outpost. And there bobbing up and down by the side of the river were these rubber boats. You climb on a rubber boat, and you whizz across, over the water, because you're at the head of the falls, and you land, 10 or 15 minutes later, by the side of some rocks, with some rickety steps, climbing up onto a long jetty which is built off the outcrop of rocks rising from the river. And the extraordinary thing is the river is only, I don't know, 60 centimeters, 100 centimeters, deep. It's not very deep at all, the river, you can see the bottom. And you walk along the rickety walkways and they end in a platform which is built on the lip of the falls themselves, so you look down into what is locally called the Devil's Throat. And you just look straight down. And there are the most amazing little birds that fly through the water, they fly through the falls, because they nest behind water. So of course I was totally smitten by this whole experience and being alone lent it another edge, which I quite liked, because I didn't speak to anybody for 48 hours, apart from thankyou and goodbye. And I took as much footage as I could. And this I'm now editing down, to use as part of the backdrop to my movie. Plus some very nice footage of Derbyshire. Because there's this great road, that Peter Riley knows very well, and that John Davis, who's another dear old friend from Cheshire, who's a sculptor, used to . . . well, he once valiantly tried to move up to Derbyshire and live in a farmhouse, and work up there, but couldn't. So he's back down in the city now. And of course Derbyshire in that area is a very curious landscape as well, because it's quite remote, it's high but not truly hilly. It's white stone walls, because they're limestone and there are these occasional, they're sort of outcrops of industry. And they're all made out of corrugated steel. And of course it's the crushing of limestone. And they exist there in this extraordinary landscape. So every so often I would scribble an idea down and there were projected words, there were projected images, there were people, and so on. What I discovered was, to hire a dance company, or to get involved with a dance company, would cost an enormous amount of money. So we had endless conversations with Martyn Ware, and so far where we're at is that we're going to perform it as a sound and light piece, rather than as a full-on piece of theatre. But I still have, in the long term, I still have the idea that it would become a piece of theatre, and that there would be all of these elements going on from it. But it would need . . . I couldn't look at anything Robert Wilson did, for years, I like Robert Wilson's work but I stopped going to see anything of his in 1999, and avoided anything because I didn't want any kind of influences. So it exists now and we're still thinking about it and Martyn and I are going to do a piece together in October for some conference on sound and television, film, stuff. So that's where *Void Heaven* exists. I look at the text now and the text intrigues me more and more because part of the text, I've only read pieces of it, I think you've heard one, there's other stuff which is quite abstract, and there's a piece which suggests it, because it's rhymed, we were talking of having it performed, not by me, but by some kind of a rap singer, because I had this kind of rhythm, but it's totally abstract. Except that it does talk about, I guess, anarchy and freedom and lots of other things, in a quite abstract way. So there were all these different elements coming in, which I was very keen, still am, very keen to explore in a larger context. So *Void Heaven* is that, and I'll get it there. It may take a while, but I'll get it there. I'm talking currently with the attaché for the Netherlands in London, because they have connections with the Nederlands Dans theatre, and they're very interested, and interesting, in terms of exploring possibilities. So I've talked with one or two dance companies since then, as well. But it's just, I'm not a producer, so the mechanisms to raise the money and put it together have so far slightly eluded me. So there we are. When I was much younger I painted a lot, and I had this glorious ambition in my teenage years of being a painter, a writer, and a designer. Now, I could have done it all, but I thought at the time that you didn't do that, and coming from quite a Puritan background, I felt that I'd got to earn a living, and be a very kind of focussed individual. So my early life was quite schizophrenic, I mean close friends knew that I was a designer but I didn't talk about it a lot, because design belonged in a commercial world, that connected me with money and a social structure that wasn't necessarily that in which the poets I knew lived. Because then they were students, they were politically active, they lived in a very very—this is my view of it, by the way—a very academic world, whereas my daily life was spent with people who didn't read books. I mean, they might . . . it was a different world. So they co-existed, but I was slightly, as I said the schizophrenia of that I didn't come to terms with until relatively late in my life. I mean, a decade or two ago was when I started to say, OK, this is what I am and this is what I do. And the consequence was that I had to own up to the people I worked with that I also . . . I didn't go in one day and say, I'm gay and I'm a poet, but I had to think, OK, if I'm working with these people who are all designers, and I go in and say things like, Did you see this movie, have you seen the clouds—I adore the sky, by the way, and light—and I would tell people, Go and look at the sky, because it's wonderful—so I had a very very bad reputation. Then I said, OK, I can't do this any more, I'm going to be one thing, and that's me. So I now will accept the fact that if somebody says, you know, What are you?, then I am a writer and a designer. If I have to define at all what I am.

It's absurd. But my background was a background of, there weren't many books in my family at all. So I don't know where this desire to write came from. Other than the fact that I had a very good head teacher at my primary school—my village primary school, there were only 28 pupils—and I would go in early in the morning, like 8.30, and we would make books. I would make this little diary and write in it things that I liked. I even discovered that

I wrote a piece of Shakespeare. I discovered this several years ago. I'd written this thing about, *And greasy Joan doth keel the pot.* What is that about? I suddenly realised where it came from. This was when I was like, ten, nine or ten. At the same time as writing that I wanted to be a pilot. But that whole weirdness of upbringing was filtering through from all sorts of strange things, because we were in a quite isolated village. And then when I went to secondary school where I wasn't terribly happy, there was an English teacher whose name was Mr Potter. I don't even know his first name. And he read to us one day, he read us a story one day, and I was amazed by this story. I just said afterwards, Who wrote that? and he said, Oh, it's this Frenchman called Maupassant. I said, I've got to find out. So I started to read Guy de Maupassant. A thin, I think I still have it, a thin collection of short stories published by Penguin. So I borrowed it, I think, from the school library, because as I said I didn't own any books. So when I was fourteen, going on fifteen, and I was interested in cycling, as in racing, I met a guy when I was cycling through the adjoining village one night, who was doing the same thing, and we came alongside each other and started to chat, and it turned out he went to a local grammar school. I didn't. I don't know why, we started to chat, and he suddenly said to me out of the blue, I've just been reading a book at school, he was a year older than me, You've really got to read it. It's amazing. I'll lend you a copy. I said, Oh, what's it called? he said, it's this Russian guy called Dostoevsky, and it's *Crime and Punishment*, you've got to read it. So he lent me a copy of *Crime and Punishment*, which I then duly read. And of course everything began to knit together from then on. But you see, you have to, in those circumstances, too, as an individual in isolation, to build your own structure, you have to create your own foundations. Because my parents didn't know about further education, or university, or any of those things. So, you know, the hunger sets in. I think the hunger must have been generated back then by other forces, other psychological forces, so I write because I need to write. And my writing is probably as close to emotion as most writing will ever be. As opposed to a stricture which I also admire very much, which is a construct of intelligence, and I guess of a desire to challenge academic norms.

I am intrigued by that. I am willing to engage with that possibility, because I know that I have set myself, in the past, tasks, to break out of a difficulty, impasse. But then I think what I've done with that construct is to only use it as a kind of key, if you like. It becomes a complex three-dimensional key that lets me open up into something else. And I know I've written— and as I say, I can't talk for any other poet, but I know I'd be interested to talk to them about it. I know when there is this curious emotion, satisfaction, which is nothing to do with an intellectual position, I think.

I'm still 16 and rebelling. There's that kind of thing that's going on with me still. Because I have to find out what it was about myself that made me do certain things, react in certain ways, respond in certain ways. I do often think that there is that rebellious teenager in many many artists, and not just in writers. If people stop rebelling when they're still teenagers, they're just conforming to society's norms and means, and I think that's the problem with society. My brother wore yellow socks, and I thought he was terrific. He was much older than me, and he wore yellow socks, and this was the Fifties, and people thought this was just outrageous. But now he conforms. And he's spent most of his life slowly conforming, and becoming more and more unhappy, to the point of being self-destructive. And I think that's really sad. And I think, better to be quietly rebellious than noisily conformist. This doesn't mean to say that everyone's got to go out there and go mad, it just means that I think if we have a society that's going to be rich and rewarding to everybody, that society needs to be one of challenge and variety and variegation and difference, and that's the best thing about it.

DUNCAN This secondary school, presumably it was in a town?

CHALONER Yes, it was in Macclesfield. The first one I went to was called Park Royal, which sounds like an asylum, and it also looked very similar to the local asylum, as well. Because we had an asylum in the town. Macclesfield had three or four things really going for it. One was the King's school, which was an independent grammar school, which I failed to get into, having twice taken my eleven plus. The others were secondary modern, I'm not sure where the modern came in.

DUNCAN Because they didn't do Latin.

CHALONER OK! fine! You should talk to that one there [daughter] about Latin, she's good at it. So you had the King's School, the secondary school, the asylum called Parkside—and there had been a workhouse, which became the Infirmary. So you've got all this kind of stuff. And my dad, who lived in this town, and who I mention in my poems, strangely, more than I ever thought I did, he knew the town in the twenties and thirties, he knew it when it still had the hangover of the workhouse. People who didn't have a job, a home, or whatever, that's where they went to. So this is Macclesfield, a mill town. Mill towns were repressive. Northern England was repressive. Northern England was a patriarchal society where the mill owner would create a very nice little village, and the village would have a little shop, and a chapel, and everybody would come from work to their own village, and they would shop in the shop, and so all they earned from the mill would go back into the shops, and the profit would go round and round and round. All in the name of altruism. Now English Heritage has got hold of them, so all the four by fours go there on a Sunday, and people walk round them and say, isn't it pretty. Well you know, what was that about.

DUNCAN You can see why people might want to forget that.

CHALONER Of course! It's why I want to forget the North! I was in the North actually on Thursday, I was back in the North, I hardly recognize it now. I still have my family up there, my sister and my brother live there.

DUNCAN I do get the impression that the North, especially the cities, has completely changed.

CHALONER Completely. I'm interested in the North from the historic point of view. I was about 28 or 29 when I left, and in the latter part of the time I was desperately unhappy. I was on all sorts of pills and tranquillizers, and they were just the legal ones. And I needed to be away. The atmosphere for both the writer and the designer was not a good one. I organised a reading, and I still have a little A5 poster to go in the bookshops, beautifully designed in Bauhausian tradition. And it was Dave Cunliffe and Tina Morris, who were the publishers of *poetmeat*, Jim Burns, and myself. And we met in, I think they were, the rehearsal halls for the Hallé

Orchestra, on Deansgate, and there were like four of us poets and three in the audience. We all read, anyway. I think this is quite good, actually, because we actually read, and we read as much to each other as to this audience of three. And Mary was one of the three. Mary and I were together, she was one of the three. You come out of that, and I used to go to an amazing club called the Amber Moon, which nobody ever remembers now. It was in a warehouse off Shood Hill, before the disgusting Arndale Centre was built, and when any concert came to the Free Trade Hall, like Thelonious Monk or Ornette Coleman or Ray Charles or whatever, quite often they'd end up in the early hours of the Sunday morning, in this club, jamming with the local jazz musicians. It was beautiful. It was open. A friend of mine, he worked on a local paper, tells this extraordinary story about Paris and Gregory Corso. Or was it Jack Kerouac? No, maybe it was Gregory Corso. Anyway, that's another story altogether. But Barry was a very good trumpeter, sadly he plays Dixieland, I'm not very fond of Dixieland jazz, but there's a saxophonist called Art Themen, he was part of the group. His brother was a cab driver in Manchester. There was a brilliant pianist, I think his name was Roy Hilton. Not Roy Hilton of the BBC, but another one. There was a great drummer whom I used to know then, I've actually only met him once since, outside of the concert scene. We both suffered from asthma, both took the same drugs, and he was drummer with the Durutti Column. That came later, but all of those guys were mooching around and hanging out, in the clubs and the coffee bars, and the pubs, in central Manchester. And even Peter Riley connects into that, because before he went to Cambridge he used to go into Manchester. He used to go into Manchester. I organised a reading at the experimental theatre club in Manchester, and Andrew Croznere and Tim Longville read with me. I read to flute and guitar accompaniment.

DUNCAN It sounds like part 1 of *Void Heaven*!

CHALONER Very much so! And there were sorts of objections from the audience, people standing up and saying. Poor Andrew was reading, and some guys stood up in the audience and said, This is all rubbish! Wasn't it Brian Patten? One of the Liverpool Poets, it was probably Adrian Henri, but, poetry should take off its clothes. It was such a stupid thing to say. I remember running out on the stage and I don't know what threatening or shouting or doing. Anyway, there was this stuff, and it disappeared. Where did we go to? How did we get there?

DUNCAN As a matter of interest, did you feel better when you came to the South?

CHALONER I did. I absolutely did. It's a dreadful thing to have to say, but for a time, when I moved south, the Lawnmower House poets, a reference to dear sadly departed Barry MacSweeney, a little poetic spat we had a long time ago, but we had this little house, which was horrible, it was two up and two down but instead of being a cottage it was a semi-detached. It was on the edge of an industrial area, brickworks on one side and a heavy engineering works on the other side, and a council estate on the other, and the railway at the back. But I don't know why I never felt at home in the North, because that was where I was raised and born, in a tiny village called Mottram St Andrew, which is still there. Still probably now full of very very well-heeled Manchester businessmen and Manchester United footballers. They're all out there. But when we left the North, I travelled up and down every week for six months, and I can remember when we'd finally moved down to London— and Mary isn't from the North, she's more from London than anywhere else, although she moved around, I remember travelling back here on my own, back here to London one Sunday evening, on the train, and getting this very strange physical feeling of relief, and joy almost, when I started travelling through Tring. Well, it was just that it was the landscape. So you see the saddest thing is, I actually remember where I was when it happened. And I knew that I was nearly back in London.

I've never felt completely in control. More so now. But I've never felt completely in control. Too many other forces out there. It's a very interesting one, because this comes back to what I said, this schizophrenic nature of my life. Never being completely in control on the one hand, and is the residual effect of my upbringing, but on the other hand I can see a point where I am totally and utterly in control. So there are two things going on here. And I'm not sure what they are. So I really really think that if I said to you, I'm not in control, that would be an absolute and utter untruth. A misreading of my own situation. I think there are times when the differences, the, you know when you get extremes, and extremes come and meet together, they go off in different ways and ultimately they come round and meet at the back somewhere. It's like the extremes of Right and Left. And when the gun-runners are selling guns, they sell them to the extreme Left, they also sell them to the extreme Right, and they're probably dealing over the same table. It's that weird structure in society. I think there is a part of me which is absolutely in control, and I know that because when I take it outside into the world in which I exist during the day, I don't have any problems about being in control. But I don't know what it is we're talking about here. Maybe it's the plastic arts, which I'm not in control of. Maybe it's words, that I sometimes feel I'm not in control of. Maybe they slip away from me.

DUNCAN Before you write the poem it is out of control, because it's unpredictable, unstable. As you write it, it gradually gets more controlled. Until you reach the end, when it's fixed. What you then do is move on to the next poem, where it all starts again.

CHALONER Maybe it is that kind of pitch and yaw of the waves. Maybe it's something I hadn't recognized as part of the creative process. And certainly people around me have suffered my grumpiness when I'm not writing well. Have said, when I'm writing well, whatever happens, I'm within myself a much better or easier person, to be around. So there, there's another thing. As I say, I don't know, what I'm finding now I'm writing, is, for me it's much tighter, more focused, it's direct. It's pared. It could be paired as well, paired with me. Maybe I'm . . . . I don't believe in all of that, I'm a Libran, cosmologically, which is balanced. There's that moment when you're a perfect balance and then it tips one way or the other. Maybe that's what it is. I think when you mention that, that's quite interesting, that the beginning of the poem is a scramble among the detritus of imagination. And then you start to pull it together. And then you're in control and you're feeling strong and positive, and you get this complete high and buzz for a few milliseconds at the end of it! And then you get back down again, into the whole morass. But I have the other things. I have design as well, you see, that works in many many similar ways. When you're looking at something to work on. And the why and the wherefore of it.

I've done this a long time. I'm quite comfortable with what I'm doing now. I do occasionally get quite nervous, but there for different reasons, it's more will I be able to fulfill someone's wishes or requirements or needs. Am I going to be able to give them what they expect. And you never know. You never know, I never assume, as I once wrote about, Where is the audience for English poetry. I never assume too much about the audience in English poetry. So it's always a joy if they're there, prepared to suffer those two hours or whatever it is, liberally sprinkled with drink. It always seems very wonderful that they've taken the trouble to be there. Lucy now goes there a lot, she and her boyfriend are there all the time, they know the barman there. They know a lot of people around in that scene at different levels, different levels to us. And it's run by people whose commitment is solid and meaningful, particularly the person I know who is mostly involved which is David Miller. Who does seem to kind of do it. It's impressive. I'm pleased about that.

DUNCAN *Chocolate Sauce.* Why the title?

CHALONER It was very much because at the time, I loved chocolate sauce. I had a terrible problem with titles, and if you look through the book, at least 50% of the poems have no title. Because I was always confused about the titles of poems, and the poetry of the time, I was reading, always had these rather onerous dramatic and weighty titles, and I could never think of a title at all. It seemed to be a problem. Should they be classically allusive, allusive, or elusive, straight on, or whatever. When I came to the idea of title, I couldn't think of anything. And I wanted the title to be unrelated to the text, and to be quite emotive. And that was the reason why I chose 'Chocolate Sauce'. It was an emotional momentary aberration. And similarly the decision to get Caulfield to design the cover. Mary and I were sitting one evening talking about the manuscript, I was saying, Oh God, what about this cover? what are we going to do? And she said if you were to choose any painter around now, who would do a cover for you, who would it be? I said, Patrick Caulfield. She said, OK, we'll give him a ring. We were still living in Manchester, so I rang up Directory Inquiries, and I asked for the names of Caulfield's who were living in London. I don't know why I assumed that, I may have read it in the press. I think I got three names. The first one I rang was Patrick. And I spoke to his then wife, Pauline, and explained to her, and he came to the phone, he answered, he came to the phone, and I explained the predicament I was in, and I said, it must be weird to get phoned by some unknown individual saying, Can you design a cover. So I'll tell you what I'll do, I'll send you the manuscript. If you hate it so much, or just find it uninteresting, just say so, and that will be it. End of conversation. So I sent him the manuscript, and he said, Fine, I like this stuff, I'll design you a cover. And the next thing was I got a cover, and the cover is hanging up on the wall somewhere, I think it's through in the other room. Andrew Crozier, who was doing this book for Ferry Press, it was my first real book, the previous Ferry Press book, *dark pages slow turns brief salves*, have you seen that? it was very much the mimeographed quarto with a cover design by me. I very much like the cover now, it was a series of parallel lines with the, further away across the field there is a split and all the lines rubbed out. It drops. But I did that. And I wanted something more special than that. So I got this. And then we labored over the cover. So then I said, OK, why do books always have words on the cover? This is my rebellious streak. So I made a decision, having talked with Patrick about it, and asked him where he felt type should go over this, on the side and whatever, and he made the decision that there should be nothing on the cover whatsoever. In a bookshop it would stand like that, and be like that, and it would have no words on it. Of course it was all part of my all-inclusive sense of what a book should be, too. So you shouldn't just be writing the words, you should also in some way have control over the expression that those words give out to the world, so they should come out on the cover. Because you can find all sorts of books with all sorts of covers that tell lies about what's inside. That was a decision that was made. The work itself was a bit of a departure for me, because at the time I remember I'd been reading a lot of Peter Schjeldahl, more now an art curator and critic than poet I think. I found my understanding of poetry was very much informed by American experimentalism. And when I first started to buy poetry as opposed to prose, the stuff that was available to me in local W.H. Smiths was actually the little Studio Vista books called the Pocket Poets. They're on my shelf somewhere. They did *Live Voices, New Voices*, they did a book of American Poems. I think they did *Jazz Poetry*, They did a book by Gene Barrow, an American, whatever happened to him. I'd seen those, but the only other one I'd seen was the selected poems of e e cummings. I opened that, and I couldn't believe what I saw. There were no capital letters. It was an extremely eccentric way of punctuation. This bizarre stuff. I thought, well, I've never seen poetry that is so free before. And it fits my desires and needs. That was way back, in 1960 in fact. This came out, I can remember the date of it, I was also obsessional about dates, 13th of February 71. These were the first poems that captured I think any true sense of solidity and consideration. And thought and self-imposed editorial rigour. Because up to that time I believed that you shouldn't ever change anything. You put your foot down and now I don't believe that. And now I go back and if ever there's a, I think OK. I'm doing my Collected Poems at the moment. I'm checking out the manuscripts, if I ever think of changing anything I'll change it. I don't believe the veracity of poems I want to see. If you want to see the original author I'm that. It's a kind of device in a way. I dislike devices but I'm editing. There was stuff at the time that I wasn't capable of changing. I didn't have the ability, the breadth of intellect, or understanding, or the expansive language use, or whatever. I just didn't have it. I was working from . . . the odds that I was working from, I was working with as a tool. Very much moving my way through the language, reading, writing letters, finding people, understanding why write poetry. What the hell was that all about. Why write poetry. Why the poem as a means of expression. So I was kind of working away at all of these things. I think this was the first true book. And there is lots of earlier stuff, I really like, but this came out of a much more rigorous attempt to understand what it was I was truly doing. And that was how I really arrived on Andrew's doorstep, as it were. And I was already meeting Andrew because he was down at Keele at the time, teaching at Keele, and said, OK, I'll look at your manuscript? He didn't say, I'll do it, he said, I'll look at it. And I was delighted when he said he would do it. I knew then it was going to be a real book. Do you want to know more about it? Well, at the time, and I'm looking at it now, there are two dated the 16th of December 1971, and two dated 15th of December 71, and I think at the time for me I was charting the changes in my life. I think in my notebooks, and I do have them from this time, I was writing pretty well a poem a day. Some of them more. And I would just be scribbling away all the time, morning noon and night. Getting up at seven and sitting down to write at eight, and scribbling away until 8.30 before going to work. But it was also about finding those times when I could do it, and I was working as well. So I would also sit and write in my lunch hour. And to my shame —and I can own up for the first time—there are two poems here both dated the first of April—three poems. That says a lot. I used to use the back of dyeline prints, because I was working in the design office. And I would tear them up—they were all A3—I think we were then moving into the A sizes for the first time. But what I would do, I would tear these up into manageable sizes and I would make a little pad, and I'd be writing all day.

DUNCAN Stealing from your employer! Your employer owns those poems!

CHALONER Exactly! That is so true. So as I say I could tell you a story that's very up to the moment about that. So I just wrote all the time. So I was kind of working away, working away. And then I would do a little bit of editing and get down to stuff. But there was one particular, 'The Swimming Pool Saga' here was written because I'd been reading John Hall, and we'd been spending time in Devon, I think in the summer of 1971, where John Hall at that time lived, on the edge of Dartmoor, and there were lots of things I was absorbing which were partly fact and partly invention. Because he didn't have a swimming pool. I didn't have a swimming pool. But there was a sort of a romantic notion of what a swimming pool might mean, in a garden. And my father, who had been a gardener, at the sticky end of that whole story, had worked in the garden of a house in Macclesfield, which I went to as a boy, very very young kid, my mother, I think she was a sort of cleaner there, and she'd worked there when she was much younger, in the Thirties, as a nursery maid, and in the garden of this house there was an area with a tall yew hedge and inside it, and I just thought it was so exotic, was a swimming-pool. With a blue surface. Empty. There was no water in it. But I used to stand and look at this thing. This is a swimming-pool in somebody's garden. 'The Swimming Pool Saga' had lots and lots of stuff coming out of it, lots of memory. There's a little piece here —

the music practice from the great hall
the listeners in the stone tower, pressed against
the silence that shifts
of voices and music and lumpy winds brimming with insects
more was crossed out in the ensuing months
attempt abandoned in favour of gruesome inertia
the flat blue surface of the swimming-pool
collecting a grim smear of debris.

Stuff like that came out of childhood memories into what I was feeling about what was going on around me. There's so much, I think, emotion in these, that it's difficult for me now, when I read them, and I haven't read them for years, to actually . . . I could go back in my diary I guess and see what on the 25th of August 1971 I was doing. I've no clue. But then this whole thing about doors was a lot to do with escape, and enclosure, and a sense of being, I guess imprisoned. One of the threats made against me in my early life. This thing about, another poem, 'Dilemma'. *What's happening above the city is a fine shuffling.* Of clouds, of course, that's what I'm talking about.

the day becomes that much more than a stifling room
where haggling voices smear the air with rabid determination
if you were here I would invite you to observe the elastic
clouds but generosity is an impossible word
and can only be liberated by the act and truth rampages
across all this demanding honesty
a messenger will reach you soon bearing this information
no reply is expected

Dilemma. The title. And there's a lot about dealing then with some unhappinesses in my early years, which have then started to pop up and haunt me. I think very simply that the poem 'Racers' is actually about cycling. And as a youth—and a lot of working-class youths did use bikes as their —

DUNCAN Bikes built in Nottingham, I hope.

CHALONER —Oh, yes of course. And I was passionate about cycle racing, and it was only one of the other dreams. Well, there were several of my dreams. One was that I would go on the stage and I flunked that because I was so nervous I couldn't go through the doors of the Library Theatre and get myself an interview. The Library Theatre in Manchester. The other was to be a racing cyclist living in France. I couldn't do that either, I didn't have the wherewithal. 'Racers' is just about the experience of being a racing cyclist and a poet. It's interesting how many people I've met over the years have also, particularly in design, have also been racing cyclists. People like, there was a designer called Jeff Banks, I think he might be from Nottingham possibly, he was a racing cyclist. I'm not sure whether Paul Smith wasn't a racing cyclist. Lots and lots of people.

DUNCAN It's very surprising that you have these feelings from ten, even fifteen, years before the poem. All these chronological layers are given such an integrated surface, like a painting. There are no labels for the chronological gaps. But I think the effect comes from the lack of labels.

CHALONER For me that's true. I did feel the difference when I was writing these poems. These are thirty years ago. Thirty odd years ago. I knew when I was writing these that I was writing differently to how I'd written previously. I was very conscious of that, and I was very conscious of the appearance and the construction on the page, and I think, as I say, they were so close to me, so autobiographical, that at the time of writing them I didn't think they were. It was only much much later, fifteen years later, that someone said, they're so transparent, they're so clear. This was a friend reading them. But I had not seen that. I had thought they were totally . . . when I say obscure now, I don't mean obscure in meaning, but I mean obscured from interpretation. But somebody who knew me, said, well, I can pick out of here all those critical elements, those critical emotional changes and differences that occurred in your life, and they are there. What I thought I was doing was digging with language. And I do use I in these, but I started, first person singular, I tried to get rid of. And it was after a letter actually from John Hall, who put this line in his letter, that I remember to this day, and he said, Writing a poem is a political (f)act. And he'd parenthesized the f. So Writing a poem is a political fact. Writing a poem is a political act. And it was just so appropriate for the time. You know, everything you did and said had this incredible meaning, this incredible significance. And that's what I feel about these. So even the word like arbiter, which is not one of, it's not part of my everyday language, but it appears there. You know, *implications*. So *Chocolate Sauce* I think was a bit of a watershed at that early time. I can't remember how old I was. Older, probably, than I think I was. '73. So, 29. That's quite late in life. Maybe. I don't know. I had this idea very early on that I had to have my first book published by the age of 20. Just in case something happened to me, like it happened to Rimbaud. That's a conceit of mine. I really really felt that if you haven't achieved something by this early age you'd never achieve it. And that was very old. And after that I think I got this just before I moved to London, we moved to London, both of us, on holiday in Scotland, were involved in a car crash. That kind of got us out of action for two years or more. So that was another period. So after this, before the next book, there was a whole lot of stuff going on.

And I think *Art for Others*, as that's next in the pile, is for me very important. Two reasons again. One is that I like its rigorous typography. The other is that it was produced by Equipage, and Rod Mengham. Important before anything, it's full of anger. Because when I had my own design business, and worked really hard, and I employed people. That was cool, I was happy with that. But the actions of the powers that be, the authorities, the banks, the Inland Revenues, the Customs and Excise, who'd come in to fuck you over and don't care, don't care about this, and don't care about you as an individual. They all assailed me in the early Nineties. Although this was published in '98, it was actually written much much earlier. Probably during 92, 93, 94, when I was going through a pretty hard time. I was out of work, I was on the dole, I had very little money, we used to live off, basically, potato soup, pretty basic stuff. My mum, who was still alive then, would send us a few quid every week, to help us out. And Lucy was tiny, Mary was not that well at the time, I was down and out, so we were just existing on the edge of doom and gloom. I was writing to banks all the time I was writing to all these authorities, and they were the most heinous people I've come across, in the sense that they didn't care. You know, I wrote to my local MP and complained, I did all of those things. And the complaining kept me alive. But out of that came these poems. How many are there? there are ten. And I really really can read these and read them spitting venom! They're really really nice for that. They have another side which engages with other things too, and the kind of geophysical nature of the city in which I was living and existing has taken hold of me, and that's London. I don't want to claim, sort of, Sinclair Ackroyd territory, but I'd been walking the streets and alleys of London for a long time, really enjoying trying to track places through. In '98, I think it was, I'd been working in Clerkenwell for a time, just wandering through the back alleys, finding ways through the back alleys. So this was very much a rampage against capitalism, against the Thatcher eighties, against . . . I designed the cover, I had this great colleague and friend Beverley Stanley to do the typography, so I like the balance. So I enjoy things like where the number is. There's a whole tension between the text and the number, for me. And the number isn't up there, it's been considered in a slightly different way. So the whole thing begins to take on a different power and emphasis as I go through here. And it's very much about typography, but I just like the way that balance exists. *A body's singular provenance. Palate of silence, palate of dust.* This is what I was feeling at the time. It's what you saw round you. You saw a lot of people very very dispossessed, and very sad.

Garden ripped from turf.
Blades, blooms, moments of stillness.
Gross dream product confronts frightened observer.

And it goes on and on. And the rhythms in it, I really got in here, I really started to being this thing of rhythmic repetition.

By this time the signal.
By this time the signs and portents.
By this time the satellite communiqués.
The extraterrestrial magic.
The ancient sites of ritual death, modem
to monitor. How scream on the internet,

transmit visions by e-mail.

Bleep god of defunct soul, pushed into the blue.

And it was almost gently stream of consciousness. So these were actively written. They were written out of anger and despair. And very very close to my heart. So *Art for Others* was very much a tongue in cheek, it's a social rant, art for others, it's about anybody's right to have art at any cost, but what does it mean and at what cost. And you can then begin to think about the context of Saatchi and the falsity of the plastic arts at the moment. All of that stuff. It was about art for others. But it had a very definitive and definite place to be, which was that perhaps art is not necessarily for others. It's a control thing, very much a control thing.

A daub's smudge catches a garment's hem,

Clay ooze lips the boot's welt.

Fringe of scum.

Unkempt strands caught and dispersed

Across broken spears.

Entering night's fragile gate.

And it's about the sort of rot that takes place, both in terms of society and personality. And it's the destruction. What I saw when I was writing these was social destruction. I met a friend on the infamous Black Wednesday, and we were in the West End, and there was nobody around. And he had a copy of the Evening Standard, and there was like twenty-two per cent in black letters. You know, the interest rate went up overnight? and then dropped again the following day? There were guys on the stock market trading money, and making billions? And we were in the Old Grey Mare on Langley Street, and there were only about four people in the pub with us. He's an architect, and he's the only guy I've known from my schooldays. John Davis I knew from a teenager, that's slightly later. We sat there, and we sat there, and said, What's the future? What has happened? because building work has stopped. Architects and designers aren't needed. Industry is slowing down. People can't afford to go out and buy the goods. The whole commercial structure that we lived in and abided by is suddenly falling apart. Then you have this hoarding, up to 22%. So we got absolutely pissed, and wandered home not knowing what

next. And it was about six or nine months when I didn't know
what next. And I read one of Peter Ackroyd's novels where he talks
about the beggars and the street guys, wandering around
Clerkenwell and so on, and I have this terrible notion, and it goes
back to my past. I realise more and more as I talk to you, every-
thing goes back to my insecure past. So when I talk about writing,
when I talk about taking risk, the risk I have in mind is that. It's
the one that was embedded into me from a truly, truly working-
class background. Mary and I chat about this now and talk about
our parents. They did not have a clue. And lots of our friends, who
were working-class too, had parents who knew that their kids had
to go to grammar school. Ours didn't know what a grammar
school was, or where it was, it's a surprising thing to say, but it was
like another world. So if you wanted to find your way out of it, you
did it yourself. You fought the battle. That's not a bad thing, but it
does lead to this kind of outpouring. So I have my social
conscience, and I have my position, and I think it's pretty clear
what my political position is, but sometimes it seems rather odd.
It's not connected in. Because I don't go around saying, I'm into
this this and this. But to me, I think I lay down some very clear and
very angry political statements in this work. And they're not, To
the Barricades!, but they are there. So throughout this demands
action.

Demands action. Breath a faint continuation
of the date. Stop.
Charmed, outstretched, dazzled.
That familiar face beyond the energy field.
has lived before. Trapped by previous example.
Fill in the forms fill in the forms
No title, no name. Obliterate difference.
Living here with loose objects.
A room constructed and demolished against a wall
of standing darkness.
Sense creates its own surface into which
you are granted access.
Pass to the embrace of a misguided future.
Realm of an uninhabited land.
Christened a name without substance,

faint growth in contours behind the eyes.
Sometimes to ponder nearby,
and sometimes to contemplate connections.
Seemingly exclusive, repeating, a command
ignored, associated with a real name.
Were there.
Multiplication of ordinary gestures.
Trees buckle and lurch to appease the storm.
You are missing.
Mind occasions such conjecture.
One road. Memory fanned like a sure hand
of aces.
Voices given strength beyond reason.
I bring you this place. It angels in hours
before speculation.
Truth as a knot falling to moments
of discord filtered through language.
Might be there yet. Sensed also
as multiple. One there attending home,
another seeking reward, retribution, escape.
Another seeking words of compliance
and don't move, magic numbers.
A line balance at the rim of sleep time.
An order against which to specify and speculate.
From which to extract energy
and by so doing embrace continuance.
Misguided to future.

So, that was what that was about. Black cover. *Art for Others*. It was written as a continuous poem of ten parts. It's a bit like outbursts of spontaneous aggression. And you do it in phases. If you ever watch people having a real row, bustup, or whatever, it goes up and down and up. And you think, oh yeah, God, that's stopped, and up it goes again.

(discussing *Projections*) Long before the language people, and somewhere, I don't know where it is. And that (poem called "Interior: Morning") is that (points to print of 'Interior: Morning' on the wall). In the back of *Projections* is a list of previous books. *Dark pages* is that one. *The Year of Meteors*, do you have that one? *The Year of Meteors* is short poems, when did that come out? probably between *dark pages* and *Chocolate Sauce*. It was getting truly truly serious. *The Year of Meteors* is a quote from a painting by Robert Indiana. And I sent a copy of the book to Robert Indiana of the poems, because I thought it was in a circle, stencil letters, what he used a lot. I don't know if Robert Indiana stands up, in many ways, to looking at in a historical context of 50s pop art, 60s pop art. That's another discussion. Anyway, I liked his work at the time. He did the infamous LOVE, with the sort of leaning O, in a square. I've got it somewhere, hanging on the wall. He sent me a very sweet postcard with the first-day issue of the stamps of this iconic LOVE painting that he'd done. *A Year of Meteors* is actually a quote from Walt Whitman. Indiana had quoted Walt Whitman. *Today Backwards*, published by John Welch. *Between the Summers*, Joe di Maggio Press, do you remember that? It was John Robinson. That was due to come out and it didn't happen. *Fading into Brilliance*, which did come out, from Oasis Books. And *After We Moved*, Actual Size press, which didn't come out. So that didn't happen at all. I don't even remember if I have the manuscript. I don't remember how I got in touch with the Waldrops, except that I was buying Burning Deck books for quite some time. And corresponded avidly, but not with any great intellectual content, I don't think, it was more like a pen-pal. And they said, Well, send something over. And I had this group of poems. A lot of them had picked up on, I think, some of it was Creeley, whom I quite admire, and all of this stuff about the Americans, but a lot of it was starting to seep in from France, and I was reading, in translation André Du Bouchet, and Marcelin Pleynet, and Denis Roche. I was reading them in translation, but I was beginning to see, in Europe, stuff that I hadn't previously seen, because my escape-route was to America, not Europe, and now I would do an entirely different take on that, like I'm listening to music from Norway or Sweden, because I like it. Michael too had been a bit European, in a way a bit like Paul Auster, who in his early career was a poet, may still be, I don't know, was living in Paris and translating French poets, and then producing them under the imprint of Living Hand. And those things were very important, for me, because they were giving me access to Europe. I'd read Rimbaud. I'd read Baudelaire, Hölderlin, I'd read Georg

Trakl, all in the Penguin translations. God, they were so important. Except that they did those horrid prose translations at the bottom of the page, which I did hate. I thought that was such a cop-out.

DUNCAN I think they were aimed for A-level students. If you look at the price, I think you realise they were fantastic value.

CHALONER At the time, I never ventured into Manchester to sort out my night life without a book in my pocket, and it was usually Rimbaud or Baudelaire, just in case I met a girl who was going to be impressed by that sort of thing. You never know. So all of this had kind of come into context, and I was beginning to get a quite serious tone of voice. I'd read a little bit of Palmer, I'm not sure how much, because he was only in little chap-books, but I really admired his ability to use language, beautifully and in a slightly abstract way. I'm pretty certain, and I could ask him this next time I see him, he was beginning to look to Europe as well. Because I know he was interested in Beckett, a lot of European writers. He speaks, I think he translates, actually. I came across a Chinese poet recently, and he'd written the blurb for it, Chinese work translated into English, and it's very interesting work, this Chinese poet. Michael has a very eclectic background, and he doesn't sit easily into any box that might have been constructed around him by the language poets. He's got far more going for him than that. And I was writing stuff, I was even using words like 'technology'. So I was writing about technology, about how it was affecting our lives, how we would change, and there was a reference here to the photographer who did the graduated movement, at the turn of the century, Edweard Muybridge.

even the stairway remains bright.
bearing the rise and fall with placid resignation
gathering in the vibrant rays
dispersing them obliquely across the angle
of two legs climbing

and it was all about the idea of movement, and the idea of technology affecting our lives. So there was a whole lot of stuff going on, and I was just absorbing it and actually spilling it out. I would.

when you admit I am lost
we take it to mean you feel "you are immune"
and the days absorb that remoteness

and it was a way for me of finding my feet, literally, because by July
of 74 I was, I'd just come out of a wheelchair, and I was in a caliper.
So I was going through physical things, and mental things as well,
sitting down, and really thinking about the future. And this was
very much, the introduction was probably informed, I think, by
Beckett's poems. I love Beckett's poetry, there is not much of it.
And I first found Beckett's poetry I think in the Sixties, when John
Calder published this rather beautiful grey covered folder. Yeah, he
was a great guy, he did a lot of stuff. Strange guy though he is. *You
are here, and here, and you are your name.* Again, it was about identity,
and the way language can describe identity, and alert one to the
fragility of identity, if you like.

sometimes a definition, and sometimes a mistake.
you are your own worst enemy,
and occasionally a conflict will persist for days,

without victory or defeat.
sometimes your name emerges

from between the lines, and sometimes
the lines themselves are its only disguise.

your own company is often sufficient,
a companion to entertain the four walls.

their pose is controlled and reassuring.
addressing you with familiarity

if friends arrive you are pleased
to see them

and it seems the walls stand back
releasing your name

So there's this emerging me, and of course '72 I'd met Patrick, and Mary had bought this print. I looked at it, and I think it was the first piece of art we ever bought. I looked at it and I looked at it, and I thought, it was just very simple, because I used to write through the night then, and I'd get up at dawn, and I'd just sit and look at that, and I knew exactly what it was saying. I recognised the light through the window-panes, I recognised the pale yellow, illuminated from inside. I recognised the ellipse of true light from under the shade. Even though it is very very graphic, and very simplistic. And once caused an incredible row between Fielding Dawson, John James, Andrew Crozier, Jean Crozier, Mary Chaloner, and myself. A very drunken night, after a reading. With Fielding saying, The glazing bars aren't right! Anyway, there we are. So I wrote that for Patrick. 'Ronny's Friend' was about a friend from schooldays, which is a little bit about sexual ambiguity, and loss. And loss related to a notion of family life that is mostly invented by sad and frustrated parents. Family life is often invented. You know, the notion of family life, the bureau and table mats and the napkins and so on. Most people have to suffer it. So there's a whole range of things that were informing these poems, and it's still rather a favourite book of mine. It was that play, and, you know, the word games.

the first restless flaws of morning.
wipe darkness from the window
a deliberate gesture
 that rewards your attention
with unhindered eloquence

here, a line that seemed to stifle
the purpose has been deleted.
And now the day you had departs,
slamming the day in your face

—which is just like the new day, and a long session of night-time creativity. And the idea that it comes to morning, and you think, Great, I've got it, and then suddenly, bam, it's gone again. Slamming the day in your face.

There's a little book, and I don't even know if I have a copy now, called *insomnia*, and it's so much about working on a page. And there was something about that that I loved, because the appeal of that to me was that it wasn't just about the intellect of the writer, putting those words and choosing to create very sparse stanzas, it was the brilliance of the way he could manipulate the white space on the page. I know people don't talk much about white space any more, but it's daring to reduce, it's daring to extract, and it's daring to allow silence impinging on the poem. And I love that idea. I do like silence. I like noise as well, by the way, but the idea of silence as a beautiful construct, silence as impossible, I do think is part of what I've worked with throughout my life. 'The fragile status of gleaming air/ recites its chill remarks/ despite a sky arched pleasurably/ above the tossed-sheets landscape.' It's good to read those again.

Delight's Wreckage was published in 2001, but actually going back into the late 90s. Pretty well after *Art for Others* and *The Edge*. I found the voice of my father and the lost voice of myself, if you like. Because I've been able to come to terms with a lot of things, but particularly the curious nature of my father's difficulties as a family man. What that means, what that leaves behind. So in here there's a much broader sweep. I broke it down into sections because it seemed to work that way, it seemed to work that way very comfortably. I'd got over my problem with titles. So not only have I got titles for the sections, usually lifted out of the poems, but the poems have titles as well, and they've got no dates. So this is very very much a wider sweep, that I felt, although I gave them individual titles, they belonged in very specific groups, there's a lot of playing with abstraction. Now I don't know where. . . there's one very very…it came long before the language people. *Raphael grins a regional fruit-lipped grin.* It's in some book of mine, I don't even know which one it is. I kind of wrote this, and I thought, Jesus, I can't possibly go with this, and there it is in one of the books. I don't know where it is now. I went back to it a long time later, and I thought, in England, and probably the Irish Scottish Welsh poets, have been challenging language for a hell of a long time, and they didn't need to make it into a movement.

DUNCAN I'm afraid marketing is very much an American expertise.

CHALONER In this section here, *Where Once Was*, this was a pamphlet from Poetical Histories, and this piece for Peter was where I'd started to use repetition more and more. I quite like repetition

because it has a rhythmic dynamic about will carry the reader.
Even if you're reading silently it will carry you if you're lost in the
text. With a lot of writers this can happen.

From nothing. For nothing, prepares a path
more pathological than loam, than darkness.
True earth. What lies. What lies in wait is the lie
of the land, crowned in copper light. Light sloping
on a ridge pulled free, pulled from free air.
Resolve. Resolve never to repeat, to return
Resolve never to return. To retrace. Never to retrace.
The lie of the land. Lost light. Last rays, slipping.
Slipping to overcast. As though to return, but not
here. As though to depart, but another place.
As though to arrive, but without announcement. As though
from nowhere. From where loam and darkness conjoin.
It is something and nothing prepares. For nothing.
To arrive. Depart. Retrace.
Resolve never. To repeat return but not here.
For nothing prepares for lies. For life. To act.
To act upon the moment's discourse. Discovery. Resolve
response. The world outlines its utterness.
Utterance to describe the world's unqualified
lineaments. To state discovery as its journey
As though return more likeness but not familiarity.
To repeat. For nothing. For nothing but the ability
to confront. Slipping light.
The instruments of response through knowledge.
As though another place. Here. As though controlling
divine fragments. In unlimited resolve. As though
thought. Ascendant spatial matrix of engagements.
Thought, response, the instrument.
Vast expanse. Language and silence. Confrontation.
Luminous planes buckle urgently.

I was really looking for that repetitious play of negative positive,
challenge retreat, and finding that a very very strong way of

getting across some feelings that the landscape of the north of England that Peter writes about a lot in his work. So it was bigger bigger sweep for me, that then went out I guess into narrative texts. There was all this stuff... at the time I was working in the West End, not far from Fitzroy Square. 'Warren Street.' Fitzroy Square was where Virginia Woolf lived for a time, among other ladies. It was just the things that happened to me informed my day. And this one was actually about walking across Fitzroy Square. It was also about the drama of the time, and what was happening.

It is an unseasonably mild December night, without frost
and moist from contrary winds.

If this is our due, our just desserts, we are done for.

Applause ripples like a wave tilting, a breeze in raucous,
leafless branches.

You walk across the square. Across the empty square.

The paving is dry. Dry and brushed and clear of debris.
A small box slides and rolls towards you. Slides and rolls
and stops. Slides and rolls towards you. You stop.

You stop in the shadow of the railings that surround
the garden. Nothing moves. The wind falls away to stillness.
Stillness transfixed. Nothing moves.

There is a sound. There is a sound. Like voices.
Like voices fading. Voices fading in a vast auditorium.

At the four corners of the square four figures appear,
simultaneously. Four figures appear and walk briskly along
each side of the square. Along each side and away
into the dark streets surrounding.

Then you move. You move. Continue to walk across the square.
Continue on your way. On your way again,
towards your destination.

It happened. It was just one of those things that I've always found
very very interesting is how things in the world impinge on the
imagination. And you suddenly find something that's almost
choreographed. Like these four people all entering the square at
the same moment, and you're there and you're at risk, and the
reason for my being at risk was entirely to do with my own affairs
and events, and it all happens and then it suddenly drifts away.
Similarly later on in the, ''Warren Street' is this thing about the
blood on the stairs. *Dull red footprints.* How people walk through
that and carry it away and how it disappears into the sort of
suburbs of London. And 'Deep Pile' is a rant against Middle
England. That's a friend who I hadn't seen for a long time and who
I visited the home of this person, and they had every thing that I
hated most in life. That I'd never seen, I'd not seen them for years.
The worst kind of place you can ever imagine. I was just angry,
because it was her inability to understand me, mine to understand
her. I just went, Wow! that's a very bad thing. *There is a place called
home. Green onyx, deep pile. Nothing, no one escapes.* It's in there, all
that stuff in there that comes pouring out, and it was a very defi-
nite resolve. The personal stuff, for Lucy, and there's a poem in a
book that's going to come out after the collected book, from Rod
again. It doesn't have a name yet. It's called *new book* at the
moment. I kept thinking, shall I put this into the Collected poems?
it didn't seem to fit. Even this (*Delight's Wreckage*) wasn't going to be
in the Collected Poems, but now it is, because it's out of print. So
Tony sent all the files over to Salt. And I'm just now doing all the
last bits of stuff to bring it together. There are things in here that
do bring me to the present in a much more comfortable way, and
in many ways a savage way, than I'd ever done before. I don't know
if you ever read 'Cause' closely. It is about birth. It is about my
mother. It is about the damage that gets done in those sort of
mother son relationships when they're not conducted in a know-
ing way, or a mature way. So it's worth just running through it.

Birth membrane shifts
across a bony flange.

Colliding moments
distanced by each dissolving second.

A quote from imminent breath.
Squeals fluctuate through swirling air
nor yet in contact, not yet seductive
nor inhaled to launch metaphors.

Though natural recognition
This being small community judgement
Speaks of sin and misses the point

Pale as linen the sky breaks gold
bronze and strained vermilion
watched from a high window.

Spasms regress dark and airless
through divine space. Far empty space.

A donation of speculative disturbance,
without dreams or inconvenient images,
without social awkwardness
or threats of retribution.

The sudden enormity of that brittle room.
The scowl of disguise, the pigment
of narrative composition.

Searching for a phrase, asking a Porter,
a News vendor, a fellow traveller.
In some way loss is predetermined,

like a claw grips its prey
a beak of daylight ravages the gloom.

So there was a lot of, I guess, the stuff that came out of therapy for
me, and understanding the positive and negative aspects of why
one is what one is and what one's early experience has been.
Reading John Welch's work recently, it's extraordinary.

DUNCAN You mean, because he was in therapy for so long?

CHALONER It's amazing to have done that. I mean, I was in therapy through most of this work. I didn't own up to it, but then I didn't need to own up to it. Through the Eighties and into the Nineties I was in therapy quite a lot. It's maybe a reason why I didn't write a lot, maybe a reason why I did write a lot, certainly it informs this work, and a lot of *Art for Others.*

DUNCAN *The cliché is that English poets don't do therapy and don't write confessional poetry. It's very dramatic how Barry took on all the conventions of therapy and really rediscovered his mojo. So much English poetry is so unrevealing and emotionally cold. Dislike of therapy might tie in with this.*

CHALONER A curious thing, because it depends why you might need another person with another skill to discuss certain issues with. Because it's not about, you do not choose to go to therapy like you might choose to go to one film or another film, or shall we do this today? maybe not, we'll do that tomorrow and do this today. It is something that becomes a need out of another space altogether. If you don't know where you are and what you're feeling, and why you're feeling it, and how therapy might help that, of course you need it. I didn't think I needed therapy. Then some things happened to me which concerned me, so, I had to go to my GP first, that's the deal. I had to go to my GP and say, Look, I'm not so hot. Would you do something, give me something? And then the whole thing opened up a little bit and he suggested I should go and talk to somebody. But I was really hostile, at first, to therapy, and indeed hostile to my therapist. But I was kind of going because I needed… the hostility was something else. So the hostility was all part of this curious distinction between not needing therapy and needing therapy. Or, sanity and madness. I mean, that's incredibly dramatic and rather curious. I mean there is madness, clinical madness, and there's a reason for that. But a lot of people suffer mightily emotionally when some help might be more appropriate. And it is a lot to do with our society. And I think if in our educational system we were a little bit more open and tolerant of emotion and discussed it more easily, it might not be such a problem.

DUNCAN There is this legend where the subjective approach produces, it's like camera shake really, it doesn't convey the process to the reader. Whereas in something like this there seems to be an external recorder who is incredibly perceptive and stable, he is like a camera taking everything in. In that wonderfully stable image there is this very emotional single line being drawn all the way through, which is the individual. Subjectivity doesn't block everything out.

CHALONER Where I think it's important for me that I can do, that is that I can be, I can stand back and be quite objective about things that are extraordinarily difficult. Not complex, there aren't many complex things in life actually. Or everything is, whichever. We're down to the fine line again. Quantum physics is complicated if you don't understand it. But I think the way you tell it is the issue here, and if it does get in the way you just get rather tedious confessional poetry. So then you come to the business of the artist, and does the artist have a function in society. Yes he does, she does, it does. And part of its skill must be to preserve very very special moments, things, images, allusions, collusions, whatever, in a way that allows them to be looked at, observed, read, without too much dilution. The ego can dilute, actually. If you read the confessional… who's a really, good, as it were, confessional poet? good as in strongly confessional? John Berryman, probably. Donald Hall. I found a book of Donald Hall, which I quite liked, actually. It was very very confessional. And I think that can just get in the way. There's another American writer, actually a philosopher, called John Koethe. And he won one of those Frank O'Hara prizes for a book called *Domes*, way back. His output has not been great, his work looks incredibly dense on the page, but it's actually brilliant. And it's very discursive. It is quite, in a way, confessional, but it's also very objective, because he's a philosopher. He teaches philosophy at Wisconsin, or somewhere like that. But the work is beautiful. The man has set up a tone that is capable of harnessing, or controlling, the negative side of confessional poetry.

DUNCAN *So much English poetry has seen these tensions and rejected them.*

CHALONER But in favour of what?

DUNCAN Something bland and suburban which doesn't say very much at all. Something which is happy not to be confessional and is just cold and emotional and doesn't tell you … And which has no core as poetry. It has no raison d'êtrce.

CHALONER Yes, I think that's true. I mean, what does poetry have that something else doesn't have? that soul doesn't have? for instance.

DUNCAN *Unfortunately, poetry has got a lot less than soul music! It hasn't got that drive.*

CHALONER That's an interesting one, which is maybe why I feel, going right back to where we began with *Void Heaven*, where I feel the need to explore some other art forms, as it were. To create a bigger thing. Create a more involving thing. Because the one thing that good lyrics can do, very simple lyrics as well, the thing is, they don't often read well. 'Interior: Morning'. Because you sit here, you're thinking about it, you're thinking about who else is in the room, with you, and what's going on outside, and why is the light on at that time in the morning anyway, and a whole range of stuff starts to happen. I think I tend to agree. The only thing for me that's different is that where the language starts to make the music in the poem, as it were. I mean, the use of the language, the layering of the language, the textual nature of the language, allows you to make a music, like the battle scene almost.

DUNCAN *I wouldn't say most poetry has that quality.*

CHALONER I think you're right. Who are the young poets who are going to challenge, or who are challenging?

DUNCAN *I've got quite mixed feelings about this. Helen Macdonald, in partic-ular, is a brilliant poet. There are quite a few very good poets. Whether it's really a dialectic opposition to the previous generation I'm not quite so sure.*

CHALONER But it will go on, and people will emerge, and that's the interesting thing for me. You mention Helen Macdonald, who's one of the people I really like the work of. Has she done anything since *Shaler's Fish*? (end of tape)

Bibliography

dark pages / slow turns / brief salves (London: Ferry Press, 1969).
Year of Meteors (Todmorden: Arc Publications, 1972).
Chocolate Sauce (London: Ferry Press, 1973).
Today Backwards (London: Many Press, 1977).
Projections (Providence: Burning Deck, 1977).
Fading into Brilliance (London: Oasis, 1978).
Hotel Zingo (Cambridge: Grosseteste, 1981).
Trans (Newcastle upon Tyne: Galloping Dog, 1989).
The Edge (Cambridge: Equipage, 1993).
Art for Others (Cambridge: Equipage, 1998).
Delight's Wreckage (Exeter: Shearsman and London: Oasis, 2001).
Collected Poems (Cambridge: Salt Publishing, 2005).

What we say after 'Innocence of First Inscription'

The BBC World Service

Today the lesson is English grammar.
It is dangerous to swim in Aphrodite's bay.
Repeat.

Why since then everybody wants to die?
It is the third world war already I think,
bit by bit, what is happening, this music.

Everybody so running to die—why?
You see this aria of Tosca, if they did,
maybe it would make them ok.

And it is dangerous to swim in Aphrodite's bay;
the razor shells will cut your feet,
the currents around the rocks are unpredictable.

Though the water is milky and clings to the skin
like a second body that slides and fits around your own,
long after you have returned to shore.

Today English grammar is heroic film;
the black and white harbour before money arrived,
western coiffure on Levantine heads.

At night I watched the ships unload:
the dovecotes, trinkets and sex toys,
the belief in mythology as fact.

And finally, more than we bargained for,
objectivity in Babylon
brought to book on the banks of the Euphrates.

DUNCAN How did you become involved with modern poetry?

CORCORAN Well, with poetry of some kind as a self deluded adolescent, in the wan hope of attracting girls—which is amusing of course—in the same spirit as singing in folk clubs, which I also did. It was an aspiration to get out of the small town in which I grew up. We had next to no books at home and not many more in the town itself, a WH Smiths with about 3 inches of shelf space for poetry—Betjeman and Eliot I expect. Bloody awful parochial suffocation and I still hate it, it's not unusual or rare is it? There was also the family situation to survive—alcoholic father, and no money for my mother to bring up five children. I've written about this occasionally. So obviously I thought, poetry is what I need, that'll transport me out of here. Turns out it did.

I went to Essex University because the prospectus laid claim to poets in residence. There was a name, Edward Dorn, for instance. I got there because I had one teacher who made me work. His name was Leonard Saffron, my English teacher. A very formal man with little or no imagination, he claimed. He was a Canadian and he'd flown spitfires in WW2—so I didn't trouble him too much I suppose. He wore spats and he used to threaten to throw me out of the classroom window if I didn't work. So I worked, and believed him when he said I was bright.

At Essex not only were there poets but there was a library full of books. Imagine the impact of that. Books that I wanted to read. Stunning. I wasn't glib about the experience, I'm not casual about it at all now either; a good teacher and books, nobody should treat these things as unimportant. I began reading the poetry that was available there. Doug Oliver was my tutor for a year, he could flatter you into saying something intelligent just by the way he listened. Just think, a good teacher in a university. I went to Ralph Hawkins' classes about reading and talking about poetry. Ralph made me photocopies of lots of poetry—Olson and Oppen I remember, and he gave me stacks of poetry magazines with living poets in them, and I was off the ground. We read lots of O'Hara, Berrigan and others. It was an absolute pleasure, it felt like my mind was working for pleasure. It was a complete revelation.

By now, as you can imagine in this atmosphere I was thinking I was a poet. The first poet I heard read was Basil Bunting, aged 75. Again, nothing had prepared me for the experience. I think I was in shock. I phoned my girlfriend and she thought I'd had an accident or something dreadful had happened. It was an overpowering experience which lit up the world for me. The sound of him reading *Briggflatts* was overwhelming. I know there are matters of style or whatever, and I read him differently now, but what a sensitive ear Bunting has, and it's all performed in front of me, sitting there with my stupid mouth hanging open no doubt. Now I couldn't be son of Bunting even if I were inclined, but add all of these experiences together and the slowest dolt in the world would write poetry I think. I found myself in a world which previously I didn't even know existed.

DUNCAN Just to put paid to all the febrile rumours, tell us about the Essex School.

CORCORAN There is no Essex school. Nate Dorward has commented on this, he's lined up a lot of the names, lined up the ducks off the lakes on campus. I imagine you could be tempted into thinking it does exist, perhaps if you read recent books by, say, Ralph Hawkins and Ian Davidson you might think it, but I don't think so. I recommend you read those books anyway. Some of the poetry I like is in someway or another, as it turns out, connected to Essex, but that hardly constitutes a school. That university, at that time, was I think different to others, certainly from what friends have said, it seems to have been the case. Tony Frazer is right about this. The interest there was there for translation and world literature, not just Eng. Lit, and of course the visiting American poets, or rather rumours of former presences. There was a door down the corridor with the name Robert Lowell on it, don't know if he was behind the door or not. I escaped unharmed. There were teachers there with an openness, a distinctive difference in academia perhaps, Donald Davie for instance. I suppose it might suit certain purposes to say the Essex school, the taxidermists could excite themselves and resort to their baleful practices. Do you think there's an Essex school?

DUNCAN I'm not sure. I think there was a lot of enthusiasm. I think at a certain moment, there was a belief that it was possible for English people to write poetry, which is very hard to find in this country.

CORCORAN I think that's right, I agree with you in that respect. That happened to me, as I explained. Yes, the atmosphere was exciting and for me empowering in the way you suggest. Not thinking that poetry is written by someone else who belongs elsewhere is essential, but it can arrive in different guises I think.

DUNCAN Right, since then you've published something like ten books of poetry besides appearances in magazines and various anthologies. Can we go through the books chronologically?

CORCORAN *Robin Hood in the Dark Ages* was published in 1985. Though I was interested in the idea of a book, as opposed to the isolated lyric, the serial poems of Jack Spicer and the book-length projects of Peter Riley then, Doug Oliver too, Alice Notley and others, *Robin Hood* is not a book, it's a collection of poems arranged in sections. Whilst I never lacked ambition for what I thought needed saying, the line was obvious, insistent and anacoluthic, running up and down—like a field full of excited horses really. *The Red and Yellow Book* was another attempt to write a book, rather than a set of isolated poems, but it was overwhelmed by my grief when my mother died and turned out differently. Those experiences made me write plaintively in some of those pieces and I think, looking back now, I learnt other things about poetry too. The idea for the title of the book originally was something like a dream or just idle thought—'it's big and bright/each poem a maze/the words in relief'. The closing run of short, lyrical pieces, called *from The Red and Yellow Book*, is an attempt to restore the project and is a way out of the book. Since then I've tended to close several books in that way, to rework and intensify the concerns in a sharper style and abandon them at the same time. There is more variety or flexibility in the line, I collage away quite happily with the domestic, the intense personal grief, Heidegger and Tracy my invented phenomenologist.

DUNCAN John Muckle said you were really into Adorno in those days.

CORCORAN I read one book, *The Jargon of Authenticity*. I read Merleau-Ponty. I was very interested in him. What I did was the obvious thing to do. I found out about what poets I was reading liked, I mean, what they read. That's the obvious thing to do, isn't it? Don't you think?

DUNCAN I never did that, but, now you mention it, yes, it's brilliant.

CORCORAN Well, I don't know. It's the obvious thing to do.

DUNCAN The obvious question is, what do you read?

CORCORAN Now?

DUNCAN At any time.

CORCORAN Well, one-click ordering has been my ruin. I read poetry. Contemporaries. It strikes me there's a great deal of good poetry to read right now. Older and new poetry in translation, Greeks and others, and Simon Smith has put me onto Catullus and Ovid. I've sailed around the Romantics recently but am having a rest at the moment. Also I've been reading books related to the September 11 atrocity, Islam and the west, and what's happened subsequently, studies of empire really. But, for your question, reading W.S. Graham has led me to Roger Hilton, unsurprisingly, and that's the *Roger Hilton's Sugar* work I've just about finished for now. I am interested in people like Martin Bernal and Colin Renfrew and I go back to Jane Harrison often. I'm concerned with ancient disputes being contemporary disputes, like Bernal's work on the Asiatic and African roots of Classical civilization.

DUNCAN *Black Athena?*

CORCORAN Yes. I got interested in them partly through going to Greece, spending time in Greece, visiting sites, and wanting to know something about the timetable a few thousand years before, which has led to patterns of behaviour we see as political now, I think it's all prefigured, I don't think that much has changed. Imagine these Bronze Age people not acting as the glorious adolescence of Europe, not being prototypes for English public school boy imperial administrators, nor models for super hero Aryan horsemen, how impertinent of them. By talking to friends in Greece and them giving me the local version of myths we know as Classical, I've suffered considerable excitement about such things. That's in *Against Purity*. Imagine that the classical edifice of mythology is no such thing but an overlaying and retelling of competing localised myths and songs, arising out of a sort of civic pride, giving back meaning to the specific group. The ancient landscape overlays the modern and I see the mythology as local and useful and not detached from the everyday. I think it's also a sort of code which tells us exactly what is happening in the present Oil Wars for instance, it is a type of ignorance to behave as though such things have not happened before and it's only in the interests of the perpetrators to act as if such things have not happened before.

My friend Yannis has told me his version, the local version, of the Helen and Paris escape, which is down this side of the Taygetus Mountains, not the other side. So they come down the mountain and escape through the village where we stay. I think that the village up the mountain, which if it's called Thalami I take to mean something like bridal chamber and the location of their first night together, is where there used to be a well which was an oracle to Leukothia, the guardian of safe voyages, and Helen's brothers used to be represented by statues on the rock out in the harbour, they also guard voyagers. It all adds up of course. Homer took a different view, not that it matters, he spoke to different villagers possibly. Troy was a trade war for shipping routes and wheat, a newly self styled western power against the east with Helen's abduction as a tabloid excuse for action? Well, however, this all begins with Yannis telling me about the chariot wheel grooves in the village they left behind.

DUNCAN You can't possibly refute that.

CORCORAN No, you can't. What happened to the chronology Andrew, the chronological skip through my books?

DUNCAN We went elsewhere didn't we? So, to restore order, what happens after the first few books, and does your sense of writing the book change?

CORCORAN I wrote more books, and yes it changed. I had the idea I was writing one long poem and that the poem in hand would find its way to the next, and the shape of the book would emerge in that fashion. Certainly from, say *Qiryat Sepher* to maybe *Lyric Lyric*, that's five years, and I was linking the last poem in one book to the first in the next. You can see this between *Qiryat Sepher* and *TCL*, for instance. Alan Halsey has said something on the lines that I seem to be writing and rewriting the same work, something like that. I can see what he means. You'll recall that time, the Conservative conservative decades, and oppositional anger was in the air, and that's taken up in some of those poems—unsurprisingly. I write the lyric, it has all my attention, imagine I'm singing, singing up in the dark. Some of those books close with the lyrical sequence I was after in *The Red and Yellow Book*, it's the same device. *TCL* is the typical book of then I think. Thinking about it now, looking back, I think *Lyric Lyric* begins a change. I think the line becomes stronger and the musicality more assured, the stress is doing a number of different things, and that afterwards prompts a different, larger sense of the personal and impersonal voice.

The other thing that started to happen after *Lyric Lyric* was collaboration with others, Alan Halsey mainly. That gave rise to longer poems I think, and formally sustained attention whether to words or graphics, the breath lengthened. Alan had illustrated several of my books and it was a response to turn it around and write back to the graphics, as in *Saturday Night in the Bardo*. Alan's poetry is obviously different to mine and he has a way of spotting something I'm doing and pushing me, it's very valuable to me. *Your Thinking Tracts Or Nations* is the prime example, and that was hard, concentrated work. Those poems begin as responses to the 14 pictures he gave me, they illustrate the pictures and then take the hint elsewhere. Now he's gone and included the *Memory Screen* CD-ROM with *Marginalien*, that's 208 graphics, how the hell can I cope with that?

DUNCAN Would you say that *Melanie's Book* also signifies another sort of move too?

CORCORAN Yes I would. The verse is less congested and I've learnt something from what I did before, there's another sequence at the end, sonnets if you like. I've always liked something Peter Riley said to the effect that in poetry, the most intimate, the utterly personal is the most common, the most shared experience. I agree. It's apparent in that book. And on top of the chaos to myself and others through divorce and a new marriage, I discover the continuing fascination with Greece. Good timing. This isn't a very technical answer to your question is it? The world of that book is bigger and more intimate than before, and I'm happy with that. It has a shape which comes out of the poems themselves I think, a serial quality I think, the love poems in the middle and the repetition of the Dante, the straight path lost, made it work.

DUNCAN And next came *When Suzy Was*? Another point of change?

CORCORAN Yes. *When Suzy Was* is another book which becomes diverted in the act of writing, rather than by events this time. It's a failed oracular book, or rather it sets out with one direction or enquiry and goes elsewhere. The wrong questions open it but the answers at the end, the *Catalogue of Answers*, another lyrical fire escape at the close, are what I was wanting to write. The book is at ease with running a range of different concerns in and out of the past of a classical civilisation, and overwhelming presence, the physical and sensuous presence of Greece. If I'm allowed to say this, I like the different forms of the poems and the variation in the line. Again, if I'm allowed, I think it shows the biggest change for me so far, I think the poetry has changed. Oddly enough I included a bibliography at the end too, though the poetry seems unencumbered to me at least.

DUNCAN I'm curious about you starting with a project, and doing the reading to fit into it. Maybe we could talk a bit about that process, I think it's something people need to know about.

CORCORAN Yes we've touched on this. Well, it's easier for me to say what I'm reading if I show you, normally it's related to what I'm writing.

Afterwards though, when the writing is finished a lot of what's been read loses its distinctiveness, and you can't even remember some of it. *Your Thinking Tracts Or Nations* is a curious example because clues in the pictures, or my guesses, prompted the reading, or made me look again at familiar material and there is a range of references and vaguer allusions as a result, prompted by the picture I'm writing to. Normally, I think, the reading and the notion of what the writing project becomes, go hand in hand, changing one another. After all, it's the most apparent element that can accompany the unknown business of what happens in the act of writing. Do you see what I mean? Unusually here though the pictures as prompts occasionally led to very direct research, an example would be number 12. I went and read about unicorns because there's one in the picture, obviously. Other types of reading are different, as the bearing of the writing on the picture is different, the connection unclear or certainly allusive, and sparking off ideas or reading perhaps already underway. Examples would be the Polar exploration material, Coleridge, Balkan politics and, I don't know, Neolithic painting.

DUNCAN I think an interview can talk about projects that never come off. I think there are some very interesting projects that don't reach fruition. I think it's important for people to realise that someone really engaged in poetry may have ten fantastic ideas, and seven of them just don't get anywhere, but that's the way to do it. If you aren't doing that . . .

CORCORAN There are three or four things I'm bothered about at the moment. I'm writing some poems which follow on from the extended sequence about Helen and Paris, which in a way allows me to act as if I'm applying findings made there, developing a world view which takes in the distant past. I've written a long narrative poem set during the end of the Peloponnesian war, the narrator is on a journey to talk to Euripides and he might go on to write odes addressed to George Bush about such things as the meaning of Afghan war rugs, or rather Hazara war rugs, but that might not happen. I've also been working on a set of poems about Roger Hilton, *Roger Hilton's Sugar*, one part of which is about going out to look at pictures by him. Often I end up looking at one picture.

DUNCAN One picture?

CORCORAN Well, that's the typical deal. One picture in a gallery in Swindon, and one in a gallery in Bath. And I ring up and check if they're open, and if the picture's on show and normally the answer is no. It's hard to find the pictures publicly available, that part of the work is called *Seeing Hilton*, an accurate title would be, *Not Seeing Hilton*. But whether this . . . this business of having several projects on the go, for which there can be explicit reasons, or not, is like thinking I was writing books and finding out I wasn't, delusion.

DUNCAN But how does that work out with the recent work, *Against Purity*, in the *New and Selected*, because that's finished isn't it?

CORCORAN *Against Purity* is in three parts. The first part is very local to a village in the outer Mani. The second part begins as a response to Alan Halsey's *Dante's Barber Shop* and the final part ends with four monologues, sliding between the past and the present, mixing immediate and distant presences. The play made with the myrio-rama game is important, it's an early 19th century pastime, it's a set of 24 cards depicting a slice of typical romantic landscape. In whatever combination you place the cards next to one another, they always make a landscape which adds up. And in the village I turn the spatial metaphor of the game into a temporal arrange-ment. So Yannis Ritsos comes into the poem, his family home is just over the other side of the peninsula. You can go and visit his house. So he's back alive. Then Shelley arrives in his boat, in he comes to tell us how to run a revolution, Shelley of *Hellas* came to live there in my poem, though of course he never went to Greece. He has a final stroll with Byron. Mythological bodies appear too. And then the middle part of the book, which is just trying to be rid of all this very local material, and it's deliberately meant to look at the world outside, but through the strange vision of Alan Halsey's *Dante's Barber Shop*. And there's an epigraph from The Melodians— How can we sing King Alpha's song in a strange land?

DUNCAN I didn't know that was how the line went.

CORCORAN You know that song, don't you?

DUNCAN Rivers of Babylon.

CORCORAN Yes, that version is the only one I've heard that refers to King Alpha.

DUNCAN And there we wail, when we remember Zion.

CORCORAN I've not seen that reference to King Alpha anywhere else.

DUNCAN Are you sure that's right?

CORCORAN I'm pretty sure. I'll play it to you later.

DUNCAN Who is King Alpha?

CORCORAN No idea. We'll play it later, and we'll see if your ears hear the same as mine, as long as you don't weep when we remember Zion. I may have misheard it.

DUNCAN Are you against purity?

CORCORAN Yes. Read the book, you'll see what I mean.

Bibliography

Robin Hood in the Dark Ages (New York: Permanent Press, 1985).
The Red and Yellow Book (London : Textures, 1986).
Qiryat Sepher (Newcastle upon Tyne: Galloping Dog, 1988).
TCL (Durham : Pig Press, 1989).
The Next Wave (Twickenham: North and South, 1990).
Lyric Lyric (London: Reality Street Editions, 1993).
Melanie's Book (Hay-on-Wye: West House Books, 1996).
When Suzy Was (Exeter: Shearsman Books, 1999)
Your Thinking Tracts or Nations (Sheffield: West House Books, 2001).
New and Selected Poems (Exeter: Shearsman Books, 2004).
Roger Hilton's Sugar (forthcoming 2005).

ANDREW CROZIER INTERVIEWED BY PETER RYAN

From Missile Crisis to English Intelligencer

(Ryan was interested in the stages before someone came to write poems
which they were durably happy with. He does not print the ques-
tions because all his interview subjects were asked a standard set
of questions. However, as well as asking his programmatic ques-
tions additional questions were interjected for purposes of qualifi-
cation or clarification.)

CROZIER During my last two or three years at school [1958–61] I began
reading modern poetry; the first modern British poet I read seri-
ously, borrowing the books from the public library, was Norman
MacCaig. (The other one I remember reading in the same way was
Christopher Logue.) So I can remember reading *A Common Grace* by
Norman MacCaig when it was published and also Christopher
Logue's translations of Pablo Neruda, and a volume of Logue's own
poems published by Villiers Press. My reason for writing poems I
think had to do with, perhaps I read a lot of poetry at the time, but
up till the summer of 1963 I did not consider that writing poems
might be a serious business, in other words it was a talent or a
competence that people possessed at which I essayed my own abil-
ities. I think when I first tried to write poems I was interested first
of all in what my contemporaries did, which impressed me consid-
erably by its competence because they actually produced a
finished text. I refer to undergraduate poets in my own years at
Cambridge, people who were writing poems then and publishing
them in university magazines, who no longer write poems and

whose names need no longer be remembered. The second influence had to do with poems I was then reading, and my understanding of poetry as it was undertaken in England at that time was partial. I might be aware of Christopher Logue and Norman MacCaig, for example, but I couldn't put them onto any kind of map together. I also read American poets and I can remember being interested while I was still at school by John Crowe Ransom. That should be seen in the context in which I read, say, Yeats and also Hopkins as modern poets, but there were no co-ordinates by which to relate Ransom or MacCaig, or for that matter Logue, to those other poets I was led to read by teachers at school. At the same time, in my first two years at university I was more directly involved in activities not concerned with poetry. I was concerned with film societies and I considered the possibility of making films after I left Cambridge. I was fairly closely involved in the anti-nuclear protest movement at the time. I certainly felt that the envisageable future in 1961–62 was not a very distant place: I had a very short-term view of the future because I think that I imagined that there would be destruction of the world in which I lived by nuclear war. What brought that frame of mind to an end was the Cuban crisis in 1962. There was no Armageddon and things resolved themselves in terms of power politics, which was an explanation of the world which up till then my politics had not led me to expect. And so I withdrew fairly consciously from political activity, from serious involvement in looking at and writing about films, and in a certain kind of hiatus in my life at that point, associated with an illness during which I read Charles Olson and Robert Duncan and William Carlos Williams, I brought myself to the point at which, by the end of my second year at university, I was interested in nothing other than poetry, and so I would date my intentional involvement with poetry from the summer of 1963 and my earliest retained, published poems from that summer. Those are the poems collected in the book called *Train Rides*, which wasn't published until some years later. Those early poems were largely taken up with experience at work, in vacation student work on building sites, with experiences on railway trains and with experience of student lodgings. The degree of intention I referred to has to do with the distinction I meant to suggest between writing poems because writing poems was something my contemporaries did and carried therefore some kind of experience which I was curious about, which would probably be the same kind of value as an experience, say, of losing one's virginity, and on the other hand writing poems with a certain degree of purposive activity because one was curious about the conclusion of the poem in relation to where the poem began. Most of the university and school contemporaries of mine who wrote poems did not write with a formal prosody as their means to completing a poem, and at that stage in my career I don't think I could have considered such a prosody as a feasible technical possibility, because it appeared to present certain rather insuperable difficulties. But at the same time was rather pointedly aware of an antagonism in the poetic world, in England especially, between the advocates of a formal prosody and their adversaries, less clearly defined, who would be the then contemporary inheritors of the technical aspects of early 20th century modernism. So that, to pin this down more precisely, I read very carefully the second *New Lines* anthology edited by Robert Conquest, which had a long introductory essay by Conquest which made a number of quite prescriptive comments about the formal organisation of poems, including an argument that there was no reason not to write in metrical forms because any restricted prosodic form nevertheless offered if not an infinite variety, certainly a very high order of variety because of the possibility of variation within a set form. My recollection is that I was not particularly convinced by his arguments, although I did not altogether understand why they did not convince me. As against the *New Lines* mode I was looking more to the example of American writers whom I had been reading since my first term at Cambridge, and the Donald Allen anthology, *The New American Poetry, 1945–60*, gave access to more recent American poets, principally Charles Olson, although I was also very much impressed by John Wieners and Edward Dorn who also published in that anthology. I also read the work of William Carlos Williams and had a curiosity about American poetry written in the 1930s which was fuelled by an essay by Kenneth Rexroth published in an English paperback anthology called *The Beat Generation and the Angry Young Men—Protest*. In that essay Rexroth mentioned the Objectivist poets, particularly Carl Rakosi, and American Surrealist poets, including Charles Henri Ford and Parker Tyler, and I recollect in my last year at Cambridge looking at some of the works of those poets, largely in periodicals. I also read Ezra Pound, though not with the sense of his serious implication in the line of poetry that was influencing me at the time—I think now I would give the same answer as I might have more tentatively given then, which is that those poets constituted the important examples for a poet attempting to write in relation to his period and his situation. That is to say—I think at this point the answer becomes complex—for the young men writing in the early Sixties in England there was also an absence of information about recent history but there was also an absence of information concerning more distant history which was nevertheless that history which would underwrite the more recent history. In other words, the poet in my position in the early Sixties probably had something like fifty years to make up in information because that information was not forthcoming to him from the publication of poetry as it then occurred. There was no clear directive to read the work of the major modern English-language poets—I refer to Pound, to Stevens, to Williams—although of course it was assumed that one had read Yeats. Of course, I read some Auden at school and at Cambridge, but there was no context into which I could place Auden apart from the immediate context of my distaste. I think that distaste had something to do with the fact that the Auden one read tended to be the later Auden rather than the Auden of the 1930s. To find out the modes of writing which are required by history, and to find out the things that poetry can say which are important to history, and the saying of those things, is tied up with that technical issue which I've touched on merely as an incident in my becoming a poet. In the first answers I was offering to your questions I suggested, in my reflections about myself, that becoming a poet had to do with ceasing to be other kinds of person. I think that my interest in becoming a poet had to do with finding a mode for making sense of and placing together a complete or a self-completing scheme of being alive. In other words, partly because other things seemed to fail, and partly because I was making certain demands, it only became an appropriate project to be a poet at the time when my knowledge of poetry began to seem to hold out some fairly complete image in world experience. In my case that had to do particularly with reading Charles Olson. I read the essay 'Human Universe' probably a month or so after my turnaround following the Cuban crisis, and it made a very immediate kind of sense to my rather political mental set, which at the same time was depoliticised because it was not preoccupied with action or political involvement in any way. I'm not attempting to say why I might now suggest that Olson is important if I were talking about him to one of my students. I'm talking about the rather occluded sense of myself in the world that I feel I was equipped with in the early Sixties, within which reading Olson occurred as some kind of light, because it was associated both with the failure or the cessation of one series of life interests, life experiences, and the possible burgeoning of another. I should also add that the kind of poems I was then writing, which tended to be short, factual, concerned with analogy so that, for instance, there's an analogy between a man seen in a restaurant car and Gérard Philipe taken out of a film, were *not* poems modeled upon my reading of Olson. It's not the case that I read the Americans and felt that here was an example to be imitated . . . They were examples of the poetic existence . . . I don't think that I would have thought about being a poet as opposed to occasionally writing pieces of verse had I not thought about the possibility of being a poet as all-consuming preoccupation, and the Americans suggested, through the very narrow representation of their work that was afforded to me in London and Cambridge at that time, that being a poet was in some way a full-time serious activity. So I'm not suggesting that there was a direct formal or technical model, and I haven't talked about Charles Olson as a model, because although I have undertaken to write imitatively of Olson, and of many other poets, it has always been in an entirely concealed, private fashion, not with the intention of producing a poem. I'm putting forward a mix of motive and experience which consolidates various essays at being a poet and various essays at writing poetry, and also the possibility of being a poet and not some other kind of person. Why American rather than English models? Because the kinds of meaning necessary to me were supplied by American rather than English examples. I think they were supplied by American rather than English examples because the history of the techniques which enable the existence of such meaning had been more availably carried forward in America than in England. The poets of the 1940s, such as Gascoyne, Moore, Hendry, would have interested me had I known about them then, I believe, but whatever comments concerning the 1940s or the late 1930s in English poetry that came my way were denigratory and non-specific in the way in which, by contrast, Kenneth Rexroth's comments about the 1930s in America were highly specific and gave me names which I could go and look up in a library. (An odd statement because I had a copy of Rexroth's *New British Poets* at the time, so I think it had zero impact.–2006) When I was about twenty I began to write poetry rather than do anything else, didn't know how to do it, and looked around to see how other people did it and used those examples not as cases of how one wrote a poem but for how one dealt with writing poems. Making my really very meagre starts with writing a few words down, realising when a certain number of words became a line and changed to the next line, and how that kind of toe-hold on a text or on a poem got to grips with something you had to say, I could look around at everything I'd read when I wasn't really interested in writing poems myself, and at things that I'd read when the business of writing poems began to be close to my heart, and see examples of poets who in the kind of consciousness their work revealed of the business of producing a poem either did or did not suggest that the business was fully absorbing. And I've meant to suggest that Olson, and the other poets whom I saw as ancillaries of Olson's, provided examples not of things which could be imitated but of a disposition towards writing which filled the business of writing with human seriousness, something like that. So my earliest poems, by which I mean the poems published from the beginning of my intentional writing career, the poems in *Train Rides*, don't, I think, imitate other poets, but still I had some sense at the back of my head as I was struggling with those texts, which were hardly anything to struggle with because they're minimal, half a dozen lines here, half a dozen lines there, of making the whole business weighty and serious and an adequate preoccupation for a person . . . it's a rather serious business to claim to be a poet. While I was still at Cambridge I would not have called myself a poet, that is to say, among other reasons if you were at Cambridge and called yourself a poet you did certain kinds of thing, you published poems in the Cambridge undergraduate magazines, which I did once. Coming back to England from America in 1965, by which time I was in touch with more people who called themselves poets or were involved in the publishing and reading activities associated with poetry, I was still not sure whether I could call myself a poet or not. But while I was in America I was in a position where, very generously, I was called a poet by various people, which introduced a certain kind of discrepant focus into my life because on the one hand here were some of the poets whom I most admired admitting me into their company, and, on the other hand, in my sense of myself as English I knew full well that in the context of English poetry I would not even have a toe in the ring. I was caught between a very real desire to go back to England because I didn't like living in America and the feeling that if I went back to England I would be failing to take advantage of what America had to offer. The most important thing was the one of self-recognition, that is to say, there was something that could be used, although now and probably then I could recognise that the poems I had written were not particularly . . . Well, simply because it enables you to keep on doing what you're doing, rather than stopping or giving up or getting tired, or thinking that you're suffering from some egotistical decision. In other words, you could realise that you were being fairly egotistical (*smiles*) but still feel that it had some value.

I think I've always known in the process of writing whether I was going to write something that was finally of interest or not, and for that reason have in the process of writing very rapidly made the decision that if I went on with the piece that I was writing it would be just to see what happened, knowing that the discovery was the terminal life of what I was doing or, on the other hand, that I was writing something which I might want to publish at some point—I think the intentional part of one's mind is very valuable because it provides continuity but at the same time can generate that kind of continuity which is edging other things out of the way. But I nevertheless am prepared to run that kind of risk in order to have some continuous experience of writing, rather than let things depend upon some kind of happy, fortunate occurrence of the unconscious or the inspirational. And furthermore, of course, as many other people probably told you, their experience I think would be like mine, those inspirational things can occur under the pressure of a fairly critical will, and applying the critical will to something which you reject, in the process of rejecting it, can peel it off to reveal something fresh beneath it.

In more gross terms the poems that I first wrote were one-off and lyric texts and from there I found myself moving, partly because I think the lyrical occasion has become more and more artificial, to writing poems in series, and also in a way that doesn't

really look as though it's on a main line of development. I had
written poems in collaboration with John James for quite a long
while. I moved to a sense of writing which was the reverse of lyri-
cal in that the authority which poetic statements require shifted, I
feel, from the person to the text, if that makes sense. And although
I keep feeling, when I get that sense of my work whereby what I've
written recently doesn't look any more familiar or, on the other
hand, any more exotic than what I wrote ten years ago, that my
work is very much of a piece, the actual writing experience has
changed considerably in that formerly my writing was rather occa-
sionalistic in its being done, and a poem whether it was longer or
shorter got written off like that. I now find—and I partly made this
the case, that I write continuously but I also write very slowly so
that I may spend a month or so writing fourteen or fifteen lines
and yet there not be any real hiatus in my sense of the integrity of
those fourteen or fifteen lines as moving from then to then. It's
like talking very slowly, as I tend to anyway. So at the moment I'm
writing a poem which is at present nineteen lines long and I've
been writing it for the last month. It's taken me that time to write
these nineteen lines and really they've been produced equally over
that time—it doesn't move steadily, I think it has surges, surges
during which new material is actively yielding its results, and then
periods of, if you like, antithetical energy in which the new mate-
rial or sources have not yet resolved themselves so that you can't
know what they are. But I find, even though I may not be spending
much time with pen to paper, that even in non-productive periods
I am, so far as I am concerned, fairly busy with writing, so that, for
instance, to talk about the experience of writing, the experience of
writing is not for me now of having written that poem and then
written that poem and then that poem, with lacunae in between
in which other things presumably happen, but rather an experi-
ence of getting on with writing at the end of which there's that
poem, and there's that poem, there's that poem, and a lot of other
stuff which never gets seen . . . I think the process of knowing your-
self is something I cast forward towards the future; in other words,
the only purpose of self knowledge is to change the future. And
changing my writing in order to give it a place in my future has
involved fairly deliberate thought about subject matter, although
fairly often, in fact more often, it's been a matter of restricting
subject matter which has become mechanical or obsessional, and

less often a matter of attaining new subject matter. So, for instance, I spent a lot of time thinking about, learning about issues of optics, sense perception, light, and so on, and that material furnished images for a lot of poems, and I know as soon as one of those images comes into a poem yet again I have to back off from it, because it's a sign that the poem is running out of energy at that point, that it's beginning to freewheel. I don't think that writing poems has to do with having a complete thing initially to say, but rather has to do with the invention of the realization of what you have to say, so that writing a poem moving from point to point is like inventing, very wilful work, very intentional, selecting from within what's available in order to make the poem continue, give it some life, and the life is entirely bound up with the poems' continuity. When I've noticed that the way I happen to be thinking about taking a poem on in the process of doing it is drawing upon a range of subject-matter and imagery which I think has been exhausted then it is a suggestion or a signal to me that at that point I'm not really thinking very hard about the poem but I'm falling back upon something that is a cliché; it's a Crozier cliché.

Writing poems was never a technical business like learning how to rhyme, learning how to get a line to consist of the right number of syllables, learning how to produce stanzas according to a common model, in a sequence because I had rejected that model of technical attainment as a means to writing poetry. And I think for that reason the term 'technique' doesn't clearly indicate the kind of learning process with a direction and an attainment that I actually feel I underwent. I think what I had to learn was what was said in the poem, and I don't mean that in a normative sense but rather what kind of unit of signification poems can consist of, and that involves management of the sentence in relation to the line, management of what is figurative in relation to what is literal, management of the syntactic forms of the self, and then, secondly, although I don't feel that it's really distinct from what I've previously been talking about, the accomplishment of that rhythmic identity which both works at the level of the line and also at the level of the transitions from line to line through the more extended passages of rhythmic coherence, of language felt as a presence which is not authorized simply by heightened delivery on the one hand, or by a metrical scheme on the other. And I think that latter sense of non-metrical rhythm is what I learnt from attention to the Americans—I would think of the relation of discourse to, say, the most significant pronoun sets and syntactic series of a poem as a technical issue, but as well and more importantly it's an issue concerning my sense of the meanings I make as a poet. The notion of 'technical' entertained here is rather that view of technique which regards it as an attainment which in some way can be instructed or conveyed by exercise and made more memorable by exercise. So I constantly think of myself as undergoing technical evolution within my work and yet at the same time I can see that many other people would not regard the kind of thing I am preoccupied with as a matter of technique rather than of content or something like that.

ANDREW CROZIER INTERVIEWED BY ANDREW DUNCAN

How High the Zero

from High Zero

Such feeling for symmetry
        in the eternal tables
where the horizon meets
the horizon in a boundary line
that surrounds us in the sky
 as in a clouded retina
in which the light is like a cataract
saturated with atmosphere
until it spills with emotion
                like a paper bag

                covered with advertisements
which its contents render illegible because
content is an illusion. So much
that can't be looked into
in these holiday transparencies.
 with their lack of foreground
and focus set to infinity
as though it was a wall
                run up by the shutter
timed to the split second

in which the sky tilts away
as the light decelerates to O
             on a soft surface
spread for such emergencies

DUNCAN (*from a letter*) Can we talk about *High Zero*? Can you talk us through its structure? Grimly Castafiore said that the title refers to *High Pink on Chrome* [by JH Prynne] and to *Striking the Pavilion of Zero* [by John James], and that your poem is also a reply to those two. Is that true? is 'high zero' the circuit of the sun in the sky? How did you get interested in optics? (Page references are to the Street Editions publication of the text.)

CROZIER (*from a letter of reply*) Grimly Castafiore is right about *High Zero*. The two flanking poems are parodies of poems in the Prynne & James volumes respectively, repeating lines from the main block of text; however, I don't see it as a reply to them. I say 'block of text' because I think of it as a square of 24×24 units: the writing procedure was to start at the top and work down, i.e. first I wrote 24 first lines, then the second lines and so on. I don't know if that tells you much. As a term 'High Zero' doesn't refer to the sun moving across the sky. Nor does it refer to a 1704 Royal Society temperature scale I've just read about in which the axis is reversed so that boiling point is given as a minus quantity. I had to read up on optics to find a way of writing about Ian Tyson's prints.

DUNCAN (*live*) I'd like to talk about *High Zero* in general. There are some more specific questions which I thought might get us going. On p. 7 "It would flout its law /saturation by the contents spread anecdotally (BAL)." What is BAL?

CROZIER It is British anti-Lewisite. Which is the antidote for a form of poison gas. At the time I could have told you what its exact chemical basis was, but I've forgotten. It has a colour, the colour is referred to there. [goes to dictionary] Lewisite: A vesicant liquid of arsenite derivative used in chemical warfare. Named after WL Lewis, American chemist.

DUNCAN Not Wyndham Lewis?

CROZIER No, but he was quite pleased with the association of his name with it.

DUNCAN So in the previous stanza 'In shock rare gases leave their stain to/ burn its bright sign on everything.' What are these rare gases?

CROZIER The rare gases would be those gases which tend to rarefy most easily. Which of course is a condition of being a gas. They're also called inert gases because they don't react chemically.

DUNCAN I thought they might be the burning gases in the sun or in neon-argon lamps.

CROZIER Not the former but the latter. So it's the rarity in the sense that in the periodic table they're obscure. There's a nod as well to 'neon in daylight'.

DUNCAN The bit about 'As if it were a lamp of earthly flame', who is that a quote from?

CROZIER That would be Melville via Prynne. 'The Confidence Man.'

DUNCAN In page 13, 'the burnished metal of your head.' I wondered what this burnished metal was. (Reference is to the Street Editions book.)

CROZIER As far as I remember these poems were written partly during a very hot summer, and that informs the way in which invention was deploying itself. Burnished metal would be any brazen head and so it's an epithet derived from sculpture applied to a living head. The sequence of the trope seems to me partly self-cancelling. To repel sunlight by staying indoors is not actually to repel sunlight. Reflection is ambiguously, I suppose, both the reflection of light by a surface and the supposedly interior transaction of mental reflection. So the head that's staying indoors has both an exterior and interior, an outside and inside. Does that go far enough?

DUNCAN Can I go on to another passage, at p.30—

Done with all that pass on
down the line of withered plants

and take a leaf from every other one
they're overdosed with Paris green
past any joke.

What is this shade?

CROZIER Paris green is another arsenical poison like Lewisite used in gardening as a pesticide, and also as a pigment.

DUNCAN I think there's a bit of some Pound poem about arsenous green.

CROZIER Green arsenic. It's one of the early poems, 'L'Art, 1910'. And the green is I guess an allusion to the 'greenery-yallery' of the 1890s.

DUNCAN I'm trying to visualise that and failing.

CROZIER 'Grass spoils underfoot.' I think it was a hot summer and the grass died. As well as being trampled on.

DUNCAN I thought it just looked sick because of the artificial light.

CROZIER It's not really summer, is it, it's more autumn and winter. You need to wipe your feet. The line on 'contents spread anecdotally' is one of the lines that stands for a line from the Prynne poem at the beginning of *High Pink on Chrome*. The poem on page 7 which begins *And the grass spoils underfoot*, which is a line I've just encountered, is in the musical sense a parodic rewriting of the first poem of *High Pink on Chrome*. Which we'll get. It's the last poem of *High Pink on Chrome*! That's right, I reversed them. '[T]he contents spread anecdotally (BAL)' is 'access by /blood spread, dimercaprol 200 mg.' Does that make sense?

DUNCAN You did explain something about this in the letter. Could you say a bit more about the taking of melodic material from *High Pink on Chrome* and *Striking the Pavilion of Zero*?

CROZIER Both those books, by Prynne and James respectively, were published in 1975. *High Zero* is written according to a very simple arithmetical format whereby the number of poems is the same as the number of lines in each poem, and the poems were not written sequentially but as so many first lines, so many second lines, so many third lines and so on. I thought I would complicate that by introducing a more definite constraint whereby some of the lines, which had to sort of graft themselves on to what was there already, at the same time had to be able to fit in the context of two other poems, those poems being based in their format on the last poem in Prynne's book, which I placed first, and the first poem of James' book, which I placed last, poems which were written according to constraints I knew nothing of. And at the time I suppose I thought that the introduction of various patterns of constraint was a stimulus. But I don't think you can go beyond that to ... I wouldn't go beyond that to speculate whether there's some kind of implied critique of either of the two books mentioned, or of the two poems chosen. In a way I regretted that the James poem wasn't a little bit longer.

DUNCAN How careless of him.

CROZIER How careless of him. He didn't know what it was going to be used for. I suppose that rather than any implication of critique, it's more a matter of engaging on a line by line basis with poems by people whom I regarded as friends and colleagues.

DUNCAN I was struck by a poem on page 31, 'the list of recurrent solutions', which Grimly and I read as being about a political demonstration. James' and Prynne's political beliefs seemed to correspond to that. This may be completely wrong, of course.

CROZIER No, that's probably alluding to the behaviour of colleagues of a different sort. I don't really associate talk of raising consciousness with either Prynne or James, so it's much more a kind of irritation with some kind of discourse inside the academic world, which might be referenced by the Sociology of Literature conferences at the University of Essex at the period.

DUNCAN I think the papers I saw were very inadequate, but they may have been leading towards something. There was a progressive nisus. I don't know if the individuals pursued that intent. Is there a relationship between the cyclical or non-progressive nature of *High Zero* and the possibly rather ill-informed revolutionary politics of the 1970s?

CROZIER I'm not entirely sure what you mean by cyclical. The question seems to allude to a very conventional stand-off between supposed modes of thought based on recurrences and cycles on the one hand and a sort of progressive history-based, teleological Left view on the other. That's always seemed to me a rather pointless stand-off, enclosed inside a discourse of the Left in any case. The aspect of the poem that you're referring to as cyclical I would mention differently, drawing attention to or mentioning that at the time part of my approach to writing was to try and think out ways of writing a poem whereby you didn't start out at line 1, although you could say that that's what happens in *High Zero*, the first line of the first poem was written first and the last line of the last poem was written last, the trajectory between those two points is probably diagonal across a two-dimensional surface. Because the thought which led to that strategy was very much conditioned by ideas about how do painters do it differently, a recurrent issue for me when I think about the practices of making anything. In making that comparison, although it's a comparison which draws attention to features of visual art which are extremely tedious for many visual artists, like the stretched canvas—Oh how boring, it's not boring for a poet to think about; and covering that surface as a kind of analogy for the way one might write a poem is not a boring analogy for someone situated elsewhere.

DUNCAN So we might think of *High Zero* as being like a canvas, the composition is allover and simultaneous?

CROZIER I think the simultaneity might come . . . Well, clearly you can't have a simultaneous experience of reading it. You always return to whatever kind of sequence you decide to set up as a reading strategy. You can read it back to front. You can read it the way it was written. And there is a version of it which resembles the way the first part of it, the first few lines, were written, called 'High Zero Quadrature', where I took all the lines I'd so far written and lumped them up as four poems. We could go back to your question about the cyclical, because I think you were picking up on something in the language of the poem.

DUNCAN Yes. Various moments in the poem which perhaps shouldn't be allowed to dominate it, but we do find for example 'Begin life again' seems to be cyclical. At the end of the line 'we begin again' is cyclical. But then 'we advance again' seems to be progress, in those terms. *High Zero* seems to reach its end without its beginning having vanished. I agree that literally if you turn a page over the previous page isn't visible, but maybe part of the informational framework in your head is. I think a long poem has to have simultaneity at some level.

CROZIER It depends how good a reader's mind is.

DUNCAN Exactly.

CROZIER But if you want to sort of get, if you like, 1970s motifs and preoccupations in the poem, there is a preoccupation with content, as on page 25—

in which the light is like a cataract
saturated with atmosphere
until it spills with emotion
    like a paper bag

    covered with advertisements
which its contents render illegible because
content is an illusion.

This particular page is obviously about perspective and our relation to horizons. The presence of light. The optic of photography. And printed advertisements on paper bags.

DUNCAN Is it the contents of the image on the bag which is an illusion? How is the content an illusion?

CROZIER Well, in the first place it is the contents of a paper bag, which is actually a simile. And the paper bag has in its role as a simile been emptied out by spilling. But then some kind of contents are restored in the poem, because they have the agency of rendering something illegible. So there's nothing there and then something.

A paper bag always holds something. But to utter as an explanation based on an implied premise, which belongs to because, that 'content is an illusion', is an absolutist utterance which needs to be read as much for its modalities as for what it asserts.

DUNCAN So there may be someone saying, Content is an illusion, but that assertion is not sustained in the poem?

CROZIER Well, there isn't someone in the poem speaking. Unless you have some kind of performance rationale for insisting there always must be. It's a form of words encountered amongst theoretical discourses and, to use later jargon, sort of pasted into the poem.

DUNCAN Could you say a bit more about that? I think this might be a source of misreadings.

CROZIER Yes. Can you give me a pointer?

DUNCAN If someone is reading the poem as being absolutely dominated by first-person experience in a way which quite an amount of recent English-language poetry has been, and if they bend things to fit into that framework, they could produce misinterpretations. As I think the perceived attack on progressive politics would be an example of this.

CROZIER So you're saying that the history of the reception of this book has been as an attack on progressive politics?

DUNCAN That would be too general. I know Grimly saw it, although admittedly most of the poem doesn't fit into that perspective. But the misreading might just be someone failing to perceive what's going on, producing a positive reading which is . . .

CROZIER In one sense this poem is full of personal experience. Fragments of it rather than a narrative about it. It was written over a certain period of time, during which I was doing all sorts of usual things one does, passing from different times of the day and night, different immediate locations, different personnel, which I then turn to as the immediate context for or source of material for the next line. And it might offer some clarification if I then go on to say I chose the word material then as distinct from content, because if there is allusion for example to a night-time walk over the Downs, that doesn't then constitute that as content of the poem, and the procedure for writing the poem works against what is drawn from personal experience. Retaining that modality because it has entered what I hope is a kind of strong field of material. And other stuff altogether, such as the series of linguistic terms which poems develop as they proceed from start to finish. And part of the strength of that field is that there is an accumulated background, and part of its strength is that there is a sort of constant displacement sideways, in that the sequence of thinking about working on material that is derived from personal experience doesn't treat it cumulatively within a particular poem that makes it relevant. I mean sideways in the sense of implicating an adjacent place in the next poem which you only get to when you've turned the page, having read several more lines of the previous poem, as though it recurs with the periodicity of the poems themselves.

DUNCAN Sideways meaning the next poem, the poem as written, adjacent?

CROZIER It sounds as though we're trying to redeem this poem, its bad reputation.

DUNCAN Well, I think probably not. Grimly was quite keen for someone to be against mid–70s progressive politics. I think this was, cough, the verdict of history, or at least the verdict of the electorate.

CROZIER What was taking place in the mid–70s? When did Mrs Thatcher become leader of the Conservative Party?

DUNCAN Well, Heath fought the 1974 election and was presumably knived quite rapidly after that. In 1975, maybe even 1974.

CROZIER OK, so this is the dying days of the Wilson government

DUNCAN I think he quit in 76.

CROZIER ... the advent of Thatcherism by virtue of her being elected to leader of the party. I did try and get a rise out of a progressive friend by asking her, was she not pleased for a woman to be leader of a political party. But I failed. What was happening in international politics at the time?

DUNCAN The price revolution, the commodities boom giving on to the OPEC price hikes, forcing oil importing economies to adjust big time. The Soviet economy doing rather well because they were an oil exporter.

CROZIER The Americans withdraw from Vietnam in 75 . . .

DUNCAN Actually they got all the troops out a couple of years before that. I think 75 was the fall of Saigon.

CROZIER The fall of Saigon. Yes. They had to sort of scuttle out to their helicopters. So fairly quiet on the international front, all in all.

DUNCAN Yes, I suppose that's true. It was the end of the thirty year boom, as we see now.

CROZIER It hadn't yet got to the kind of late 70s distresses of downsizing, destocking, cutting retail prices.

DUNCAN It was more fighting over the division of the wealth which was seen as being freely available.

CROZIER Well, perhaps it is appropriate to this. One of the reference frames is the turn taken by unorganised left-wing politics through the higher education system, and it would also be the time that the academic world was being hit by the juggernaut of Theory. Sometimes more politicised than it had been at source. But no-one talks that way any more, and it would be antiquarianism to seek to retrieve and rehearse the jargon of that time. (When did you last hear someone called out for believing in transcendental signifiers?) As a kind of professional discourse about literature which encroached on me at precisely the point where it made political claims for itself.

The thing about the juggernaut of theory is that it did run on wheels, in the sense that it was characteristically a mediated, second order activity. I think I came across a lot of that for the first time in Jameson's *The Prison House of Language*. Taking more of a backward look at these matters, I suppose the most up-to-date of French theorists to engage me directly, on the basis of my own inquisitiveness and curiosity, were Lévi-Strauss and Merleau-Ponty in the 1960s, both already by the 1970s pretty passé. I also read a lot of Sartre in the 1950s, as one did, stopping short of the *Critique de la raison dialectique*.

I was saying that the progressive politics of the academy were associated with interests which excluded most of mine over the previous 10 or 15 years. It may actually articulate a generational difference, insofar as I would see that little group of writers who emerged from Cambridge in the first half of the 70s—Wilkinson, Mengham, there were others who have sort of faded away or gone in entirely different directions. I see them as to a greater or lesser extent shaped by the immediacy of all those theoretical discourses.

DUNCAN That would certainly explain a lot.

CROZIER Don't think you should draw the conclusion that I was obsessed through the 70s with what some of my near contemporaries were thinking and saying and doing, because I think the characterisation I've given of the preoccupations in writing *High Zero* indicate that I'm continuing to think along long established, already established, lines. I have *High Zero* as a kind of theatre in which certain knockabout characters can be rapidly led on and led off.

DUNCAN I like the 'rapidly', Andrew. There is clearly an affinity between decentralising the text and talking about a strong field.

CROZIER That's right.

DUNCAN But the wish to set up a strong field in which the composition surprises you rather than being a memoir of things you've already experienced could well come from quite other directions. Probably did, in fact. For example from the interest in visual art. That is, static visual art as opposed to cinema. Can you expand on that, because I think this transition to a strong field is quite a deep cut in English poetry which a lot of readers don't understand at all.

CROZIER I think it a restatement, on different terms, of notions and suggestions which were still quite potent and suggestive and stimulating, which nevertheless might now be considered when put baldly to be dated. Such as for example the autonomy of—awful phrase—the work of art.

DUNCAN So autonomy also from biography?

CROZIER I would say that taking autobiography broadly, *High Zero* contains a great deal of material which might be thought of as autobiographical, although it's not actually been put together as a narrative, so if a biography means some kind of narrative about a subject, so you might want to allege, or want me to allege, that the material then ceases to be autobiographical, as a result of the kinds of pressures I've described. On the other hand, 'Free Running Bitch' is in many respects quite directly autobiographical, and yet I wouldn't feel that in the way those poems are conceived and written, that they allow for any notion of strong tension between truth-telling, by virtue of narrative, on the one hand, and the autonomous work of art on the other. I don't think those two issues need be in tension, except when they're defined in such ways that that tension is turned into a stand-off, and they're treated as though they're mutually exclusive. Which is what I mean when I use the term stand-off. So coming back to the question, if we're talking about modernism, then part of the background is the inescapable belated novelty of much of foundational modernism for people growing up in the 1950s and 1960s. I think the sort of modernism you come across depends very much on your social circumstances. For example, those educated at universities would come across the novelty of Ezra Pound and William Carlos Williams in the early 60s, two or three generations too late; whereas others might in museums and public libraries come across other things.

DUNCAN We were talking about the difference between speaking with your own voice and a strong field, and about politics coming in big-time in the 1970s and making things very teleological as opposed to . . .

CROZIER Does Ryan's extract from his conversation with me reproduce what we discussed in relation to the Cuba Crisis?

DUNCAN It certainly mentions . . . I've got a transcript here . . . [reads from transcript].

CROZIER Why did Castafiore want to see it as a critique of 70s politics?

DUNCAN I think Grimly has a line of criticising 70s Marxism for the same reasons that most people I know do.

CROZIER Including 70s Marxists.

DUNCAN Well probably, yes. It's hard to think that those tactics or concepts will prove victorious now when they didn't then. This opens up a whole world of data but perhaps its relevance to *High Zero* is limited.

CROZIER Correct. It's not a basic premise of the poem, merely part of the ambience of the times. This is an anecdote but it may not be completely without interest. I went to hear Arthur Scargill talk to a Labour Party meeting in Stoke on Trent Town Hall, probably 1982, quite late on in the coal strike. Very crowded meeting. I was sitting in a balcony at the back. In the side balcony on the length of the hall there were a group of miners from the South Staffordshire pits and a group of students from, not the University of Keele, I think some institution in the south of the county. This group were ultra-radical in their interventions when Scargill was speaking. It ended up being something just short of an outright onset between the two groups, the miners and the radical students. It was rather like having the supporters of two football teams on the same terrace. That seemed to be very striking as a comment on the anthropology of left-wing politics at the time.

DUNCAN They were probably both quite turned on by confrontation. I mean, I would see that as a political failure, but they wouldn't necessarily.

CROZIER No. What the group of miners were saying was, Butt out of it, this is our struggle.

DUNCAN The original edition of *High Zero* has got a painting of a Carrara marble quarry. Does that shed light on the poem?

CROZIER It's a very large monochrome wash drawing of quarries by Ian Potts who is a Lewes-based painter and a friend of mine, and he produced a large number of such drawings in the mid 70s, of various sizes. They're monochrome, which is not strictly typical of his painting, in order to represent the very high contrast of black and white in the quarries under Mediterranean sunlight, reflected light and shadow. And as well as the rather impenetrable shadows there are a whole series of reflective surfaces which are variously rubble, stacks of marble waiting to be sold on to sculptors and other consumers, and there are a number of places in the poem where my looking at these drawings is part of that experience of everyday life we discussed earlier, and drawn upon thus. So talking about light falling upon things, which I think goes on throughout the poems, may be about daylight, dawnlight, if you like, light as experienced within the diurnal cycle. So you get your cycle in that way. But it's also about the experience of looking at and reading Ian Potts's transcription of a very different quality of light, in particular the way that perhaps engages with a certain content as represented by the rubble or blocks, which the light articulates just as much as does the shadow. The drawing actually reproduced on the cover wasn't chosen particularly for what it represented so much as because it could be bled off at the edges to yield an image which would fit the format of the dust-wrapper. Nobody else illustrates that . . . the kind of thing I'm talking about, but perhaps not as forcefully as some of the other drawings in a more conventional, less landscape format, although of course actually as folded around the book they're not landscape format at all.

DUNCAN The procedures which allowed you to build *High Zero* are the key information not printed in the book. It's not that people would want a volume of Collected Procedures, but I'm curious to know more about how you devised such a procedure, and other procedures you used, because I think a lot of people are unfamiliar with this approach to writing.

CROZIER It should be self apparent that the number of poems and the number of lines per poem are the same. Although that doesn't then lead to understanding of the actual sequence of the writings, it should suggest that there is a relationship between the two. I very easily see that relationship as being rather like that of a grid on a square format, in which the number of divisions on each side is the same, not unlike a square of an Ordnance Survey map, for example. It's also, I think, self-apparent that the first and last poems in the book, which are different in shape to the other poems, stand outside that format, while nevertheless having all their lines repeated, or recurrent, within the poems that make up that format. So both of these features of the writing, it seems to me, are completely overt, and provide strong clues to something about the character of the writing as conceived or as intended. Anyone reading the book at the time might quite reasonably have also been expected to have read books by Prynne and James so that although there's no direction, other than a kind of hint in the title *High Zero*, to specific books, there's a reasonable expectation that that kind of dragging one's coat-tails, let's say, will be picked up on, as it appears to have been picked up on at least by Grimly Castafiore. And of course also there's the dedication of the book to Prynne and James. Therefore I think I can say that the features of the writing and the way they contribute to a reading of the poem, are fully candid, certainly for the readers I was able to envisage at the time. Then of course anyone can come along and say, are these things actually exhaustively true? and certainly there was a problem at one point, in sending the manuscript round, when I lost a line from one of the poems, and there's one of the poems which visually on the page looks much more erratic in its disposition than the norm. And it would I think be quite apt to ask, was this written in quite the same way as the rest? To which the answer must be, No, it's an erased poem.

DUNCAN This is . . . (leafs through the book to p.28)

CROZIER Yup. Or what's left after a certain amount of erasure.

DUNCAN I think erasure is back in fashion.

CROZIER Let's change erase to obliterate. To be exhaustively detailed, what I held in the back of my mind while doing that was the cancellation or obliteration of text performed by Tom Phillips.

DUNCAN *A Humument.*

CROZIER *A Humument* and other things where . . . he used a kind of stripy column of words which he certainly intended to be read. So that's a bit of a throw-back to an earlier connection to Tom Phillips's books and to John James.

DUNCAN Because John knew Tom Phillips, or exhibited his works?

CROZIER No, because John James and I produced a series of collaborative poems which were published with the text on one page and then a sheet of versions of the text by Tom Phillips on the facing page, called *In One Side and Out the Other*. You've not seen that?

DUNCAN I think I may have been shown it.

CROZIER I think my copy is at work. It was published in 1970–71 and Phillips had been working on these treated pages of text, in particular W. H. Mallock's novel called *A Human Document*, which becomes *A Humument*. This was in the late 60s, I would say, and a number of these had been exhibited in a Critic's Choice exhibition at Arthur Tooth's gallery, I think, round about 1969, 1970, so I approached Tom Phillips and said, You know, we've got this book of poems, we want you to illustrate it, produce a visual collaboration to go with it. Which was the sort of thing you would do in those days.

DUNCAN What changed?

CROZIER You could approach people out of the blue and they'd say, Yeah. Don't you think it's all changed?

DUNCAN In 1969 I was still at prep school so it's hard for me to say.

CROZIER Perhaps artists just get successful younger.

DUNCAN Perhaps there was just more trust. Fewer spreadsheets with quarterly objectives.

CROZIER Off the record ... (deathless perceptive comment summing up thirty years of change to general satisfaction, suppressed)
 Am I digressing? I think as it stands there are no missing words, so in relation to words that were there before, and which you might say have gone missing, what remains is in a similar relation to that between the repeated lines and their separate contexts.

DUNCAN It's hard to look at it without having a kind of shimmer of a different text it's made out of.

CROZIER Yes, I think that's why I left the words disposed on the page as they had been previously, that's the trace of before. There's a point we haven't touched on at all which we should touch on, which is that these poems ... the way the group of poems is set up as a formal object recurrently involves drawing attention to the significance of the line, to the line of verse as a unit, and to the line of verse as a unit which can perform different roles in different contexts. Leaving aside the question of lines of verse as things which can perform different roles in different semantic contexts, which is something which individual words also are required to perform, I think very important to understanding something about my poetry is the attention I pay to lines as units of composition, and relations between one line, and the preceding line, and the next. And that raises inevitably the topic, it seems to me, of what is referred to variously as metre or metric or prosody or rhythm or measure. Those matters which are if you like a component in the technical material of poetry as a medium. I don't think I go as far here in ensuring or attaining a kind of absolute autonomy for individual lines as I do in a later poem called 'Humiliation in its Disguises', in which each line could stand in isolation as a kind of caption although the way they're put together brings out a kind of syntax running through the poem as a whole.

DUNCAN It could foreground the act of combination as well as disjunction?

CROZIER It seems to me one of the most interesting things about poetic language is its conjunction or bringing together of larger or smaller units. Or bringing together of elements into smaller and larger units. Thus drawing attention away from the largest unit as the ultimate verification of what meaning may be, which I think is one of the things which a notion of full and complete utterance or a bit of a sentence or a bit of sententiousness or an intended communication falls short of, overlooks. I hope you can put that back together as a sentence.

DUNCAN So these are the units which are to be disposed and the field is the way in which they can be disposed? a set of relationships which they're going to enter into?

CROZIER I would probably think that having demonstrated that a line can be repeated in a different context and remain integrally itself and at the same time have its weight and significance affected by a different context, that it ought to be possible to go on doing that indefinitely with any particular line. And if a line on the one hand is unique in itself and at the same time not unique in its context, then the other possible contexts in which it might play a functional role rather than remaining true to itself ought to be thought of as indefinite, without a theoretical limit to the number of possibilities.

DUNCAN So the 24 poems point to a much larger, even indefinite, set of possibilities, which they're a sample from?

CROZIER Treating the book as something read from cover to cover, then the reader's experience would presumably be, Read the first outlying poem, go on to read the main block of poems and have an experience of déjà vu, and then read the second, closing outlying poem and have recurrent senses of déjà vu throughout, since all those lines would have been encountered already.

DUNCAN They might pick it up and they might not. Is it a motet where one systematically . . .

DUNCAN A catch, or a round . . .

CROZIER I think a musician would probably pick that up much better. I don't think music enters into my calculations here. I probably have a very naïve set of understandings about music which would regard it as wild and novel. Not subject to artifice of the sort I've been describing. Which I know is perfectly opposed to the case of music, but nevertheless my experience of music tends to ignore that fact. Which means I'm not a skilled listener.

DUNCAN I'm a bit surprised, because Zukofsky and Bunting were so preoccupied with music that . . .

CROZIER Indeed, and, when I was initially formulating ideas about the poetry of my epoch with a view to carrying on post-graduate work, it was in terms of the analogy between poetry and music, because that was so strongly solicited by amongst others William Carlos Williams in his later writings on measure, quantitative verse—but I came to the conclusion that what one was dealing with was at best an analogy rather than a strong structural identity. Partly because, as I've increasingly come to think, poetry is something which is read rather than heard. I think that's the condition in which we experience poetry, certainly the condition in which I experience poetry, although I can in reading it put, imagine, it in the context of being voiced, I can read it aloud, or I can read it inwardly, obviously that seems to me an incidental material enrichment rather than something which contributes to either the poetical form or the poetic significance. Which might seem to beg the question, What can I possibly mean by talking about prosody? It means I still think that there are formal features associated with language's material qualities which are the basis of rhythm. And I don't think performance is necessarily a very good guide to anything other than the rhythm of the performance. Certainly not to the sort of authentic rhythm within a good text.

DUNCAN I think a performance is a social event, and the people in the room compose a large part of the meaning of the event, rather than just the text. It would be a bit paradoxical to argue that they're simply amplifying it. It's hard to believe that.

CROZIER It used to be frequently alleged in the 60s and 70s, and no doubt subsequently, that by hearing poets read their work a reader attained to a much clearer and authentic understanding of the rhythmical character or signature of the text. Which I don't think could possibly be true. Many poets are very bad readers, and bad reading can have all kinds of qualities, including too strong a commitment to sounding good, and even contradict what one might think was the evidence of the written page in front of one, as in comparing the two by following the score at a concert. So I think that that whole line from Pound's early insistence that the separation of word from music led to poetic degeneracy, down to Bunting's reiteration that the pleasure of poetry was in the sound, not the words, is unhelpful, certainly unhelpful to me, and I don't think it stands up to scrutiny when looking at the work of either. And I think since you mention Zukofsky that, although he may have had both a kind of, I want to say spectrum, but I should probably say ratio, that runs through speech as a lower limit to music as an upper limit, and although he has described several of his poems, the shorter ones, as songs, and he has talked about *A* as the equivalent to Bach's St Matthew Passion, he's also—I don't know whether it was Zukofsky or someone else, perhaps James Laughlin, described *A* as an epic of the class struggle. And Zukofsky's whole tendency as a poet seems to me to be towards the semantics of the lowest semantic function of language, by which I mean the semantics of enunciation and audition. I don't think that can be equated with music. I think that's there in his Catullus translations, it's there in late poems like '80 Flowers'. Anyway, let's not pursue that, because I haven't thought my views through entirely in relation to Zukofsky.

I've introduced the point about the line, which seems to me to follow from the account I initially gave of *High Zero*, because I suppose I think of myself throughout as a poet whose practice has been led by thinking about prosody generally and prosodic decisions locally, on the assumption that those things are the irreducible identity of poetry, and that this in turn means that my range of tolerances when reading poetry is tested when I fail to discern the presence of either prosodic effects or prosodic decisions, so that I am at a loss to recognise where the language is coming from, because it comes from those matters in the first place.

Bibliography

All Where Each Is (Lewes: Allardyce Barnett, 1985).

He fills his head with culture; the moon shines bright on Scott LaFaro

Afghan Ghazal

wave of the long grass
as the wind shakes it

small dance of juniper
on the brecciated ridge

on limestone conspicuously abundant
old shells littering the ground

jewel-cases under stones
highly polished and heliciform

on walls in worm-burrows
in flood-plain exuviae and silt

plethora of their remnants
hard glossy and polished

pondering foot of steppes
think slow and act slower

ascend in thin light
perfect and complicated

unconsidered but not lost
the connectives not seen

refer to their tiny skyline
distance opens up

hoping for the principle of hope
in the diaries of these snails

for Tony Baker and Richard Caddel, their *Monksnailsongs*; thanks to Blanford and
Austen, *Fauna of British India: Mollusca* (1908) and Simms, *In Afghanistan* (2001)

DUNCAN Aspects of the scene may get missed from the interviews if
people talk too strictly about their own work. My concept was to
interview you as the Consumer of Record—that is, you would talk
about your career as collector/connoisseur of Cultural Goods. This
would act as a commentary on how you came to write your own
poetry, and simultaneously illuminate a landscape which abid-
ingly surrounds poetry.

One tries to carry out this task at a generalised level, and
realises that all the rich detail only exists at the level of an indi-
vidual—and, anyway, that generalisation has to follow collection
of primary data. The task is less to pile up lists of records, films,
etc. than to capture the procedures by which pleasure is self-
administered—the symbolic acts underlying individual acts of
capture of the desired object. There is a magazine called *Inventory*
dedicated to essays about cultural consuming—which I find
inspiring.

GILONIS I was at the launch of Issue 1 of *Inventory* . . . though I confess I
haven't kept up with their activities. Their reprinting of things like
found street detritus neatly squelches fetishised consumption.

DUNCAN The 1970s are a vanished era. People really don't understand
what was going on in that decade. But consuming art objects was
probably part of it. Can you recall the 70s? What music did you

listen to? what books did you read? what were you proud of owning? how did your taste evolve? were things changing fast? did you expect art to undergo its own revolution?

GILONIS You write that 'the 1970s are a vanished era'. Well, let's start by fretting at over-easy chronological models. I have a long essay on the artist, photographer and writer David Bellingham's work, much of which is an attack on measurement and its hypostatisation.[1] Having just come back from 6 rather gruelling days walking the Dingle Way in Éire (plus the much more gruelling Cork Poetry Festival following . . .) I was struck yet again by the lunacy of such physical models. Someone draws a line on a map and people insist on walking 'all' of it, as if it had some *a priori* existence, like the Nile.

So I'm unhappy about the '70s' as a notion. Guy Davenport put forward the notion that the 20th Century ended with the Somme. The 70s were, I think, split between before-the-OPEC-oil-price-increase —which took some time to kick in fully—and after it. We think of this shift, if at all, as coterminous with the arrival of Thatcher and its -ism; but that wasn't wholly true. When I went off to university in 1974 it was self-evident that a graduate in anything at all would be employable somewhere. By 1977 when I graduated, post-OPEC but pre-Maggie, that was evidently no longer the case. Perhaps this cusp, too, separates happy smiling prog. rock—a dinosaur by 1975—and punk.[2]

So I'll address your questions as best I can with this bifocal in place.

DUNCAN ('people really don't understand what was going on in that decade. But consuming art objects was probably part of it.')

GILONIS Again, the allure of hypostatisation; but let's jump on to consumption, just as if it were the 80s we were speaking of.

---

[1] see 'An Indeterminate Vision: Notes on David Bellingham's Phenomenology of Mensuration' in David Bellingham, *ASP [All Spare Parts]* (Kunsthaus Nürnberg, 2001).

[2] (Which, lest Ben Watson pass by and try and canonise it again, was mostly really really crap, bad rockabilly or roadhouse music with inevitably lumpen drumming. As Mark P. eventually grasped, the *wrong* three chords will make for a very dull band. The great feature of Rock against Racism gigs was *always* the reggae bands, who were *always* the support acts. Curious, that.)

DUNCAN (Can you recall the 70s?)

GILONIS Well, dimly; I was there, but not conscious of their 70sness (see above, interminably). Partly, of course, because that decade began with me aged 15 and ended with me aged 24, which is probably as hefty a jump as a consciousness can make. I wasn't really listening to music at all in 1971; by 1980 I think I had made the majority of the formal discoveries I've yet made. (Though I like uglier and noisier music now than I did then, I think.)

DUNCAN (What music did you listen to?)

GILONIS An avant-garde composer, Chris Dench, was working in a very ordinary record shop (back in the days of vinyl . . .) in the nearest high street in the London suburb I grew up in. I went in to buy Caravan and Soft Machine, the sort of things the hipper kids were listening to at school (though the *really* hip were already listening to Beefheart, which I couldn't yet fathom—knowing nothing then of the American musics he drew on). Chris pointed me, immensely helpfully, to a rack of Shandar imports; so I was the only kid on my block to go away to university with a LaMonte Young LP as well as Soft Machine *Third*. Through Chris I'd got to know the UK contemporary music avant-garde; they were virtually unrecorded then, and remained so for many years to come; but I had heard some (Michael) Finnissy and (Brian) Ferneyhough—the former having just been rediscovered (for the first time), the latter in a very different mode from that shown in parts of the current and—I think rather questionable—Walter Benjamin project. The overseas product took longer, curiously, and sometimes I met it in idiosyncratic order. I'd heard the (*ridiculously* obscure) Yanni Christou before Iannis Xenakis, for example.

The now often-regarded-as-twee-or-pastoral (don't get me started on *that* word) Canterbury rock scene did throw up its own contradiction in Henry Cow, a group capable of employing violin and bassoon or non-4/4 time-signatures with the best of them (but somehow never pompous; even 'Solemn Music' wore its solemnity lightly, and for a clear rhetorical purpose); but also capable of wholly exhilarating full-on playing; and free improvisation, too. I

---

* At the time this project, to be called *Shadowtime,* was incomplete, known only from a few sections. I still have reservations, but at the time of this e-mail interview they were more inchoate.

didn't 'get' this when first exposed to it, I suppose around 1973 or
so; but found it again by another route, again by happenstance. I
went to an Arts Lab Jazz Evening in autumn 1974, on spec.; and
caught Derek Bailey solo, plus the (Evan) Parker-(Paul) Lytton duo.
Both wholly altered how I listened. Particularly the latter, heavily
noise-based as they were; Lytton played an amplified drum-kit
including a whole, contact-miked bicycle. In the light of Ben
Watson's remarks in his Bailey biography—in other respects an
excellent book—which highlights the contribution of Tony Oxley's
drumming and seriously misread *and* undervalued Evan Parker, it's
worth stressing the astonishing effect of this material at the time.
(Retrievable after the effect on a couple of fine CDs of live playing
from Emanem, plus studio recordings, put out in the 70s by Incus
on LP and re-issued on CD by Psi, distributed by Emanem.[3]) This was
I think the first music I met with a seemingly explicit implicit poli-
tics (can't put it clearer). It suggested the ludicrousness of hierar-
chies, the necessity of collaboration, the fatuity of enforced formal
models. It foregrounded the liminal, the between, noise over pitch.
If I (or anyone) could write like this music plays . . . ! Chief access to
this stuff was the LPs put out by Incus, the UK's first musician-
owned recording/publishing label. Another good place to start
thinking. But vital though recordings were, it was, as Ben Watson
says, a live phenomenon more. Which encouraged you to go and do
it yourself. So I did. Another vital jump.

I was also involved in the avant-rock scene; which also, perhaps
Incus-inspired, had its own musician-run label and shop and distri-
bution outlet, Chris Cutler's Recommended Records. (Still going as
RēR Megacorp:<www.rermegacorp.com/>.) This distributed record-
ings by overseas bands of like mind; and also promoted gigs,
helped set up festivals, etc. A great hands-across-the-ocean enter-
prise. Who in the UK would have heard a Swedish rock band doing
free improv. without them? Cutler's RecRec acted in tandem with
another project (neither just his, the usual shorthand) Rock in

---

3   Something of Parker-Lytton's out-there-ness might be gleaned from the instru-
     mentation, collectively something like this—Paul Lytton: percussion, live elec-
     tronics, air horns, dog whistles, harmonium, klaxon, etc.; Evan Parker:
     soprano & tenor saxophones, sheng, dopplerphone, ocarina, voice & voice
     tube, cassettes of prior performances. (Is it just my memory, or did he whirl
     the cassette-player as it played, like a bullroarer?)

Opposition, which existed to act against the developing
Thatcherite enterprise. I'm not sure I have the stamina (as in, I
know I haven't) to rehearse the debates about music and politics
which surrounded it at the time; Cornelio Cardew was still alive,
active, playing electric piano (a very un-punk instrument) in
Peoples Liberation Music, which took what now looks like a very
'tanky' line on the way politics should act within music; simple
tunes displaying clear ideology was about it. ('Smash, smash,
smash the Social Contract!') I rather dislike this sort of thing; but
it is worth highlighting the considerable strengths of e.g. Cardew's
critique of indeterminacy, graphic notation, etc., in *Stockhausen
Serves Imperialism*. The devil doesn't have all the good tunelessness.

Another important 70s moment was the London Sinfonietta
concert series at St John's Smith Square, *1945–>1975*, where I first
heard important small-orchestra pieces by the likes of Xenakis,
Stockhausen, many others; well-played, too, as this was the
Sinfonietta in their hey-day.

(I ought to say, in case I seem always to have peaked just soon
enough, that I had a really good track record in the early 70s of
going to Prom concerts the day or two AFTER the unmissable
thing; I missed Soft Machine but went to hear Beethoven 6; I
missed the Scratch Orchestra doing some of *The Great Learning*, but
turned up to hear Brahms.)

Punk was important to me more for the second generation,
where the liberty *not* to use currently popular forms (prog. rock,
heavy metal) wasn't just the requirement to use others (garage
rock, etc.); I was, and remain, much taken by PiL, The Raincoats,
The Slits, This Heat; also by The Fall and The Pop Group (both of
whom I didn't really get to know until after the end of the 70s,
shamefully). Almost as important for me was the locally-strong
South London squat-rock scene; lots and lots of tiny fissiparous
groupings, using noms-de-plunk to avoid dole difficulties. I mean
bands like Amos and Sara, ... And The Native Hipsters, The
Homosexuals, Mama Dada 1919, Prag Vec, Scritti Politti; not all
from S. London, but that's where I first met this stuff. RecRec and
These Records (the shop) both supported this material, a lot only
now being properly released. Again, an implicit politics;[4] a great
sense of inventiveness; a naturalisation of arthouse discoveries in

---

4   Not least in the highlighting of production, distribution and exchange. The

more popular formats. Much of this material came out as cassettes, very low cost and easy to transport and sell. A sort of echo of what Writers Forum, say, was doing just across the river (though I knew nothing of it at the time).

I haven't touched at all on jazz; I did the probably far-from-unusual thing of buying lots of late Coltrane and working slowly back through the stuff that seemed tamer, seemed a given in the face of what followed it; a sort of reverse chronological learning-curve. I can't claim any real insights into what was going on in this area; I liked what people who liked that sort of thing liked; Ayler, Coltrane, Ornette. I did find Sun Ra quite early; copies of *Heliocentric Worlds of Sun Ra* vols. 1 & 2 found for 50p each in a local junk shop (sending me off to the recently-remaindered Impulse! reissues elsewhere).

Chris Dench's local record-shop also had the also-remaindered Unesco and Phillips ethnic music LPs for £1.99 apiece around the end of the 70s; I got my hands on a lot of African, Arabic, East-Asian, etc., musics.[5] Some enduringly part of my head—The Toraia Orchestra of Algiers' North African semi-pop, for example. Some less seemingly less user-friendly, even arcane—Watazumido-Doso's *The Art of the Japanese Bamboo Flute*, since highlighted in *The Wire* as fantastic. Often what wasn't conventionally 'user-friendly' could still have an immediate allure. It wasn't always Difficult Listening Hour, where you had to sit bolt upright in a straight-backed chair for something relentless and impenetrable. When *The Art of the Japanese Bamboo Flute* was played in my local record shop a friend and I, hearing the initial notes, ran instantly to the counter to buy it. One copy left; I won.)

Which seems a suitably churlish point to stop for now.

first Scritti Politti single detailed on the cover not just the (*theoretically* empowering) costs of recording, mastering, pressing, label, cover, sleeve, etc., but also told you the names and addresses, so you could, practically, go and do it yourself.

5   I mention this in part because of recent piffle in the *Guardian* about the 1980s, if not 90s, creation of 'World Music' as a genre by a cabal of journalists and record-biz honchos.

DUNCAN This is really interesting. I think it opens the way to understanding that, like tragedy, modern poetry may have its birth in music. The customs around consumption of objects of culture help to show us how, later, creative cultural acts are partly inevitable and loyal to shared conventions, and partly spontaneous breakouts into uncoded territory. The acts of classification and identification involved in cultural shopping are a training ground for the acts which bring the poem into being. The conventions are in fact trophies of victorious shared trips, the heat organs of 'warm' loyalty groups.

(What books did you read?)

GILONIS Let's stick to the second half of the seventies here; unless you really want me to try and exhume and comprehend my fondness for J.R.R. Tolkien. (That said, my parents' bookcases were never off-limits; I'd read Freud's *Totem and Taboo* before puberty, which may or may not have been a really good idea.) I couldn't at this juncture tell you what I went to university already reading. I remember reading *Ulysses* on a ferry steaming past Ithaca, which I found rather pleasing.

A lot of—to me, then—important political literature came out of a radical independent bookshop called The Peace Centre. It also sold fiction; and I there met my first taste of radical chic. (Or do I mean label queendom?) Certainly enough literature I thought highly of was published by the new Picador imprint; and friends and I came to trust it, and buy new Picador books automatically. (With a shudder I recognise that this may well have been brand loyalty.) Meeting books by Calvino was a shock; I'd read Gore Vidal's essay on him which described *The Cloven Viscount* and *The Baron in the Trees*, and I was sure he was a spoof on the then-realist Vidal's part . . . I think, in fact, that I may have met these first as US imports. I wish I had a better recollection of what turned up in the US imports category. Translations of Queneau, certainly.[6]

Weird imports were—increasingly occasionally—to be found in The Peace Centre, but always in Compendium in London. What a

---

6 The almost-utterly forgotten Richard Farina suddenly comes to mind. 'What a civilisation! What a civilisation! No-one even remembers who wrote *The Moon Pool*.' (Googling has of course entirely abolished this rhetorical figure, here borrowed from Kenneth Rexroth.)

fantastic place. I remember being shocked to the core when a friend shoplifted from Compendium. That seemed utterly unforgivable. Compendium mattered too much to do that. When I first went in (and I cannot do a *Je me souviens* and say how I got to know about it) there were in fact 3 Compendia; two, I think not adjacent but one shop apart, on the NE side of the road, and one across the road next door to Honest Jon's (where you went to spend what you hadn't spent on books on weird jazz or rock music. Good place for Sun Ra LPs, then). I didn't spend *much* time in the occult branch, nor much more in the politics shop (though I spent a long time scooping up, over many years, fugitive pirate editions of Situationist classics). (I even reprinted some myself; but that's a story I mustn't tell in print. . . .) This was before Mike Hart joined Compendium, and the poetry section wasn't yet all that exciting; but they were terrific for fiction. American little-press pamphlets of Burroughs I recollect in particular; taking home (and finding almost incomprehensible) *So Who Owns Death TV?* or *APO-17: A Metabolic Regulator.* Some of these were I think published by the wonderful Aloes Books imprint (also responsible for making available pirate editions of the otherwise completely unavailable early Pynchon short stories). Of course some of this stuff was Little Press activity; but it didn't foreground the fact. It hadn't occurred to me before now, but I suppose the world of small political pamphlets made me ready for this as a mode of publishing, instead of being puzzled that books didn't always look like *proper* books.

It occurs to me that I should mention that, just as beer was absurdly cheap then, so too (though not *as* cheap) were books and records. It was easier to take a punt at something; or, indeed, to publish or issue it. Adventurous record labels like Virgin Caroline (*not* the same thing as the tubercular-balled main enterprise)[7] were much more feasible. And the collapse of the larger little-press poetry publishers in the late 70s after the price of paper went up dramatically is a matter of record; the mainstream became much, much drabber thereafter, and the avant-garde were forced for financial reasons into tiny editions, with initially unappetising production values, in formats — first duplicator, then photocopy — for which there were few if any stockists, and no proper distribution.

7 (Prince Far I sang that Branson was a pickle with no place on his plate . . .)

I found no very logical way of structuring this reply; and realise that at some point I ought to have uttered a strong paean to the public library. I spent years of visits to Wimbledon library picking *The Cantos* off the shelf and opening them at random, finding the contents somehow strangely unlike John Betjeman (our teacher's particular favourite for 'O'-Level English). The same library held copies of the Cape Robert Duncans, which I bought for a song purely on spec., knowing nothing of him, when they were sold off as tatty and unwanted. I just missed Cape's two-volume Zukofsky shorter poems; it took me many years to make good that mistake. I took the old Faber edition of the *Cantos*, the one with the red cover, to university; and spent a year or more annotating it in my spare time. First-off from the library's copy, which no-one else seemed to want to read, of Edwards & Vasse's *Annotated Index to the Cantos of Ezra Pound*, an infuriating book to work with, as everything you wanted to look up appears in alphabetical sequence, not as you meet it in reading the text. It certainly induced a model of the *Cantos* as a less-than-linear event, somehow both simultaneous and disparate at once. So my model of great poetry was polyglot, fissiparous, and by someone dead. It was to be years—safely into the 80s—before I made the alarming discovery that living people, in the UK, were writing interestingly. I had thought it simply axiomatic that that couldn't happen.

DUNCAN (What were you proud of owning?)

GILONIS Now that's a very sneaky one; and indeed a very tricky one. Much hangs on the valency you give such pride. I vied with a friend up in Northumberland for a while in owning obnoxious 7″ singles; so, yes, I took pride in owning Little Jimmy Osmond's *Long Haired Lover from Liverpool*, just as he in possessing Hilda Baker and Arthur Mullard's joint cover version of *Save All Your Kisses For Me*. But I'm not sure that's the same sort of pride as I felt in having the (early, good) Steve Reich album on Shandar, with its cover still from a Michael Snow film. So I'll need to tread carefully! There was an obvious status pride; 'I'm the sort of person from the kind of background that listens to classical music'. I did grow up in a household where that was true (although it was also played, which gives you a very different slant). I did buy stuff in the early 70s because *I'd* discovered it—in the sense of discovered it for myself. I don't recollect being played Beethoven 4 in the same way that I evidently was the 5th or 6th symphonies; and I remember buying the vinyl LP. From a series with sleeve-scenes of the British countryside; their Bruckner albums always had better covers than their Vivaldi; a sublimity thing, I think. My folks said they could remember the previous time Sibelius had been discovered; but I enjoyed having the 2nd Symphony—and enjoyed knowing that the best recording was, implausibly, by Brits—the Bournemouth Symphony Orchestra under Alexander Gibson. (Nowadays I suppose you *have* to buy Neeme Järvi, or they sneer in the shop.) Mahler I came upon independently of help; and was able to go to all of Simon Rattle's first big cycle of all the symphonies live, back before he was a Sir and lost the plot.

A variant of this would be peer pride. Nearly everyone at school at a certain point had Deep Purple *Live in Japan*, though they might now take some pushing to admit it. (The same crew also had, though I'm sure most would now either deny it more hotly or fail to recollect the band's existence, *Argus* by Wishbone Ash . . .) So it was tricky if you didn't own these; but you could at least take or fake an interest. There was some status in it being *your* copy of such albums that was being played on the school common-room gramophone. Those with pretensions to musicality might have a Genesis album—this was before they attained world hegemony. You could side-step being *too* obvious by listening to their near-clones, like Greenslade. Somehow *in* but not quite *of* that category were Caravan, Soft Machine, Hatfield and the North. (I think their occasional whimsy let them down. We *are* serious when we're seventeen.) I remember Softs *Six* creeping occasionally onto the school gramophone and being most intrigued. That of course was a good example of the next rung down, coterie pride. You were interested in stuff that was vaguely prog., it set you a bit apart. The categories weren't clearly defined, it certainly didn't involve close listening. But . . . your question was, what was I proud of owning. Which also invites vanity, big-time. Yes, there was of course some gratification in being able to play people LaMonte Young's *14 VII 73 9:27:27–10:06:41 PM NYC from Map of 49's Dream The Two Systems of Eleven Sets of Galactic Intervals Ornamental Lightyears Tracery* and watch them edge towards the door, somewhat worried; just as, a few years later, I could do the same thing with Evan Parker's *Saxophone Solos*. This was I think also partly about their hard-to-get-ness;

which didn't strike me fully at the time. I happened to have found them; so I didn't think about the mechanics of their supply. I probably at one point owned as many LPs from Incus (then the home label for free improv.) as from any other label, possibly from all other labels . . .[8] Buying stuff at gigs or mail-order seemed basic, seemed ordinary. Given that I do own quite a lot of STUFF, it is curious—to me at least—that I'm not particularly collectory about it. I don't have every recording or book for more than a handful of particularly important people (admittedly they include Derek Bailey and Allen Fisher, and to be absolutely completist about either would be a life's work on its own).

The micro-coteries, though—now I was firmly ensconced in several—were usually so arcane that *snobisme* within them was pointless, or unfriendly. I don't remember anyone bragging about having, e.g., Japanese LPs—there was a solo disc of Evan Parker's, and Derek Bailey's much nicer 'Live in Japan'; to have succeeded in finding these was a source of satisfaction/congratulation. If there was a scene of taping-and-trading I never met it; except for taping-and-trading gigs, which was different, and harmed no-one's livelihood. I'm aware that we haven't spoken of visual art; but I certainly didn't own anything 'original' in the 70s, in either sense.

DUNCAN Fantastic! I will write a more intelligent Gosh Moment when I get a moment. We should reveal that the Musicians' Co-op in Gloucester Avenue was a few steps away from Camden High Street (and Compendium).

GILONIS It actually shouldn't be confused with the Musician's Co-op, a different groupuscule; the Collective was indeed in Gloucester Avenue. I must say, as a regular attendee (and regular performer) I scarcely thought of it as being in Camden. You didn't go up the main road, the Compendium-and-Honest-Jon's axis, but went off at 90 degrees down Parkway, which led you nowhere except a rather tame Young's pub and a chip-shop. The distance was indeed small; but if you were carrying gear you went straight to the venue (especially given those substantial, ricketty external stairs). Certainly

---

8 Incus must have been the first label that I fully realised *was* one. Product of one issuing body, indeed one taste. The commercially desirable false-catholicity of mainstream labels—or publishers—blurred any sense of their having *a*, or *any*, taste.

the folk I knew saw it as a venue with no real hinterland, except the absolutely necessary pub (indeed crucial, as the LMC had no loo).

DUNCAN In fact, I thought of writing a work in 2 volumes: *1, Poets culturally based in Camden; 2, Losers and Weirdos.*

GILONIS I could bang on about meeting Scritti Politti in a pub in Camden, but who remembers them from back when they weren't a him? ('Who remembers who released Opec-Immac'?)

DUNCAN (How did your taste evolve?)

GILONIS Not sure that this can be answered; either it involves a self-scrutiny Proust would wither at contemplating, or it amounts to banalities. Let's go for the latter. We all know what navels look like . . .

BANALITY 1: You find out about stuff people you know know about. A girl I knew barely at all—hello Siobhán—owned only 2 items of recorded sound; so visiting her, you heard one, or the other, or both. One was Nico's *The Marble Index*; the other, Planxty's *The Well Below The Valley.* I knew Nico from the first Velvets album; but didn't know she had worked solo, wasn't remotely prepared for her style, or for John Cale's astonishing orchestration. This set me off to chase up her other recordings, some of which I still quite enjoy; plus those of other ex-Velveteers, specially Cale. Planxty I knew nothing of, and had heard nothing like. Set me off again; but just chasing their recordings, nothing else, as I had no other source of recommendations. You need to know where to find enthusiasts!

COUNTER-BANALITY 1: You don't find out about stuff no-one you know knows about. Being a long way from Ireland, knowing no-one Irish (Siobhán was definitely English or very Anglicised, despite her name), I had no source. World music, such as it barely was, was much more directed towards ethnographic recordings; and although I did get some Irish material thus, it tended towards a very conservative model of listening, and was, curiously, rarely as well recorded as was, say, gamelan or gagaku! A similar accident kept me from picking up on The Fall until well after the end of the 70s. (Only extensive psychoanalysis could explain why I rarely listened to John Peel. It certainly makes no sense on a conscious level.) Small technological excursus: Siobhán's recordings were pre-recorded tape-cassettes. I don't think I knew anyone else with *just* a cassette-player. I almost never bought pre-recorded cassettes— their poor quality was legendary. An early introduction to tape-as-a-medium (which I abused in performances later) came about when I listened, inadvertently, to a commercially-released reel-to-reel tape of a Dvorak symphony in reverse. Some sounds were distorted (the now-cliched sound of backwards-cymbals) but the predominant sounds of strings, wind and brass were by and large still plausible. So you heard the melodies in retrograde; which did them no harm, and me a power of good.

BANALITY 2: You find out about stuff that accompanies stuff you know about. I've mentioned earlier the business of buying Picador books on trust—until they started selling stuff that wasn't as good. (The same applied to Virago for a while, until it became clear that not *all* 18th or 19th century women novelists were geniuses.) This is really an extension of Banality 1, except that the contiguities are those of goods, not people. So let's personalise the commodity, why not. I trusted Picador books; I trusted Calder (& Boyars) titles; I trusted—still trust—Incus. It also worked through trusting certain shop-buyers. I will as a courtesy to your presumed readership omit the 15,000 words on the role of the little magazine, similar on the poetry anthology. See Görtschacher and Tuma, *passim*. Also there are contiguities in time. You go to a concert to hear Debussy and they also play Messiaen; so later you go to a concert to hear Messiaen, and they play Boulez. Commoner in avant-garde classical circles, as the difficulties of funding and affording proper rehearsal time mean pieces tend to be about 10-15 mins max. So the mixed billing is very common indeed, and more heeded than support-acts.

COUNTER-BANALITY 2: You meet stuff you really *don't* want to know about too. They *will* play Adès or Turnage on the South Bank.

BANALITY 3: You find out about stuff because humans are find-outy kinda guys. My reading the dedication to Pound's *Guide to Kulchur* led me to its dedicatees, Bunting and Zukofsky, 'strugglers in the desert'. Not that I wouldn't have got there eventually, but it saved time. And then Bunting writes a poem to Niedecker ... and so you proceed. Pound's letters got me to Olson; Compendium got me to the Olson/Creeley correspondence ... which led me to

Creeley, where I might reasonably have started. Chinese whispers, Pound hearing from Fenellosa.

COUNTER-BANALITY 3: not all enthusiasms can be, or should be, shared. (Note absence of any examples.)

BANALITY 4: you find stuff; because there's a lot of it out there. Serendipity; my finding *Heliocentric worlds of Sun Ra* volumes 1 and 2 for 50p each on a stall outside a junk-shop. Could have happened to anyone; happened to me.

COUNTER-BANALITY 4: you miss stuff; because there's too much of it out there. Another junk-shop had four Pierre Henry albums for a pound each. I'd never heard of him; and, because one was his collaboration with Spooky Tooth, I left them there. I could probably retire on the resale price of them now. On which forlorn note/tone I fade out again.

DUNCAN (Were things changing fast?)

GILONIS Well, that's a pig of a question. If your typesetter can do a 'Welsh-white-trash' font, then cue Dylan Thomas in the States, meeting a Professor of Comparative Literature. 'So what do you compare it to?' [Last word pronounced roughly 'teeuw'.] The 70s lacked the almost glacial stasis of the late 80s; so it seems now. But— see very beginning of this blether—I'm chary of any such time-span generalisations. (I think the early 60s were still the 1950s, even in swinging London; certainly reading Barry Miles's book on the 60s, and the recent biography of B. S. Johnson, would suggest this.) I'm not sure that the implicit model of change as following a set speed (or even set acceleratory pattern) is helpful. Things were perhaps jerky; or, even, there were sudden bursts of extreme high-speed. Some changes occurred in—*pace* Eldredge and Gould— 'punctuated equilibrium'. I'm thinking chiefly of the shift from pre- to post-punk, in which even those who had no truck with punk in its purest forms (as I didn't; it was mostly bad garage-rock) still moved, as punk had, through an absolute change of consciousness, which seemed not to occupy actual time. Punk 'happened' for a couple of months, really, if that. Before the first summer was out there were Sunni and Shi'ia punk tendencies. There were almost instantly the political (including, lest we forget, those with the wrong sort of politics, as e.g. 'Oi!') and the apolitical, including those who were too much in it for the beer and skittles, or were just too dim to notice the implications of what was happening. And there was bandwagon jumping. I can remember photos of The Clash with swastika armbands; and the first title of 'I'm So Bored with the USA' was 'I'm So Bored with my Girlfriend'.

Certainly big changes went on which didn't need talk. To take a trivial example, in punk and post-punk the state vector was one in which you couldn't have keyboards in a band any more. Tim Hodgkinson's organ-playing, a big feature in Henry Cow, was replaced by flat-guitar in The Work (a key group, btw, if you want to consider how ideas re-entered post-punk music. Along with This Heat, the pair seem to me crucial. But then my brother played guitar with the former.) Other things were perhaps slower. I don't get the feeling that 'the novel' was rocketting along at the time. Some stuff lauded then—John Hawkes—looks a bit dodgy now. I wasn't always on the ball—although I read B. S. Johnson bright and early, I didn't read Brooke-Rose or Alan Burns until the 80s. I'm not sure, then, that 'were things changing fast?' offers a line of enquiry one can productively pursue. Things changed (as they do); some at different rates (as it so often happens). Some things seemed to move with lightning rapidity. [9]

It may be that speed (or change) is a function of paying attention. If you go—as I did for some while—to see gigs at the LMC at least weekly; or to see John Stevens' residency at The Plough in Stockwell every Friday . . . then you spot things happening as they happen. Is this a function of certain eras? Historians of Cubism claim to be able to see ideas propounded and then modified or refuted in the call-and-response of canvases in the glory days of Analytical Cubism. Was that a magical moment? Or were they just those kind of guys?? I paid, then as now, no attention to dance; so

---

[9] for a while I thought I could follow Derek Bailey's changes in guitar style as he moved from investigating one area to another . . . In part this was a fiction generated by the obviously patchy sampling created by recordings and concerts; though there were clearly the years when, e.g., he was investigating his '19-string guitar', after which it was set aside, I felt there were less-clearly defined periods when, for example, he made particularly strong use of harmonics. But I certainly wouldn't, now, want to try and lay down such a model of periodicity; even the notion of early- middle-, late-Beethoven, which has always seemed to me logically unassailable—has recently come in for stick. Bailey seems to go back to things later; or integrate lots of micro-enquiries from his whole playing life into a cadence—I'd hesitate to say narrative. End of excursus.

when I saw—on TV—the Twyla Tharp Company performing David Byrne's *Catherine Wheel*, I couldn't say that it was an 'advance' on anything at any time, ever. But it seemed to be 'contemporary'. Perhaps you can be contemporary and get stuck there (like Brian Eno) until you aren't contemporary any longer. (We are more used to this model in artists who start out retro and get more so, like Meatloaf.) I suppose the whole question could be turned inside out. If the perceiving self alters, then a static perception will be seen differently; and, more complicatedly, an altered subject looking at altered states will see their altering differently at different points. I certainly expected different things of music in 1979 than I did in 1974. Probably 'heard' differently.

DUNCAN This is terrific & will shed light on all the interviews in the book & on how at some point the Poeticus breaks free from conventional art, as violating his dearly-held values; and at other points is completely pliable, becomes enthusiastic about what makes the other people enthusiastic, pays attention to things in order to be polite and cooperative, hears the music because it is there. So that poetic taste is not just 'preferring red to blue' nor just 'singing along with the group', but an intricate mixture of wilfulness and pliability. And some works reshaped the landscape.

GILONIS Looks like I'll need to read a bit more sociology (as Ez would add,'drratt you!'); I suppose the field of cultural production is one we all have to get our boots muddy in. Of possibly some slight relevance; I'm currently reading Pierce Ferriter, 1601–53, the westernmost adherent of International European Baroque. (Hard to see how anyone could trump him on that—he lived at the western end of the Dingle peninsula in Éire, 'next parish America'). He was executed after illegal seizure by English troops. Here's his prison stanza (translated by Pat Muldowney):

A dia na mbuadh an truagh leat mise mar táim,
I bpríosun fuar is nach mór go bhfeicim an lá,
An braon bhíonn thuas i n-uachtar lice go hárd
Ag tuitim im chluas is fuaim na tuinn lem sháil.
　O God of Excellence, am I a pity to you as I am
　In a cold prison, and I shall hardly see the day

The drop above that is on top of a slate on high
Falling in my ear and the sound of the ocean-waves cutting me.

Once you grasp that rhymes are vowel-based only, it gets clearer what's going on in the Irish. What I like in this is the similarity to Zukofsky; heavy use of vowel parallelism, a very tight syntax and sound-frame, a *literal* rather than merely metaphorical musicality. How much of this is an unheeded survival of early Irish verse practice? How much is a reflection, and how accurate a one if so, of International European Baroque? Is it just my wild misreading? And if so, would it matter?

DUNCAN Mention of The Peace Centre reminds me that there was—I *think* there was—a whole circuit of alternative bookshops in the 70s, which were visible proof that liberated people existed, and which were the proof that there were useful jobs which were not wholly compromised. It's reasonable to think that the words of underground poetry were meaningful because they embodied the safe knowledge of this network of people (and of rules for relating to each other). They were, quite prominently, not empty or self-referential gestures. Compendium enjoys its fame because it was an uneroded relic of what had been a whole plateau. Sheila Whiteley has written about 'psychedelic coding' to describe how in psychedelic music, intense meanings about the life one wishes to lead are burnt into musical and verbal ornaments, and how much people desire to see such gestures. Underground poetry had a code which was accessible to individual poets but which had been programmed by hundreds, or thousands, of people. I was never ENTIRELY clear what it was! The redefinition of bookshops into high-pressure capitalism was a symbolic event—the 'alternative bookshops' closed by the dozen. At one time, those shops had stocked small press books and magazines by the yard.

GILONIS I must say I don't *remember* them stocking interesting poetry! (Ginsberg, yes; but more usually Brautigan.) But they did induce, bizarrely, a strange sense that there were businesses you might trust. I mean, I bought Picador books or LPs on Virgin Caroline with scarcely a second thought—for a while. Not sure you could say that of any enterprise of like market-penetration these days; though they all *act* as if you could; and indeed as if you DID. The public lingo is that of happy friends together in this shared enterprise. Loyalty-cards replacing party cards. The whole enterprise as doomed as its (Free) Herald.

DUNCAN (Did you expect art to undergo its own revolution?)

GILONIS I suppose this question begs you to futz with hindsight, which is a term with no counter-term. In the strictest sense, no; any more than I expected, in 1975, that there would be an April 3 1978. Had I been *asked*, I'd have said I thought there was every likelihood . . . but I wasn't. I didn't expect art to do anything, really; just be there, *ut doceat, ut moveat, ut delectet*. I did notice that it altered over time. I went through the same steps everyone else did, wanting the new book/album to be the same as the last one, being disappointed that it wasn't, and then learning to love it anyway . . . but *revolution*? Not really sure. I didn't foresee, say, punk; nor the British Poetry Revival. Certain things seemed immutable—bad music, the *Daily Telegraph*. And so they were. What, precisely, might you mean by revolution, anyway? (Don't have my copy of *Keywords* to hand.) Are we speaking of an accelerated rate of change? Or an alteration in an acceleration? Are we talking gradients, or vectors? I don't know that I expected art to *be* revolution(ary). There's one exception to this; free improvised music. There was a rhetoric, I think ultimately anarchist-inspired, which spoke of the experience of small-group improvisation as akin to the way non-hierarchical social organisation would work; with degrees of plausibility, basically depending on the ensemble (saxophones are innately more conscious of rank than are acoustic guitars, apparently). Some of this got wound up with assertions that music is a language (it *isn't*, but there's hardly space to debate that here)[10] which would assist one in thinking of it as communicative, socially binding, etc. My thinking on all this is a lot more based on Adorno than it was in the 70s (when it wasn't at all; he was scarcely on the map) but on occasion anyhow I saw improv. as a way of doing sociability, one which had implications for being social. Perhaps the interview, too, does this?? (Or, my turn to ask a question . . .)

---

10 Cf. Adorno's 'Music and Language: A Fragment', in the 1956 essays on music, *Quasi una Fantasia*, Englished by Verso.

DUNCAN We should have at least something on your own poetry. In the public interest, etc. Can you talk to us about that renga you did with Tony Baker?

GILONIS Yes; *from far away* was published very handsomely by the much-missed Ian Robinson's Oasis Books. Literary reference played a part therein, as it does in traditional Japanese verse, where the brevity and inconsequentiality of a lot of the writing is either heightened or countered (I can't wholly make up my mind which) by delicate allusion. If you fail to spot a reference, the poem should 'work' anyway; but it would be a hallmark of being cultured that you would notice.

I cannot and would not claim the same for my, our, writing in the renga; it wouldn't be possible, given a far wider and far less 'common' culture. We thus ran the risk of writing *obscurus per obscurioris*, and there are certainly stanzas which are 'just' a web of allusions:

rainheavy and pissed on by the *púca*—splats –
rips web—*De Lineis insectabilibus* only hope
unless it rains—tatters—Brier Spider
unhoused—ditto *Oothops* in my teapot

—I noted in the afterword to *from far away* that

My master-copy [of the poem] got slowly tattier and tattier, with illegible asides to explain the jokes. (How else could I remember that *De lineis insectabilibus* is a typo in Latinised-Aristotle, to do with indivisible lines, not spider-webs?—And who could need to know that??)

I would hope that the speed of mixing blackberries, leprechauns, Aristotle, Captain Beefheart and Uncle Remus (or, elsewhere, Krazy Kat and the Fall of Man) makes this writing closer to Zukofsky's 'Poem Beginning "The"' than, say, *The Waste Land*. The collisions should generate more than their unpacking—probably impossible —would benefit. Ultimately, as I wrote in the afterword to the book, 'what matters most—as far as I'm concerned—is the noise it makes as it goes past your ears.'

So although it is the case that, as the critic and publisher Peter Quartermain once said of my poetry, 'I collaborate with my reading', that is getting less helpfully true. I don't expect my reading material to respond directly to what I write; but if one is, for example, looking up the words of a Japanese haiku in a Spanish dictionary, the findings should alter what you might have been thinking of writing. (Cf. the *poem for cecilia vicuña* in my Booklist.) An increasing confidence in taking diabolical liberties has moved what I do away from interlingual writing to something more complex, occasionally nearer to glossolalia, if not always immediately evidently (as in this stanza from my *unHealed*, derived in various dubious means from an old Welsh poem, the *Canu Heledd*):

The houses of Basra collapsed and burnt
for profit and power
syndicated gulf-wide.

In the original Welsh:

Eglwysseu bassa collassant eu breint
gwedy y diua o loegyrwys
kyndylan ac eluan powys.

which might roughly translate as:

The churches of Bassa have lost their honour
after the killing by the English
of Cynddylan and Elfan Powys.

You can see that 'collassant eu breint' doesn't *mean* 'collapsed and burnt', though the latter derives from the original Welsh, if illicitly; likewise, 'eluan' (modernised 'elfan') suggested 'Gulf'. There is a clear link between the texts, evident without knowledge of the curiosa of Welsh orthography and pronunciation (which I sometimes chose to ignore—'syndicated' is an English-only eye-echo of 'kyndylan', which it does *not* resemble to a Welsh ear).

I should perhaps say a little about the poem at the head of the interview, *Afghan Ghazal*. A ghazal is an Arabic verse-form used throughout a lot of the Muslim world; made up of free-standing couplets which are unified by mood rather than narrative or other modes of thrust. I can't claim 100% to have observed this; re-reading my poem it is clear that a co-creating reader might infer grammatical subjects being carried forward. The genesis of the poem was seeing a pre-release white-label copy of Tony Baker and Richard Caddel's *Monksnailsongs**, a sequence in part revolving around, obviously enough, snails. I immediately remembered one of the little poems inset into Günter Grass's novel *From the Diary of a Snail* (his hymn to gradualist politics). From memory—haven't read it in two decades plus—it goes something like this:

'And what about Hegel?'
'He sentenced mankind to History.'

'And what about Doubt?'
'Oh, they just laughed at him.'

—which appealed, still does, to the anarchist and non-systematiser in me. And the certainties with which Bush and Blair were—are—addressing the world made this stance seem curiously *radical*.

Back to the ghazal. Somewhere in the back on my mind was the way that Pound excavated luminous details from ethnographical research in the Chinese border country. I suppose in a way it is 'local colour', but, hey, if Pynchon could describe cities he'd never visited on the basis of old Baedeckers, then. . . . So elements which recombine into the descriptions of Afghanistan are lifted from visitors' accounts, chiefly that of the poet-naturalist Colin Simms. These were broken down into minute increments; I don't think you could find a phrase taken over intact. (I hope not, anyway.) But these mix with snippets from a standard work on the snails to be found locally to Afghanistan. I can't now tell, and a reader isn't supposed to be able to, whether, e.g. in the couplet

on limestone conspicuously abundant
old shells littering the ground

the descriptions are contemporary eye-witness account or century-old technical description. (And, to labour the point, there is an unsettling pun on 'shells'.) This, I think—hope—takes the language into another way of working, leaves the thing non-specific. Which in a way is also what the 'free' couplets of a ghazal are; so it isn't

* Subsequently published by the admirable Wild Honey Press, one of very few such enterprises in Eire.

inappropriate, even if the mode of working isn't an exact transfer (e.g. I haven't fretted over monorhyme, or 'signing' the last couplet with my *nom-de-plume*, a strong ghazal convention).

I'd thought I could now go through the poem now and as it were 'unpack' it; and find I can't. It would be vanity to suggest this is wholly because the poem 'works' when it need reflect no more than bad memory and/or poor record-keeping. But I hope it works; and suggest that if it does it is because of a clash between my writing and other writing. The (brief) bibliographical note is not intended to send a reader off to look for the bits of DNA that go into my poem, but rather to instill worry. If you can't tell, and often you can't—I can't—which bits are which, then you are left *less* sure of the text, not more. If I were trying to show off I'd try and let the reader think I'd been to Afghanistan, knew a bit about snails. (And, indeed, would have pointed out the allusions at the close to Ernst Bloch's *The Principle of Hope* and the Günter Grass novel; not to mention the misquote from Buster Keaton. . . .)

Perhaps by now I've made quite enough noise move past your eyes.

Bibliography

POETRY

Afar / Alongside Simple Vice
Axioms (with David Connearn) Ankle Press
Forty Fungi (with Erica van Horn) Coracle
from far away (with Tony Baker) Oasis Books
The Incriptions (with Ian Hamilton Finlay) Wild Hawthorn Press
Learning the Warblers Writers Forum
Pibroch levraut de poche (reprinted by Morning Star, with Gaelic
        translation by Maoilios Caimbeul)
Reading Hölderlin on Orkney, Grille/Simple Vice
        reels levraut de poche
Reliefs hardPressed Poetry (reprinted by Pig Press)
*six translations of the same haiku by Matsuo Basho inside a poem for
        Cecilia Vicuña* Grille
Three Translations from Sappho, frame publications
walk the line Last adanA
words for Webern, perhaps Form Books formCard

PROSE

Ian Hamilton Finlay, Works in Europe 1972–95 Editions Cantz,
    Ostfildern
*Finlay's Metamorphoses: variations on several themes in the work of Ian
    Hamilton Finlay* Fundació Joan Miró, Barcelona
'Inscription and the Shipwreck of the Singular' (one of a set of
    pamphlets for a boxed catalogue, *Where is Abel thy Brother?*)
    National Gallery of Contemporary Art Zacheta, Warsaw
'History Sculpture'—*Ian Hamilton Finlay's La Révolution est un bloc*
    [privately published]
*Printed Paper (folded and unfolded): one hundred and one sentences on
    David Bellingham* Centre for Artists Books, Dundee.

EDITED

Louis Zukofsky or Whoever Someone Else Thought He Was [Zukofsky
    10th anniversary] North and South
Soleil + Chair [Rimbaud centenary] Writer's Forum
Horace Whom I Hated So [Horace bimillenium] Five Eyes of Wiwaxia
Pieces for Howard Skempton [50th birthday] as issue of Spanner
    magazine.
All of these are anthologies with contributions by composers,
    performers, poets and artists.

There is also a collection of poems and papers *For the Birds:
Proceedings of the First Cork Conference on Modern Irish Experimental
Poetry* published jointly in Éire and the UK by hardPressed Poetry
and Mainstream Poetry.

Reminds me of a sweaty Yorkie Bar

Railway

What a difficult railway track you are,
no rails! How easily you kill,
what a fool if I chose to
to die for you—beckoning
your kiss across a battlefield.
No engineer could deliver you

heaped with unwrapped things.
Have I the courage to imagine
and deny you? Constantly—
until I can't help myself
pulling off your wedding ring,
your skin at its white hinge.

I want a pillow where your belly
sets a beacon on the map, a taste
where trouble breaks its wings.
I want a night on your lace,
on your margin. I want to greet
each broken object when it sings.

ALLEN David, can we start by discussing your collection, *Each Broken Object*. It was the first time I encountered your work in substantial chunks and I was struck by its 'chunkiness' . That solid feeling it had was down to many factors, not just the style and matter of the poems themselves but also their presentation, their package. Was that deliberate?

GREENSLADE I wanted *Each Broken Object* as a material 'book' to remind anyone who handled it that it was a made thing. I was able to work with artist Jim Noble who designed the book with extraordinary attention to detail such as across the hinge graphics and also fore-end illustration. Air-brush historian Andy Penaluna did pencil drawings and Antony Rowe Ltd of Chippenham printed and bound it. All this was made possible by Two Rivers under the benign eye of the late Pete Hay. I can't imagine many publishers making this solid sculptural aspect possible. Yes the packaging is consciously in support of the text. The cover is based on the Colonial Tools Catalogue for Contractors and there's no mistaking the borrowing. We wanted the book to display ambiguities that are ascribed to poems. Our job as a team was also to make the book fun to handle and to read. So yes it is chunky but it's also slippery.

ALLEN Slippery? Slippery chunk, reminds me of a sweaty Yorkie bar. And while we're on the adjectives could you say something about the 'broken', as in 'each broken object'. Is it as simple as the objects have to be broken, broken into and/or broken up, in order to write about them?

GREENSLADE Well the word 'broken' has an underlined significance because it's in the title of the book. This collection did not start off or even work its way forward with the title *Each Broken Object*, there were other abandoned titles along the way. That phrase though, which is in the final line of the poem 'Railway' (the sentence is 'I want to greet / each broken object when it sings') did become the title of the sequence for a reason. This phrase and also ideas arising from it puzzled me and I felt bound to go where there was more to be had. This single image led in a productive direction. These studies led me back to Heidegger's famous essay on 'The Thing' which I read with new interest. I really wanted to avoid the Coleridge's walking stick kind of poem. You know, that situation where a stick is just a stick but then you find out it was 'Coleridge's stick' and so the thing gets a projected significance in the wake of an associated personality. Heidegger's phenomenology, translated as the hilarious 'thinging of the thing', proved relevant and I was relieved to have made most of my own commitment to these poems before coming under its influence. I suppose breaking the object means bringing it into human joy and suffering but without domesticating the object's wilder virtues and integrity. In a way 'broken' could be structuralist shorthand for defamilarisation, but that seems a bit inaccurate for what I was attempting. For example, an obsolete object has freedoms other than function—becoming decorative, nostalgic, dumped, mistreated, incomprehensible and so on. An object commandeered away from usual use e.g. applying a knife as a screwdriver, or a toilet as an object of art allows other reflections and insights. The thing becomes differently visible when it is refracted away from states connected with forgetfulness. This is Heidegger's indication. I was already enjoying as many options as I could while also disallowing the 'Coleridge's stick' approach which was too sentimental for this project. Opportunities for regarding the object occur when it shifts into perceptive and critical states of feeling, measurement, memory and so on. We hurl ourselves unthinkingly or not at objects all the time. I tried as many forms of attention as possible for as long as the connection lasted. Ultimately it's relational and so somewhere unstable between the hermetic and the erotic. I spontaneously called them 'broken objects' at the climax of 'Railway' because this was a very rhapsodic moment of particularly impossible love.

ALLEN I found 'Railway' a scintillating little poem, and it was only the second poem there. I remember, on reading it first, that the singing broken objects made me think of the singing rails and then of something/one broken by being cut in two by a train. It seemed to be a heart-breaking love poem too, a poem of the night, a dream of steel and arrival and loss, highly surreal, and the 's' word is not something I use lightly. Yet the poem also seems to me to be crafted in a quite conventional way. Could you say more about that.

GREENSLADE Surrealism as a method has limits for me. When, via Bachelard, I discovered the concept of the oneiric, I felt this was closer to my way of combining various forms of observation with registers of projected fantasy. Oneirism helps with craft because it moderates relationships within the mind. I try and phrase small conceits as they arise—without compositional censorship, allowing mythic, psychic, metabletic, semantic and other needs to have their say, each of them leading me though drafts as though these functions were a band of friends and I among them. Oneiric awareness possibly bonds organic fictions with the metaphoric choices that make writing pleasurable. I think MacDiarmid's 'Esplumeoir' is an example of this. When my attention first begins to regard something I credit the 'object' of my attention with greater resources than mine; resources that will inform me and, at this point, if I'm lucky, some lyrical phrase might occur to me. Lyrics though (like many forms of purpose) can tend to push a rhythm forward at the expense of what I might be trying to be lyrical about. So I resist this hypnotism while also cradling it because it has given me something. I think the conventional craft aspect of 'Railway' is apparent because essentially it is a song of praise, a fiercely longing, direct address to a desired but unattainable object. So your fictionalising towards seeing someone more or less strapped to the tracks is intuitively close to the world of these three verses, even though such a specific fantasy was never mine. I'm fascinated by your response, but remember the railway track of this poem has no rails—it is an impossible material thing but it is a semantic object and also a psychological object for this poem, which explores folds between material and psychic reality. When the person for whom it was written read it, at first there was very little recognition; when read aloud, however, the reader was very moved. I'm convinced it was conformity to lyrical music that enabled the mystery of this poem's contradictory language to make the violent breach that Blanchot teaches us is the sign of a poem being read.

ALLEN You mentioned Bachelard, and Blanchot, do you read French, are there French poets who have influenced you directly? How do you see the relationship between literary-philosophical theorists and poetic practice, in general terms, your explanation of the 'oneiric' in relation to your own work, was fascinating but isn't that a very rare thing for a British poet? Or don't you see yourself as a British poet—Welsh? European?

GREENSLADE I don't speak French so I have to read René Char, Francis Ponge, Jules Supervielle, Lucienne Suel and other favourites in English translation. I can't explain why but for a while some French writers started to interest me almost obsessively. I think it was the way they seemed determined to explore ideas in a highly refined way, so refined at times as to be extremely difficult if not impossible (for me) to follow—particularly a fascinating figure like Anne Marie Aibach for example. This degree of abstraction is quite removed from Welsh poetry which is very much read, appreciated, admired, composed and discussed at all levels of the community still. I love this and writing in Wales is as satisfying as anything I read and re-read, particularly the work of Robin Llywellyn (novelist) and Gerallt Lloyd Owen (poet). I think it's likely that French writing has interested me partly because these writers seem to enjoy testing their language as a medium for a poetic epistemology (Guillevic and Jabès particularly) as well as the other expectations we have of poetry—praise, meditation, expression, etc and so on. I don't think this kind of interest is rare for a British poet. The challenge as always, it's been said before, is to absorb the delight of these writers and devise an idiom of our own. I don't think there is a direct influence but there may be a motivational one. I certainly don't enjoy being comforted by poetry so that finding Larkin (whom I appreciate in a similar way that one 'appreciates' Charles Bukowski) being elevated because he confirms etiolated aspects of our British way of life is a bit puzzling to me—I can see the cultural logic but I can't buy into it. I wonder if R.S. Thomas (the Anchorite) will get this same fairly lazy iconic recognition. Theorists engage me in the same way as poets do. Reflections on poetry I get from poets themselves. Bobi Jones is a hero of mine. Charles Simic has dazzling things to say. Bly can theorise enthusiastically and he does so with plenty of evidence. Bachelard is generous in a different way. Denise Levertov I found to be practical and helpful. Rafael Lopez-Pedraza applauds poets with very little theory and one learns a lot from him. Then Paz the great romantic. There's no end to it. I do enjoy reading thinkers who enjoy poetry as opposed to aggressive theorists who feel they have to compete with it. I have learned a great deal from people like Hans-Georg Gadamer and other hermeneutic readers whose passion is to explore how it is that repeated reading is possible rather than seeking to pulverise the poet, which is what I feel some theorists tend to do. While 'ideas' can spell the death of an essential erotic aspect, dancing, making mistakes, falling in love, taking risks, being foolish and pointless and so on, they needn't. And the best ideas don't, which is why I invoked Gianni Vattimo on the jacket of *Weak Eros*. That title is his phrase but I got it from Gemma Corradi Fiumara whose manifest interest in poetry is wonderfully oblique.

ALLEN You mentioned *Weak Eros*, your latest collection (Parthian 2002). Love poems? True love? What do you think of Andrew Duncan's comment in *The Failure of Conservatism in Modern British Poetry* to the effect that it is impossible to write good love poetry these days? Is he wrong? Have you proved him wrong? I know that when I first read the poems in *Weak Eros* I was struck, even more so then by *Each Broken Object*, by the available levels of interpretation, I could see those poems winning friends in many different quarters. Has that been the case or not? And tell me more about Gianni Vattimo.

GREENSLADE Gianni Vattimo teaches in Turin and more of his work is becoming available in English all the time. Vattimo is extremely courteous towards thinking that differs from his own and I remember James Hillman pointing out that levels of courtesy increase according to levels of tension and conflict so, as I considered the implications of my love poems—issues of desire, brutality, exposure and reception—I sought his work out. The concept of being 'weak' is central to Vattimo's entire project and he labels himself as a 'weak thought' philosopher. Regarding love poetry, Andrew Duncan isn't the only one to say that love poetry is close to impossible in the present climate. While I recognise the difficulty I've always thought that this can't be so as long as people still fall in love, which they do. So the challenge was to find a ground that I could write from. The poem 'In That Country' got me going and that poem arose from the object writing. We live in a highly literalist age confirmed I think by the sinister and comic literalism of television. Those who eat light breakfast cereal float into the air. Commercial literalism has contaminated our expectations, particularly the interaction of self and others. Oneiric literalism on the other hand dwarfs the foolishness of television. At the same time we have writers like Julia Kristeva who reassure us that imaginal instability, particularly around self, sex, the body, gender and text also obliges us to treasure a sense of personal resistance. These ideas inform the love poems. I very much wanted to write in this difficult zone and when I realised it would be something I'd commit myself to I carefully considered the various templates that might be available to me. I drew on my own experience where appropriate and linked these with opportunities that other writers have made known to us. Just an example—the poems 'Tulip Medicine' and 'Five Children' were not inspired by a book called *Sex Crimes in Seventeenth Century Venice* but they were, during composition, given context by that remote material. Then 'Five Children', because it features a teenager at a garden gate, has an allusion to Ezra Pound's poem 'The River Merchant's Daughter—A Letter'. 'The Car Behind' is a combination of experience and the meeting of Pwyll and Rhiannon in the *Mabinogion*. A vocabulary of display and concealment, of fountains, roses, kisses, letters, food, drink, clothing, pursuit, secrecy and declaration remains essential to this kind of writing but the challenge is to make it of our time. When the manuscript was ready I made sure I showed it to female poet friends and our conversations were very frank. A few difficulties in phrasing arose but not many difficulties of sentiment. As for access to the work—I do try and make the writing such that a reader can return to it which, yes, is a way of trying to make it available at different levels, since we read differently at different times. The collection has won praises except in *Planet* in Wales where the reviewer accused the book of being only about sex—this is not much of an accusation but it is reductive and I resist it. Sexuality is not the only way to notice the erotic and in my opinion a lot of contemporary sexuality is either superficially Dionysian or plain anti-erotic.

ALLEN Could you tell me more about the Welsh scene, particularly concerning your own development as a writer within that, or as a resistance to it. How do the tendencies to look inward and backward in Welsh poetry square with your highly modern and European outlook? Is that contradiction something which dialectically drives your work? And what do you think of the Welsh poetry scene in general, in comparison to the current English, is it healthy? Is it changing?

GREENSLADE The cultural ecology in Wales is totally different from that in England and it is healthy—the novel is going through a very exciting period especially the work of Mihangel Morgan. Poetry, and in Wales finding the new implies a sense of historic connection, is buzzing with optimism especially on the hands of a new generation of Eisteddfod-linked performative writers. Welsh writers are not parochial. I might as well say at the start that being a practitioner in Wales without entering the language community is, to me, a snobbery that too many writers and artists seem to feel they are licensed for. This kind of resolutely English-only writer, painter, performance artist or whatever (arrogant wimp?) is simply out of the loop as far as I am concerned. There is an avante garde in Wales and mercifully there is enough going on that remains ungathered, undocumented and unpublicised so that a person can be fed by very radical ideas and events. The publishing house Y Lolfa is well connected with emerging literary talents. What is lacking sometimes is a cohesion to these newer programmes so that occasionally some magazine or group might coalesce. Also because the demographics are so very different from majority expectations, 'free radicals' if I can call them that are often quickly folded into an institutional embrace. This isn't always so of course—the extraordinarily talented writer, painter and organiser Iwan Bala seems destined for exclusion precisely because of his stature. Avant-garde writing doesn't really have the same definition as it does for majorities but to compensate there are possibly more collaborative opportunities in Wales because communities overlap quite readily. The painter William Brown, for example readily shows within Wales at very modest venues and outside Wales at prestigious commercial galleries. His ability to combine the absolutely local with a very erudite and perceptive international vision is just the kind of balance that working in Wales makes possible. He is a painter who works with writers and pushes the writer to an edge, alongside his, which combines tradition, the new, the local and the remote. His is a very compassionate radicalism and that's what seems to drive much of the successfully new. Novelist Angharad Tomos could never be described as avant-garde but her radicalism, inseparable from her work, has taken her to prison and got her into intense political and personal trouble. This is what I regard as real aesthetic boundary pushing—the ability to identify and articulate the unique joys and difficulties of working in Wales. This is just too much of a challenge for the writers at Seren who seem to be stuck in a precious English-only bubble. In 2004 I worked with Marc Rees, a writer, performer and producer very interested in text. Marc assembled some of the most innovative interpreters of ideas, text and concepts at work in Cardiff and locked us all in a house together where we generated a simultaneous and theatrical text performance based on a novel by Michael Toppings. It was wonderfully different and became a seminal event. Because of the nature of community in Wales, Marc was been able to enlist participants from very separate worlds for what was an oral tradition venture given a powerful new turn. What is really amazing about working in Wales is that one might find oneself working at a basic level—on say a school's project, or a local pamphlet—alongside a writer of real reputation and achievement. RS Thomas served as secretary for The Cyfamodwyr (a very uncompromising group busted by the British police). Rhys Nicholas, hymn-writer, poet, essayist, editor, close friend of Waldo Williams—read manuscripts of mine when we worked together on a magazine. The concept of avant garde in Wales involves facing immediate shadows as much as being daring enough to react against them and look further afield. This is not only possible but it is encouraged. But narrow English-only factions, wherever they are based, and they aren't hard to find, remain grossly unaware of what it implies to fully work in Wales. This dynamic is central to my sense of belonging and of exclusion. But I also work outside of Wales and my friendship with the Two Rivers co-operative based in Reading connects me with the best of what it means to work in England

ALLEN I'm wary of entering this ground David, feel that I'm intruding on someone else's problem, but it is obvious from your last reply that there is a deep political project here and your conception of yourself as a poet is, through the Welsh Language question, intertwined with that. Aren't there both radical and reactionary factions within both Welsh and 'English only'? Are you saying that if an individual writer happens to be Welsh he/she has no choice but to orientate themselves with regard to the dual language question and that if that choice happens to be 'English only' that automatically makes them 'narrow minded', or, at least, not truly radical. I might have misunderstood you but I am worried by this, as I see it, far too direct and binding link. Doesn't it fly somewhat in the face of the more typically international notion of innovative poetic activity that tends to see language as a vehicle of freedom?

GREENSLADE Of course there is no one single response. Speaking a language is not a key to virtue. I am saying that since language is meant to be a concern of writers, then to be at work in Wales obliges a writer to take a look at this complexity, without monolingual prejudice. Fortunately our literary magazines *Planet*, *Poetry Wales* and the *New Welsh Review* currently have editors who can tolerate these tensions. But until very recently this wasn't always the case. I have been shocked by the vehemence of English medium bullying in a Welsh context, but the atmosphere is starting to change. Of course it would be convenient to forget that it has changed because young Welsh language activists have gone to gaol in order to secure these rights. I'm afraid I don't understand the last part of your question at all—it implies that if we all speak one language and call it internationalism then we face a wonderful collective future and that to resist it is somehow reactionary. I don't think so. I'm happy to be geographically who I am and intend to let this maximise my freedoms not confine them.

ALLEN Thanks for dealing with that so frankly David. Let's move on. What are you working on at the moment? Is it a project/collection in the same sense as *Each Broken Object* and *Weak Eros*?

GREENSLADE After a relatively quiet patch things are picking up again. What I really need is a full time day job but since the scandalous collapse of Creative Writing at Cardiff University I can't find work and despite my worthy record schools seem to be suspicious of me. In 2006 I'll have a book out combining punctuated verse and unpunctuated prose, from Parthian, the most exciting English medium publisher in Wales these days. The book is called *Adventure Holiday* and I'm particularly pleased with it. Another verse manuscript, *Zeus Amoeba*, is doing the rounds. I wrote *Zeus Amoeba* after seeing the sort of poetry that gets into school text books these days. It has the support of some name zoologists. My novel *Celtic Hot Tub* is being translated into Czech which should lead to other contracts. My work in Welsh and in English is being translated as it seems to interest people who come to my readings. Some readings tend to be consciously theatrical, even if it's just working with solo or choral voice or actual props such as video and audio tape, vegetables, objects, human beings etc. Writing in Welsh is of central importance to me and a work (*Lladd Nadroedd*) I wrote for a visit to Sorbia, a minority culture on the border of Poland and Germany, has just appeared (June 2005) with art work by Pat Gregory. My work is attracting the interest of a small but growing audience who, because they like it, often collaboratively include me in their projects or otherwise help move my writing forward. I have a very fruitful relationship with Kevin White and the music composition department at Napier University for example. So I'm looking forward to two or three years of presenting new material and finding new ways of doing it—especially with time-based workers and their very interesting physical experiments.

Bibliography

Lladd Nadroedd (in Welsh) Y Wasg Israddol.
Celtic Hot Tub (novel) Gwasg Carreg Gwalch.
Weak Eros (poetry) Parthian.
Cambrian Country ('essays') Gwasg Carreg Gwalch.
Each Broken Object (poetry) Two Rivers Press.
March (poetry) Y Wasg Israddol (in Welsh).
Old Emulsion Customs (poetry) Y Wasg Israddol.
Yr Wyddor (poetry) Gomer) (in Welsh).
Creosote (prose poems) Two Rivers Press.
A Love Letter (poetry) Y Wasg Israddol.
The Sorcerer Receives a Cutte (poetry) Two Rivers Press.
Panic (Poetry) Red Sharks Press.
Burning Down the Dosbarth (Poetry) Y Lolfa.
Fishbone (prose poems) Y Wasg Israddol.
Pebyll/Pavellons (poetry) Y Wasg Israddol (in Welsh and Catalan).
Iolo a'i Farcut Coch (for children) Gwasg Carreg Gwalch (in Welsh).
Iolo a'r Llythrennau Groeg (for children) Gwasg Carreg Gwalch (in Welsh).
Gloria a'r Berllan Bupur (for children) Y Lolfa (in Welsh).
Welsh Fever (non-fiction) D Brown and Sons.
Adventure Holiday (Parthian) forthcoming.
Zeus Amoeba forthcoming.

When I hear Ella Fitzgerald sing it

and all the time . . . (from CHANGING LINES)

*a*nd all the time you are

*b*e

*c*oming

blin*d*ly

impossibl*e*

a machine *f*or

carryin*g* distance over sound,

a desired lover *h*oves to

your ra*i*nbow

*j*ailor's eyes

*k*een type of the

specu*l*ative

te*m*per

a liste*n*ing

y*o*u can

*p*lace

*q*uietly with the dead

*r*e

s

ting

under

cover of

whitening flesh

experience has

coloured your

prized words

(A version of Changing Lines is on the *Great Works* website)

ALLEN John, your essay 'Writing and Not Writing', deals with your years of not writing, with silence, and this state, the state of writing and/or not writing seems to be a constant theme in your work. Could you begin by talking about your very early 'writing' and 'not writing'?

HALL I am interested in your remark about writing/not writing having been a constant theme for me. I would have to go back to what I was writing up until the end of the 70s to see if it seems to me that way too. Because early on I wasn't silent at all—in the very earliest years producing much more than made its way into book publication. But of course being silent and being interested in silence as a modality (or set of modalities) of exchange between people are quite different things. And I am sure I have always been interested in the latter.

I suspect that silence is a topic you might want to come back to so I'll duck it for now and head straight for the easier bit of your last sentence.

How does any writer characterise their own coming into writing in relation to a phrase like 'very early'? I wasn't one of those who started writing in childhood. I certainly *used* writing in adolescence and had I suppose one poem that I was serious about by the age of 18—a long one that, as I recall it, had been invaded by Eliot in his meditative mode. I've still got the first line in my head now: 'Winter with all its chaste beauty / Untouchable . . . .' The writing I still acknowledge, with whatever reservations, started when I was

20, perhaps 21, and some of it is there at the beginning of my first book, *Between the Cities*. I was at University and lucky enough to be in a place where a number of things were coming together and usefully apart. I was taught by Jeremy Prynne. Tim Longville was in town. Later on John James took up a job in the town. Andrew Crozier was back from his time in Buffalo and visited regularly to do some supervision. With Jeremy's help Andrew was starting up *The English Intelligencer*, duplicated corner-stapled foolscap sheets distributed to a small group of writers. I then met many of the people on the distribution list. Very few people had had anything published in book form by then.

Not-writing didn't come into it at that stage. Reading, writing and conversation were very closely connected. If anything it was much more a case of writing too much, that is indiscriminately, often overexcited by the feel that writing could have a purchase beyond itself. It is probably true that much of what I wrote at that stage was some sort of **reply**—to some reading, to something someone had said, to a film. This was not a silent time.

ALLEN Could you say more of what lies behind that little phrase, 'I was taught by Jeremy Prynne', or perhaps try to pinpoint what was going on with that group of names at that time? And what kind of direction might you have taken if you had not been 'taught by Jeremy Prynne'?

HALL I suppose the first thing to comment on is that word 'taught'. At Cambridge at the time—and I'm sure it's still true—responsibility for teaching was divided between the University (I suppose through its academic departments) and the colleges. The University Department must have been responsible for the examination syllabus and a lecture programme; the college for providing personal contact through advice and supervision. Although Jeremy did give a number of lecture series which were most exciting my main contact with him was in the other mode, either one-to-one or with very few of us. There only were six of us studying English in the college in the year I started.

Almost certainly one of the things that would have happened if he hadn't been there is that I would have left. I had some very unrealistic expectations of university, mostly bound up with my own take at the time on what cultural studies people later came to call 'really useful knowledge'. I was distressed by the reification of a literature syllabus as though it was part of a self-contained circuit and the exclusion from it of other forms of enquiry, or of literature as itself a form of enquiry rather than as something to study. Jeremy helped me in this predicament in very practical ways— first by managing the institutional side of the problem for me, but mostly, as I remember, through putting a pile of books that had nothing directly to do with a syllabus in my hand with the expectation that I would read them.

This opened up all sorts of things and very much included a way into that US line that took both Pound and Williams as differing reference points. This way I came to read all of those writers who were anthologised by Donald Allen. Even though Prynne had been in very close touch with a number of these people, including particularly Olson and Dorn, there was no way he was trying to be a pseudo-American in Cambridge. At the same time, Andrew Crozier had come back keen to make sense, it seems to me now, of what was already UK-based writing activity and to instigate more without this being satellite. So at the very time that people like me were getting very excited by models that were in many senses *open*, the question was also in the air about the specificity of the then island situation. Hence, I think, the title *English Intelligencer*—though the list included at least some born in Wales and Scotland.

Very much to the point too was that Jeremy was at the time writing the poems that were to form part of *The White Stones*. Some of these were appearing in the *Intelligencer* and circulating too in photocopies of hand-written versions. So it was a kind of nexus, a place and a moment—one that was, I suspect, over quite soon. Better Books—with readings as well as poetry in its shelves—was soon down the railway line in London. Through *Resuscitator* (John James and Nick Wayte) there had been a node in Bristol, owing something to Charles Tomlinson. And in the north-east, Basil Bunting had been a presence for Tom Pickard and Barry MacSweeney (the latter by then based in Hertfordshire and a fairly frequent visitor to Cambridge) and the Mordern Tower readings were already happening.

Nothing had formed firmly enough for it all to be too inward-looking (that enclosing Cambridge that features in so many John James poems) and there was an exhilarating sense that study was every bit as much to do with making something as it was with examining the past—that these two directions needed each other.

I have no idea what direction my work might have taken without all this and I don't know how to know that kind of thing. It is no good looking at people who found their own way in; you just find different stories of accidents and connections, about which you could ask 'what would have happened if . . . '. I was thinking of Roy Fisher and tracking back to his 'Antebiography' to the first contact with Gael Turnbull. But he was already putting himself where that contact could happen and he already was playing jazz.

ALLEN I am interested in that situation in which the main influences were coming from the Americans and yet, as you emphasise, 'there was no way he (Prynne) was trying to be a pseudo-American'. For example how did Crozier's concern, 'to instigate more without this being satellite', work in the practical sense? If writers such as John James were already writing work that was distinctly British why was there the anxiety? Was there a real problem in handling the 'open forms' in a manner that did not sound American? I get the feeling that the English poets, especially those who read English at University, had to struggle harder to feel comfortable with novelty and that the fruits of that struggle are very much the character of the Cambridge end of the British avant garde. And if I can bring this back to your own work, in the poems of *Between the Cities*, which you were writing at that time (1968), isn't there a trait that is common, in one way or another, to the majority of the poets you have so far mentioned, that of being continually and quite consciously on the cusp of different choices?

HALL This was all a very long time ago now and memories have probably diverged—by which I mean there is no reason to trust mine. And the answer to how it all worked out practically is perhaps to look at the work being produced not only through the *English Intelligencer* itself but also through magazines that were either already going or were about to start up, the small press book publication and the meeting up of people. There was I am sure a considerable amount of work that was attempting to apply objectivism or Olson's or Dorn's geography to a UK experience; Robert Creeley's line was certainly caught in many an ear. I think a lot of UK writers at the time had simply given up on the writers associated with the so-called Movement; were not even faintly afflicted with an anxiety of influence that related to a just previous UK generation. It took some time to connect back by other routes. Bunting was very important; so was David Jones, I believe for some. Grosseteste published some Scottish poets. It was later, wasn't it, that people—including Andrew Crozier—started to go back to the forties, that Tony Lopez did his work on W.S. Graham?

Your remark on John James's Britishness is interesting on two counts—firstly his Cardiff Welshness (do you know his *Welsh Poems* from this time?) and secondly the way he started only slightly later in the 60s to work with what he learnt from Frank O'Hara.

As for myself, it may be relevant to this topic that I did not spend my early childhood in the UK. I was born and brought up in colonial Africa, in a country whose colonial name was Northern Rhodesia. I had realised by about the age of 18 how little I knew England, of life in England—or rather, perhaps, how I was caught between exilic narratives of what England was and class-inflected and geographically limited first-hand experiences. Some of that sense may be in *Between the Cities*—certainly a feeling at that time that a poem could be a place where you found things out. I like your phrase about being on the cusp of different choices. Of course that can be an illusion if what you are doing as a writer is rehearsing the procedures that accompanied other people's choices— especially where the cusp of choices is embodied in formal—i.e. syntactic and prosodic—decisions.

ALLEN I think, John, what I want to know is, what was it that made some British poets' response to Olson and Creeley look distinctly North-Atlantic while others, particularly those we have been discussing, produced something a lot more English in texture and weight, even though it was a million miles from the Englishness of the Movement. Welsh John James: OK, what shall I call it then, guided by the American but, to my mind, distinctly not American. I was not referring to the classic 'anxiety of influence' but to this new one re American open forms; and maybe that is one of the fundamental things that have separated mainstream British poetry (classic anxiety of influence) from the innovators (new anxiety of American influence). You said, 'it took some time to connect back by other routes', so let's return to what you were doing in *Between the Cities* by way of asking what other influences were working on you at that stage.

HALL Everybody gets their initial 'method' from somewhere. Method may be a rather clunky word there—some sort of anticipatory sense of being in language and shaping it. Another and a different way of putting it is that most young writers start off by inhabiting some version of the poetic behaviour of an earlier writer or of earlier writers. At an extreme that can take the form of mimicry—an imitation of the outer effects without an understanding from within of what moves the shapes into being. As soon as there is a sense of procedure, of method, of poetic, then there is a better chance of transformation through attention to specifics. John James, for example, may very evidently have adopted some of the devices and spheres of reference from O'Hara, but in my view he puts them to work, to his work.

But back to *Between the Cities*. Apart from the twentieth century English-language modernist stuff, I was at that time very taken with some of the Middle-English texts that I was encountering because of the English Literature syllabus. I particularly remember *The Pearl* poem and *Sir Orfeo*, but also much of Chaucer and dream narratives. Also with Elizabethan (and earlier) sonnets and other forms of lyric. Shakespeare was always there. Still is. Campion had come through by way of Williams—I think—and Creeley. Prynne was terrific on Wordsworth. *The Prelude* became a real excitement. I have a feeling that if I were to track back through those early poems of mine and try to compile a booklist of what had prompted them or woven into them it would show how excitable I was by the kinds of unofficial syllabuses thrown out by Pound, quite differently by Olson, and through my contact with Prynne. There were at least two lines to this: the absorption of prosody—quite a self-conscious ear-training—but also trying to take on something from an epic line that was to do with knowledge and history; and how do these come together. It seems obvious to me looking back at the actual poems that lyric knowledge—what an individual sensibility might know in a song-like form through a formal convergence of experience, affect and percept—was still driving many of the poems. That together with attempts to try to move into preferred attitudes—to use poems as places to try this out rather than to settle into them as places already marked out for some sense of the sublime.

In a University town, and reading Pound, Olson and the Prynne of the *White Stones* era, it was tempting to respond to the feeling that quite other forms of knowledge could be activated within poems. This may have been more a matter of the kind of environment that I chose to see as around my writing at that time rather than something that was truly their mode of operation.

ALLEN I immediately recognise that wanting to move into poems as places to try things out rather than, 'settle into them as places already marked out for some sense of the sublime', and I see how the practical freedom offered by that can result in a poem of such rich freshness as 'Remember the City?', but what is 'lyrical knowledge'? It is the kind of thing the poet in me might say, and probably has, but another part of me has absolutely no idea. From your description of it I understand the 'formal convergence' but why does it have to be 'song-like'? Are we talking about mental short-circuits here? Is the 'song-like' a kind of poetry within poetry, becoming known, becoming a strange knowledge, through an awareness of the poem's internal relations?

HALL What is lyrical knowledge? Or what does a song know? And why does it have to be song-like? I'm not the only one to have been bumping into these questions for years now. Let me try 'lyrical' and 'song-like' first, since they are almost the same, it seems to me. Literally, a lyric is a kind of song sung solo to the accompaniment of a lyre. If the words of the song can get by on their own without the lyre, lute or guitar, without that transformation of voice into a singing game of pitch, timbre, dynamic and melody, but if the situation of the utterance is still dramatised within the utterance, then it still gets called lyric. The OED says, 'the name for short poems (whether or not intended to be sung) . . . directly addressing the poet's own thoughts and sentiments'. In putting it this way—'poet's own'—the OED buys into a notion of authenticity or sincerity which rubs right up against another characteristic of song-like utterances—their repeatability and their appropriation by other 'singers'. ('Every time we say good-bye I die a little'. I love that song. I 'know what it means'. And I have known what it means to feel that. I don't feel it often, and yet I love that song. And when I hear Ella Fitzgerald sing it, her skill as a singer was such that it is the song that knows, and the singer only as manifest in the singing. Whether all those other parts of Ella Fitzgerald that are not present to the singing also know this, well who could possibly know?)

In putting it the way I did and by invoking the notion of knowledge I was trying to get at a difference between propositional knowledge (relying on modes of *argument*, when at all elaborated), narrative knowledge (which doesn't explain so much as exemplify and whose most compressed mode is perhaps a proverb), and this other that I called 'lyric knowledge', that oscillates between two conditions of language: its 'sound shapes', whose intrinsic patternings are always tempting to play up, and the utterance state of speech—that if there are words then someone must have said / be saying them. This oscillation is often pleasurable as a tension between shapeliness and 'truth' or—and you may have seen some of my framed pieces putting these words into visual play—artifice and candour.

Another way yet of putting this is that 'lyric knowledge' is always a performance of existential knowledge—knowledge in a process or moment of being. As performance this can be 'as if'. And this kind of knowledge can have all the intuitive conviction of epiphany; can be caught in its own play of doubt; or manifest the bad faith of alien occupation of an already given shapeliness.

And does it have to be song-like? No. But given sound-shapeliness, this is most likely. What Pound called melopoeia. Think of Creeley's 'A Song', early in *For Love*. Or Prynne's 'Shadow Songs' (in *Poems* between 'Oil' and 'Concerning Quality, Again'! But with 'Price Tag Song' not far behind.) It can equally be picture-like (imagism?, 'concrete'); object in a world of objects; machinic.

ALLEN OK, let's move along a few years to 1971 and *Days*. You mentioned 'concrete' and here a certain concrete element is feeling its way along with what is, at times, an almost chatty directness. The effect of both makes poems that are at the same time lighter in tone yet texturally animated. There is more language-play too, something that tempers and slightly twists the love poem angle. Can you tell us something about the circumstances that lay behind the particular turn of those poems?

HALL I very much enjoyed that set of comments on *Days*!

There was quite a bit of writing between the last poems in *Between the Cities* and the sequence of *Days* poems. It may well be a good thing that they have disappeared from view. I was having to adjust to the changed contexts of my life—temporary jobs that I wasn't enjoying and the company of people—many of whom I did enjoy very much—who were either not interested in poetry or wanted to know why they should be interested in poems that looked and sounded like mine. I struggled from time to time, too, with something that many have had to deal with—the quality and shape of time that was available for writing. All of these factors produced a decision that I would write a daily poem, that it would use whatever was at hand as its materials, that if it was drawing on any references it would give them an anecdotal context, not assume them as shared knowledge, that it would settle for contingency and tentativeness where that's all there was. Of course I didn't write a poem every day and many of those I did write—especially at the end of a long pub visit—were terrible. The book itself is a selection as you can see from the numbering—1, 2, 4, 10, 13 . . . Tim Longville had originally set far more pages than were eventually used. I am sure I have every reason to be grateful for his editing down.

And what you call the 'language-play'—in this book, the poems seldom set out to be a play of language; it was more a matter of finding the play that seemed to be lurking there in banal or conventional formulations. Rather than starting out with any idea of line length I remember trying to gauge intuitively what sort of run, what sort of momentum, the lines needed.

I felt at the time too that no one numbered poem had any autonomy. They all needed a sense of calendar-like narrative. Not the story-like narrative of 'yes, and then what?' but a sense that all this was coming out of a same life and its vicissitudes. It was a mixed time in my life, full of some very good and exciting things (love poems, with a twist . . .) and the pleasures of company but also uncertain, lacking a sense of direction that I had perhaps briefly enjoyed.

ALLEN So much of what you just said, for example your asking why anyone close to you, 'should be interested in poems that looked and sounded like mine', and your talk of the struggle for time, brings us to the issues you focussed on in the 'Writing and Not Writing' essay. When I first read that I was astonished by the clarity with which you discussed a situation that was very familiar and yet one that I could not describe myself and had never seen described. Most writing about writing ends up as clichéd biography because the writer takes their writing for granted, or rhetorically appears to, and that renders it as 'special' in precisely the wrong way. You were doing the opposite, so what was it in your experience of writing and not writing which led to your being able to formulate what was happening? Where did that realism and analytical focus, that ability to step outside both internal and exterior ideologies, come from? It is something that English poets are not supposed to do, people get suspicious.

HALL Suspicious of what, I wonder. Maybe there are at least two transgressions involved and of a completely different order: one that takes many forms but broadly goes that writing's costs and debts should either not be spoken at all or, if spoken, should take the accepted contours of melodramatic narratives of driven, damaging but exultant artists. The last bit of that sentence gets close to the second: that head and heart dichotomy, according to which 'analytical focus', to use your phrase is completely the wrong register for dealing with matters of strong emotional significance. On top of all that, isn't there a problem about letting autobiographical material get too close? What was that phrase of Alvarez's when talking about certain US poets for whom writing poems and contemplating suicide were closely related activities? Was it depth psychology?

You can see that I share some of the suspiciousness and that I am avoiding that question 'where does it come from'? I'll try and answer it but I don't know that I know. I am very flattered by the way that you put it. Because that felt a very vulnerable piece both in the writing and in the letting go.

Some of it is almost certainly a matter of temperament and 'upbringing'. I think I am at heart a literalist, and as a literalist can be captured by the specifics of a question, as though nobody had ever thought of it before. In the case of that article it really was answering a question. Denise Riley, the editor, invited a contribution on 'processes of writing'. I thought hard about the invitation since at the time I had not been 'writing' and realised very quickly that for a writer not to be writing was just as much a processual question as if s/he were. So I really did want to address the question but knew that it would be difficult to do so honestly and in a way that could belong to conversation rather than confessional monologue.

Looking back, there was something else too, and this came from the material I was engaging with as part of my teaching. I left university in 1967. I suspect that this was a matter of months before 'theory' began to drift across on the cross-channel ferry. Nine years later I found myself working with art students on a course that had 'social context' in the title. They were not particularly expected to re-produce theoretical thought on the topic but were supposed to respond within their work. For some this was fairly straightforward conceptually (and I know that this doesn't necessarily mean also straightforward in practice): 'context' could mean 'community' as in 'community arts'. I found myself most interested by those who found the question problematic and so in a problem solving way I got myself involved in those kinds of texts which together came to make up 'cultural studies'. This was before it had quite become (just) another slice through institutionalised knowledge. I became taken with an understanding that in 'studying' culture you could never be studying something outside of yourself; that the very act of 'studying culture' was a cultural process and therefore a practice.

This may seem long-winded but I really am trying to answer your question! I had tried to bring some of this together in a sequence of poems called *Repressed Intimations* which Tony Baker published as an edition of his magazine, *Figs*. It still feels like unfinished business, that sequence. I could well go back to it, perhaps try to translate it. Ten years later the invitation to produce a prose article on these processes felt like a licence to be completely literal and to apply the questioning to material I knew best, my own experience. Isn't that what prose is for? (Let me withdraw that absurd rhetorical question without actually doing so). More than ten years after the article, the questions are still alive for me, as you remarked earlier in the interview. I think that that act of writing helped me to work with the questions in different ways, through different forms of writing (and I am sure of not-writing). One of the sub-themes won't go away. In 'late capitalism' writing is bound to be caught between being a medium of exchange between people—symbolically performative—and being a commodity operating in market exchange networks. No easy way out of that, nor into it either.

ALLEN Yes indeed, the problems of writing within this late capitalism context—or whatever other term can be used for it—go deep; I have trouble reading so much poetry written since the mid 80s (rough date) that does not engage with it, does not even nod in its direction, is not reflexive. So could I use this point to jump off into questions that revolve around the binary issue of mainstream and innovative? You are a poet who is perceived to be of the latter, so what are your thoughts on this? I know that most poets instinctively knee-jerk against pigeon-holes, just as they are ready to embrace the comfort of being in a 'group' when feeling delicate, but for me the differences are often stark, whatever attitude and picture of him/herself the individual poet creates. So, a stark question: what is it that you do that disqualifies you from being mainstream?

HALL Is there a poetry 'mainstream' in the UK in 2004? Really? I have difficulty with the metaphor, anyway, because I try to visualise it as a pattern of tributaries flowing into a 'main' stream and this doesn't work. It feels the wrong way round. Isn't the idea more that there is a grand flow of literary history which occasionally branches off into unimportant little side streams but even so the grand ole river just keeps rolling along? Something like that. It works better if 'stream' is taken as 'current' so the clever people are there where the current moves them on and the others are left in still or slow moving side waters.

Certainly it is a root, trunk and branch metaphor rather than a rhizome one and it is difficult to see how it could make any sense in a contemporary post-industrial society. I think it gets in the way. Even so it might still mean something if there was an evident hegemony made up of networked poets, corporate publishing houses, journals, broadsheet reviewing cabals, school and university syllabuses, radio and TV programmes, chart lists . . . I don't see it. I see residues, for sure. Broadly speaking what I see when I hear these terms are two traditions that are most easily defined in relation to modernism(s): one that is an oxymoronic tradition of the 'new' that is still energised from either the 'Pound era' or from the concurrent European modernism very much including Dada and surrealism; the other sees these as aberrations of posturing aesthetes and goes back for its early twentieth century source to (non Pound-) Yeats and to Frost. In terms of a sociology of literature what separates the two 'streams'. At first glance not a lot. Might even be tempting to try a familiar psychoanalytic line using the Oedipus trope. Yes, I like this one, especially as both traditions have been so male. One lot, with whatever subtle waverings and adjustments for filial transformation, claims paternal heritage. Just think of all those 'my father' poems. The other lot disclaims and not only that, behaves in such a way that they can ensure disinheritance. As if.

Raymond Williams commented in one of those earlier books of his that the European avant-garde was a formation of migrants, refugees, generally displaced people. That makes a lot of sense, I think. Not just that a place has to be 'made new'. It has to be made. It doesn't exist prior to the act of writing. No mimicry of something before will do. I love those early Reznikoff poems in which with wonderful deliberation he misapplies to Manhattan an OLD Testament pastoral aesthetic.

It is not the 'new', the innovation, itself that counts in this. It counts for nothing unless it is a response to make it and for a writer this is to make it in and through language. 'Innovation' is just as open to being a re-branding trick performed by a tired marketing department. I don't recogn   ovation' as a drive for me.

Always at stake is a   mmunity, of speaking for one (out of one), of speakin.   ne (hopefully) or in despair of lost community.

So why am I disqualii   n? Perhaps I have just demonstrated! Obviously I havei   produce the artefacts recognisable in that 'mainstreai   ou h I am not all happy to be found obscure. The answei   ways lie in the banalities of literary politics (i.e. not nece   y have anything to do with poetics); and it might have everything to do with poetics. Taking the terms of your binary at face value I know where I like to do my reading. And I am aware nearly all the time of dealing in some way or other with lines of movement that feel like displacements, outside of any belief in a settled place of language, even one settled enough to be troubled in.

ALLEN Well John, I don't quibble with myself about the aptness of the metaphor, I actually find most metaphors misleading, even stupid, part of the wonderful absurdity of having to use language. For me the word mainstream refers to something broadly understood as existing, much as you describe it as a questionable hegemony that you say is now 'residue'. What is important is that after doubting the existence of such a thing you go on to demonstrate in your answer more than one way in which it does seem to exist, via those different heritages. And I agree with you about the word 'innovation', but then, you said before that you are a 'literalist'. Before we move on I want to ask you what you mean by 'community', why is it, 'always at stake'?

HALL Yes you've certainly caught me in a vagueness with that always vague and always ideological term. And I'm sure I'm about to get into even more trouble in trying to explain my way out of it. I got there by way of thinking about 'mainstream' and assuming that one of the things implied by it as a term is that the people in it are understood because they speak out of—perhaps even *for*—some shared social experience, even if that is highly individualised. When the topic is 'personal experience' and recognition of this experience is expected from others then there is a 'community' of sensibility invoked that goes way beyond the literary. People who are bound together in repeated plays of shared recognition form and sustain a sense of 'in common' that is carried in the word 'community'.

One of the many difficulties with the word is that it implies a kind of social gestalt. And where nostalgia and loss—or indeed nationalism—are in play then there is probably always also a sense of whole. Isn't it true that rhetorical acts—any language acts whatever—have at least a double engagement with the world that they take place in: their specific situations of utterance—who is talking with whom, where, when (and in relation to what); and then the fact that the medium—language—only works because it has been around and carries a world with it. And the world it carries is not just the referential or associative world, the world implied by its vocabulary and formulations; it carries with it too all of the accumulations of its pragmatics in that world—how it has been used, for what purposes and so on. 'Community' is very likely an unhelpful word—worse than 'mainstream'!—but you will see what I am getting at. What I am calling 'recognition', when that is wholesale, relies on cultural relay to sustain a sense of collectivity. There is, by default, a whole attitude to the past entailed, though it does not need to be specified. The same goes for a repertoire of generic manœuvres for dealing with sameness and difference.

A wounded sensibility can resist recognition (I suppose I am using this term instead of Althusser's 'interpellation') and operate as a dissident member or even an outcast. Any more systematic refusal is far more problematic; it will need company and it will at some point need affirmation. I am wondering how much I am still being drawn here by Olson's 'polis'. I think there has been an idea that resistance within language can somehow operate affirmatively all on its own even when 'within language' really means 'within poems' and little account is taken of the social pragmatics of exchanging poems. Poems happen between people or not at all and they have limited powers to keep at bay all the other things that happen between people.

ALLEN Tell me about Dartington, that world where your life as a writer and your life as a professional came together. Or did they? I called the college a 'cut-off hot house', or something similar, in one of my hot-tempered Brit Po spats with cris cheek.

HALL People who have heard of Dartington often don't realise that there are—and have been—a number of different operations that go on under the name. I was talking to someone on the phone recently who said, Dartington, isn't that the Rudolf Steiner school? My connection goes back for years. I went to readings there—organised by Peter Kiddle, I think—long before I worked in Totnes as a school-teacher. My first formal connection was through the Arts Society which actually had a panel to oversee a poetry programme. I was asked to do the planning one year when Peter Kiddle was away and got explicit permission to do it my way—by which I meant inviting only poets I wanted to hear myself. This was extended for a year or two. You would recognise all the names of the people who came down. This was great but rather in a vacuum when it seemed to me that the College—Dartington College of Arts—would be the obvious source of audience and I only had connections through the Arts Society and a few friends.

    In 1974 I went on to part-time in the school-teaching job and was immediately invited to do a day a week at the College of Arts with art students in writing workshops. What a treat! I had to go back into full-time the following year which meant letting this go. But a job came up at the College in 1976 that also involved working with music students. I was in an odd position. There were no writing courses—just classes within other courses—and at that time staff belonged to departments more than they did to the

College. I got more and more sucked in to things that were institutional rather than sectional. Eventually this led, in a crisis, to being asked to take up a management role as Vice Principal. I did this for twelve years and only stopped with an early semi-retirement in September 2002.

As far as the coming together of two versions of myself—the writer and the professional—is concerned, for much of this time this happened no more than when school-teaching, just differently. There were years in the middle when I did not directly teach writing.

In 1994 we got going an undergraduate degree which we called Performance Writing. I chaired the group that planned this—an interdisciplinary group of volunteers. That exercise was one of the greatest pleasures of my professional life. I was director of the course for its first two years. All of this was not just a pleasure. It was a chance to apply to the teaching of writing everything I had learnt from a much broader engagement with contemporary arts, especially one that had an emphasis on performance, composition, installation, and on context. All of that, and then working with Caroline Bergvall, Ric Allsopp, Brigid Mc Leer, cris cheek, Alaric Sumner, Jerome Fletcher . . . (the list goes out and on—Peter Jaeger, Dell Olsen, Mark Leahy . . .) and the many people who came down on teaching visits, really helped to put me back in what felt like an immediate context for writing. This did bring the two (writing and teaching) together, though Performance Writing was only supposed to be a small part of my job and I wasn't able to give it all the time I'd have liked.

I very much enjoy teaching—both the face-to-face aspect of it and the design work behind the scenes.

I know what you mean by both 'cut off' and 'hot house'. From the inside that probably gets translated as 'no time' and 'very intense'. But I don't think the Performance Writing project was ever cut off as in 'insular'. I think it is more that the pattern of connections has been very spread wide with the effect of some neglect of the closer to home. Paradoxically there are almost certainly people the other side of the Atlantic and in mainland Europe who don't at all feel that Dartington is cut off. There is now a new arm to the institution with the job of connecting into the region. This should eventually make a difference.

An illustration that touches both of us — since my semi-retirement I have very much enjoyed participating in your Plymouth Language Group discussions. This wouldn't have been easy earlier.

ALLEN Can you say something about your visual work; do you consider it concrete poetry or is it hybrid? For me the pieces have an almost Zen-like quality but at the same time I am reminded of psychological tests.

HALL I just call them visual poems or sometimes framed poems and am probably still too close to say anything coherent. I'd much rather ask you about the 'psychological tests'. Do you mean that the poems have a kind of riddling effect from their elliptical form and that this suggests that they are prompting an answer?

I got into them by a number of routes — one of them a negative one. I missed out on art almost completely in my rather strange schooling (until the end when I sought out the art teacher who became something of a mentor for a while) and indeed on any hand/eye activity except sports. I have put some of this right since, partly through picking up some basic wood-working skills in a Devon boat-yard and partly through refurbishing at least one house with the help of a very experienced father-in-law. I came really to enjoy making or adapting things.

I had done some playing around on a typewriter but really it was buying a BBC computer in 1983 that let me play with letter forms for the first time with any confidence. In those days like everyone else I was using a dot matrix printer with no colour. It wasn't until a few years into the 90s that I had access to an ink-jet printer and Windows style fonts that showed up on the screen and I think it was probably in 1995 when one of my sons acquired a colour printer.

If that's two factors, then a third was an interest in — perhaps envy of — those kinds of made things that could play a visible part (not just visual) in everyday social life. Making cards came first; then making things that could hang on the walls of a home.

A fourth factor could well have been that their minimalism offered too, as it were, a minimal step from not-writing, and also a means of getting away from full sentences and their propositional entailment.

The hybridity you include in your question, would that be between poetry and visual art? If so, then not hybrid. In a recent article that touches on this whole topic I found myself using the phrase 'playing up the visual'. They are only hybrids with visual art to the extent that visual art has taken typography into its means.

ALLEN   What have you been working on recently?

HALL I set myself two lines of activity when I semi-retired. One was to read much more current poetry than I'd been managing, especially to read the kinds of things that I had put aside because they needed a different kind of time and attention than I'd had. The other was to go into a sort of fitness training that might take me back in the direction of longer page-based poems: to try out again a writing that builds up movement—momentum—over time rather than one that operates as kinds of interruption or punctuation. Mostly this meant trying to get back to sentences (I mean sentences in the context of lines).

Much of my time in the last eighteen months has taken the form of a reading towards the writing of articles. So far as the second aim is concerned I have not got as far as the kind of poem writing where one sentence follows another. My fitness training has more been to do with playing with lines. A set of variations called *Changing Lines* has gone up on Peter Philpott's Great Works website. The pull of the visual is still strong and one main reason for sending the variations to Peter is that a website can easily handle colour and different typographic decisions. This is still more of a problem for magazine and book printing. I am in the middle of adapting the same pieces for framing at about A3 size each, possibly to show as part of the Exeter Text Festival (tEXto4). And in a different format still the variations are contributing to conversations with composer Edward Cowie that might well lead to a collaboration (not necessarily making direct use of the poems).

I am hoping too at some stage to get into a conversation, through writing, with some drawings of Heather Cowie's.

I need soon to learn to work directly for the web and to use its possibilities for moving text and giving it a time signature ('animation'). I did one piece using PowerPoint as a contribution for a memorial event for Alaric Sumner that I wasn't able to attend. So there are other kinds of training I need too.

ALLEN To bring this interview to completion John, can I ask what young poets, or new poets, have particularly impressed you recently, and where do you see English poetry going over the next quarter century?

HALL I can't help treating your two questions together. I was re-reading Doug Oliver's puff on the back of Denise Riley's *Selected Poems* again the other day: 'Poetry's future probably lies in the direction Denise Riley is taking . . . '. Because of what is likely to be in store for the next 25 years I don't myself have that kind of sense about 'the direction' in relation to any individual writers. This is not because there aren't some younger (a good bit younger than me that means) writers whose work interests me greatly—or just gives me pleasure—but because I think that the directions will be multiple.

I am sure that serious writers will go on working on pages with book publication in mind. Andrea Brady is a poet I expect will do this. So perhaps is Helen Macdonald. I suspect that with Print on Demand publication now changing the poetry publishing world there will be two kinds of books and that these are likely to diverge even more than they have already: the get-them-out-there POD books where the only design differences between examples are cover and thickness; and the individually designed book that continues the twentieth century's small press tradition and allows all sorts of material decisions to be part of the writing.

The www is already becoming more and more significant. The bulk of the poetry on www just uses the environment as an alternative to print, and in the case of e-books as an alternative route to print. I will be very surprised if there isn't more and more writing, like some of Michael Atavar's recent work, that works directly with the formal possibilities of software and screen, with the lit quality of the screen, with the possibilities of animation and sound.

I hope too that there will be more and more poetry that gets itself thoroughly entangled in the visual art world, and the other way round. I'll be following Brigid McLeer's work with interest in this respect.

And then there is a reconciliation of great possibility between textual poetics and a poetics of performance. This isn't a single possibility—as in say, 'theatre'. The forms are already multiple. Just think of Aaron Williamson, cris cheek, Caroline Bergvall, Lone Twin, Dell Olsen, Fiona Templeton. There won't necessarily be anything to see on a page.

I have come at the question so far from the angle of different *textual* environments. Every bit as important will be the economic, political and social environments and the relations poetry activity does or doesn't have with currents of power, with the often violent negotiations that compress together political, ethnic and religious futures. A difficulty with the mainstream / modernist dichotomy is that it is coming increasingly to look like a parochial conflict. Will UK-based poetry be mono-lingual? Or, to put it another way, will there be very different postures within UK-based English language writing? Will writing in English make a pitch to speak within the vast language 'community' of speakers of English, whether this be as a first, second, third . . . tongue? Will it be possible to restore a specifying use of plural personal pronouns (this links back to my muddled thoughts on 'community') within concrete rather than abstract senses of social difference?

I went back to Nicholas Johnson's *Foil* anthology in thinking about this last question of yours. Apart from Caroline Bergvall's recent *Goan Atom* work, which certainly deals with aspects of what I am talking about, I'd like to see more of Khaled Hakim's writing. I like those pieces in *Foil* very much.

Bibliography

Collections of poems or separately published
      sequences:
Between the Cities (Lincoln: Grosseteste 1968).
Days (Lincoln: Grosseteste, 1972).
Meaning Insomnia (Leeds: Grosseteste, 1978).
Malo-Lactic Ferment (Lewes: Ferry Press, 1978).
Couch Grass (Bishops Stortford: Great Works, 1978)   .
Repressed Intimations (Durham: special issue of Figs No. 6, 1981).
else here : selected poems (Buckfastleigh: Etruscan Books, 1999).

Included in the anthology, *A Various Art* ed. A. Crozier & T.
Longville (Manchester: Carcanet, 1987 and London: Paladin,
1990).

'Featured poet' with 'A Lone Knower's Disavowals', in *Poetry
Quarterly Review* 20 (ed. Derrick Wolff and Tilla Brading,
Summer 2003), unpaginated and unstapled centre spread
(A3 visual poem in fifteen frames with accompanying prose
text).

ARTICLES AND CHAPTERS INCLUDE:

'Writing and Not-Writing', in *Poets on Writing: Britain 1970–1991*,
ed. Denise Riley (London: The Macmillan Press, 1991).

MICHAEL HASLAM INTERVIEWED BY ANDREW DUNCAN

The Hallowed Cloughs of Haslamabad;
Time Sprites

ALUNE
and the Idle Gardener

ALUNE,
Alune Alune
the phantom and companion of an idle gardener,
his private tune
a dream of this ghostess.

Alune, an idulum, an eidolon, the gardener
had let her grow,
soft moss over hard rock.
A She of natural Felicity. Alune.

An idle gardener spent years of afternoons
observing stones behave like garden gnomes.
The panes of green-house glass grow algal
and obscure nostalgia, cracked or absent,
fallen out. The moss root eats.
The wood frame rots. The biggin's shot.

Since she re-seeded the long grass
across the ghost-bed by herself

wilt pales the leaf. Her dying off
awakens all his idle misbelief.

She flowers, but if flowers have no ears
she may be deaf. She takes whatever
strength of wind with hardly any sound.
The perfect form whatever is
an idle gardener has found Alune.
    The hawthorn creams, the hawthorn bare
the hawthorn buds. Each year has left
      an idle gardener bereft.

Alune came under cover of the river-flanks.
Her sex alone could generate hypnotic spooks
enough from living flesh to make the wild bush blush
for crying in the field. Let us get real.

It was on Longworth Avenue, beneath a moor. Her father
snoring in the room next door. The baby put to sleep on Ruby Port.
    A lust upon the lip of an abuse. If shame
were shady, shadowed blame, then this disgust is more
your watered dust. We never sinned in language.

    Daydream heads. An idle gardener
rose blackberry from bramble bed.
    Then scratch the theme. The heart feels losses
if it bleeds.

Untended legumes droop. The nettle spreads like reverie. Alune,
    If I put by my fork and rake we might
mulct silence of its metal shine and share
a conscience, mutual reluctance, palming fingers
for a hold to hand, and watching midges do
    their dazzle muck-dance in a shaft of sun,
and after-shower air, and honour consciousness
    that puts us on the spot. The trick is here.

The more I'm reticent to fight the slugs, the less is lettuce.
    Let the creepers ply.

A mope came to an end of term, and there let fly
attacking roots with violence, attaching cries,
    I cry, I miss you like a tune Alune.
The clearing stars, the riving stops, the seasons close relapse,
    the balsam pops. And I do not.

Before sunrise, Alune, the pattering
    departure of late revellers
from off a party lawn
in leafage under early rain, midsummer day,
the first rays greening grey. You know,
I am alone. **Are you Alune?**
The ruby rubbing out occlusion,
flash on occasion,
furnishes arcaded gold.
Art thou. Are you. Touched cold.

Run through bright winter sunset too Alune
with frozen water and the sky a wine maroon.
A dusky pink, a rose of smoke about the street
at lighting-up time, afternoon,
the sun peaks orange to the pitch
    of tune set song to screech set on
the drone of power-generated electronics.

I have been active too, Alune. I have been planting tunes.
A planet blues shone through the trees. Alune
A phantom face receded to the whiteness
    of the moon on sheets. A real live face.
The attic skylight lit. Alune,
I find thy loveliness dramatic, and a song
    Alune Complete.

DUNCAN How do we get up to the point where you moved to Hebden Bridge? What was really happening in Cambridge in the late 60s? And do you have any reminiscences of Martin Thom and Ulli Freer? in fact, what was happening in Hebden Bridge?

HASLAM (*letter dated 18th February 2004*)

I agree, let's not talk about abstract principles.

There are time-spirits. Take that as literally as you like, Andrew— I am writing this reply in rhetoric, which is a resource of spirit riding syntax. Of course I don't talk like this: my auditors could not have stood, or understood, my tone. As a written statement, this is what I believe. As though on oath: I swear, if I write at all, I can't help—oh I can help—writing poetry. The placement of the self in rhetoric invites the spirit to come forth with, in my case, possibly codswallop, spawn, or possibly something salty from the far blue sea. A mental or medical condition that brings such happiness, as I'd incline to decline a cure. This is the pretentious person of myself, of which I'm proud; of his charlatanic skills.

In Cambridge in the late 60s something happened as certainly as it did in Paris, Chicago, Prague—not true; not quite so certainly— since I'm as if on oath. There was a revolution in Left mentality. An immense disaffiliation swept a generation.

The true story is made of names of people and places. I was in Paris in the summer of 1965. I liked to sit by the river, reading poetry in English or in French and idly relating to clusters of international beatniks who'd be passing through or hanging round the Rue de la Huchette. Meanwhile, in Edinburgh, as I've heard from several sources, the ecstatic Festival fringe was happening in poetry. Young enthusiasts, fresh out of school, some of whom were bound for Cambridge in the fall, discovered each other. And the star poets were not much older than the schoolboys.

Here was a nucleus for the gang I was to encounter and link up with, via Labour Club bread-and-cheese lunches. We had enough in common. Poetry. Jazz and blues, CND, etcetera. Provincial grammar-school products. Class-fashionable types, in jeans and donkey-jackets. As a gang, we went off the rails. I was the only one to take a degree. My reading had drifted far off course. I sat the finals in blithe indifference. Someone later told me, they thought I got a Third.

The earlier leavers went down to Notting Hill. When I graduated I joined them there. A slightly different cluster, but with common factors. I was maybe the only one who had let go of poetry. I was a poet. It's a vocation. You argue with it, and you lose the argument. There were poets around. Lee Harwood. Michael Horovitz. Pete Bland (one of two poets of that name, this was the 'lost' one—who knows what became of him?). In Cambridge I'd known Jeremy Prynne, John James, Andrew Crozier. But I thought I'd drifted far from them. There were poets around. There was a culture thick with poets and poetic aspirations. David Stringer. Mark Hyatt. And such. But it was following the adventures of a gang of friends, more social than literary, that led me to Foster Clough, Hebden Bridge.

Meanwhile, Pete Bland had told me to send some of my work to Peter Riley in Denmark, who might duplicate it, sending copies to the editors of various tiny magazines. This happened, and my work was picked up on by editors such as Kris Hemensley, Paul Buck—and Martin Thom. From then on, I had a new sense of an epistolary gang, which linked back with those I'd known in Cambridge not long before. I could see it as like a guild within a greater league. What the gangs had in common was perhaps a sense of practical, workable alternatives to Capitalism, shorn of revolutionary delusion. This lasted until Margaret Thatcher told us, we were all still quite deluded.

The names of two lapsed poets I might mention. Alan Green. Nick Makepeace. Alan first made the links with the Cambridge poets, and fixed up our tutorials with Mr Prynne. Alan lasted the three years but simply declined to sit the exam; and he made contact with the ex-Situationists, Chris Grey and the King Mob Echo crew. Nick led the shifts to Notting Hill, and then to Foster Clough. I didn't follow him to Wales.

There was a slightly younger cluster of Cambridge poets, a gang of Nick Totton, Ian Patterson, Peter Ackroyd. Denise Riley tells me I met her in Ed Emery's room in my college. Martin Thom, I think, was younger yet, and an in-law relation of Ian. As an editor, he liked my work. I don't know why. He had liked a book I aborted, called *Melanie, Melanie Klein*. He published *various ragged fringes*. A good person. A good writer. He lived in Halifax for some years, a decade later on. I stayed over with him in Cambridge for the Peter Riley 60th birthday celebrations.

Peter Riley. A name to conjure with. An example beyond opinion.

Ulli Freer? Ulli McCarthy, as I knew him, when he lived at Boulder Clough. He used to visit a poet called Paul Buck, who by calamitous mischance had come to live next door to me. I admired Ulli's performances. I may be wrong, but I took them as wholehearted exhibitions of incoherence. I admired the idea. For myself, I still fancied my chances with coherence. I might be wrong.

What was happening in Hebden Bridge was that there was a severe and chronic contraction in the once-substantial local textile industry, even while there were plenty of jobs in the economy elsewhere. The local workers left their rented houses to follow the jobs, leaving empty dwellings, hollow liabilities on their landlords' hands. Some local councillors were minded to knock much of the town down around their own ears; there were 'slum-clearance' grants available from central government. There were also improvement grants, for buyers and occupants. The more liberal councillors favoured making use of these. Then they offered 100% council mortgages, on houses going for a few hundred pounds— until local Local Government was abolished, 1974, and building societies relaxed their rules on back-to-backs and underdwellings.

A part-time job or the dole could buy you a house outright, within a couple of years, in my case (I had a private mortgage, 'Pay when convenient.'). Visitors would come to see me, and buy a house while they're here.

So this astonishing town and its surroundings were discovered by a mix of spiritual dreamers and refugees from the English version of '68, and blended their alternative alternatives. The magic of Marian O'Dwyer and the political legacy of Guy Debord. A City of Refuge. It was the hippy side that set the tone for a future property boom. Now, alas, we're nearly up there with Wilmslow and Prestbury. You could say we were unwitting agents of Capitalism, as we had been back in Notting Hill. In the newsagent, piles of The Guardian stack higher than piles of The Sun. The communes and most of the co-operative are gone. It's a knowable, therefore a lovable, community, locals and offcumdens. It has made sense. Maybe Thatcher was right, and there was no Alternative. We've had poets. Asa Benveniste, for example, who's now up near Merlin's mum, and saint Sylvia, in Heptonstall churchyard. February 2004. I've had two funerals this week, of friends who went back over thirty years. I was late in hearing, too, that Jeff Nuttall had died. It used to cheer me to run into his portly frame, at the bar of The Albert Hotel.

Andrew—Traversing your questions seriatim, I find I'm invited to go back again, and recover this same old ground. What could only be an ideal, of existentialist authentic living. Dada. Surrealism. Situationism. Then how I was sunstruck with a millenarian lunacy of reverence of Revolution. I stood alone in a white-painted room in London, W.11, 1969, and felt the process of my own disaffiliation from everything, including the beliefs of self and friends. I'd been distanced from poetry, as a backsliding from lived authenticity. From here on I should let poetry and its angels save me, time after time; as they had done in my adolescence, so they should again. It was a moment of full self-consciousness that would serve as oracle and guide hereafter. I had loosed a grip on radical critical analysis. I distrusted myself, I dissolved myself. I did these things lest I destroy myself. The way from here now just seemed just to be *drift*—to not resist whatever took my mental fancy. If drift were to lead me by ley-lines to flying saucers, so be it. It didn't quite do that in fact. I did a decade of sleepy drift through Celtic dreams. I'm not ashamed of that.

It was also a decade of the personal but systematic application of Freudian theory to the writing of poetry. This was a rather less intelligent mistake.

Critical analysis wanted some way back in.

The 1970s were in many ways a time of general drift. The Labour Party. Alternative Hebden Bridge. My wrong ideas about my own writing. Sexual relationships.

Indulgence in the cultivation of nascent superstitions had produced some repeatable, edible results, but had led me to the furzen borders of a paranoia—over mournful mountains with their schizoid flags. I don't do things, don't do that, quite so simply, any more now, these days, now, today. By 1979, I knew things had to change.

I left the checkpoints to decay.

I set my poetry on its current course of continual song.

I had been drifting on the time-spirit. I thought to stop the drift.

I opted out of drifting with the dreaming caravan.

I wanted a figure that would stand against time.

I remembered my own cold point of utter disaffiliation. I grew to like touching that spot. Then from 1981 I had the looking-after of my own then nine-year-old son, a benefit book, no need to sign on, and time to write a continual song.

And not to forget the desolate spot. That dot. That antidote to being overwhelmed by waves of a proclaimed love.

DUNCAN Can you tell us maybe about the scope of the Anglo-Saxon, Norse, and Celtic tripos?

HASLAM The Celtic Thing, I think, for me, sprung thus: north Wales was my parents' favoured holiday destination. I was privileged enough to spend at least six summer weeks each year at Porthdinllaen, in Llŷn, from the age of five until I left school. In the smoky 1950s, the utter beauty of the Lleyn peninsula contrasted strongly with Bolton's pollution. At the same time, I could sense the awkwardness of my situation. I hadn't the words for it. Colonialism. Nefyn was being colonised by Wilmslow. I loved Wales. I suppose I could have gone to live there, on an early hippy wave —

— an interjected note: Jack Hirschman, poet of the US, and occasionally of Hebden Bridge, was puzzled by my use of the word 'hippy'—a transitory '60s fashion, that died with the Manson murders, he'd say. The incomers to Hebden Bridge didn't call themselves hippies; the locals did. There was a phenomenon that needed a name. The locals won the name game. It survived as a descriptive term at least into the 1990s. —

I can take being a Lancashireman in Yorkshire: we can have a clean fight with different shades of wit. It's like meeting George-a-Green with staves, and knocking him off his log. As a kid, I didn't like being a colonist in Welsh beloved Wales. I'd not then go to Wales, or to Drumnadrochit in the 80s, or to West Cork today, except a visitor and tourist. I might extend my own identity some way up the Pennine chain.

DUNCAN Can you tell us about the design of *Continual Song*?

HASLAM *Continual Song* began when, after a decade, I knew I meant to carry on living at Foster Clough. Withdrawing from the Celtic illusion I looked at the Calder Valley, and what I saw were no remains of Elmet. And not so many Vikings either. Mostly Forest-Christian English. I would ground my references in the Carboniferous Pennines. I concocted eighty-odd pages of such newly-focused stuff. I had a brilliant mad idea about the number 84. That glowed with me for more than a decade. I thought the number 84 could stand against the flow of time, and be a backbone, and a hilly backdrop to my love affairs. It was like a Zodiac of my own, and quite impersonal. Did it work? Did it work though. I don't know. I return to the asymmetry of time. The Continually Sung Thing Runs From In Time From Front To Back—and I tried to lie, and persuade my readers otherwise. Like Tony Blair, I maybe didn't know I was lying. I still like many of its pages, though. And I sympathise with my vain attempt. If I ever were a Structuralist, then 84 was it. But it was an Haslamic thing, and owed nothing to developments in France.

DUNCAN The archaeologist Cyril Fox, in *The Personality of Britain*, talks about the continuity of culture in the west, as waves of innovation from mainland Europe arrive in the east, dissolve the previous culture, attenuate as they wash across the island, and simply mix with what was already there as they approach the Irish Sea. There are distinct differences between England and the cultures to the north and west. Do you think Lancashire belongs with the west, in this sense? Do you feel your poetry is continuous, as well as being continual?

HASLAM I'm familiar with Fox's notion. It's seemed plausible. I guess other scholars will have contested it. Historical conjecture is a weak ground for belief. I believe I've believed it, since 'letting drift' has led to sense of allegiance, and allegiance's attendant prejudice. There are two images I like to hold in the same frame. One is that void point of utter nothingness, a shining hollow cylinder of inwardness; and the other is an imagination of the actual Irish Sea, which fills me with an unaccountable sense of love, which, when I try to put it into words, comes out as Manchester Liverpool Dublin Belfast Glasgow. Preston Docks. That feels like home. And Hebden Bridge, a Yorkshire town, with a history in cotton. I'd like to imagine all the planet in such detail, but I've not the brain, time or experience for that. And I don't think the tragic end of the

Pennine textile industries (in Christian-Muslim discord: Oldham, Burnley, Halifax, wherever) quite matches Fox's pattern. You'd need to refocus on the layers of a carboniferous dome, the misadventures of a British Empire, the drift of capital, and the demise of a socialism that could, if not change, at least explain it. Maybe mulct it of some cash for us poor folk.

And I don't know how far Chinese cockle-pickers stain my legend.

My poetry is continuous in the sense that I continuously write it, in the hope that a continual recycling of the world may in due course discover publishable shapes: discrete shapes from continuous practice. I do this because I enjoy it, and dislike not doing it. I'm ashamed to say that, in periods of dire poverty, I've felt resentment that what I do do generates next to no cash, but my resentment is most correctly focused on the character of my genius itself.

I've had gratifying reviews, but the one that made me think was Peter Larkin who wrote 'There is no true witness or wilderness in Haslam.' I want to refute that, but my genius eyes the stares and puts its foot down like a jackdaw, and emits its jacks, and swallows the verdict whole.

And to the wilderness is only where I go.

There were moments when self-consciousness seems so complete, it's quite impersonal, and solid as the Askrigg Massif.

DUNCAN Larkin wouldn't know a wilderness from a wireless set.

What are 'offcumdens'? I know what forest churches are, we have those in the Borough of Charnwood, and they also have to do with enclosures, of the wood. But what do you mean by Forest Christians?

HASLAM Offcumdens are incomers, off-comed ones. These were rare through the long postwar textile decline, but we swamped the place in the 1970s. Many of our children today are broadly local, once again, though my own son's become a Virtual Irishman.

Cultural Speculations take brief flight each night. I know no trusted tone for prose.

'Don't start me to talking; I'll tell everything I know.' (Rice Miller)

DUNCAN I'm wondering if poets in Hebden Bridge interacted poetologi-
cally, or if it was just a benign place to be alone in. Don't you think
there are quite big similarities between *The Bloodshed, the Shaking
House* and *Continual Song*?

HASLAM *The Bloodshed, the Shaking House*, I remember, was good. I'd have
to dig that pamphlet out to check. It's in a box, since I lately had
the hippy wiring, circa 1972, renewed. Possibly the common
ground might have been some objective social time-crisis we both
had passed through. And a shared range of literary inspiration. I
can remember once, in the early days—I can't date it precisely—
Martin, Denise Riley & Child, were visitors. And we lost each other
up on Midgley Moor. And there they were, figures under the
skyline, in a moderate wind, but in the mind forever.

Constricted by bounding moorland townships, Hebden Bridge
is, or was, knowable; not big enough to sustain isolate consen-
suses; not small enough, or rich enough, to exclude variety, poeti-
cally or socially.

Forest Christians is too cryptic. I might have said Ancient
Greenwoods.

You'll have heard of Ted Hughes. He's still the local Question.
Countless times, in the pubs, I've been asked for my opinion of
him. Nowadays I say right out, he was a bloody great strong poet.
But I used to read him at arm's length, and have been known to
deny him his due, lest he influence my own developing prosodic
line. He is a true witness to what this place was still like, as late as
the time I arrived here, 1970. He took no interest in the change
that overtook his homeland thereafter. I imagine him hugging the
grime of the hopeless past of it, close to the heart in his coat, even
against the fresher winds over Dartmoor.

I was reading the same books as he, over a decade later. Classical
Anthropology (in my case, by drift, on no set course). And seeking
some authentic and original, primordial, poetico-religious rite.
The Wake of Frazer. Jane Harrison's Kouros. Eliade's Shaman. But
by my time, that whole edifice was crumbling, pretty much the
way the cord and moleskin mills were. Hughes had had, like me, a
weakness for contemporary intellectual fashion, until he got
depassed. Sexy were Pagans, Vikings, Celtic Saints and Jungian soul
Journeys. He painted these figures of meaning into his bony verbal
landscapes. It's become almost the official tourist information:

here were Celts and then came Vikings. What I believe I've seen are the forest margins of long Anglo-Saxon Christian religion and administration; less violence, an equal poverty, but largely peace.

One writer I read saw late Anglo-Saxon administration as a blooming great chrysanthemum decayed. I thought I saw the browning petals curl. Bare Erringden of course became a Norman chase. The Greenwoods, Redmans, Sutcliffes, these had been offcumdens once, from god knows what neighbouring kingdoms once, but these were of the ancient greenwoods, forest Christians for the nonce, for they had been inside a church, if but the once. This might be sentimental nonsense.

DUNCAN Can you talk about the cynghanedd thing.

HASLAM The cynghanedd thing is an outcome of evolving lines by natural selection. I cross my writing out, and try again, a me and a thee, the imagined interlocutor, my genius, as ready as a dog to play. The spinner and the cutter of the cloth. The line should harmonise a chord of three moods of errancy and judgement, and survive. Our dialogue is largely forest comedy. My genius fancies itself a Dawkinsian Meme, having a pool of woodland nymphs to please. I tell it to cut that out, but it charms me with its rhymes and jokes and doublings of sense. If it charms me, it may just charm another reader too, and I could take the credit. (Supernaturals don't need the money.) It's like a spirit of poetic image, and it often leads me back into the Classics.

Another poetic scientist who comes out with comparable results is R. F. Langley, with his *Jack*. He's so economical in fact, I envy him for that. No way so awesome as Hughes's *Crow*, my it can look like a discomfited rook.

DUNCAN Can you tell us more about your study of Celtic cultures, and also about the ley lines line of country? is this sense of drift related to the notion of ley lines as part of a whole web of forces unconsciously guiding activity, a Neoplatonist order beyond, or perhaps beneath, the personality and the will? How close is this 'subjectless action' to what you describe as your Structuralism?

HASLAM I went on a good number of walks and excursions with ley-line or earth-mystery folk. I always preferred squiggles to straights, but they could countenance that. I published a couple of scraps about spirit with them. The last involvement I had with them, they were looking for the Significance of Beauty.

Unconscious webs of force. I do not know. I cannot say. You tell me.

I think I said *If* I ever were a Structuralist. That *if* might be a locked gate. In a sense most modern thought, since Marx, Freud, Frazer, Darwin, and the like, has been Structuralist. I never cared for what got built on Saussurian linguistics. I've had young folk inform me definitively, that there's no thought without language. If that were true, I am exposed as an obscure, unsuccessful charlatan, or a fool of the delusion of translation into language, from beyond.

DUNCAN Christopher Gray (not Grey) was co-author of a 1967 pamphlet (credited to 'The English section of the Situationist International') which says 'Most of the crap passed off as culture today is no more than dismembered fragments . . . of the débris left by the collapse of every world culture. This rubbish can be marketed simply as historico-aesthetic bric-à-brac, or alternatively, various past styles and attitudes can be amalgamated, updated and plastered indiscriminately over an increasingly wide range of products as haphazard and auto-destructive fashions.' It sounds like the hippies' *détournement* of derelict properties in post-industrial Hebden Bridge.

HASLAM King Mob/ Angry Brigade. Don't make me go back down that pit. It has collapsed. Oh, OK. King Mob did not turn into, but was overtaken by A.B., which proceeded to smash, causing a bloody great spiritual pile-up. I didn't know what was going on, but there was cowardice in my choice of ignorance.

Educated youth inhabits academic years. There were ex-situationist elders. I literally sat at the feet of Messrs Gray, Clark, and Nicholson-Smith. I was told I should live on my wits, which hinted perhaps at a career in petty fraud. Could I have done that, I should not be who I am.

King Mob was an ungated thing. There were some creative types who hung out with Chris Gray, dreaming up amusing political wheezes, like opening, de-railing private London squares in fancy dress, and insisting on wearing costume in the dock. To break the law, and openly mock. Play-space for kids was a popular issue.

The angry lot were mostly my juniors by a year. I expect they thought we were frivolous reformists. Initially various, a hard extreme consensus formed. They would be serious, and do something really real. They blew us up more effectively than they did with any Biba shop.

In fact, I'd already been saved for Poetry, and my association with the angry circles had to do with a plot to use an offset litho to publish a book of softheaded love poetry, written in the innocence of summer '67. I'd been regathering my poetic past. In this period I moved to Foster Clough, where I meant to keep an open house, a safe place of escape from the paranoid terrors of London political life. I knew something disquieting was going on, and felt the clash of conflicting allegiance. I sat tight while the crisis passed, thinking moorlands, sex and romance.

I like the Chris Gray quote, its tone of high scorn. I can't breathe in the single tone of scorn. I can't believe in it. It's not enough. I wanted polytones, but, given which, I could no longer maintain the position of extremist. A touch of scorn, though, was a good inoculation against rising plagues of guff. I chose, not Grosvenor Avenue, but Foster Clough. That was an easy choice. I preferred variety to a tightening mental consensus in aversion to the known world.

We can't, I thought, fight the spectacle by spectacular means. We could live without. One black-and-white television set served six cottages, and could be dusted off each week for Monty Python. We lost track of popular music. It took a rising generation of toddlers to begin to change this way of seeing things.

DUNCAN The ley line thing is a wished recapture of the Neolithic, the Celtic thing is somehow a recapture of the Iron Age. Both are 'collapsed . . . cultures'. Updating them involved an idealisation of myth, the deep past, and the village community. What I'm wondering about is a milieu where libertarian Left, neo-authoritarian Left, Counter Culture, New Age stargazers, are all in the same pub. I wasn't in that pub.

HASLAM A life outside the spectacular media consensus may also drift free of the scientific one. I was shocked when a friend declared himself a hollow-earther; I could eat geology myself. Other flocks went bleating off after various Hindu gurus. Poets could only follow hollow-earthers in their dreams; some of them had eschewed the traditional ambition of Fame.

The years we're speaking of were LSD years. I took a tab three times between 68 and 71. In Notting Hill I laughed for three hours, and then wandered off to find a typewriter. From Grosvenor Avenue (the place was awash with the stuff) I went via Speaker's Corner, thence to find refuge with my old college rival and chum, Peter Fuller. From Foster Clough, I looked at the valley and thought, This Will Do, then set about fire, food, and blankets for visiting friends who were rolling naked on the wet October moor. That was enough. A dangerous drug. There were friends I watched programme themselves mad. It lent a certain coloured loopiness, to taint the atmosphere of everyone who was taking the adventure.

How come we're still stuck in say 1965–75, or, more focally, 68–71? I've shrugged off all my writing from that time, and all I retain of the self I've been is just the talisman of Fool. I've dropped any brief I may have held in the defence of me whom I was then; I only hold some continuities of poetic image. Answer: yes, those times were crucial. Half-a-dozen times the strange angel of poetry arrived to effect salvation. Poetry is happen the only world religion to grant full grounds to scepticism, while proclaiming experience. I have a soft spot for the hypnotism of the cross, as what bare body and soul can bear, and like the gests of family ghosts in found or lost redemption, the memory consults the guilt of folly as an oracle, in order that some self may shine, a sinner saved by slight grace.

DUNCAN How do we get from Situationism to drop-out communities in Calderdale? what is the link between this collectivist ideal and the individualism of *Continual Song*?

HASLAM The collective/individualist split didn't seem to apply up here. The terrace of Foster Clough was open to all visitors, but was basically a common sense building co-operative, financing a string of house-renovations by pooling improvement grants. There was a kind of vague collective, like, 'Freaks', but membership was merely checked by intuition. Eventually a local tone, of the whole place, would re-impose itself, and re-assume us, changed. After a decade I realised I was still in The United Kingdom.

DUNCAN 'mournful mountains with their schizoid flags'. Help! what does this mean?

HASLAM It's a fault. The electronics in my brain have flipped forward by twenty years, and it's during the first (John Major) IRA ceasefire, and I'm travelling by bus between Dundalk and Newry on my way to visit my son Merlin, and his girlfriend Fiona, in Belfast. The army checkpoint. There are no other signs to say where, exactly, the border runs. Somewhere, on the UK side, there's a hilltop village, off the road, decorated with the Republic's tricolours.

At the republican caff at the top of the Falls Road, in West Belfast, I'm asking a Sinn Feiner if it's the prospect of European Unification that has changed things and made a ceasefire possible. He firmly confirms that idea. I'm happy with the fashionable neo-liberal idea of fuzzy boundaries and multiple identities. Writing the way I do, I could hardly deny it. But it's a fault. I blipped from how things drifted in the '70s, to how things had changed by the '90s. Merlin married Fiona Ryan of Cork. They are modern Dubliners now. Fiona and her friends tend to regard the Celtic Dream thing as so much baloney (which my dictionary says is not Irish, but Italian sausage). They're critical of the old deValerian vision. I like the size of the modern Irish republic, with or without fairies, smoky bars, or folkloric illusion. For a kind of atheist, I'm an instinctive Protestant, and it's odd to catch the strains of my visceral thinking. I'm still wishing for the world's divisions to come together in the fifth act of a Shakespearian tragicomedy.

Meanwhile way out west, I call where she lives Upper Leesdale, the Gaeltacht Muscrai of the County Cork, inhabiting a poor English colony, lives my old lover Chris (who drove the van in ragged fringes days), growing vegetables, a fine session fiddler who went out there from Lancashire, via Hebden Bridge, and who still has Celtic Dreams. I wouldn't want to lose touch.

But schizoid flags another slice
or sleight of brain. That village
in gorsed mountains, Mourne in Down, split
into visionary pleasures of a present heaven:

I hold an outpost, as I have the use of a garden delph, and it's here in summer that I like to take my pen to write. I have an hosepipe trained from the syke of the clough into the quarry, to soak a cluster of yellow iris flags.

Then schizoid flags another split as iris flags or sandstone slabs. And iris eyes and rainbow fracture, shower-spectral, smiling at a flight of stone steps.

Bibliography

The Fair Set on the Green (Bishop's Stortford: Great Works Press, 1975).
Various Ragged Fringes (Oxford: Turpin, 1975).
Son Son of Mother (Cambridge: Lobby Press, 1978).
Continual Song (Hebden Bridge, Open Township, 1986).
Aleethia (Hebden Bridge, Open Township, 1990).
Four Poems (Cambridge: Equipage, 1993);
     A Whole Bauble (Manchester: Carcanet, 1995).
The Music Laid her Songs in Language (Todmorden: Arc Publications, 2001).
A Sinner Saved by Grace (Arc Publications, 2005).

ALEXANDER HUTCHISON INTERVIEWED BY ANDREW DUNCAN

Melodic Cells

An Ounce of Wit
to a Pound of Clergy

Let's begin our panegyric: weft of wool
and warp of cotton. Tow a drogue at your stern
so you won't broach to. Abandon your tails
and cheek pouches. For loft, for distance
put the baffy back in your bag.

~

Who wants this mush of meat and fat: poets
of the pemmican (dried and pounded) school —
with bugger the berry to give it some taste?

Where it's grind me to powders, and cankering
creeds—with never a blink of primrose banks
never a hint of beech woods building.

~

Strip off your rags and bend the bow.
Get your ordinance *full and flowing.*

~

And scrape me rather some pepperpots of potency:
the grains of Paradise, the cubeb, the chili
the cayenne of Guinea, the pods of Sichuan.

≈

Put worms to work, and moles to mark them.

≈

I'd have us smile like a parcel of seraphs.
Not lolloping loose; not dying duckies.

≈

Ladies in sable, come up, come in —
take the weight off your feet, take ease
of all your rasping parts.

≈

Warty newts and fire-bellied toads
continue your aquatic and sociable ways.
Natterjacks of heathland and dunes (your loud
rolling call like a ratchet). Corncrake
of bogland and grasses; fugitive, invisible.

≈

Aspect of all aslip and aslither: things
that tremble, things athwart. Come gastropods
come snails and limpets—sallow, blanch
and black-avisèd.

≈

Things that scuttle, that squeal, or puff
themselves up, or launch themselves through
the air at intruders.

≈

Take root all sprouts of pseudoplatanus.
Protophytes and protomorphs, let's get a move on.
With hooks and burrs and green helicopters.

≈

Set with ardour bright and clear
beams, jambs, lintel and moulding:
an architrave of red-hot promise.

≈

Eager and apt we bristle, we burgeon.
The hand of the glazier puts putty to the frame.
The pastry-cook pounds out his faintest concoction.

≈

Knit up the bones of computation.

Let like kiss like.
Let bright affinity walk
in anklets of amber, in fillets
of silver.

≈

Not ten go, but twenty posts out of your way.

≈

Cool and open and tempting the vista.
The spiral of the condor vast and leisurely.
The bat at noon (anomalous) in twittering loops.

∾

Let all things fused
transparent, opaque
enjoy diversity.

Snaps and scraps of quick allurement.

∾

Stone-crop in succulent rosettes
of yellow-pink and crimson-green.

∾

Penetration of the optic:
when all the down-draft of wintry webs
is wafted away.

∾

O, the women in dove-grey
swimming suits!

the roundel windows
admitting the light of day.

∾

(This poem was first published in *Stand* magazine.)

DUNCAN The obvious thing to focus on first is the meeting point
between rhythm and phrasing—can you talk about your way of
thinking on this? And as to style, is the runic serpent band on the

cover of *Deep-Tap Tree* a reference to the laconic quality of Norse poetry—or to west Norse elements in Scottish speech?

HUTCHISON What would I say about rhythm and phrasing? I'll go along with Bunting's insistence that emotion is aroused by the *sound* of words—though not when he adds 'and next to nothing to do with their meaning'. At an extreme he would claim poets were only good for arranging syllables—and occasionally I'll endorse that too. Certainly if you are tone-deaf or cloth-eared in any context you might as well pack it in.

The memorial rune as an emblem on the cover and inside *Deep-Tap Tree* did point to the Norse material as a base for several poems there, including start and close. It also is a sign of interlaced decoration or embellishment—which I can talk about later. It was commissioned by a Viking in memory of his mother—there are two serpents, one large, one small, entwined—and if I remember right he was an admiral for one of the emperors of Byzantium.

In terms of language, the cryptic, reductive, ironical character of the saga-speech and related dialects was around very early I suppose—a typical winter's evening exchange of pleasantries in my home-town of Buckie, with the boys taikin up or doon the brae, could easily go: 'Fit like, man?'—pronounced *min*. And the response: 'Aye, it's a caal hoor o a nicht'.

So laconicism *was* a native element of style. And if that's the case you have to be sharp to come back, alert to shifts in tone and emphasis. It was a while, though, before I actually read the saga material and the *Hávamál*, for instance, from which the 'Death of Odinn' and its epigraph quite obviously derive.

At the same time, in another aspect of the Scottish, northern European tradition there are the extravagant and scabrous exercises you can find in Dunbar, or in Urquhart of Cromarty's versions of Rabelais: flytings where everything is piled on for outrageous wounding effect. I've been pulled into that also, early and late—from 'Mr Scales Walks His Dog' to 'Unfinished Business'. (Though Scales' dog has Christopher Smart's cat Jeoffrey as a kissing cousin.)

DUNCAN What sort of approach do you take to pieces like those?

HUTCHISON *Sauve qui peut.* Just set the margins wide to lay it on thick and heavy.

Drawing up catalogues is diverting and pleasurable, but you still have to keep a proper tension, and at least an elemental blocked-out design. Mr Pound, talking about the link between emotion and poetry, said there was an 'absolute rhythm' which corresponded precisely to the emotion or shade of emotion to be expressed, that this was 'interpretative' and so in the end ought to be your own, 'uncounterfeiting, uncounterfeitable'. You need to vary the textures of language; and there's no reason to suppose that even when a thing rolls on at length and apparently at random it can't be built up from a pattern of melodic cells or intricate effects. Part of the astonishment in the Tara brooch is the recognition that what you have is worked within as well as without. You can aim for that in lyrics; you can get it in longer or larger forms too.

DUNCAN What about sources? Any contemporaries or near contemporaries that you looked out for in terms of a road to take?

HUTCHISON When people start queuing up in the High Street it's tempting to head for the closes and back wynds. You can sometimes predict who you'll bump into; less easy to figure just where you'll come out.

Basil Bunting, W.S. Graham and David Jones were the older poets who drew me in different ways—though they all had depth, humour and resourcefulness. It was a pleasure to me the other day to find that Bunting had a strong regard for David Jones. And it was unexpected: I hadn't heard him mention Jones in conversation, and I didn't remember any particular reference in the printed sources.

All three seemed to have known straitened circumstances, sometimes for very long spells. I'm not recommending that, of course, but it must have contributed in each case to the texture and resilience of their work, and to their character. None of them congenial to certain strands of critical opinion; but all central to me, and in their work real gifts and power.

Behind those three you don't have to go too far for links to Eliot: who was publisher to both Jones and Graham, and acted as a referee for Bunting on at least one famous occasion when Basil applied for a grant and was able to put down Yeats, Pound, Eliot and Ford Madox Ford, I think, but didn't get past the first hurdle because the fellowship people thought he must be taking the piss.

I ended up doing a dissertation on Roethke, and Theodore— loopy, ecstatic, despairing, competitive (he could bust tennis balls by *stamping* on them, and used to cross himself before important points just to rattle opponents who knew he wasn't Catholic)— never made it into Eliot's circle. A particularly *American* barricade was set up for him I suspect. However, the stories I like about Eliot also have a surreal edge. Like when he was desperately unwell, and used to add a bit of green to his complexion to make himself look *iller* (though this deceived none of his friends). Or the time his old college pal Conrad Aitken visited London, and both took on so much alcohol at lunch that when Eliot was ferried back to Faber and Faber by taxi they discovered for some reason he couldn't uncross his legs—and had to be lifted bodily out, over the pavement and up the back stairs to regain his seat in the office.

DUNCAN You went to Canada in the sixties, and lived in Chicago for a while between 1968 and 1970?

HUTCHISON That's right, and went back for a bit later. It seemed we were right in the thick of things early on: the Democratic convention riots and trial; Judge Ostler and Mayor Daley; The Fred Hampton shootings. Plus the Art Institute, Sölti conducting Mahler; Janice Joplin in a concert wailing out between prolonged biffs from a bottle of Southern Comfort.

DUNCAN What about the poetry?

HUTCHISON I fed for a long time on American verse of the middle 20th century. As I say, I wrote a thesis on Roethke, looking at what I called a 'context of illumination' in his poems, though I didn't reach a strong, governing idea until about two-thirds of the way through writing it. Which was that his work could be seen to spring from two sources or tendencies. The *immanental*: in the greenhouses, visions of childhood, the affirmation of earth and all its particulars, with links to a long Romantic line of celebrants— Whitman, Wordsworth, Emerson, Blake (and Palmer, I nearly said— though Samuel Palmer would fit, along with Traherne) plus Hopkins in 'morning's minion' or 'long live the weeds' mode; and the *transcendental*—where he went darker, and numinous in a different way with the Metaphysicals, Dickinson, Yeats, Hopkins of the 'terrible' sonnets, and on via Evelyn Underhill to the mystics and the archetypes of the *via negativa*, where ultimately the images are wordless—or you have 'a darker dark behind the sun' and things like that—not always great territory for poets.

DUNCAN Where do you think that duality came from?

HUTCHISON It wasn't just manic depression—or maybe it was—but the first vein was richer in some ways for him, though he wrote fine love poems and elegies in both. Still, his impulses emotive and spiritual appealed to me, with openings like: 'I knew a woman lovely in her bones'. Or in an earlier genre:

>   Bees and lilies there were
> Bees and lilies there were
>   Either to other
>   Which would you rather
> Bees and lilies were there?

And his long-lined discovery pieces. Whitman you could obviously say was better at it, with those astonishing juxtapositions:

> Sure as the most certain sure, plumb in the uprights, well
>   entretied, braced in the beams,
> Stout as a horse, affectionate, haughty, electrical,
> I and this mystery, here we stand.

But Roethke had me thirled or hooked on the same wavelength, and was nearer geographically, as it happened, in the Pacific Northwest—though I never met him, and hadn't even heard of him until I got to Canada in 1966, three years after he had died.

DUNCAN He had worked in Seattle, at the University of Washington— and that was right across Puget Sound from you.

HUTCHISON For a period in the 1970s and 80s I lived up near Oyster River, and Black Creek and Miracle Beach on Vancouver Island where he had holidayed and fished, and where he based at least one of the beautiful meditations from *The Far Field*. Roethke said he wanted a 'language ... complicated yet passionate, full of auditory shocks and shifts'—and I would still opt for that too.

DUNCAN Anyone else you would mention?

HUTCHISON Robinson Jeffers, John Crowe Ransom, Williams, Berryman, Wallace Stevens and Marianne Moore were the poets I taught by choice round about then. A fairly mixed bag. Poems like 'Boats in a Fog,' 'Bells for John Whiteside's Daughter,' 'Mr Bones' Diversions', and 'The Idea of Order at Key West'—which is very moving as well as being a liturgical baroque *tour-de-force*.

Marianne Moore is probably the one I go back to most frequently. I mean, I turn a notebook page and find 'Armor's Undermining Modesty', 'Propriety' and 'Voracities and Verities: Sometimes Are Interacting' in fair copy and wonder how many on the block at the moment can string that kind of stuff together. And I remember the last poem has a reference—gratifying in a peculiar way—to Colonel Jim Corbett's *Man-Eaters of Kumaon*—one of the very few books I had read with close attention in my early teenage years.

Although I say these things, the question of influence in particular is very hard to assess, except here and there—like the short-lined skinny arrangements in some poems, which I probably derived from Creeley's *For Love*. I recall sending a copy of a four poem pamphlet *Link-light* to David Jones in 1974, not long before he died, which was a clear acknowledgement.

DUNCAN What sort of things were you hoping would rub off from some of the poets you have listed?

HUTCHISON Rigour and dexterity, elegance of expression and neatly turned syntax—a combination of these things has always been attractive. Coming back to one of your first points, though I can ramble and be exorbitant, for me: 'compression is the first grace of style'. I liked Violette Leduc's line about wanting 'to achieve the brevity of a fowl pecking at a single grain of corn'. And sticking to the birds, here's Bunting on vultures, for instance—almost a haiku in the middle of 'The Spoils':

Lean watches, then debauch:
after long alert, stupidity;
waking, soar.

Keep it *too* spare and you might be drawn into over-refinement, so
what you produce is cryptic or costive. And I would repeat there's
nothing against letting out the slack from time to time. But I'm
still inclined to slim it down and go with Stevens (the former Vice
President of Hartford Accident and Indemnity, after all) who
would have us invest in 'ghostlier demarcations, keener sounds'.

DUNCAN Say a bit more about structure and putting things together.

HUTCHISON In the early days I didn't know a lot of the time what I was
up to: just feeling my way into things, and relying on sound—
whether the piece made a whole sound in my head—to determine
some kind of integrity. Now I'm more practiced (even if you're lazy
like me, you can fall into it) I miss that kind of foraging, though I
hope I'm still capable of it. It's probably what I was getting at when
I praised Edwin Morgan a little while ago for operating *much of the
time in an area of fertile uncertainty, where 'the unknown is best' (as a
stimulus to invention), and where the elements of song are somehow there
in welcome support.*

As to 'the reason-for-being of a poem in its shape,' and what
determines the tone, or a sequence of variation in tone, or 'a grad-
uated kinship of moods' in Hardy's phrase, you have to find the
language and you have to find the form. Where you pick that up is
anybody's guess—but the provision of 'luminous detail' is some-
where in there too. If that sounds haphazard, well, that's a word
worth reckoning: as part of an event, an action, a fate, a thing
occurring joined with chance and risk, and random in connection.
The art isn't random; but the subject matter may well be. Unless
you want to insist on it; and then you can insist too far or too long.

If the concept of fate looks out of place or out of order I still
don't know a better word unless it's providence for what befalls
you when you strike a line or phrase or mood and the poem
emerges. As I said before, sound for me works all the way through—
with sense and nonsense, plain or fancy, free or fixed, many-
centred or interwoven.

DUNCAN Any literary laws to lay down?

HUTCHISON I've never been one for manifestoes, or general theorising. In fact when I was a literary academic I shut out a lot of developing theory quite deliberately—sidestepping hermeneutics and most of those French-based contrivances. I didn't want it cluttering up my responses to poetry, and I don't feel I missed all that much. Whatever has shaped the words has been personal and not schematic. Though I'm not against criticism *per se*—especially when it happens to be true, or makes you smile.

DUNCAN Can you nonetheless be drawn into some theorising about what contributes to the effects of poetry?

HUTCHISON At the level of language, the energy of poetry—its emotional and intellectual energy—springs from a mix of the demotic and the hieratic: joining up or breaking away. If one gains ascendancy, or settles in, the other will soon enough appear as a corrective. MacDiarmid and Joyce both worked to extremes of each, that's part of what makes them pre-eminent—the range and subtlety. But if you don't look out, or have no wish to stop, you can end up talking to yourself.

DUNCAN Maybe we can go back a bit to look at the region where you were born and brought up. Do you think there is a northeast tradition, and where would you place yourself in respect to that?

HUTCHISON What do I make of the poets of the area around where I was born? Especially those writing in the Scots language: in some cases almost sharing the idiolect I grew up with. *Ten Poets of the Northeast* was in my hand for the first time just a couple of weeks ago, after the question was raised. Plenty names I knew, but whose work I didn't know except in small selections, anthologised elsewhere. Charles Murray was in my childhood, and relished by local concert parties and so on, but I'm slightly abashed to say the poems by other names—Flora Garry, Violet Jacob, Hunter Diack and others— well known enough, I didn't really know.

    The Scots is familiar and personal to me in many ways; the subject matter too, though my upbringing wasn't linked closely to farms or agriculture. John Morrison Caie caught me by surprise with a poem beginning with the name of a farm township: Nether Dallachy. It turns out he lived about 4 miles from where I was born; his father was a minister in the parish of Enzie (pronounced Ing-ee). When I was a boy I had howked and picked potatoes on a neighbouring farm during the school Tattie Holidays, and remember the tractor's jolting approach and the forks of the digger curving through the dreels to churn out our work. We filled buckets, the buckets filled sacks or harn bags, and the harn bags filled the horse-drawn bogie.

The school represented in *Ten Poets of the Northeast* is decent, artful, humane and humorous, with an interest in folk and how they live and work and interact. The level of art for me is mostly equivalent to genre painting: so that without being deficient in motive or perception or power to entertain it nevertheless misses something absolute about it—something deeper or darker, more lyrical, and beyond the edge of practice here.

The thing is: I have written poems in the Buchan dialect all through my own poetic practice—and probably have used it best in translating others. One of the first things I did when I came back to Scotland in 1984 was translate a handful of Catullus's *carmina*, followed by versions of four sonnets by Ronsard. The Catullus pieces—foul and fragrant, and directly in the speech of the 'weel-kent sites', drew a positive response from a variety of people. The Ronsard versions (which after the first came out about one every twenty minutes) could fit right in to *Ten Poets of the Northeast*. On the other hand, 'Catmaw' and 'Hyne Awa: Nae Howtowdie', printed together with those translations in *The Moon Calf*, are in what you might call a modernist goliardic vein—caustic, up to mischief—which has irritated some reviewers: principally those with no native spoken Scots, nor any notion of what has changed in the face of the world. I would say I'm a better craftsman than a critic; though I have cause to know my own verse and all its limitations pretty well.

DUNCAN The north-east is a 'thick' area for folklore, unlike most parts of the British Isles, and more like Scandinavia. I'm not wholly convinced of the joys of this; I wish Hamish Henderson had written more books of poems and done less collecting of folklore. I'm worried about the conservatism of folk-based forms. There does seem to be a problem with poets who want to abolish poetry, and withdraw inside the conventions of song. What are your thoughts on that?

HUTCHISON The folk revival took off in the late fifties and early sixties—though, as you say, the northeast of Scotland is a 'thick' area for folk tradition. I heard Jeannie Robertson sing live only once—but her rendering of the first line (and most of the rest) of 'The Four Maries' had the hair up at the back of my neck—and I said at the time quite honestly that the experience was like falling into a great pit, there was such an overwhelming sense of unbroken tradition, and vocal flourishes (her extension of the word 'hairrit' for heart) that came from such a long way back.

She was a great spirit on the folk scene, and her importance to Hamish Henderson and what he wanted to show forth was unparalleled. MacDiarmid made a mistake about the folk tradition—he claimed at one late point that 'no European artist of any significance owed anything to it'. Henderson said to me (and plenty others) he couldn't understand this—why MacDiarmid 'wanted to kick that ladder away'. He described a conversation in the Café Royal in Edinburgh when he had indicated some of the ordinary punters in the bar and said 'You see those boogers over there—they don't know about you or about Jeannie Robertson—but they *will* care, *because* of Jeannie Robertson'. MacDiarmid didn't like that, and came back dismissively—'Scotch dismissive' Henderson described it—'I don't care about them'. 'What *do* you care about then, Chris?' said Hamish, and got the measured response: 'I care about carrying my own thing through to the end'.

So clearly, if I use the terms I brought in earlier, he was booting out the demotic, and nailing up hieratic colours—disparaging his early sources of inspiration for what he saw as some higher purpose. Henderson had every admiration for MacDiarmid, thought him a great poet beyond question, but had to fight him on this because of the risk to what he wanted to save. He thought that interest in the folk tradition was at some level an interest in *poetry*—and that any attempt to bury that tradition would diminish the arts in general.

DUNCAN What did you think of this?

HUTCHISON I'm on Hamish's side on that one. As I've indicated earlier, as far as the demotic and hieratic dimensions go you don't want to dump either one. Henderson wasn't seeking to 'abolish poetry and withdraw inside the conventions of song' as you put it—he wanted both to flourish—and I don't think he would agree with you for one minute about the balance of his own activities. The poems he *could* make, I suggest, he *did* make. The things he re-discovered, collected or puffed back into flame were a central activity not a sacrifice of his own talent.

DUNCAN Okay—I wouldn't argue about that—but I still wish he had written a second great book of poetry.

HUTCHISON Of course, I wouldn't wish to talk you out of your regrets on that. But he took on MacDiarmid because he had to—and after a while he relished it. In their public flytings it was ding and dong: and, as Hamish was fond of quoting, in these terms 'great blows are delights to the mind'—and he would give an exuberant brief throaty cackle to underline that.

DUNCAN Maybe we can change tack again. Who would you say you are writing for?

HUTCHISON Who do we want for an audience? 'Proper places and noble souls'—that was what the Irish vagrants Clement and Dungal replied to Charlemagne when he asked the price of wisdom. Well: attentive, willing to be carried along, but not palmed off with pap or sophistry or special pleading. What I want on the one side is plenitude and universality, and on the other it needs to be particular and near (and said or read so you remember it). Marianne Moore put a key dilemma neatly when she said: 'I think the most difficult thing . . . is to be satisfactorily lucid, yet have enough implication in it to suit myself.'

DUNCAN And what about performance, readings, getting the work across?

HUTCHISON I would say most poets don't read their work very well, even when it's well written. There's too much modish display, or straightforward ineptitude. Sorley McLean had a true bardic presence, with a few unconscious eccentricities, and MacCaig made a virtue of relaxed self-deprecation, and deliberately didn't make things *difficult* for the audience—though a touch of the crocodile was never very far away. But too many contemporaries convey no presence at all: nothing is heightened; there's neither growl nor benison. They rarely give the sense of being moved themselves by what they write or have to say, so the most they can hope for is polite acquiescence.

As an aside I'd say actors over-egg it. Not all of them—but most of them do.

DUNCAN What about University—we mentioned Chicago when you were attending Northwestern—but you were an undergraduate at Aberdeen?

HUTCHISON I wasn't a sophisticated reader of poetry at all as an undergraduate—and certainly not in the first two years. Patricia Thomson was my tutor in Advanced Special English, and I wince to remember at an early tutorial wading in with both feet to rubbish Dunbar's '*Done is a battel on the dragon blak*', before she gently put me to rights. I suppose I improved. In my final year I wrote essays on Marlowe and Johnson (with Voltaire) and gave Dunbar his due as well. The year before I had been fired up by Blake: *The Marriage of Heaven and Hell* was the first piece I consciously took as a model. But it wasn't until I was transported to North America and started teaching undergraduates myself that I came at all to grips with contemporary verse and fiction.

DUNCAN And then how did the writing go when you got there?

HUTCHISON *Deep-Tap Tree* was written through the seventies while I was living and working on Vancouver Island. 'Mr. Scales Walks His Dog' was written when I came back to the coast after the two years in Chicago—sometime in the winter of 1970 or early spring the following year. In the summer of 1977 Will Carter of the Rampant Lions Press in Cambridge had printed *Four Poems In Broadside*, and Courtland Benson made up folders with a beautiful selection of papers and beeswax finish. Those poems made up the final section of *Deep-Tap Tree*, which came out in 1978.

DUNCAN How does *Deep-Tap Tree* appear to you now?

HUTCHISON Looking at the book now it seems to me northern, Scottish and metaphysical.

DUNCAN How do you mean metaphysical?

HUTCHISON How does anyone mean metaphysical? More than the rustle of leaves in a bag. Not information only, however elegantly sliced. Exorbitant; singular.

DUNCAN Okay, okay, hold on—anything else?

HUTCHISON Of the book? Satirical, romantic, unfashionable. I can see various things in the background a bit more clearly now. Have already mentioned David Jones—not just the poems of course, but *Epoch and Artist* and the preface to *The Anathemata*—and either he or my friend Patrick Grant pointed me on to people like Jacques Maritain, whose Mellon Lectures on *Creative Intuition in Art and Poetry*, for instance were a model of clarity and practical wisdom, without ever jabbing with insistence under your nose. Patrick certainly put me on to Michael Polanyi's astonishing essay *Personal Knowledge*, which is the longest and most emphatic periodic structure I have read, and which I am still unpacking. So I wasn't stuck for precepts and models of complex intellection. But who's to know what predominates, or when something important—or unimportant at the time—goes in, and just how it comes out?

Round about the time I was reading Jones and so on I also loved poems by Robinson Jeffers: his *austerity*; for instance; and there is something irrefutable and flinty in what he has to say at times. His mother was Scottish, and probably mineral too. He has an extraordinary poem about Iona and the early burials there, which the professional Scotophiles will not relish, when he refers to 'jellies of arrogance and terror' to conjure the monstrous presence of the kings long gone.

DUNCAN Do you see anything that provides links to themes, or pins to structure in what you were writing?

HUTCHISON Venery is a thread through *Deep-Tap Tree*. The myth of Actaeon has always been a clue for me—though it doesn't figure directly in the book. It did in the nasty wee pastiche *Mr Scales at the Auction*, where the central figure is brought to a similar sticky end. I took a look at Ted Hughes' versions of the *Metamorphoses* when the book came out, to compare it with Rolfe Humphries' translation and other people's. Went straight to the dogs (as you do)—the list of hounds lined up to sink their teeth in—and was straightaway disappointed.

DUNCAN A bit bland?

HUTCHISON Well, a missed opportunity. Sometimes I feel my personality is still basically rooted in the Medieval or just later. Plenty evidence of that in *Deep-Tap Tree*. Maritain I remember was a good source for quotes and stories too—like the one where Michaelangelo gives advice to his pupil Marco da Siena that he should always make his figures *pyramidal, serpentlike and multiplied by two or three*—and of course you don't have to trip too far to turn that kind of stuff into poetry. I liked the high-mindedness of those Catholic poets and commentators—and I liked their spirit too, if I can get away with saying that.

Here is Maritain in a pure, clear, antiquated style talking about the *unprecedented* nature of the thing made—or on *poesis* in the wider sense: '*The great witness of it remains Cézanne. More to be sure than Manet or any other, he has been the liberating figure in contemporary art: precisely because he was so totally, he seemed so obdurately and desperately intent upon that bound, buried significance of Visible Things, which he felt perpetually escaping him in proportion as he took hold of it.*' That word bound is the key link to religion in Maritain's sense—*religio* means a binding—and around material like that I warmed to the idea of art as a connatural habit of self and spirit.

DUNCAN But you don't haul that baggage around with you all the time do you?

HUTCHISON Hardly—there's plenty else going on right up to Leadbelly, loblolly, Cullen skink and dirty dancing.

DUNCAN Sounds a bit like a line from 'Unfinished Business'

HUTCHISON I guess that's part of the point. I thought in that piece
maybe I could make a final reckoning in that satiric vein, mopping
up some choice bits, but there's always more turning up and stink-
ing out a corner—determined to have a good time!

On the one hand you can't get much more hieratic than
Maritain's descriptions of prudence, say, as '*the straight intellectual
determination of something to be done*', or poetry as '*a mineral purity*'
(shades of Jeffers again). But there are divinations of various kinds,
under different auspices, some of them raucous, some of them
psychotropic (I have this by report) and, as far as the dedication to
that poem goes, I could even suggest that Paracelsus was at the
head of the queue along with *CMG*, as well as several others. There
is always a potent, disreputable or anarchic side that's liable to
stick—'like a burr, sir,' says Lucio in *Measure for Measure*.

In all this, though, I would still agree it is '*by love and not by
obscure collusion*' as Maritain maintains that we find ourselves in
what we make or do. In fact, I put that thought into a small poem
in memory of George Mackay Brown—who of course is right in
line with Jones or Hopkins and that particular dimension. In a
quite different but explicit way it's also in a poem for Norman
MacCaig, 'Didn't Do', which gets off to a fairly indecorous start.

DUNCAN And can be read as a corrective against the standard kind of
mush for tribute, I assume.

HUTCHISON I would say so.

DUNCAN Anything you would add?

HUTCHISON I wanted to say something more about interlacing. I'm not
sure if it is a sustained device or not—it certainly was meant to be
in 'Helix'—which never really looked as good on the page as it did
in my head or in the air. I tried twirling the lines round a central
axis—but the software wasn't there then. I remember setting it all
out on the floor of a cedar-built house about half a mile along the
beach from the mouth of the Oyster River. Late seventies; early
eighties. It was a long zigzag trail of paper. I didn't think anyone

else would take to it. 'An Ounce of Wit to a Pound of Clergy' came out of that spell too, though it was a long time before it found its way round. Gael Turnbull liked it, and made a pamphlet, 'Carbuncle's Culinary', out of it in 1992.

So what's interlaced there? In terms of personalities, there's Roethke—with Oyster River. Then W.S. Graham, whose poems were coming out in the *Malahat Review* in Victoria, published from the university where I worked—'Johann Joachim Quantz's First Lesson', maybe pieces from *Malcolm Mooney's Land*, *Implements in their Places*. Robin Skelton as editor was taking these pretty well as they were produced—at least that was the impression I got. Also I met Basil Bunting when he came as a visiting writer to Victoria in 1971. August Kleinzahler, Brent Mackay and Terry Humby would give me news of what went on in Bunting's classes, since they were students of mine too for a spell.

DUNCAN So you were teaching there at the same time?

HUTCHISON I was teaching there *exactly* at the same time—that's why I couldn't sit in on his classes! Anyway I was lucky to meet him, and liked him a lot, then and later. By contrast, I pretty well dodged Sydney Graham when he came to read and stay for a short while in Victoria. I was working up-Island then and didn't drive down. His own accounts of the trip will tell you how that was probably a good thing. Out of nerves or drink or something Graham behaved badly and felt worse. My pal Lawrence Russell fell foul of him at the reading and still won't hear a good word. The university library at Victoria has quite a collection of his stuff, and later I discovered his compensating virtues. His poem to Robin's children is ominous and touching. He put most of his best impulses into his poems—and his letters as well. People are jumping on the band-wagon at the moment, and that's okay: but it's been a long haul for proper recognition to come round at all, especially in Scotland.

DUNCAN And interlacing in the poems themselves?

HUTCHISON Well, I touched on 'Helix'—but there's a different kind of construction in 'Lyke-wake' which is much earlier, and combines images from the landscape of my childhood with various other deposits—some early historical, some almost mythological. At one point the poem carried a dedication to my father and grandfather, and my maternal grandfather figures in the opening, overlooking the town and harbour from the Hill of Maud, with a view to the west of Buckie and across the Moray Firth. This 'real' landscape is picked up again in the final section before a ceremonial close.

In the middle sections among imagined medieval settings, there are interwoven glimpses of a triptych of the 'Annunciation' by the Master of Flémalle, which hangs in The Cloisters in New York. When I went to see the piece I found it in a room where it was the only art work hanging on the wall, but there was an oak hexagonal table—I think it's hexagonal—like the one in the painting, and on it an Italian faience vase with Easter lilies—again just as in the work—so the fragrance in the room was the same as in the painting. The only other people there apart from me were a large, black, uniformed security guard, and a kid from Harlem doing a high school assignment.

What's implicit is always hard to sort out—but of course there was the impact too of all the people and places I knew during that period—though they don't make explicit appearances. It doesn't matter for the poem's sake in 'Undertow', for example, that the two feathers first circled the river pool in a civic park in Nanaimo. Or that copies of 'Construct by Simple Succession' had been pinned up in all six elevators in the Hyatt Regency in Vancouver during a conference on alternative lifestyles (which had Sufi dancing, Chief Rolling Thunder, Ina May Gaskin and Spiritual Midwifery; even buzzards and bald eagles circling overhead). And that as I went up and down with my sheaf of poems I never went in to a lift but I had to post another one up.

Coming back to decoration and stylistic devices, if you jump forward a little there are signs in poems like 'Incantation', or 'Mao and the Death of Birds' of an unembellished style: even though one piece totally dispenses with irony, and the other leans on it rhetorically at key points before an unmistakably straightforward conclusion. I would just say again you need both options, and I'm happy to vary the textures as I also said before. Melismatic or unadorned: that's another important spectrum to reckon with.

Select Bibliography

Mr Scales at the Auction (Victoria: Soft Press, 1972).

Link-Light (Victoria: Morriss Publishing, 1974).

Four Poems in Broadside (Cambridge: Rampant Lions Press, 1977).

Deep-Tap Tree (Amherst: University of Massachusetts Press, 1978).

Flyting (Mission: Barbarian Press, 1982).

Inchcolm (with 5 etchings by Alfons Bytautas) (Edinburgh: Bonfire Editions, 1988).

The Moon Calf (Edinburgh: Galliard, 1990).

Surprise, Surprise (Edinburgh: Galliard, 1991).

An Ounce of Wit to a Pound of Clergy (Edinburgh: Minimal Missive Maximum Missile Publications, 1991).

Epitaph for a Butcher (Kirkcaldy: Akros Publications, 1997).

Sparks in the Dark (Kirkcaldy: Akros Publications, 2002).

NICHOLAS JOHNSON INTERVIEWED BY TIM ALLEN

Falls from the ceiling: intact and impetuous

from PELT

on dead lime
of farmed fields we kids
scrap and build

in tall corn
we hide and yellow lines
go cross
our faces

we get shoved out for trampling crops,
learn always go round
field edge   come back
then jump over
river where a collie decomposes
in a sack   in the woods
pikies live
in the caravan
there
we play with them lots

on dead lime
of razed fields we lads
scrap and build

ALLEN Nick, I would like to start this interview near the end, so to speak, with a question arising from your penultimate collection, *Cleave*. What is its purpose? Now I know that is a most irritating question for any poet to attempt to answer, but I ask it because of the direct and rather intense link between the poems and the foot-and-mouth disaster.

JOHNSON *Cleave* is not a collection; of discrete pieces linked or unlinked, but the [failed] attempt at an assemblage. The material did not suggest a long poem, which in the case of *Haul Song* (1989–93, rev./expanded 97), and *Show* (94–01) does entail a laborious process of keeping material in the head, writing aimed at what I presume the 'long poem' to require; work that changes its nature, and then has to be pitched against the rest of the book.

There was not the time for this in *Cleave*, because on the one hand it was an Arts Council commission; so there was a time-constraint, and second, the materiality of the subject could date. As it happened, its publication coincided with Love, Labour & Loss an Autumn 2002 exhibition (Cumbria / Devon) to restore confidence in farming purportedly, and an exhibition concerning the culling on one farm; both at Exeter—so, the book had already taken on a retrospective nature.

Cleave ultimately is a botched, journalistic attempt to write something a potentially wider readership could understand, and runs contrary to the way I think and naturally work. The notion of prose breaking up the work was a good idea, and of having pieces that were abstract enough to contrast the Foot and Mouth material was fine in principle, and a sturdy enough template for a necessary revision of the book, but its purpose does not result in something which is able to take the reader very far.

Its purpose was to document what I saw, heard and experienced. But what I didn't see, hear and participate in was carnage— and would to me relate to 'ghosts of lyric' rather than anything overt. Since *Cleave* came out in Autumn 2002 I've been freed to approach Foot and Mouth in my own temporality—and language. J.H Prynne's *Acrylic Tips* is a real poem on Foot and Mouth.

ALLEN With regard to *Haul Song* and *Show*, why did their material suggest the long poem and how difficult were they to write, for example what was the personal cost of writing them? And were you pleased with the final results?

JOHNSON To answer that, you need to know what *Haul Song*;—written first, is pitched against. The early poems, written between 1982–1990 are either stanzaic; setting out what needs to be said in 4 to 5 verses, or blocks of usually uninterrupted verse which run for between 20 to 100 lines.

I very much wanted 'The Telling of the Drowning', initially written in 1983, to be as long as Eliot's *The Waste Land*, to which it's indebted, and due to the variety of its material and its cadences, constitutes a long poem. But it took 15 years to resolve a version, 'contained' in *Land*, like, 'Vortex of the Nightingale' and 'Hienghene'.

Restoring long poems for *Land*, was only possible, because I'd learnt how to handle longer material, such as *Haul Song*, *Show* and *The Lard Book*, in the intervening years. Once I'd written the group of poems *Listening to the Stones*, and was still young in practice, in 1989, I was simply writing lyrics again, in 3 to 4 verses. They had a start and a finish, and seemed similar in tone to each other. I approved of their unity, but where could I take them except round in a circle? Perhaps I'd cottoned onto the idea of a circular, long poem. The following year I wrote, in one take, something that by its opening lines suggested terrain of a journey,

Guitar string follow
stars on the lake,
the clover road . . .
I'm weak as a shoe lace,
falling to sleep
beneath lovely stars
full of white cockerels

and had no End. I left it, and these pegs, the lyrics—similar as anchors until something else positive (as poetry) occurred.

In Easter 1991, like the next visitation from the same ghost, the next 'section' appeared, again the equivalent of six sides of foolscap. I wrote this at the poet Seán Rafferty's desk. He kindly sat in the kitchen with my family and his lodger while I did so. In retrospect, they were the only two sustained sections I had, and would constitute the fifth and sixth sections of the six-sectioned book. The rest of *Haul Song* was composed of scenes, partial or

complete; that often petered out, handwritten then put away—
permitting myself to forget where they were going. I kept up this
process for a couple of years, interspersing these stanzaic 'pegs'
with more sculptural blocks of text.

Haul Song was published in 1994. Three years later, the edition
out of print, I looked at all the pieces I chose to leave out, and the
poems I wrote concurrent with *Haul Song* that I had not
published, because they seemed lodged into the hip of *Haul Song*,
and fused them all in, to get the version I wanted. Once the first
version of *Haul Song* was published (in October 94) I wanted to
write another one. As a parent, you can accept being interrupted
in a long poem by a child. A third child was imminent. I wanted
to write another long poem. If *Haul Song* encapsulated personal
biography and topography, plus stories of several friends, it soon
appeared that I'd no real narrative for *Show*. I'd used up my 'story'
in *Haul Song*.

If I planned outright for long poems I'd be disappointed in
myself, but should I keep fragmentary ideas in my head, eventu-
ally something falls from the ceiling: intact and impetuous. Odd.
So you're curious to go on. There are many false starts, and dull
parts married to what's gone before. But once I'd written 'Silver
Hounds', after nearly two years of scratching like a rat in a tunnel
I knew I'd got something. It's to do (again) with address.

 Clouds silver hounds pursue
haring to the Goddess' tits
quick and tumultuous

Gets silent
beneath stars
        when ploy s over

 Aeons anticipated.

A very winter.

And so return.

It was a 3 & a 1/2 year process then, of trying to build up on that; a
variety of 'lyrics' which I didn't use intact. But the bulk of its

published form was written in the last six months I worked on it. I accepted that incidents would occur and form poem sections. *Show* took seven years to write, copy out, re-write, assemble, re-assemble, delete, what I eventually published as a 'work in progress.' By that phrase I felt able to let it go, if I showed I was humble in being tentative. What got left out, to be resolved later, either as a lost section or freestanding piece, but precious to me; is entitled 'S.W.'. I don't know if it would join the poem it was once in an earlier (or another) form expelled from.

All this illustrates difficulty, from a flathearted feel of the potential for wasting my and everybody's time, and adapting interruption into the process of writing—which is nothing to do with the privileged artifice of textual interruption referred to in other questions.

Then you read a poem of seven lines or 19 words by the Toms Pickard or Leonard, or Gael Turnbull, and you wonder how you got into such water. But bits chip off as short pieces in their own right, like 'on dead lime / of farmed fields / we kids scrap and build', which closes my fifth long poem, *Pelt*, as a simple, final breath to a complicated work with many long lines, to bring it all back home. Rein. Rein.

I like *Haul Song* the most of my books, because it's my story. My roots. *Show* may be more sophisticated and subtle: it possesses humour and wordplay, has sharper contours yet it still contains other people's stories, however private, which don't lose their resonance with time. But *Haul Song* is more popular. At readings, with its audience. It still sells. People say it's a young person's book. I'm glad I did one of those. I didn't realise till I finished my degree at Dartington, aged 34, that the visual work I did there with completely different methods, strategies, tactility, materiality, was *The Lard Book*. I've performed this a lot. Sarah Simblett and Brian Catling made a film of *The Lard Book*, in 2002. But it was also a 'long poem'. These long poems can be performed in 25–35 minutes. Shorter than Ben Hur.

Tho' what can you do with 96 sides of A1 tissue paper, handwritten, with colour, drawings; bits of material stuck onto its sides?

Since the tumult behind *Cleave* subsided, in 2002, I've been free to root about again, more guardedly and been enabled by doing a

MA in Creative Writing to write a new, two-sided long poem, which deals with material I thought I'd already filleted: childhood. If you put all that together, that's five books, 15 years. Publish that as one book, it's a similar length to Alain Fournier's 3 part novel, *Le Grand Meaulnes*, a neoligistic punk version of Fournier, an assemblage of the lost domain.

ALLEN Do you see yourself as a modern rural poet? Do you see yourself as a modernist? In connection with that would you agree that there is a tension in your work between an essentially rooted subject, change and loss in Britain's countryside communities, and the expansive poetics you appear to be heir to?

JOHNSON I do not think I'm very modern. I enjoy myself too much. It's probably easier to chuck in mist, hedges and rowans in a poem, than whatever constitute the furnishings of a city. Roy Fisher in CITY fuses both, & he is exceptionally a Romantic poet. Perhaps I'd term myself that way too.

There are various poems, where the speed and pace of the language indicate something that feels faster than the 'slow burn of time' traditionally associated with the rural. The Margarete Sulamith Cycles of Anselm Kiefer, Loup, Gillows Mohr, Slide Show & Abduction come to mind. I don't think I can be seen as a modernist rural poet because the private interests that go into the work definitely ain't rural when they're in the imagination. Tension, yes, between an 'essentially rooted subject' but the expansive poetics I'm heir to? I'm not sure what expansive poetics are. And why they're plural. There's playfulness as well as a paying respect, or just filching, in taking other writer's lines. As in *The Waste Land* they got to serve a purpose.

ALLEN I suppose the poetics are expansive simply because you are giving yourself space in which to imagine, speak and discover, in contrast to a poetry which forms itself around an aesthetic of pre-determined limits on formal and mental activity.

JOHNSON In hand-copying the poems over and over again, I can bring in asides and discoveries. I'm happy at certain junctures to interrupt my poetry, sometimes this is playful. Or artful.

ALLEN And 'plural' because an expansive approach is going to give rise to quite divergent practises.

JOHNSON It's about getting the surface to gleam or be muddy, but the poetry has to have a surface. I admire poets who work in diverse mediums, either because they are film makers and visual artists; or because they have ancillary activities to being poets, they keep a pack of hounds they run a builders merchants they are a tailor or they coach tacklers at football. But the reader shouldn't know this. I used to do collage and voicings of other poets—because there were writers I wanted to inform myself, and thereby the reader-hearer in. Now I've run out of comment on other poetics in my work. My own poetic is diverse enough.

ALLEN I take your point about, 'the private interests' not being rural because they are in the imagination, so could you expand (ha) on this? What do you mean by private?

JOHNSON Once you've absorbed the snapshot (1840s term) your eye has taken, this goes into the imagination and therefore becomes private. Nearly all my work is private. The rare occurrences of public-spirited work, such as CLEAVE, only require me afterwards to rewrite it later, to introduce my own bill of privacy, flanking a subject sideways on rather than headways.

ALLEN You do expect your reader to work fairly hard don't you?

JOHNSON No reader works as hard as the writer. What the reader does is private, and it's up to them. The imagination is, at the end of the day, what's held to account. That has its own conscience. I don't follow the reader like Malry's ghost, telling them Rethink, Rethink.

ALLEN Sound is very important in your work, and performance of it brings that home, but you have been criticised in places for letting the aural qualities take over on occasion, and praised for it of course. What is your view of this? Do you see sound—I like that, 'do you see sound'—as an enhancing vehicle for what you want to say or do you see it as something of value in itself?

JOHNSON 'The melody! The rest is accessory' Zukofsky

ALLEN OK, perhaps, but when you perform your work there is a very
definite coming together of strands such as timing, pace, pause,
pitch, emphasis etc. How much are those things written into the
work on the page? Does it behave like a musical score, intended to
guide the 'silent reading in the head' of your reader, or is it more
concerned, on the page, with the page, with the visual?

JOHNSON There is a lot written into the work, which I see when reading
it aloud, and yes I think it would be a musical scoring that's always
needed which is physical, and of my seeing my body of work as a
body, just that, a block of sound which is aural and oral—but I'm
not responsible for approximating the visual element of the page.
That's up to the reader. I'm performing it and taking it somewhere—
and keeping the relatively small body of short poems alive, as well
as the (excerpts) from the long poems, interpreting them accord-
ing to the nature of the evening, the acoustic, the audience and
the location.

ALLEN I'm not sure if you've answered my question Nick—live perform-
ance gives a listener an extra dimension to ride through, ride on,
but is that what it really is, a vehicle, a tool, something to connect
listener/reader to meaning, or is it of value in and of itself?

JOHNSON There's not much point dragging yourself out for an evening,
to hear poets who read like horses with a feed bag. You can
perform anything, so long as you perform it well, Caroline Bergavll
told me that as my tutor, when I was trying to ascertain how to
pull off a mooted performance in a launderette. I can't recall if I
called it a Laundarama, or a Washathon, but I encouraged the
audience to bring 20ps to get the driers going. All poetry derives
from song—it's a base art, it's a base emotion. Sound, be it
Shwitters or Messian, blocks out information. Plus the heavy rota-
tion of a fast-spin. So if you accentuate your accent in a live read-
ing, and use your ear to report how you found things sounded and
your pen-brain to show the reader-hearer other ways of sounding,
then that's what you do. Therefore it connects the listener/reader
to meaning, and I place value on it. But I refer you back to:

i] the matter of asides and discoveries

ii] The melody! The rest is accessory. Zukofsky

ALLEN As well as being a poet you are a very energetic publisher and champion of others' poetry. Could you tell me something about the relationship between the development of your own writing and your parallel activities as publisher and promoter?

JOHNSON Initially—in 1992 with the first of the Six Towns Poetry Festivals—it represented a setting up of a personal university, and there existed an older, senior generation to work with. Twelve years on Dorn, MacLean, Coffey, Weiner, Gascoyne, Oliver, Rakosi, Cobbing, Barry MacSweeney, Tom Scott, Hamish Henderson, Turnbull, Rafferty—someone starting where I left off, would find other poets—but I was extremely lucky in the way things fell. And the way things fell came out of a lot of luck, tact, listening and hard slog—and it was Romantic, to use that term again, to build that companionable environment. There were many instances of kindness and humour with poets. Editing of FOIL was the antithesis of that; but I'm glad I tasted both. Obviously there are some wonderful presences and voices left, but quite a few who embraced the radical shift which began in the early 50s, or represented a prewar optimism in humankind are no longer about. So. That, plus the enjoyable 3 years studying performance writing and visual performance at Dartington, taught me a lot—and offered its own companionable milieu.

The autumn tours and festivals always, when the dust had settled, engendered a new poem, one a year, 'The Heron', 'Accidental Sightings', 'For The Locker', 'The Steerer' and 'The Stars Have Broken In Pieces'. I wanted to learn, in the same way that Tom Pickard did when he set up The Morden Tower with Connie. I still want to learn, but I've served my apprenticeship. I enjoy the travelling, seeing the world from Skip's (etruscan typesetter/ roadie) trusty white car.

I have learned most from hearing all these people read, and how they related to an audience; and because I need to watch performances. I like the sound of the human voice. Pyle, the auctioneer.

My only fear—with the editing chiefly, was to leave myself enough space, or, get the balance right, between reading too much contemporary work in the way that it is a very close reading, in terms of design, layout, typo spotting; and make sure that I kept on with all the antidotes to that, which sometimes the poets you're editing provide, from what they teach you and send you too. May that balance continue. I've also learned, and it was a hard lesson, that you can only get so far with a dream; a dream is difficult to distribute in the terms I'd like to.

ALLEN Why was editing *Foil* the antithesis of 'that companionable environment'?

JOHNSON The companionable environment of a poetry festival, stands as a celebration of the hard labour of the poet—and it is something people enter into, and leave, in the evening. They take the sound, the feet, of the poem, the presence of the writer; crucially the sound of the voice. They belong to that reader for the duration of their reading-life.

The responsibility of the festival curator is to be unobtrusive, link the writers together craftily; know where the fire exits are, and pay the bills. The anthologist is also a curator—but might end up being more obtrusive. I might be good at gathering work, at designing a book—but I might be more sensitive to designing an original single-author volume. To work with 33 writers simultaneously is quite a task. *FOIL* was necessary, and I took it seriously, but it is also tongue in cheek in places the thesis boys might not look.

To have an array of presences entering the loft where the book was edited, and to have a generous response to the endeavour, by the poets, was emboldening. The writers were juxtaposed to make sparks fly.

ALLEN To finish Nick, tell me something about your latest, *Pelt,* which I heard you read in its entirety in the middle of Dartmoor.

JOHNSON It's a book of two opposites. The first 'book' is a poem of accumulation, written as clearly as possible (see author's poem) and takes the protagonist up to pre-libido. The second 'book', 'Sure Body' will return the story back to the coast where the first page began and therefore, to an extent, the book is circular. This second 'book' leads you from 13–19 in age and remembers a school friend, hanged in a children's home. However, this second 'book' doesn't hope to make things simple for the reader. I wrote it for myself and myself alone. Overall *Pelt* honours my first family, my upbringing, location, loves and peers.

ALLEN I take it as 'pelt' meaning skin, a rendering.

JOHNSON Pelting of rain and hail. 'Pelt' in order to escape and in being pelted in the stocks.

Pelt explores the notion of a good child, and what kind of person emerges from a doubting of trust, a feral and unruly childhood; and notes the acts of cruelty within the milieu of the farms we worked on. So, as I pointed out earlier, it's a kind of neologist, punk *Le Grand Meaulnes*.

Bibliography

The Telling of the Drowning (London, 1987).
Listening to the Stones (London: Many Press, 1991).
Eel Earth (London: Writers Forum, 1993).
Loup (London: Writers Forum, 1994).
Haul Song (Bath: Mammon Press 1994, revised edition 1997).
H (London: Writers Forum, 1996).
Etruscan Reader I: Helen Macdonald, Gael Turnbull, Nicholas Johnson
        (Buckfastleigh: Etruscan Books, 1997).
Hassel (London: Writers Forum, 1998).
Land: Selected Poems 1983–1998 (Bath: Mammon Press, 1999).
Show (Buckfastleigh: Etruscan Books, 2001).
Cleave (Buckfastleigh: Etruscan Books, 2002).
Pelt (The Two Brothers, Shore Body) (Buckfastleigh: Etruscan Books
        2005).

Folds Pack Away

Depending on the Weather

The hurry to bite that runs over the spare
text, with his head high, with his bulging eyes. He
swerves with the weave, expecting his next success.
Premise:—the beetle believes that he knows what
the wasp is thinking. The beetle believes he
knows what the wasp is thinking of him, the green
beetle, what she sees he might mean, his needles
winking and the wicked cut of his jaws. The
beetle believes he knows what the wasp thinks the
beetle is thinking. About them both. All their
embroidery. His nip. His stitch. The set of
grapples in his grin. The rich twist of his you.
His green me. Two to embrace. Then the toils we
intended to trace. The last clasp. About how
clever to run though what needs must be done, to
be stitched up as them, as the beetle and wasp,
woven deep in and ready to work. But what,
we remember, both, as anyone should, is
this shock of this buzz of these silvery wings.

The classic malevolence of the evil
fairy, or your own ill-treatment of the poor.
She passed by the door, speaking nothing. Then she

instantly returned with a like look, and in
the same silence departed. The new wheat-cake
I was chewing fell from my mouth. Myself in
a trembling. Myself off my stool, sewed in a
stocking. Stuck in my fit. I believe the old
widow knew well enough what went right to my
heart. What I ought with my cake. For the sake of
a silent rebuke. My neighbour, the witch, who
is after my cookies. Eye on me, as if
she were Atropos. Green as a beetle that
studies to bite through these golden curls. The twirls
of a wasp round a hot pocket of sand, as
if it were checking its property, combing
out honey. The kingdom of spin and snip. A
bobbing goblin. The hank and the quill of our
hungry fate. Escape that. We both think we will.

Imagine the beetle imagining the
wasp imagining what would be involved in
keeping a diary. I should have risked more. Done
nothing. Taken half, maybe. Never the whole
bake. But, it's a fact, no peas would then grow in
the field. They were unable to make butter,
or cheese. And that was it. A fly—always the
same fly? In summer weather it would shuttle
through the glints and darkness looming in her room.
Far too familiar, they said. Doubtless a
part of her repertoire. Some point of view, some
plenitude and cogency. Really? Nonplussed
on the glass, it knocks against the white outside.
It taps. His angry finger nail. Tap, tap. Some
privy agony? Eleven women, all
acquitted, and, it seemed to me, believing
nothing of the witchery! He sat up straight
as if the sky were resting on his head. The
wasp reads on. The beetle rips up what is read.

The beetle believes that you are watching it.
It lifts its chin, looks at you, and gets ready
to unsheathe its wings. The fascination of
a magician is ever by the eye and
to the heart. Mine aches. Dread hunts my ground as a
tiger beetle, reeves my quiet as a wasp.
I learn their manners and disguise myself as
them. But their movements figure out themselves. They
never choke on cake. It's a mistake to wish
that they could speak. They pass on this and that. Most
of this kind do take to the air at once, not
saying a word. And he cheerfully greeted
the more sensational testimony, with
the remark that he knew of no law against
flying. Staggered, they went out into the day.
Blind. Reeling with freedom. Who cares what they thought
that they thought that they thought? All such repertoires
are put to bed. The blanket design was an
old one, easy to pick out, worn to a thread.

WALKER There's a lot of 'tackle and trim' in this poetry—phonetically, in the technical agility, the rhythmic care, and the range of vocabulary: is Hopkins a conscious influence? Would you like to comment on influence in general?

LANGLEY Well, yes, Hopkins is, yes. Because by the time I left school and went to University I think Hopkins was my favourite poet. Partly because he took the outside world and got it into the poem in such a bright and immediate way. I was just impressed by that whole imitative affair. But then, I didn't, in my early poems, that got published ... they were not particularly Hopkinsian at all!—I thought of him as part of my academic life rather than part of my writing life.

I didn't start writing until I found out about American poetry. There was Donald Davie at Cambridge who talked about Pound. But Davie never talked about Olson. It was really Olson who convinced me that I might write something myself.

So that something like 'Matthew Glover' is a fairly naive attempt to do a minuscule Olson in an English setting. I'm not sure that I even thought that as I did it, but it so obviously is now: with willow warblers instead of kingfishers and an open verse system, a field verse system, moving in open paragraphs. Not much Hopkinsian tackle in that, is there, so far as I can remember? I used to respect so much that Olson remark about 'the dance of little syllables' and I used to think at that point that the Hopkins was rather heavy compared with that. So I was trying to watch little syllables that weren't particularly onomatopoeic or imitative in any particular way at all back at that stage, and think primarily about 'areal subject matter' as Dorn would say. I pretty soon ran out of that line of business, but that's really what got me off the ground.

So Hopkins, yes, to start with, and then a lot of Wordsworth I used to like enormously and then Shakespeare all the time. That sounds fairly ludicrous, but I suppose if there's a single person that's influenced me steadily all the way through, fed me, as it were, day by day, it's Shakespeare. Because I have to teach him every year again and again, the same plays, or the same small number of plays, and they get richer and richer in the whole way they . . . that's influenced me more than anything else, I would think: pure Shakespeare: quoting from him, and image themes and basic ideas, yes, he cuts through and underlies the whole lot. But when you've said that, that's the major range, I would think. And it did start with Hopkins, yes.

WALKER Pound, generations ago now, spoke of the need to 'break the iambic pentameter'. You seem to have mended it.

LANGLEY I've slumped back into it, that's what I've done. I'm absolutely conscious of that. As I've gone on and allowed more rhyme into the poetry again, and become more concerned with the structure of it, the body of it, I've been unable to use anything but the iambic pentameter. I've pushed it around and split the lines differently, but I feel rather an amateur actually at the whole business of the formal structure of the poem still. And the iambic pentameter is so insistent that I have just used that in the last four or five poems particularly, shoved around a bit, counterpointed with line endings, not corresponding to them, but I've allowed it to happen and actually felt quite uncomfortable when it hasn't happened. And I've constantly thought I ought to be breaking this and doing something more adventurous with it, but feeling that I wasn't ready to get out of it again yet. And that I rather desperately need it just at this moment, to give me an interwoven system.

I don't think I actually had it early on, did I? Right back at the beginning of things I wasn't particularly thinking of any sort of rhythmic . . . I mean it was so much . . . I used to have in my mind in those days those ideas about composing by the . . . like Campion, you know, and Creeley, that you compose . . . that's Pound as well isn't it? 'Not by the metronome but by the musical phrase.' So I wasn't feeling rhythm as an iambic anything in those days, but lately I have, I have.

I've got the feeling that I'm losing Modernism bit by bit where I shouldn't be. And falling back into more traditional modes. And I think the iambic pentameter has got to be the thing I fall back into at the moment.

I have been influenced in that by quite tangential things. I don't know whether to launch into that or not. But one of the things I've been thinking about over the last couple of years is an essay by Wollheim on art history, nothing to do with poetry at all. Because, you know, since the very beginning when I used to be interested in Pound, the days when I first got interested in Pound through Donald Davie when he came to give a talk to the Jesus College Literary Society, steadily, I got more interested in Adrian Stokes than in Pound. When I went round Italy I was looking at the things Adrian Stokes admired most, and he seemed to offer the first coherent aesthetic that I'd ever met. So I've been looking at him [Wollheim] and at Melanie Klein as well, and Bion. There've always been a string of people that I've found interesting since Adrian Stokes who have been, you might say, preoccupied with object-relations.

Anyway, there's the last chapter in his [Wollheim's] book *Painting as Art* where he talks about how a painting can become a body. He invents the word 'metaphorize', the painting metaphorizes a body, you see, and he says things like the skin of the paint becomes the skin of a body and what's inside the frame becomes a metaphor for the body. He admits that he's not prepared to explain why it should particularly, and that a lot of people won't go along with this, but he hopes they'll go along with him as far as they can, which is the sort of remark I rather like. And then he talks about how painting becomes a body. And it turns out not to be one coherent way in which it could, with one line of process in it, but lots of little ways in which it can become a body. Lots of the things that Stokes used to notice about [Agostino di] Duccio's carving, perspective distortions and flattenings out as well as the way in pictures you handle the colours and the paint in general: they all add up to the fact that the painting becomes a body. And the paintings he thinks do become a body are superb ones like Bellinis and De Koonings, pictures that I've always liked anyway. So it rings true. And it just occurred to me that—this is getting round to a simple point in a rather complicated way—that the poem might become much more of a body too. And that my poems weren't very body-like. And I might find . . . the things that would make the poem body would obviously be the small formal elements, wouldn't they? It's easy to talk about sound effects in terms of imitation and so on, but there are millions and millions of assonances and consonances and rhymes that have got nothing to do with imitation at all. They're not open to the subject matter in that sort of a way. And what they're doing, I suppose, some of them, is something like those little things that Wollheim talks about that make a picture into a body and pull it together as a structure and give it a head and a tail and make it exist.

You see what I mean? So I thought I would start paying a lot more attention to those in their own right and play around formally to get a unit like that, something that exists within the frame of the poem in a body-like fashion. Does that make any sort of sense at all?

WALKER What contemporary poets do you read and admire?

LANGLEY I read them with trepidation because I feel so out on a limb, rather than in the midst of them. But ah well, I admire Peter Riley often, for instance. And Douglas Oliver as well. And I've always admired Prynne, most particularly. Michael Haslam. I've liked W.S. Graham. He came along as a sort of post-Hopkinsian influence. Frank O'Hara, Spicer, Barbara Guest, some Dorn, some Creeley. There are a few people who amaze you and make you want to do things. Douglas Oliver, for example, when he was doing *The Diagram Poems* and he gave that little talk, called The Three Lilies, that was a moment when I felt there was someone who was personally engaged in the sort of way that was exciting. Yes. Really, I suppose, I'd go back to the Objectivists, Oppen in particular, and to Carlos Williams and to people like that again and again. And Tom Clark [Thomas A. Clark]. Yes, I must say I like his readings especially. I would like to find a way to talk about the density and difficulty of these poems.

WALKER Could I ask a series of questions with this in mind? The first about reference.

LANGLEY I rather hope that the reader could miss almost everything and still get something out of it. That's what I was aiming at, certainly. So that if you didn't know that the Mildenhall Dish had Hercules in the middle of it, simply the references to it in the poem would carry enough, to carry some sort of meaning along with them. 'Saxon Landings' is a particularly vulnerable example there. I think that is a pretty specific set of references. The general references in my poems tend to be towards autobiographical things, don't they? Places, and things that have happened to me. And they're quite often subsumed entirely into structures and themes. And that does make it slightly impossible for me to imagine how other people might be reading my poems. I'm never quite certain about that. If ever I get into explaining, I sense there's discomfiture around because I do this. So I think well, you know, this poem must've done something before I did all that explaining, and now I've either spoilt it or made it better. But I don't like to give away too much. I don't like to surrender. But on the other hand I've never managed to go as far as, say Prynne goes when he is down 'the mallet path'. I've always thought that was pretty terrific: to have a 'mallet path', but I've never managed to get on one, a path where there isn't, I mean, you know the word 'mallet' there just hasn't got an immediately referential thing at all. I find that magnificent, justifiable and powerful, but I've never managed to go off down that path myself. It's always stayed tied to Mildenhall Dishes, where I could actually say what I was looking at and why I'd said that and it would be fairly simply referential, if you wanted it to be, if the threads were in your hands . . . [comment on low redundancy of poetry].

WALKER Is this particularly true of post-modernist poetry? Is there a danger that there is so much collocational oddity that the text becomes willfully meaningless?

LANGLEY I think by the time you'd read four of my poems you'd be able to fill in the holes in the fifth almost. And I'd say that that's probably one of my major weaknesses: that I keep reworking the same territory and finding the same contexts and the same words even, the same vocabulary quite distinctively coming round again and again. But I'm not sorry about that at all, because I think it's a strength too. So while I rather wish I was more unreadable—I mean I spend my time wishing I was more unreadable in precisely the sense that you're talking about, I'm also glad I'm not.

My poems are led by things extrinsic to the poem, I take it, though they are interested in not being so led. I mean I like them to be transparent and get the outside world in: first of all from the stuff that goes into journals, the actual experiences that I've had. And if I haven't got one of those in the poem I feel that the poem runs the risk of being slack in some way. I feel that it ought to contact some sort of a reality in a simple Wordsworthian sort of a way. So that there's some feed-in coming from that. And I'm quite conscious of the fact that the poems where I don't do that are nothing like as good. Because they can't, to that extent, surprise me. There's got to be something to push against, something that gives you something more than you knew you were going to get, or can theorise that you could get, and biography is one of those areas: 'To break the loneliness of thinking'.

And the other way which is more germane to what you're talking about now is etymology, isn't it? because I never write a poem without having etymological dictionaries around and—I don't necessarily look up every word—but wherever I find myself at a point where I feel something else is there or I must expand in some way, etymology is one of the major places to look. Ever since I read Hopkins and ever since Skeat's etymological dictionary first came into my hands, I've found etymology important. And let it lead me. That in a way is a sort of answer to what you're saying, isn't it? Because the words I use are etymologically relevant. Always. So I don't take risks beyond the etymology. The etymology sometimes takes you a hell of a long way, into mournivals and gleeks, I mean into fairly obscure areas, but not actually untraceable areas. That's what I don't dare do somehow. I stick within those parameters. Because, I don't know, I don't want it to feel any more subjective than that. In addition to the virtue of direct experience, I want to feel, to some extent, authorized by etymology.

WALKER These poems are for the most part a very long way from
     accounts of daily experience ... Even where there is direct speech
     it is rarely clear who this is coming from. Where is the writer in all
     this?

LANGLEY Although it may mean that some readers are disorientated,
     there are objections to positing the self as the primary organising
     feature of the writing. And I am necessarily aware of and impli-
     cated in this debate. The poems are not straight memories. There
     is a lot in them of 'sounding language from the inside'. Only the
     kind of resonance I'm after is quite often just an old fashioned
     matter of what you might call punning. 'Folds pack away', for
     example, when you've been talking about clothing and cupboards
     and wolves and sheep, and how things might be arranged so that
     they will keep for ever, because someone has died. Very serious
     punning: 'where a ghost took a breather'.
         As for human extremism and the lyric ... Hmm. I was at the
     cinema the other night watching The Piano and I thought 'Why
     don't I like this film very much?' at the end of it. I find something
     like that exhausting because from moment to moment one went
     through these extraordinary climaxes and there was not a
     moment that wasn't full of suspense and emphasis and I couldn't
     take that. I spend my life trying to avoid that extremism and I just
     felt I'd rather watch a film of enormous quietness where there
     wasn't that exposure of human intensity and distressed voices
     coming over all the time, even in apparent silence.
         Marion Milner used to make her diary at the end of day and put
     down what had happened to her, and she always found that it
     wasn't the dramatic bits that mattered at all. It was just some
     small item that she wouldn't otherwise have remembered that
     she'd written down. And she collected that over months, didn't
     she? And decided that she ought to redirect her life, because, obvi-
     ously, the importance of her life was in areas she'd not suspected.
     In my case, it might just be pure escapism, and I want to avoid the
     tensions. That could be it. But I'm quite sure, I know because I keep
     a journal, that the things that would go into the journal as being
     important would definitely not be moments of confrontation and
     extreme dramatic voicings of that sort. They would be objects and
     situations which spoke very very quietly and implied things but
     didn't.

WALKER There is a lot of wonder in these poems. Is this wonder an important part of the inspiration for the poems or of the moral value of poetry as you see it?

LANGLEY Yes. Oh yes. It's the chief thing, isn't it? The thing I value. Marvellous. Yes, wonder is quite a good word for it. Joy, Wordsworth might have called it. It's . . . let's think of one or two, go back to the obvious example, Iris Murdoch in *The Sovereignty of Good*: where she talks about how Goodness and Beauty might be the same thing, because they strike you with wonder, because they take you out of yourself. She's got a passage about a kestrel, which would take you back to Hopkins again, wouldn't it? You're wrapped up in your own affairs, you're screwed up by your own subjective feelings, and you know that you're colouring the world with your own thoughts and resentments, and you see a kestrel outside the window hovering and it—what does it say? 'The world becomes all kestrel' or something. And so you forget yourself . . . and she's making the straightforward case that's central to her thinking too, isn't it, that at a moment like that, what is beautiful is also good because it takes your selfishness away, removes your self. And that's really what this wonder would be. She quotes: 'Not how the world is, but that it is, is the mystical.' It's the opposite of existential nausea, isn't it? Instead of being sick that it exists like that, it suddenly becomes extraordinarily wonderful that it exists like that. Ever since I read Wordsworth I thought that it might do that and it does do that from time to time, yes. Particularly in those quiet moments, things do shine like that. If there's nothing there, then I'm misdirected, really. That is where I want to find it and that's where it seems to be. Yes.

WALKER I know 'Matthew Glover' is almost a youthful poem among the ones collected here. It seems more obvious at a superficial reading what this poem is about. Do you see this as a development or a loss?

LANGLEY Yes. That's right. And I think I see it as both. Yes, I would like to do that sort of poem again, It very much came to me as an extension of Olson and a real Dorn poetry to start with, and I needed a fairly fixed scenario to operate in, because I wanted very much to tackle something on a large scale with wider interests. So I just assimilated the whole thing. Without knowing that I was doing it quite so naively as that.

But yes, I like it myself. I like it because it was the first poem of mine that anybody listened to and took vaguely seriously. And I would like still to able to . . . well, I do find my range limited and one way of widening it would be to go back, because you can include wide issues there, obviously, political and social issues. So I have got quite a lot of material like that where I know that I'm interested in the past, usually in pretty obscure people: like Edmund Bohun, who lived in Westhall and got into trouble licensing pamphlets when William and Mary came to the throne. And yet lived in this extremely remote place and was a very irascible and unpleasant person who lived by words almost entirely, so that his whole life was obsessed by definitions. He argued in the market place about definitions every day and he hardly 'saw' anything in his whole life. And he got himself into enormous political trouble. And he was deaf. And I've got extracts from his journals, and I know where he lived, and I've looked at the place. I do feel tempted to go back and work on the implications of his story.

And of course, Mrs Coke herself, in 'The Ecstasy Inventories', comes from an inventory, and the poem was largely stimulated by knowing everything about her, everything she'd got in her house, on her tables, in her presses, the clothes she wore . . . And coming to terms with her, not by writing a dramatic monologue, but in a dramatic monologue-like sort of a way was a major notion. Yeah. But I do think the things I've written since have been a good deal subtler and if you can sink that kind of subject matter deeper into the texture, as it were, and yet it's still around somewhere, that's certainly what I've preferred in recent years.

WALKER There seems little of what many poetry readers might think of as imagery in these poems. Would it be true to say that your poetry does not operate in this kind of way at all?

LANGLEY Well, if by imagery you mean a concern for the visual, I'd like to feel my poetry had it all the time. And I do also think that I am very aware of the metaphorical, metaphysical aspect, which wouldn't be surprising, bearing in mind when I was at college and what sort of things were admired. And the people I used to talk to at that time. So that I wouldn't be at all surprised to find myself taking knucklebones and making a throw of dibs, or whatever they call that game, and turning the world inside out and upside down in some sort of an emblematic metaphorical form. I would do that. But I wouldn't find that the best part of what I did. And I'd rather try probably not to do just that on the whole. I would tend to prefer 'The Red Wheelbarrow' sort of imagery where there isn't that sort of metaphorical foisting. There's just an opening up to what is there in front. With things mattering about it.

[Interviewer asks for a 'thread outside the labyrinth to each poem'.]

LANGLEY So in 'Man Jack', the most recent one, it is the telephone call that Barbara, in fact, made to Jane from a telephone box at night with an owl sitting on the telephone pole watching us doing it. To find out if Jane had had the baby. And in fact we couldn't get through. Jane couldn't hear us, but we could hear her. So that there was this peculiar—Jane's voice actually in the air, in Suffolk, in the dusk, with an owl sitting looking and Jane unable to hear what we were saying. It didn't occur to me really, at that moment that the situation in a telephone box making a call would be a central sort of thing. Peter Riley. Isolated telephone boxes. The 'conduit theory of communication'.

Anyway. And the first half of it is something I'd had hanging around for four or five years. Maybe the poem falls in two. I mean the bit about Jack himself. One inspiration for that is simply the dozens of columns in the Oxford Dictionary on the word 'Jack'. And everything you can do with Jack, a sort of commonality of humanity that Jack might represent. And all the different combinations he's been in: the names of flowers, Jacks and Jills, and Jack in the Beanstalks, and jack in the boxes and how Jack turns into Tom and all the rest of it. You know who Jack is don't you? he's that little figure you see running along beside the train jumping over the hedges and swinging from the telegraph poles.

Then 'Mariana' is called after the Tennyson poem, because she's a woman inside. I like Tennyson's 'Mariana', a nice symboliste sort of poem. Mine is the opposite of symboliste. It's about a bedroom that I've been in often, which has really got exactly what it says: it's got martins, well, it did have in those years, that nest under the guttering outside the window. So that every time they fly up to the window their shadows shoot across the floor of the room and up the far wall and then back across the ceiling and then meet them at the top of the window. So much happens inside the room at an

immense speed perfectly synchronised with this little body arriv-
ing at the guttering outside. And I've lain in bed watching it
happen again and again. That isn't in the poem at all, actually, but
it might have been!

I often count things, don't I? There are 13 trees, or 8 bench ends.
Because the Sanskrit root 'pu', from which we also get our word
'pure', means 'compute' and counting things is the purest way
you've got of knowing things. Just to put them into numbers. And
it's either adequate or it's not adequate. So I quite often strip
things down to just counting. And then see what the opposite of
counting might be. The search for certainties. That's what it's
about. As usual. That's the major biographical bit of that.

The next one is 'The Upshot' and that stemmed from a sentence
in Proust's *A la recherche du temps perdu*: 'We leave unachieved in the
summer dusk'. And that sentence in itself appeared to me so excel-
lent—because it's so unassertive and yet it's got such fine syllabic
things going quietly in it and it's also so sad: to leave without any
sense of achievement and at a time when you wouldn't expect to
leave, like a nice relaxed time, like a summer dusk. The absurdity
and horror of life is so deep in that. And also 'unachieved' is such
a splendid sort of word because etymologically it'll give you 'chief',
which'll give you 'head', which'll give you 'captain', 'caput',
which'll give you innumerable things, the point of life, the chief of
life, bringing life to a point, understanding it. That line itself
seemed so excellent that I just played it into a biographical situa-
tion where I went to Westhall church in Suffolk with Kate and
Nigel Wheale and they were looking around the outside of the
church and I went inside alone. And being extremely patient
people they didn't obtrude on me, and Kate walked past the door
which was open, a little Norman round-headed door, through the
dusk outside, in the halflight, without even looking in, after I'd
been standing silently inside for about half an hour.

And so everything in that poem is really about the inside of
Westhall church. It's about the bench ends. The number of bench
ends sticking up. And, as I say, I don't like to think that I have to
say that, particularly in this poem, because I'd like to think that
the notion of 'captains' would do, without knowing that they were
bench ends. Though I do call them 'poppy-cock' at one point,
which is cocked-up poppy heads etc., so I practically say so. But I
feel slightly disappointed if I have to explain what they are. But

that feels unfair, because I myself enjoy the poem because I do know what they are, precisely, and how close every detail is to what was really there. Like that strange little creaking noise which your sleeve sometimes makes when it rubs on wood if you're leaning on it, which sometimes sounds like a seagull making a noise a long way off. You know I love things when they're incredibly precise, and yet move off all over the place as well. The tighter the wider. So that's, yes, the bench ends inside Westhall church.

And, oh yes, that little bit of a Gombrich article on art and the difference between pictures and maps. So when the poem says 'there are no maps of moonlight', that's another of those phrases I knew I'd have to get in a poem somewhere, because it was going to be pretty significant. 'Maps of moon-light',—what a marvellous notion that you can't do that. So I was waiting for that to crop up as well.

And then 'The Ecstasy Inventories'. That great Nicholas Stone statue inside Bramfield church. When I came back from Italy thinking that I'd never see any good statues again, because I'd been looking at Donatello, I then found Nicholas Stone was a good sculptor. An excellent one. So Bramfield became a particular place for me because of his statue of Mrs Coke, which is one of his very best. So I was interested in her as a work of art and as a person. Although the church records were missing for the years when the Cokes were there, Nigel Wheale found for me, in Suffolk Archaeological Society records, the inventory left when Mr Coke died—so that I had an account of his house and every room in it and all the objects that were on the tables. And objects in a way take you close to people, I suppose, and yet they don't as well, of course. So that was the stimulus for that. All the things mentioned in the poem, like 'paragon' and 'scarlet gown' and habits and costumes and a lot of the vocabulary comes from the actual 17th-century inventory. Petticoats, waistcoats, spots like pinks: she really did have gowns with spots like pinks on them. 'Worked with eyes' means, in one sense, it'd got little eyes sewn on it. There was really a picture in the house of, the inventory says, An Moore on horseback, and you can't tell now whether that means a black man on horseback or a woman called An Moore on horseback. A footnote suggests it might be Anne Moore of Stansted, who later lived in Bury St Edmunds. She was around at the right time: 1561. The inventory gave me a lot of the poem.

And then that connects up with the beginning of *Adam Bede* when a carpenter is carving a mantelpiece singing a hymn. Kermode writes about how you read a book and what details you pay attention to when you read it. And what you don't. How you just dismiss some of them as background realism, but you pay close attention to others, because they're going to be character and plot. And that again is the basic question of what you pay attention to, and what sort of an interpretation you make. And that's very much the question of an inventory and how much you could understand from one.

So those two locked together and they led to the *Phaedrus,* where Phaedrus supports poetry, but Socrates says frankly Boreas and the rest are only myths: Boreas never carried Orithyia off, she was just blown off a cliff. He suggests rational explanations. So it went out from having the inventory through all the other things I was reading at the time. That's one where for about seven or eight weeks everything I read seemed wonderfully pertinent to what I was doing, and although I was in the middle of a school term teaching at the same time, nevertheless in the evenings I came home thinking 'I've got some more, this is the next verse'. Even a *Scientific American* article about wolves protecting their pack areas from the next pack of wolves so assiduously that around the boundary that they don't have time to hunt the deer around the boundary. They only hunt the deer in the middle of their territory where they feel safe. So the deer survive precisely because the wolves can't pay any attention to them where the wolf packs intermingle round the edges. You know I really think you're going well when everything you read like that suddenly pops into place and you feel that your life's making sense for once.

Then there's 'Juan Fernandez'. That's the island where the original of Robinson Crusoe was wrecked. He took the idea of a man isolated on an island, making sense of the island, coming to terms with the things around him. So that's why it's called that. And that's what it's about again. It draws on Heidegger. The Jug, the Earth, Sky, Man and Divinities are in a lecture given by Heidegger on 'The Thing'. That's what I'd been immediately reading when I started doing that.

It's a denser sort of thing altogether. Biographical bits are about the bench ends in Westhall with the little spiders' webs on. That have been there for 30 years now, to my knowledge. They can't really be the same ones, but they look as if they were blowing, 'A mite of quicksilver rousing in the threads'. And then little birds again. A spotted flycatcher that came into Gislingham church and nested in its roof there when it was practically a ruin. Bringing in beakfuls of wriggling legs. And flickering to its deep nest. And then connecting up with Iris Murdoch's kestrel which suddenly takes you out of yourself: 'The brooding self with all its vanity disappears'.

So these things are merely bits of reading in one way, but extremely close personal experience in another. And that's when it gets good. So that's 'Juan Fernandez'.

Then Matthew Glover, yes, is the man who didn't know whether to vote for the Open Field system, or for redistribution of the fields in 1800 in one particular parish near here. So he's a man who didn't know, which seemed to me at the time to be a crucial frame of mind to be in: not to know. But to gather together ways of looking at it. So we needn't say too much more about that. That's got actual descriptions of the parish, of course, and it's got some more birds in, fizzing and so on. I can remember the evening when I saw those, they were in some willow bushes on the edge of the parish in the dusk. On the boundary. Then it's got Clare in it. Quotations from Clare, as he was objecting to the enclosure movement. But that's more open and obvious than most of the poems, so much for that.

'Saxon Landings' as you know is about the Mildenhall Dish. I mean quite simply about the Mildenhall Dish. And possibly a play about the Romans having to pull out of England under Saxon pressure, *The Long Sunset* by (R.C.) Sherriff. I think it was just having listened to that play on the radio that made me suddenly feel the trauma of throwing away a structured existence, bonfires going off at the bottom of the garden, and pagan shadows playing against them, and the likelihood of being massacred at any moment. And that's what got that going.

'Arbor Low' is about the stone circle in Derbyshire and is just a little postcard piece, really. I was fooling around with a way of writing it rather than anything else. Though again Arbor Low's a pretty sacred sort of place, I must admit. And the birds fart because they're wheatears, of course, which means 'white arse'. Yes. Yes.

And then 'The Long History of Heresy'. It's long. When I wrote it I was pleased with it. There are bits of Lévi-Strauss on Totemism, I remember. He cites Bergson saying that the creative energy stops, and the stops become the appearances of living things and places, comparing this to the beliefs of the Sioux Indians: 'Everything as it moves, now and then, here and there, makes stops.' The god stops. The sun is one place where he stopped. It's a footprint. Thousands of grains pressed into a pattern. So are all other things. I'm back with Man Friday without saying so here. I'm particularly fond of the last bit involving Ford Madox Brown when he was painting his landscape 'Gathering Corn'. It's in the Tate and it's a very small, wonderful landscape of a field full of stubble and carts on the other side, in the afternoon light, meticulously painted. And he left a journal at that time about how he was trying day after day to catch that, but the weather conditions kept altering. 'I can make nothing of the small screen of trees'. And he said it would be better to be a poet rather than a painter, because poets didn't have to possess things. He obviously did feel that he'd got to get the truth of what was out there and hold on to it. And he couldn't because the weather conditions altered, and because they cut the corn and took it away when he was halfway through painting it. 'Found the turnips too difficult to do anything with'. It's an attitude which I sympathise with, but can see is hopeless. So the poem ends up at that moment: 'the warmth of the uncut grass, in impossible furrows, in tufts, near green, dove grey, an unusual rosy pink in the unmade hay.' Those are parts of his journal worked in there.

And some of the rest of it comes from a Kurosawa film (*Kagemusha*). The image of a prince-figure who could do practically anything. He's the opposite of Ford Madox Brown. He's the guy who could make anything mean anything; ride straight through and give it the significance he wants, put his footprint where he wanted it. It was just simply an image from the film of him on horseback followed by his retinue going past an enormous stone wall. And the sheer confidence of the man. Isn't there something about him substituting for somebody else as well? So that he's not really the man they think he is? So he's being played off against . . . well, they're two types of knowing, really. Zen versus Thomas Hardy.

And sitting under a tree in Suffolk again, with lights going through the leaves. Oh yes: standing under a tree for an hour and a half. One peculiar evening, that's the biographical centre of it: I walked out of the village at dusk and, as is extremely unusual nowadays, I stood for an hour and a half by a track and no-one came anywhere near me. And it just occurred to me that I ought to stand without moving at all for that length of time and see what happened. Not even turning my head. A lot of rabbits came up and sat on my feet. And moths whipping about within inches of me. A feeling that you might get through to what was really there if you stripped off enough.

I thought that was an interesting experience: to be alone and perfectly still. As soon as you move things take on meaning, don't they? because things becomes things that you've got to step round or walk over or something. They instantly become part of your map, as it were. Whereas if you stand absolutely still, then they might not be part of any map at all. You 'see' the place when you haven't got any designs on it . . . 'coolly', as something independent, . . . as Stokes says. I just found it interesting to strip it down and see if there was a way through. Although knowing that there wouldn't be, of course. So that's 'The Long History of Heresy'. The title comes from Bion's *Attention and Interpretation*. Then Blything is the name of the area in Suffolk. The Blything Hundred. With Blythburgh Church at its centre, which is a splendid place. It's just a little bitty poem, which again I like because it's short and spikey and sort of opens you up a bit. Like Carlos Williams writing *Kora in Hell*, to open things up a little bit occasionally. So that's full of different fragments. There are bits of Darwin reporting from The Voyage of the Beagle, which got in there, since he made quite a lot of the things around him. Yeah. And then 'Rough Silk' is about drinking in The White Horse garden in Westleton in the evening during our holidays. One particular time, again, stimulates it: where there were particular light conditions, and the poplars were opening and closing themselves gently. My brother had just bought a complete edition of the works of Dryden, I remember, so a lot of books got into it. 'Rough Silk'. That's a sort of quiet drinking session, that is, which didn't turn into an orgy. In fact it's one of my very controlled orgies on the whole.

'The Gorgoneion', the last one, that's another heavily worked up one, which is either too worked up or rather good. I'm not quite certain about that. That's done in Wales. I had the experience of going somewhere where I hadn't been for thirty years and seeing it again. It had been altered a bit, but not a lot. And I knew that I would never come back again too—in another thirty years I'll be dead, obviously, so you can't have an interval like that again. So 'The Gorgoneion' is actually about waking up in that cottage in the morning, and seeing the things again and coming to terms with them, or trying to: the fact that they're going to be of no importance afterwards, the absurdity of them as usual in that existential sort of a way. And what patterns you might fit them into. That's enough. I'm a driver who enjoys being talked to too much.

WALKER Would you be prepared to be more open about how you actually write these poems?

LANGLEY Yes. How do I write these poems? I try to snatch some solitude to start with at a time when I'm feeling that my practical life is going quite well. That's pretty essential. I don't like writing out of a moment of stress. Well, I can't. I've got to be reasonably relaxed. Which means it doesn't happen very often. That's absolutely necessary. Then, I've usually got bits and pieces lying around, and sometimes over a period of 10 years or more, say a line or two, which got thrown aside from a previous piece, or an alternative start. Something that something might be made of. Sooner or later. And I pick these up and keep reading them. It's that Valéry business: that the poet is the reader of his own first line. You only need a first line and you read it again and you react to it like a reader would react to it and then that—it's a composite business between you and the first line then. And it doesn't really matter if it's the first line of the poem or if it comes halfway through, obviously. So long as you've got a little nugget to start from. That can be like that one in 'The Upshot': 'We leave unachieved in the summer dusk.' There'd just be sufficient feeling and sound in it to make me want to go on, and connect it with other things.

And then, as a system of discovery I'd use an etymological dictionary, obviously, to help sometimes, and I sometimes reread my journals: though I can't just pick chunks out of them and put them across. But I keep getting reminded of bits and then I might read the whole journal again by accident and unexpected bits come in which I'd previously not thought I was going to use at all. Ford Madox Brown in spite of all. But caught up in a process.

WALKER Could you offer some broad manifesto as to how you see the role of poetry in history, society, the life of the mind?

LANGLEY 'So much depends on a red wheelbarrow' . . . still I think that's true: the sheer opening you up to the outside world. Like this: 'From the earliest period of my recollection, when I can just remember tugging ineffectually with all my infant strength at the tough stalks of the wild succory on the chalky hills above Norwich, I have found the study of nature an increasing source of unalloyed pleasure, and a consolation and a refuge under every pain.' That's Sir Jasper Smith, the founder of the Linnaean Society, quoted in the Rev. John's *Flowers of the Field*, 1890, the 27th edition, under the entry for chicory. That tugging at the fact, absolutely typical and deep-rooted, hung up in the wind . . . suspended after samphire.

WALKER This poetry is very English. I find it difficult to imagine in translation. Do you find foreign poetry interesting or accessible?

LANGLEY Oh yes. I have an interest in Rimbaud, for example. But I would at the same time be pretty sad if I thought my poetry would translate without considerable loss.

WALKER What is it like to be bringing out your first collection in your fifties?

LANGLEY Well, I'm just delighted, that's all: that feeling that anything that's private to one could interweave into a larger scenario, that life might cohere on a larger plane. I don't ever expect there'd be more than a few readers, really. Was it Peter Riley who said there won't be more than twenty or something. And I expect that's right. But I don't mind that at all. I like the poems to be available in case, that's all. That's why I've collected them together. I didn't want to call it 'Collected Poems', because that would suggest that I wasn't going to do too many more, to me it would anyway. And I'd like to think that I might do quite a lot more.

WALKER What can we expect from you next?

LANGLEY Well, I don't know. It's difficult to predict. That would spoil it if I could. I might say I might go back to writing something with a larger body of subject matter again of the Matthew Glover sort. I have got the material ready. But I honestly can't find a way of doing it.

Bibliography

Twelve Poems, (Cambridge: infernal methods, 1994).
Jack, (Cambridge: Equipage, 1998).
Collected Poems, (Manchester: Carcanet and Cambridge: infernal
    methods, 2000).
More or Less, (London: The Many Press, 2002)

Picador, Piccolo and Pan

In Memory

I missed it. So much did they make of this news,
Jean Tension and Steve Fray on *Terpsichordia*,
precisely the tone we were looking for.
You have over two month's salary for a word –
here's one coming through now: Allen Ginsberg,
a cramped hotel room in the late sixties,

Black sticky opium. Nobody at home.
The numbers going sideways are train times –
'*Melancholia* has a plastic core.' You know
it's funding that makes us aspirational:
external validation and review.
Where are you now Allen Ginsberg? Who is pumping

Your harmonium? Elgar Alien Pcoet?
We speed into the tunnel expressway
but can't read the graffiti, Allen Ginsberg,
your senior conductor speaking. Formica Zen
always being torn down and rebuilt, for what?
Not some future perfection: everyone does it.

'Anyone can write' you told John Drew. You, a man
who cared to know what happened and made poetry

without hope of any hope but what is constructed
herein. Part-exchange on detached homes and yellow
silence of three months. Who cares whether any of this
is happening? Allen Ginsberg, you can do it!

You can find the brand name guru and holy ghost,
as we go past the gas works, a tongue in your ear.
Ribbons of scrubland by railway lines and razor wire –
a new lead on the free state. We have yet to make it,
Allen Ginsberg. I'm at Alexandra Palace.
What thoughts I have of you just now, what fantasies:

Of deluxe sentiment and men in tights,
with hiking boots and hanging baskets put forth,
an ivy-leafed geranium. Allen Ginsberg,
faintest touch of lips on the big name
of your generation. My heart skips a beat
at the speed-up through hypertext to real time.

What difference does it make if you're getting
the best head you ever had, Allen Ginsberg? Muggers
snatch a few dollars but leave your manuscripts
so you go down on your knees in a bio-pic
we're currently developing. Imagine that:
Starving, Hysterical, Naked Productions plc,

The best minds of our generation. Can you
see it? Where is the expiry date printed
on these verses by Allen Ginsberg, Gent, BL?
Before Language: little black and white books
passed round in school, real songs of insolence.
This is Bill speaking on Thursday at nine, your time.

Allen Ginsberg, the very name is like a phone
ringing in a train. And because you'll be awake,
the doctor will be able to talk to you throughout.
These faint echoes of Moloch, Sammy, patch me through:

Mohawk, Motown, Mohican, Motivator,
who's fixing your juice in the hereafter?

Everyone's a little bit heterosexual,
now that planning is making a comeback
in the upright position. Allen Ginsberg,
the photograph reproduced on page seventeen,
sometimes a curly shepherd lad, should be a
vertical image, head down, facing pastures new.

Gordon's London Dry or *Tanqueray* pink gin
ought to be the drink we toast your memory in.
Were you able to raise that conference call
Allen Ginsberg? Are you rotting in Manhattan?
Or cast upon the Hudson river to fade away?
Where are those howling verses that used to be?

Allen Ginsberg, what peaches and penumbras!
What price bananas and sunflower sutras?
Singing a Blake song, chanting mescaline dreams!
Setting your poems in the supermarket
of eternity! Re-inventing prophecy!
I'll see you later, Allen Ginsberg, wait for me.

from *Devolution*

ALLEN Tony, I was discussing your work once with John Hall and I was trying to explain why I thought you were essentially a descriptive writer. He was arguing that the montaged aspect of your work was paramount but I was bypassing methodology, the various ways in which you construct and frame, and focussing on what was there in front of me, a description of mediated existence. I likened your poetry to hearing the news read by the weatherman.

LOPEZ My poetry is a response to the world that I see and experience, but it is not usually an attempt at description as such. I have written poems about how it feels to be living through a particular event or set of events, and there would be description involved, things happening and lived through: 'We got the back pay/ And are held in fear under dripping trees.' That is something that happened at a particular date and time. What John says about montage is true also, and probably more consistently accurate. I have written poetry that is largely made of pre-existing language collaged together from different sources and fashioned into a new continuity. *False Memory* is made in that way, though it is a mixed process, and such procedures are bound to be another kind of response to the world we experience, but still a response. The writing has an emotional structure that comes from particular things and ideas put together under pressure. It is a new experience in itself. Reading the work in performance puts that into play for me.

ALLEN I think it is as a 'reader' that I find it descriptive. Any description is a series of prompts and matches and your poetry often seems to me to be a faultless re/creation of how the world gets into my head. But it comes balled-up, pleasurably aestheticised yet strangely angsty and bleak. As you said, it becomes something else, a 'new experience in itself'. But let's stick with your creation of the poem, as opposed to my reception, for the moment: montage/collage is purposeful, so what is the purpose behind your use of it? What can it achieve that another method cannot and how do you see your use of it as being different, or similar, to other poets who work in that vein?

LOPEZ The purpose seems sort of dumb, but it is to make poetry. I mean that by now I have an ongoing project to make poetry because I have been writing steadily and publishing for more than thirty years and there is a demand for new work. In order to make a composition that takes a step beyond simple self-expression you have to use a method, some kind of technique, that allows you to work. Otherwise it would be like personal confession or moaning or talking to yourself. So when I was writing *False Memory* I would strip bits out of a broadsheet newspaper, say the financial pages, or property pages, or medical reports, or an issue of *Nature*, or *Scientific American*, in order to begin to work with what's out there, what's happening. But I'd also use rubbish sources as well, just old books, and printed stuff, labels, anything. I'd copy things out and re-arrange them according to patterns of rhythm and meaning. There is a kind of passive relation to material that already exists, you read it on the look out for something that seems to be typical or remarkable or something that contributes to an emotional effect that you are looking for or singling out. The process of combination of sources is different and more control is needed. I need to be involved with the material in a certain way but the process of working partly establishes that involvement. The other thing that happens is that I exhaust working methods all the time. I couldn't really write anything like *False Memory* now. Immediately it was finished I started casting about for other working methods and I produced all sorts of different things, using programming and transcription from talks and other events. I am interested in using materials that don't seem to be 'poetic' and I have been combining those materials in reconstructive processes to make poetry that has a political ambition. Beauty is important in this process, making something unforeseen and finding ways to develop meaning until it shimmers. I like to read lots of different kinds of poetry and I don't find just what I want to do anywhere. I really enjoy reading the poetry of Kit Robinson, Tom Raworth, Denise Riley, Lyn Hejinian, Bob Perelman, Charles Bernstein, Allen Fisher, Fanny Howe, Jeremy Prynne, David Antin, Alan Halsey, Gavin Selerie, Peter Gizzi, Jennifer Moxley, Carla Harryman, Liz Willis, Andrea Brady, Barrett Watten, Keston Sutherland, Ron Silliman, Rae Armantrout, Michael Davidson, Douglas Oliver, John James—but this is going to be a long list and is getting pointless. I was trying to say something about the purpose which would have to be to delight and astonish, to make something affecting that wasn't there before.

ALLEN There is much there that I would like to follow-up, but could we begin with what you said about 'beauty', something many poets avoid referring to, they will allow others to talk about it for them, maybe. You called it 'finding ways to develop meaning until it shimmers', now that is a fascinating way of putting it. Could you say more about the 'shimmer', or the 'shine of surface' I called it once when trying to describe the texture, particularly of American Language work. And what is 'developed meaning' as opposed to 'meaning', or even 'undeveloped meaning'?

LOPEZ There are surely a large number of ways in which language can be made to seem inevitable: compression, deformation, acoustic patterning, repetition and variation, rhetorical embellishment, apparent plainness, adopted persona, dramatised fragmentation and so on. If you choose a highly specialised vocabulary then you have the option of moving away from it to another specialism or moving to a specialism from another register. So the mix will create emotional effects like aptness, incongruity, comedy, banality, disproportion. I don't choose what kind of effect I'm looking for but I am affected by the way the piece works when I read it back to myself and see whether it goes or not. The capacity of response is learned I think and not always in balance, certainly not for me. Emotional eccentricity can be written in as a pattern, in fact it probably must be written in. So it is one thing to agree that a statement is correct and it is another to be moved because that point is made effectively by a figure that is surprising and seems right, it is yet another thing to be engaged with the current sense in that way and to be pleasurably surprised that connections are made to other thoughts and ideas that are already elsewhere in play in the piece you are reading. A kind of harnessed and layered meaning that works in a musical sense as well as providing clarity and depth and complexity, that would be developed meaning. But so would a mode of plainness in such a context, like Patrick Caulfield up against Expressionism. Of course the sense of complexity is only beautiful if one cares about what is at stake, so the sense of beauty we respond to is always a combination of emotional and formal or intellectual power.

ALLEN Alright, so developed meaning, in your explanation, and pretty evident in the poems themselves, is language based, because you talk exclusively there of literary methods, ways of organising and manipulating texts, 'compression, deformation . . .' etc. And whereas a poet utilising collage methods would once have juxtaposed images or transparent words you do your tiling with 'specialised vocabularies'. When did this shift towards the textual take place in your work and how conscious was it? Were you aware at the time of the theoretical swirl that stormed behind such poetic surfaces?

LOPEZ I started to collage material to make poetry in 1973 or 74. I was working on a book called *Snapshots* that was published in 1976 and I started cutting up text from a field guide to the sea shore to make

a poem. The book patches in bits of letters and quotes as well as poems made from particular sources. I think everything I published from then on was at least partly cut up, though the work is not really successful. The pulp fiction I was working on (to pay the rent) had quite a limited set of sources and the first book was very sub Burroughs. Five novels were written very fast with scenes rehashed from factual crime books, bits of language, place names, dialogue, were crucial. So I was stealing from crime novels as well. Then I worked as a proofreader for a scientific abstracts journal and had access to other journals in the office that I worked over in my lunch break or when I was underemployed to make weird poem-stories that didn't quite work. I didn't really know why at that stage. I worked for a while in the production department of Pan books, collating proofs and copy editing books, I think the process of putting proof versions together for the printer and changing bits for different readerships (say an American cookbook into English), children's books and literature (we produced Picador, Piccolo and Pan) all of that was very formative to my idea of composing a book. I worked on some poetry books for Trigram— Asa Benveniste, Oasis—Ian Robinson and *Spanner*—Allen Fisher but I needed money and took on freelance projects for more commercial firms. All of this was a continuous activity for me and not theoretical but my job. So in different ways the poetry books I published were based on cutting and pasting: *The English Disease* (78) very much so, *A Handbook of British Birds* (82) is exclusively material taken from field guides and juxtaposed with pictures of things that turn up in the figurative descriptive language used by the original authors. I was a student at Essex from 77 to 80 and I remember making new cutup works specifically for readings then. One project in 78 was a splicing of Keats with Marx and Engels I called *Idiot's Endymion*, a punk artefact really, some of it was published in a mag called *The Heretic* that my friend Paul Brown edited, pretty dreadful I think, and I came across a typescript copy in a library recently, but that was unpublished and I was surprised to find it. I wouldn't mind if I had been paid for it. I was working on American Literature, mostly, as a student and I went to Cambridge to do a PhD, originally on an American topic but switched to writing on W S Graham, whose work is very explicitly involved with language. Do you know his poem that begins
What is the language using us for?

Said Malcolm Mooney moving away
Slowly over the white language.
Where am I going said Malcolm Mooney.

I was writing about his work for some time, years, and I was teach-
ing small groups of students. The abstract sense of the page as a
white space filling up with text, the misleading and paradoxical
direct address to the reader and the idea of language as something
really large that you plug into, all of that was in play. Theory was
just beginning to be professionalised into English studies in
Universities and different approaches became fashionable one
after another. I used the Cambridge lectures and seminars
designed for undergraduates to find out what was happening. The
libraries are wonderful of course. My earlier writing practice
wasn't really driven by theory but I had every opportunity to find
out what was happening. I did read Americans but not the
language writers, not until much later. I met John Ashbery in 1976
when I went to America for the first time and I read all his work. I
got to know Ed Dorn quite well because of friends at Essex. I
invited Tom Raworth to read at Essex (he was well known there
and had been a student and a writer in residence) so I read the
work of his that was published on the west coast: *Logbook, A Serial
Biography*, etc but not (at that stage) the writers who had been his
main friends and contacts there. Douglas Oliver was at Essex and
so was Anthony Barnett. It is astonishing really, given how things
are now, but connections were very accidental and meetings often
went nowhere. I went to Cambridge in order to work with Jeremy
Prynne, mostly because of what Peter Ackroyd and Doug Oliver
said about him. That was good enough for me. But anyway, the
shift towards the textual was always there, it was the work that I
started to get published from scratch, before I had even any kind of
education.

ALLEN Your use of the word 'education' there gives me the opportunity
to pose a series of questions on that topic. What do you mean by
education, are you referring to academic education, an education
that made you reflect on what you had already been doing? Did
your poetry change with that education? And, connected with
this, you said that early on, 'Theory was just beginning to be
professionalised into English studies', so how do you now rate the

influence of that 'professionalised theory' on the subsequent development of experimental and innovative poetry? Has it been for the better or the worse? And could you say something of your binary role as poet and professor.

LOPEZ Yes, in that answer by 'education' I meant higher education. I went to a London state grammar school at first but had a disrupted and fairly chaotic time, my family did, when I was in my teens. I didn't get round to going to University until I was 27 and I had by that time been earning my living writing and doing various jobs for some years. When I went to Essex to be an undergraduate I was paid a mature student grant (which was a big income drop but still enough to live on) and all I had to do was write an essay once a month. This was clearly the way to go. I think that the process of studying with exam deadlines and so on fills up time and it is difficult to keep writing new poetry or fiction at the same pace. But academic work was interesting and pleasurable for me, I mean talking about poetry and novels and writing essays, as an occupation, was better than anything else I'd tried. Then I got a grant to go to Cambridge and be a research student, and I was much better off there. It was strange socially but it was lively also and the resources were terrific (they are even better now, even when the rest of education seems to be going down the tube). Writing a PhD is not really conducive to creative work, but I don't think you get spoilt for creative work, it's more a question of what fills up your time. You need to concentrate to bring the academic work to a conclusion, which is usually the problem with research. I think the way that I used to imitate things that I liked was cruder and more dependent early on: education was part of the process of complicating that response, as well as just having more sense of what has been done by whom. I decided to stop working on W S Graham after my PhD was revised and published because I didn't want any one area of scholarship to become the main thing. Graham's poetry is wonderful and there would be plenty to do but I didn't want that work to become my life. I had opportunities to work on other serious and more substantial academic projects for publishers but I decided to concentrate my work on poetry. I had a number of temporary teaching jobs that meant I was spending all my time doing job applications—but once I was through that and got a permanent job I started to write much more. I think that ways of reading and arguing, constructing an argument, imagining opposing arguments, going back over what you are working on and researching it further, taking the time to develop things properly, all of that process which is involved in academic writing, that has had a profound effect on my writing—not least the wish sometimes to break free from such structures and write something spontaneous or irresponsible. I have been writing mainly poetry for a long time now, but I do also write essays on modern and contemporary poetry and publish that work in books and journals. Lately I've done more commissioned work in poetry and performance than ever before and I'm interested in that.

It's difficult, you know, to respond fully to the idea of theory as an influence on 'experimental' or 'innovative' poetry. In one sense theory is just another text, just another vocabulary set, for poets to play with and cut up. I think that the political positions and the standard moves in argument, those can be adopted and adapted by all creative artists including poets. I think that there are many poets whose work is a kind of theory—and not just the so-called experimental poets. Carol Ann Duffy or Jo Shapcott are feminist writers in their way just as much as Rae Armantrout, Denise Riley, Susan Howe or Rachel Blau DuPlessis. The treatment is somewhat different but theory is everywhere, it is a fact of life in our time. I think that there is another question here about the implied readers of some kinds of demanding contemporary poetry. I mean a lot of contemporary poetry is just dull because publication is so easy now. As to my roles of poet and professor—well they both clash and complement at the same time. Any poet needs a day job, wouldn't you say? Otherwise you'd need to have a string of residencies and be always hustling for freelance reviewing and so on. It's good to do some of that work when you want to but I wouldn't want to rely on residencies and chat sessions in festivals or teaching courses for commercial writing schools, turning out biographies etc, not for the main income. It would be a weary business having to work as a freelance unless you were really very successful. Working in a University is sometimes very demanding and that can blot out the space and time you need to do imaginative work. But students are very interesting to work with and colleagues also, I can't imagine any other working environment (I mean other than higher education) that would be better.

ALLEN That definitely answers the question about your personal negoti-
ation with 'education', but isn't the relationship, which has devel-
oped, between academia and innovative poetry more complex? I
would agree that, as you say, theory is another text, but I am not so
sure about it being 'just another text' because theory, when in its
academic context, touches on questions of power. Indeed, what
many mainstream poets do (as those you cite) is put a very narrow
theory into practise, only they don't call it theory, they call it 'how
it should be done because it is normal and natural', when it is not
normal or natural at all, it is particular and artificial. But that is
quite different to the percolation of theory into poetic practise as
mediated by academic institutions. Isn't it a fact that over the past
decade innovative poetry, particularly the Language and post-
Language strains, has become largely institutionalised? I am talk-
ing about in the States of course, but by extension doesn't that
increasingly include us Brits? And wasn't this something that Lee
Harwood and Tom Raworth, in their own very different ways,
warned against a long time ago now?

LOPEZ Of course theory is all about power, though sometimes you might
forget it as you peer at the seamless and seemingly endless streams
of self-aggrandising jargon arranged in flawless chiastic sentences
that emptily echo the cadences of Derrida redoing Heidegger.
What? If you nod off at a conference you can catch the same
phrases coming back at the end of the paper, quote marks acted
out with curling fingers held aloft. What does it mean to say that
poetic practice is mediated by academic institutions? That Bob
Perelman has to work to bring up a family and pay his kids' college
fees? That Lyn Hejinian was finally recognised as someone we
could learn from and offered a steady job? That no-one could be
better than Susan Howe to teach you Emily Dickinson? That there
are academic books published about and by these authors? That
they all somehow manage to keep writing wonderful poetry? Or is
it that I might ask my students to read those poets rather than
some others who are in my view less challenging and interesting?
Thus my choice and the imposition of that choice on students
from my position of power is self-interested? Is that it? I'd like to
know just what Tom Raworth and Lee Harwood said or wrote to
warn us. They are both excellent poets who have themselves been
supported for considerable periods by academic institutions: earn-

ing reading fees and teaching fees, being graduates in English (Lee from London University) and Translation (Tom from Essex University); both of them have been writers in residence and teachers in academic institutions. I see them and hear their poetry performed when I book them to read in an academic institution or when a colleague books them in another. I'd like to have them both supported by the state and have them come to meet students and inspire them. They both have a lot to give. Where will their poetry go unless into University libraries and archives? Why worry? It is important for the theory of the avant-garde that there is a state of permanent opposition. But you would not want Bob Dylan, the Rolling Stones or the Sex Pistols to be still making demos? There is a very strong anti-intellectual prejudice in English society that is bound up with old-fashioned class loyalties, deference, and proper suspicion of leisured gents in universities. It's not like that any more. Larkin, Amis senior and their cronies had this resentment in spades. It's a reactionary position, a kind of nostalgic Tory romanticism, as if we could take to the open road with only our banjos and songs. Remember Donovan? I bet he's a Tory in his Surrey mansion.

ALLEN The 'anti-intellectual prejudice in English society' remains as strong as ever, but I do not think it is entirely 'bound up with old-fashioned class loyalties' and 'deference', it has other roots too. Yet class is a big player, for me, in respect of the weird nature of the British poetry scene so I think the extent of my agreement with you on this subject would be more telling than any disagreement. Nevertheless I do, personally, think there are problems even if they are at base problems of perception; for example in the US there is bad feeling between some of the new young-bloods and the older generation of poetic innovators, and their arguments are framed, more-often-than-not, in terms of establishment privilege. While we are touching on the subject of 'power', can I bring you back to the political aspect of your poetry, something which really hit me when I read *Devolution* where it seems you are dealing with, or playing with, or using, or negotiating with aspects of Thatcherism and the daily experience of living through late-capitalism. Earlier you said, 'I am interested in using materials that don't seem to be 'poetic' and 'I have been combining those materials in reconstructive processes to make poetry that has a political ambition.' So what do you mean there by 'political ambition' and how does it relate to actual poems such as 'Jump Start' and 'Stress Management'? Do you have a sense of the poems masking themselves in post-modern flatness, the material that doesn't 'seem to be poetic' perhaps; in order to subvert its power, unmask it by default?

LOPEZ Well as it happens I think both of those poems are political in quite straightforward ways. 'Stress Management' is much earlier, made from news stories, principally news images from national and local news, but also radio 4 news stories, I can't exactly remember but I think all on one day. In fact there was a story that the Cornish tin mines would both close and all the miners would be laid off—but then there was a reprieve a couple of days later and one of the mines stayed open much reduced. At that time the first Gulf War was on, most of Kuwait was burning, covered with clouds of black smoke from the sabotaged oil wells. There were picture stories about implements of official torture in Iraq, families all over Britain were having their homes repossessed and Mrs Currie, a minister in an elected British government, the same day offered her opinion on national news that too much money was being spent on school meals in Derbyshire. So I guess she was putting someone, some particular local councillor or councillors under pressure for her own ends. But it is obvious I think that the poem relates threads from various public things happening and runs them together. Even if they are not all completely recoverable by the reader, there is an account of a specific time and set of events. Naming both Mrs Currie for her work and also naming Mr Gandhi watching his mother burn is important in that poem, it tends to show these huge forces (as in twenty thousand prisoners) bearing on individuals and what they might feel. So the beginning image of the children walking is written over and over with what is happening in the day and in adult consciousness of the day. 'Jump Start' is written years later and is much longer and more ambitious but looking at it again now there are some definite similarities. I suppose that the setting is at times virtual and imaginary and at times located in real travelling environments, road signs, landscapes seen from the air. The text is cut in with material on crowd control, child care, public announcements, wage negotiations, gun crime, phone messaging services, political process. I think that both poems are very much concerned with daily life, ordinary things that happen. Now that I look at it again I think that the flatness you speak of is factored in strongly by beginning with a virtual reality scenario which becomes a kind of emotional default setting, that and the use of ready-made text that can be funny, or horrible or just blank. 'Don't you just love / the slide into abstraction' is actually moving into a site of political public disorder: when the normal political channels have broken down. That's where we are much of the time. I have been writing things that are just dead obvious lately as a new discipline.

ALLEN Yes, I can see how your work tracks that process where 'the normal political channels have broken down', and as you say, it is where we are much of the time, which is why I find your poetry descriptive, an exotic form of description though. I want at this point to touch more on the thorny subject of post-modernism itself, and ask you if you consider yourself to be a post-modern writer, or not. And could you tell us more of your new material, the 'dead obvious' you mentioned?

LOPEZ You know Tim that for many academics now that question seems to be beside the point. I mean that they have just let the question die because postmodernism quite suddenly became an empty category as modernism was extended into the present and is now seen as an unfinished project. It just happened and I realise now that that was what I wanted to happen when I wrote about W S Graham, to prove that modernism was not over (that it was over used to be the orthodoxy in the 1980s) that it was still happening. What was being described as postmodernism has apparently become less compelling. It has quietened down as a field, though there are still courses called postmodernism in universities, but modernism and 'late modernism' are expanding together. But I do expect that there will be a series of 'slight returns' and maybe big ones, until we discover some other discourse to deal with what is recent and contemporary.

Some of the features of postmodernism as a descriptive tool still seem useful to me: the notion of an eclectic mixing of styles, of deliberately 'broken' or monstrous works, of works that cross genres, of decentred and rhizomic replication as opposed to hierarchy and high artistic autonomy. Yes, the mixing of high and low.

The idea of an authentic personal voice or style is alien to me as a writer. I don't think I have an individual style: but maybe one will appear in retrospect. I try one approach to writing for a while and exhaust it for my own purposes (or just can't see how to continue) and then try something else. Postmodernism is not what I think about when I am writing, not at all, but I have read Jencks, Lyotard, Jameson, Foster, Baudrillard, Blanchot etc. My work is motivated by certain experiences that have a lot to do with authority and the lack of authority, lack of belief, displacement, with social and psychological damage. All of this comes from the second world war ultimately. I grew up in a family patched together out of world war two displacement and the landscape we lived in was made by the blitz. The social order was deeply and inescapably wrong in every particular. So growing up in Stockwell and Brixton in the 1950s as a first generation immigrant (my father's English was a second language, my grandmother never learnt to speak English) I knew all about hybridity and the legitimation crisis before I had a language for it. So I trace the consumer society we live in back to the second world war, it is the post-war era, and that era is I think expressed in postmodern art: Joseph Beuys, Warhol, Ian Hamilton Finlay, Christo, Kienholz.

Thinking of the 'dead obvious', this recent poem will be the opening poem in the autumn issue of *Poetry Review*, see what you make of it:

In Photographs

A pair of Iranian twins joined at the head
far from settling this increasingly bitter row
swiftly and grimly appeared to transmit the story
because it had been in the public interest
an inquiry into the good faith of one man
from Hereford to London misrepresented the situation
when an express train hit a transit van
the politics was driving the intelligence
when an express train hit a transit van
let me tell you how the scores have changed
possibly pronounced 'STROOD' as far as I know
three people, believed to be fruit pickers, died

and may have been acting in good faith
although we were divided on that issue but otherwise
supporters of the gay priest now not-to-be Bishop of Reading
Iraqis provide information about attacks on Americans
the veracity and honesty of our government
I wondered whether that was worth saying
whether or not the claim was well grounded, well founded, I
    mean
either a cow or a woman with a cow's horns
became prime minister in 1958 and was assassinated
back in apartheid days
Mr Straw calls for an apology from the BBC
let me tell you how the scores have changed
fourteen to Mr Good
this long-range ballistic missile travels 800 miles
without seeing the actual documents
about whom we know nothing
nor do we know his motive on the basis of evidence
whether there was undue pressure
and where exactly is Kim Bauer now?
if the claim was not well founded
chemical or biological weapons could be launched
whether politics was driving the intelligence
which he had typed up on a very long roll of paper
taken from the foreign affairs select committee
in a transit van: a clear and present threat
needed to be established or not
and the evidence was to the contrary
that the 45 minute claim
could have been avoided
and the people were misled and the parliament was misled
denied access to witnesses
about whom we know nothing
and Jack Straw hangs by his thumbs then passes out
tries to pull the rip-cord but passes out
is shocked by a security man rogue element
falling on a dodgy dossier, he passes out

he looks worn out but handsome in Arab dress
they hang him up again by the thumbs
and he is interrogated by Robin Cook
who wants to know about allegations made
by a gay priest from Reading called Elizabeth Bishop
whether politics was driving the intelligence
making this 45 minute speech
or whether it was in fact a sky-dive
a man addicted to risk
making a complete *Horlicks*
falling out of the sky
but acting in good faith
like a certain celibate not-to-be Bishop
serving on the joint intelligence committee
and not the other way around
Mr Bauer called for an apology between 2AM and 3AM
when the bomb went off in the desert
as far as possible from Los Angeles: maybe Phoenix
maybe Tucson, maybe Basra, maybe Janin
the verdict NOT PROVEN
I wondered whether it was worth saying
whether or not the claim was well founded
how much it would cost to get a bulldozer
how much should I allow on the arts council application form?
what would be the appropriate delivery system
to get it over the level crossing
and into the settlements in good faith?

ALLEN Umm, I would not have recognised that as one of yours Tony. It's like a poem of yours that has been unfolded, has had its extra dimensions opened out and spread and exposed. I like it. I like the idea of Straw hanging by his thumbs. Yea, 'dead obvious'.

Bibliography

POETRY

Poetry: Equal Signs (Cambridge: Equipage, 2004).

False Memory (Cambridge: Salt, 2003).

Data Shadow (London: Reality Street, 2000).

Devolution (Great Barrington, Massachusetts: The Figures, 2000).

False Memory (Great Barrington, Massachusetts: The Figures, 1996).

Negative Equity (Cambridge: Equipage, 1995).

Stress Management (London: The Boldface Press, 1994).

When You Wish . . . (Cambridge: Poetical Histories, 1992).

Mortal Heart (with U.A. Fanthorpe) (Exeter: Spacex, 1991).

A Theory of Surplus Labour (Cambridge: Curiously Strong, 1990).

Abstract & Delicious (London: Secret Books, 1983).

A Handbook of British Birds (with Mary I. French) (Durham: Pig Press, 1982).

Wish You Were Here (with Lee Harwood) (London: Transgravity, 1979).

The English Disease (London: Skyline Press, 1978).

Change (London: New London Pride, 1977).

Snapshots (London: Oasis Books, 1976).

CRITICISM

The Poetry of W. S. Graham (Edinburgh: Edinburgh University Press, 1989, paperback 1990).

FICTION

As 'Vincente Torrio'

The Politician (Sevenoaks: New English Library, 1976).

The Executioner (Sevenoaks: New English Library, 1975).

The Dealer (Sevenoaks: New English Library, 1974).

The Bootlegger (Sevenoaks: New English Library, 1974).

The Second Coming (Sevenoaks: New English Library, 1973).

Hold that Golem

There's a Carnivore in Heaven

The room a fabric of words, old stain
of something let happen in toner, self
-coloured lamb's caul that the checkerboard
takes to a new level and praises

outwits the concrete, only hour of sun
among animals, painted itself
by torchlight, ground in fat, from memory.

To know nothing, in clear light, but remedy
(for the dead, one) read this badge:
it is a project for a sketch of the whole wall.

Detergent predigests the tell-tale tracks
of paralytic breakfast on the endless vest
of no mind; in the place of mind, an attic
harbours the colon in a belly lock /
the rocks are star-fucked. Shit, I know my name

ALLEN Peter, I first came upon your work in the mid 90s, with your
editorship, with Robin Purves, of *Object Permanence* magazine.
Around the same time you began sending those distorted mirror
computer graphics to *Terrible Work*. But what is the story that leads

up to those points? I notice your bibliography begins in 1991, with a poem in a Glasgow mag called *Northlight*.

MANSON I did publish some work in Scottish little magazines in the early 90s, but the experience was never very encouraging: the better-known magazines seemed to be permanently full, and the smaller ones, while they did occasionally accept my work, always seemed to take the weakest thing they were sent. The problem certainly had a lot to do with the kind of work I was writing at the time. I was very influenced by the traditions following on from Ezra Pound and William Carlos Williams—especially Louis Zukofsky's poetry—but didn't have any direct contact with contemporary innovative writing. On the other hand, the Scottish small press scene seemed hermetically sealed to the Outside: there was almost no information available about the kinds of experimental press I later came into contact with. I made the most of the data that came my way: I remember reading a review by Edwin Morgan in *Lines Review* of Veronica Forrest-Thomson's *Collected Poems* and spending ages trying to track down every name he mentioned.

Between 1991 and 1994 I was signed up to write a PhD thesis which I eventually abandoned. Very early on, I went to visit Tom Leonard, who was the writer in residence at Glasgow University, and Tom really got what I was trying to do (got the humour of it too, which people often miss!) and was able to point me at a lot of writers and artists who became important to me later. I remember Tom performing Jackson Mac Low's *Six Gitanjali for Iris Lezak* at the creative writing group, counting the pauses between stanzas under his breath. Amazing. Around the same time, I met Robin Purves, who was also then a postgrad and interested in a lot of the same kinds of art, music and literature as I was. We haunted the library, gleaning where we could (Glasgow University library still contains almost no works of innovative poetry written after the 1960s). Some time in 1993 I acquired my first PC, and wondered out loud if the easiest way forward might not be to set up a magazine of our own. Robin turned up the following day having found the addresses of a dozen experimental poets, so we basically just wrote to people and asked if we could publish some of their work. Most people replied, and the magazine took off from there. The thing that pleases me most about *Object Permanence* magazine, eight years after the final issue appeared, is the amount of contextualising information we managed to surround the poetry with: every issue had more listings than the last, we reviewed a lot of books, and told people where you could buy them. Readers found that useful at the time, and the back issues give a real sense of the context in which the poetry we published was being produced.

My own writing began to feed on the work that I was exposed to (Clark Coolidge, Bob Cobbing and Barry MacSweeney were in the first issue and remain big influences), and the experience of physically making the pages of the magazine fuelled the visual work I'd started to do on my PC. I'd been a very amateur programmer since my teens, and discovered that I could subvert a simple Mandelbrot Set program by feeding it all kinds of rogue equations. The first image I made went on the cover of the first issue of the magazine, and that made an immediate connection with Bob Cobbing and the people connected with his press *Writers Forum*. I published a lot of visual work over the next couple of years in little magazines: the poetry was still developing.

ALLEN   Your description of how starting and editing a magazine actually brought what you were seeking to your doorstep ties in with my experience with *Terrible Work*. I would never have made the contacts or been exposed to that material, to that degree, if I had not made that move. You mention three of those 'exposures', Coolidge, Cobbing and MacSweeney, but these are three very different writers, can you say more of how they impacted on your development, especially considering their differences?

MANSON Bob Cobbing was an influence in a lot of ways. I think it's very easy for a writer who is just starting out to mistake the nature of small-press publication: if editors keep returning your work, it's tempting to attribute more power to them than they actually possess. As we now know, Tim, small-press editors and publishers tend to be one or two-person operations, often run by writers, who usually have fairly well defined tastes and very limited budgets. Bob's press, *Writers Forum*, was a publisher degree zero: he had a photocopier in the basement, which was the same machine he used to produce his own visual work, and the processes of creation and publication were, for him, inextricably linked. If Bob believed in your work, he'd publish it, and you'd generally receive a proof copy of the booklet within a few days. Once you've come into contact with someone who takes the process of publication so seriously but treats it in such a matter-of-fact way, you lose the sense of 'publication' as a mystical goal. A publisher is just a person with access to a photocopier who knows some other people who buy books.

Bob's own practice as a poet and performer, especially as an interpreter of his own non-verbal visual poetry, was an enormous influence. The discipline of accepting that all aspects of the text on the page, visual, verbal, whatever, can be used as keys to influence the performance of the text in real time, is something that can be just as useful in the performance of more purely 'verbal' texts as in visual or soundtext performance. Once you accept that all written texts are open to interpretation (even the simplest sentence can be grammatically ambiguous, and tone of voice can change meaning entirely) it seems to me that there are two options. One is, don't give readings at all, because it's impossible to translate a written text into speech without collapsing its ambiguities, and an audience might be likely forever after to restrict the possibilities of the poem on the page to the particular route you chose through it that night. The alternative, which is more risky but much more rewarding, is to embrace the openness of the text, study it from the point of view of a reader not a writer, recognise the points where your interpretation of it could branch off in one of several directions and use every cue available to you in the moment of performance to decide which one to choose. As one of Bob's poems puts it:

Every poem is an experiment—
The tightrope—
Sometimes it comes off;
Sometimes you come off.

Barry MacSweeney was a poet whose work I discovered in the Paladin 'Re:Active Anthology' *The Tempers of Hazard* (these very influential books, containing a substantial Selected Poems by three writers per volume, were edited by Iain Sinclair in 1992 and 1993. *The Tempers of Hazard* suffered the distinction of being withdrawn and destroyed within weeks of publication, when Paladin axed their poetry list). Robin and I asked him for work for the first issue of *Object Permanence*, and he responded with an incredibly beautiful suite of poems from his sequence *Pearl*. A year or so later, he phoned me out of the blue to read me the first poems of *The Book of Demons*, a sequence about the alcoholism that eventually killed him. He couldn't have known at the time that I was having similar problems, but we kind of bonded over that (I remember us rattling our little bottles of Librium down the phone at each other) and remained in pretty close contact—usually by phone—for the next two or three years. I have misgivings about *The Book of Demons*, which I think became as much a means of concentrating on his drinking as of fighting it, and I suspect it wouldn't have been written if he hadn't embarked on a horrendous, almost monthly, cycle of bingeing followed by Librium withdrawal, which must have wrecked his health. Even *Pearl* isn't a sequence you can read innocently, as it's about a mute woman being 'given' the power of language by a man . . . On the other hand, it's a dull hero that you can accept in all their aspects, as Barry would be the first to recognise. The main thing I learned from Barry was not to be embarrassed by beauty in language: Barry's work processes the language of English Romanticism through the sensibility of Jack Spicer or Frank O'Hara, and the result is as great as anything produced by the amazing generation of writers he grew up in. I've seen unpublished work written after *The Book of Demons*, and it's among the best he ever wrote.

Clark Coolidge is someone I've tried and failed more than once to write about, and I find it really difficult to explain why he's so important to me. I think it has a lot to do with the semi-independence of the surfaces of his poems from the larger structural moves going on underneath. I can't think of any living poet with a more powerful sense of what happens to words when they're placed next to one another, and for me Coolidge just has the *funniest* ear for word-collocations in the language. I remember when he first sent us a poem for *Object Permanence*, we stared and stared at it and I said to Robin, 'They're going to crucify us'. But the poems teach you their own mode of reading, and there's a kind of joy to be found in distractability. I think quite often that the things you resist most as a writer are the things that have most to say to you. I've always had a strong dislike for Surrealism, which always seemed to me to be all depth and no surface, making its points through analogy and metaphor rather than embedding them in the material properties of the language (Surrealist poetry in English always sounds to me like poetry in translation). The very earliest poems I wrote emerged out of a kind of post-adolescent angst that far outstripped my ability to make it into interesting language. After a while, this was replaced by an interest in formal play within language, as much influenced by the *OuLiPo* as by Zukofsky, but which in my case tended to delete any personal or emotional content, to pretty sterile result. Eventually, and I think largely due to Coolidge's influence, I found a synthesis where I could use my formal interest in the language surface almost to 'distract' myself from the often quite personal material which was being drawn in underneath. It's not quite the 'pure psychic automatism' the Surrealists spoke of, but it's the only way I've found of making poems which stay interesting to *me*, in that I don't feel that I stand in a particularly privileged relation to them: I have to work at them, and with them, in the same way any other reader would. I'm usually the last to know what they're about.

ALLEN Can I pick up on something you said about Cobbing first? You mentioned how he was someone who took the process of publication seriously but treated it in a matter-of-fact way, losing 'the sense of publication as a mystical goal'. I find that very interesting because doesn't that contradiction, or working contradiction to be more precise, mirror a certain orientation of the poet/artist to the status of the work itself? I have always found it very difficult trying to explain to people how poetry is, for me, something with huge importance in my life yet something almost entirely demystified to the extent that as activity it is on the same level as anything else I enjoy, such as watching football or walking the dog. The same thing comes up in your comments about Coolidge, what you called the 'semi-independence' of the poem's surface from the larger structure beneath, so maybe what we are both referring to here is something essentially tactical, a way of inducing a psychological trick upon ourselves in order to open ourselves to language.

MANSON I think one thing that I probably share with a lot of the people (not to mention poets) I feel closest to is a basically materialist view of the world, coupled with an overwhelming sense of the ramified complexity of absolutely everything that isn't man-made. It probably sounds quaint and a bit dated to say that I got that sense from the time I spent in the early nineties getting into as much of the maths behind fractal and chaos theory as I could follow (I've forgotten most of it now), but that's what happened. The visual work which came out of that period pretty much cured me of the desire to draw or paint, which I'd nursed for some years, as the results were just so much more *interesting*. Though I don't think I realised it at the time, that work also gave me a taste for language-surfaces that weren't necessarily impenetrably dense or difficult, but were in some fairly obvious way unstable, open to interpretation. I think experimenting with things like the Game of Life, where simple cellular patterns are allowed to interact and evolve over many generations on a computer screen, did away with my belief that I could have any real control over how an object as complex as a poem would finally be interpreted, when almost every move from word to word involved the reader in an interpretative decision whose outcome I couldn't predict. And to answer your question, yes, I do think on one level it's a trick I play on myself: I'm so used to looking at language—all language—up close that I see ambiguities where most people wouldn't, my censor goes to sleep and I discover I've written with a candour I couldn't have attained by more direct means.

One of the most important functions of art is the way it acts as a transitional object between human consciousness and its material basis: art is matter, it's not alive, but it's marked by consciousness and the only things more complex than the interactions people have with art are the interactions they have with other people. I'd like art to approach the complexity of the human mind as closely as possible, if only to remind myself that things as complex as the human mind are materially possible, that we really are children of this world, with no-one to rescue us if we fuck it up. Hold that golem.

As an aside, as if that wasn't an aside, I think all this correlates interestingly with a change in the dominant scientific metaphor that the arts use to understand themselves and the world. A very influential stream of 20th Century art, from Dada to John Cage and beyond, was concerned with ideas of acausality, indeterminacy and randomness which ultimately derived from quantum mechanics. Then, some time in the 1970s or 80s, the concept of randomness was called into question when people became aware of ideas emerging from chaos theory—the possibility of unpredictable behaviour arising in simple physical systems which are so constructed as to be extremely sensitive to their initial states ('The Butterfly Effect'). I think an artist like Cage was very much of his time: where he used chance operations to isolate objects and events for contemplation outside of any system or causal chain, a contemporary artist would be more likely to start from the premise that nothing can ever be considered as outside of a system or causal chain, that all the elements of a work are mutually interdependent and the ramifications of their interaction are more complex than an artist can hope to control.

ALLEN I didn't fully understand it when you said, 'I think quite often that the things you resist most as a writer are the things that have most to say to you.' You then cited surrealism as, 'making its points through analogy and metaphor rather than embedding them in the material properties of the language'. You are right, there is a sense in which surrealism was all depth and no surface, after all the classic surrealist motif was the pointing hand, this way to the subconscious, or, this way from the subconscious, either way the signpost is clear while the road is foggy. So was your strong dislike of this lack of surface, this 'image on top', due to a kind of metaphysical discomfort? Was there a secret fascination then? If you resisted it, as you have implied, was this resistance dialectically resolved for you by some of the things that were happening in Language Poetry?

MANSON I think I just have an aversion to Breton's squeamishness about an art that prioritises its material properties over its metaphorical payload. I was going to draw a contrast between two statements, one by André Breton, one by Stéphane Mallarmé, until I realised that I hadn't a clue where the statements came from . . . I'm not even sure the Mallarmé one is by Mallarmé, but they've been floating round my head long enough to have become part of the furniture:

The most sublime word we possess is the word 'like' (Breton).
'Like'—the very word should be struck from the language
  (Mallarmé).
If you're used to paying extremely close attention to the way language works as you move from word to word in a poem, anal-

ogy and metaphor start to look like incredibly lazy substitutes for transformation. Look closely enough at the words, and they don't just suggest other words, they actually *become* other words. There's a line by Johan de Wit, 'Wind sucks tunnel vacuum parts' where each of the words can be read as a verb, or not, as you choose. You get to the point where you can't decide where the material of the poem actually *is*—is it the exploded totality of all possible paths through the poem's syntax, or is it just the black curls on the page (taking us back to Bob Cobbing and soundtext performance).

I think what I came to through the influence of Coolidge and others wasn't orthodox Surrealism, but simply an openness to a not especially theorised version of the unconscious. I've never understood the desire to communicate through poetry—it just doesn't seem possible, given the infinite scope for interpretation of the finished work, and why on earth would you want to do it anyway, given that you're a reasonably articulate adult and know how to have a conversation, unless you don't like being contradicted and prefer to emote at a brick wall. 'No one listens to poetry', as Jack Spicer wrote. Ultimately, you're alone with the text, whether you're the writer or the reader, and as a writer the most interesting and addictive thing I can make the text do for me is to draw things out that I didn't know I had to say. I can only hope that the combination of unexpected statement and finely-measured openness gives the reader something good to play with too.

ALLEN The differences between Symbolism and Surrealism are complex so your pairing of the Breton and Mallarmé quotes is neat. I'm wondering if it is misleading though, particularly with regard to the gap between Mallarmé's poetry and the proliferation of less pure symbolist practices. It is also the case that the achievement of Mallarmé's supreme materialism of language was one of the things that Breton saw surrealism aspiring to. In the first half of the C20, to my knowledge, no poet from any avant garde talked about Language in the same way as we do today, yet Gertrude Stein and Zukofsky both pointed to those ways of exploring 'surface' that eventually changed the expectational textures of avant writers so that 'direct' and 'indirect' became functional conduits for each other, therefore, as you say, you can, 'make the text . . . draw things out that I didn't know I had to say'. But can I ask you why so many of these things you didn't know you wanted to say are so funny? The humour in your work was the first thing I noticed and I think in some review, somewhere, I referred to a piece of yours as being hyper-satire, or something—*Adjunct: an Undigest*, for example, which I've been listening to on your CD.

MANSON *Adjunct* is a book that tends to divide people: they either like it or they can't work out why they're being shown this thing. I started working on it in the early 90s, just as a way of recording particular bits of ambient language which appealed to me, but as time passed I found myself putting more and more of what was happening to me, and around me, into the book. I've always had a soft spot for language that manages to communicate something completely other than what its originator meant to say, and I think the way *Adjunct* was written (each entry was placed on a page determined by a random number table, so I never knew which sentences were going to end up next to one another) helped to multiply the absurdity. I think sometimes people see it as betraying the seriousness of my more formal poems, and certainly those are *worked* over in a way that *Adjunct* wasn't even slightly (though it was edited down rather carefully after I finished it). To me, the same processes are at work in both kinds of writing: the formal poetry is often built on found language and is full of deliberately distracting word-collocations which mess with the reader's attempt to parse the text. I'm really an almost completely facetious person, and I like the way *Adjunct* enabled me to draw everything that was happening to me up to and into the language surface. There's only so upset you can find something when it's resting next to the sentence 'Jobby by Hans Arp'. It's another form of the distraction we talked about earlier, a psychological trick, but it's probably saved my life on a number of occasions. Actually, the way I think of *Adjunct* now is that there comes a point in most poets' lives, I think, when they realise just how little of what makes them interesting as human beings finds its way into their work. You often find, somewhere, some anomalous blow-out work, whether driven by anger or love, where they just *let more in* than they usually do. Whenever I tend to be over-obsessive about minute details of language—which is usually—*Adjunct* is there as an example of what I might not be seeing for the trees. Whether or not I let more in than anyone needed to know is another question.

Bibliography

Peter Manson was born in Glasgow in 1969, where he still lives. His publications include:

iter atur e (London: Writers Forum, 1995).

me generation (London: Writers Forum, 1998).

Birth Windows (Cambridge: Barque Press, 1999).

Two renga (collaborations with Elizabeth James, in the Reality
    Street Editions four-pack 'Renga +') (London: Reality Street
    Editions, 2002).

Adjunct: an Undigest (Edinburgh Review. An audio CD of Peter
    Manson reading from *Adjunct* was released by Stem
    Recordings in 2004).

For the Good of Liars (Cambridge: Barque Press, 2005)

Before and After Mallarmé (translations, The Gig/daemon,
    forthcoming 2005).

With Robin Purves, he co-edited *Object Permanence* magazine (1994–1997). The imprint has more recently been revived as a publisher of booklets of new poetry. His website is *www.petermanson.com*

DAVID MILLER INTERVIEWED BY TIM ALLEN

Shuffling of Revelation and Occlusion

– Anastasis, they queried; the name of a goddess? False stories were put into play. Bicycling through the city, with his ears painted red.—I was seduced, seduced myself, into living through illusion.— What would that mean? I asked. I put little credence in the story that he buried some of his writings in a tin can in a corner of the schoolhouse. Sleeping under mounds of white netting strung over the bed. Night, the shadow of a tree on the pavement—leaves moving in wind. By his own admission: a painter of blue puddles. He wanted to learn ancient Greek so that after his death he could converse with Heraclitus, Socrates and Plato. Each page of the stolen thesis was retrieved from the river, then taken home and ironed. Lines and patterns of dots, in wax on cloth; colour in abeyance. Reflected: you and I together in your room, while you painted. Sitting on the sand near the quay, surrounded by geese. He asked us to look away when he rose from his sickbed and went to the bathroom. When we heard a knock we said: Come in; and the visitor who came in saw us sitting huddled together, our eyes still averted, and left without a word. A gathering-up of stray thoughts by a potlatch thinker, or so it was rumoured. Marble or limestone slab, doorjamb or lintel. Finger or eye tracing what remains, what's shown.

From: *Spiritual Letters (Series 2)*.

ALLEN David, I rate your work very highly, as you know. Whenever I am asked who my favourite poets are your name is always there, always in my top 10 so to speak. Yet your name means nothing to those poetry readers who do not engage with the various innovative and experimental scenes, especially in the UK, despite the fact that you have lived here since the 70s and have written a fair number of collections in that time. Bearing in mind the 'colour' of your work, its beautiful accessibility, how do you personally negotiate with that mainstream ignorance and neglect?

MILLER Actually, my name means nothing to many poetry readers who *do* engage with the innovative and experimental scenes. I don't think that this is a black and white situation, where the mainstream is set over against the innovative and experimental in any absolute way. I've occasionally had very good responses from more mainstream poets when I've read at 'mixed' readings, and I've had interest and support from innovative and experimental poets. I've also come across a great deal of ignorance or indifference—or downright hostility—from poets of either general tendency. You've probably noticed that my work has not been represented in any anthology in the UK, apart from *the new british poetry*, which Ken Edwards and others did back in 1988, and Tony Frazer's *A State of Independence* a decade later. (On the other hand, I've been in recent anthologies in the US and Austria.) We're obviously talking about very general categories here when we talk about the 'mainstream' and the 'experimental', and it's always worthwhile considering the variety of approaches within such categories. At the same time, there are some very sectarian attitudes firmly in place amongst many poets and poetry readers. There are ideas and expectations about poetry, involving literary allegiances and connections, both at the level of the writing itself and at the social level. This can range from the sort of writing your work connects with (whether Language Poetry, Cambridge School, etc.), the presses you publish with, the poets and critics you group yourself with socially, and so forth. Many writers are excluded from serious consideration on this sort of basis—for example, they don't fit in with dominant attitudes or aren't allied with the 'right' poets. If I belong anywhere, it's with various poets whose work is similarly 'outside', for example Paul Buck and Stephen Watts (to name two UK writers)—as different as our work is from each other's.

How do I deal with ignorance and neglect? I keep on writing and publishing and giving readings. I'm also active in running a reading series in London, Crossing the Line. (I run it in collaboration with two younger poets and friends, Sean Bonney and Jeff Hilson.) I form and maintain loyalties, based on respect and friendship—rather than in relation to dogma and reputation. In other words, I keep doing the things that are *really* important to me as a writer.

ALLEN You are quite right, of course, and I must admit I smiled broadly at your reminding me that the innovative and experimental world is itself rife with splits and prejudice. But, 'downright hostility', that's strong. What is it that you do, how could your writing be so different, to cause such a reaction? Is it something to do with what some people might call its spiritual qualities? Your work, it has always seemed to me, is also related to the French avant heritage, I've drawn parallels before between your material and that of Mallarmé for example. There is a quietism in your work which contrasts sharply with some areas of English innovation and maybe that 'beautiful accessibility' that I referred to has something to do with it, after all, there are those for whom both beauty and accessibility are anathema. And I hope you don't mind me calling your work accessible, I was not being ironic, your poems hit the spot directly and there is mystery in that.

MILLER I was very pleased by your reference to Mallarmé, though I would not have dreamed of drawing parallels between his work and my own. It's a great compliment, needless to say. More generally, I think that a comparison with French poets might come to mind because so much of my writing is what might be called poetry in prose. So many significant French (or French language) poets have written in prose, from Baudelaire and Rimbaud through Michaux to Jabès and so on. However, this would be to ignore the rich heritage of poetry in prose in English language writing, starting with Thomas De Quincey but also including precursors such as Thomas Traherne and John Donne and also the translators of the King James Bible. I think you know that Rupert Loydell and I edited an anthology of poetry in prose, *A Curious Architecture*. There are a number of poets in that book whose work I admire and relate to, in whatever different ways. I'll just mention a few: Robert Lax, Thomas A. Clark, Fanny Howe, Rosmarie Waldrop, Keith Waldrop, David Rattray, Ray Ragosta, Guy Birchard. . . .

I think you're right, that some people find the spiritual dimension to my writing anathema (others, I suspect, just think of it as a bizarre eccentricity!). Not that my work ignores the physical in any way. Tim Woods, in a long essay in *The Poet's Voice* a few years ago, referred to my 'spiritual materialist poetics'. I accept the paradox. You may also have been thinking of some of the poets who come out of Language Poetry, as admittedly my work is very different from theirs. But the two poets I was thinking of when I said that I'd encountered some downright hostility were reacting from a different perspective. Something I have no interest in—at least as far as my own writing is concerned—is elegance (of language, form, etc.). Elegance is clearly very important to the two poets I have in mind. But beauty and elegance are quite distinct, and if you find my work beautiful, obviously I'm pleased. At the same time, I think of Jack Spicer's remark to a young poet who told him his writing was beautiful: Okay, it's beautiful, but what does it *mean*? (That's from memory, by the way, and may not be exactly right.) Not that I'm accusing *you* of stressing beauty at the expense of meaning, of course!

ALLEN Ha, 'stressed beauty', and meaning can get pretty stressed too. Part of the problem here David is that I know beauty, by which I mean I am acquainted by experience with the string of notions that the word 'beauty' can vaguely represent, but I haven't a clue what 'meaning' means, not in this context. Do you actually want me to ask you what your work means? I think if I was asked in the pub, 'What does David Miller's work mean?', I would shout the drunken reply, 'It means the experience of the dream.' Dreams, of course, lack elegance but are often filled to bursting point by beauty. Dreams are lack too, and edge.

MILLER I don't really believe that you don't know the meaning of 'meaning'—you wouldn't be reading if you weren't in some way engaging with meaning—with interpretation and understanding. Otherwise you'd be staring blankly at indecipherable marks. At any rate, that would be the logical conclusion of the position you're invoking. I wouldn't want you to ask, What does David

Miller's work mean? But I would be happy with the idea of some-one asking themselves about the meaning of specific texts—in terms of a detailed rather than a general consideration, and in terms of *possibilities* rather than anything fixed or final. (I'm think-ing of the title of a book by a friend of mine from many years ago, the songwriter Sydney Carter—*Nothing Fixed or Final*.)

Dreams and dreaming—I've always liked your comment about 'the act of writing becoming a way of dreaming more fully' (which I think was in a review of my book *Tesserae*). Also, Tim Woods has emphasised the importance of dreams in my work (in the essay that I mentioned earlier). And Joel's mention of dreams together with visions and prophecies in relation to a pouring out of the spirit has always struck me (*Joel* 2:28). But as Tim Woods goes on to discuss, I am most interested in disclosure—which I would happily gloss with your remark about 'a continual shuffling of revelation and occlusion' (from that same review). I've written about this a good deal, especially in the essays that were collected as *Art and Disclosure*.

I guess I should go back at this point and say that when I talk about 'understanding', I mean an understanding that remains 'open' rather than a comprehension that seeks resolution, closure. I'd also want to say that writing can definitely exhaust or surpass interpretation and understanding—not just any single act of inter-pretation, but as a whole. However, my approach to this is by way of negative theology (especially Dionysius the Areopagite) rather than any materialist textual theory.

ALLEN Yes, in the *Art and Disclosure* essays you explore the topic, but mostly in relation to others' work, not your own. Could you say something about your choice of the prose poem as your habitual vehicle, though I look more upon your work as a form of poetic sequencing than as a conventional prose poem. And your poems that do look like poems, like familiar free verse, are not, are not free verse as such. There is a marvellous tension built into them by the highly formal quality in symbiosis with a relaxed prose.

MILLER That's true, the essays in *Art and Disclosure* are about writers and artists I admire, although 'The End of the Kingdom of Necessity, Servitude and Inertia' gives an indication of my own concerns. I've talked or written about my own work in a few places, including the interviews with Andrew Bick and James Crouch in *At the Heart of Things* and a piece called 'Concerning *Spiritual Letters*' in a recent issue of *Poetry Salzburg Review* (no. 4, 2003).

South London Mix, which is mainly in prose, was a sort of 'break-through' for me. I wrote that in 1973, and it still feels relevant in many ways to what I do now. Oddly enough, I concentrated on poetry in lines (to get away from the expression 'free verse') for some years after that, and then wrote both in lines and in prose. The prose took over eventually, although I still write the occasional poem in lines and also incorporate poetry in lines into my prose texts. I don't really have a problem with the term 'free verse', to be honest—to me, it just means that one is avoiding conventional (metrical) forms. It's somewhat similar to the term 'free jazz', which just means that one is avoiding, e.g., conventional (harmonic) structures or chord progressions as the basis for improvisation. I agree with you about the need for some sort of tension in poetry. However, I think that when I write in lines I'm really writing something that's quite different from prose, e.g., the language is more spare and compressed, the rhythms tend to be more pronounced, the movement through the text is very differ-ent (especially because of the line breaks), and so forth. Why do I write in prose? I like the idea of achieving a very real integrity while also incorporating variety, range, discontinuity, etc., and I find I can do this much more in prose.

ALLEN For me, now, so-called free verse is one of the strictest and most model orientated ways of writing poetry, but with the added prob-lem that the writer imagines they are being free, which can lead to a certain degree of bad faith, in the existential sense. That was one of the reasons why I moved towards examples of avant formalism, the search for what I can only call 'honesty', and which you seem to be calling 'integrity'. Can you say more about this? How can one way of writing have 'real integrity'? Is it something to do with engaging with variety, range and discontinuity without homoge-neous pretence while yet aiming for an aesthetic homogeneity?

MILLER I'm afraid I misled you when I used the word 'integrity'. I meant it in the sense of 'entireness, wholeness' (*Chambers Dictionary*). Yet as you know, I work a good deal with the fragmentary and discon-tinuous, so there's a tension there—one that I hope is fruitful. Do

I believe in integrity in the other sense, in relation to writing? Sure, I believe in keeping vigilant with regard to what I'm doing. I also believe in the idea of an ethical poetry (in the sense of an ethical vision of things that's realised in the language of the writing, rather than in the sense of trying to put forward a particular moral code).

I've never been interested in writing in conventional forms (such as the sonnet), though I don't have a problem with others doing this, especially when they re-envision these forms. I'm interested in bringing certain structural determinants and notions into my writing, as part of the compositional process. (This is something that I discuss in the essay 'Interrelation, Symbiosis, Overlap' in *Art and Disclosure*.) You can see this in poems such as 'Focus' and 'Devotion' and in some of my prose, especially *Spiritual Letters*. However, the determinants are in my case very simple and scarcely very constraining. In fact, they hopefully give a sense of structure but they also *enable* me to do certain things. I'd rather not give examples (although I seem to recall that I was guilty of doing so somewhere in print). But I also should say that I've written—and still write, at times—without any specific guiding lines at all. I don't feel that there's any need to be rigid or dogmatic about these things.

ALLEN Recently Singing Horse Press, from Philadelphia, published *The Waters of Marah—Selected Prose 1973–1995*, [published in the UK by Shearsman 2005] a beautiful book in every respect. The large format gives the work room to breathe, which I think suits it very well. Was the large format your decision? Are you pleased with it? And could you say something about the choices you had to make when selecting?

MILLER I'm very pleased that you like the book. I can't take any credit for how it looks (apart from the cover image, which is by my painter friend Derek Sprawson and which I chose). The publisher, Gil Ott, was responsible for the design. I really didn't know that it would look the way it does until I received the book in the post! I think Gil did a wonderful job.

That book incorporates what I consider the best of my poetry in prose through to early 1995. I stopped at that point because there were a handful of uncollected prose pieces from later in 1995 I wanted to publish elsewhere. Also, *The Waters of Marah* doesn't include anything from the *Spiritual Letters* project, which I began in late 1995 and which I felt belongs in a separate space. However, it does include a longish piece of poetic fiction—I'm not sure how else to characterise it—called 'Tesserae'. (It's 27 pages in Gil's layout. 'Longish' by my standards, at any rate!)

ALLEN What is 'poetic fiction'? I ask because I've been reading Barbara Guest's *Forces of Imagination* in which one of the little essays, 'Poetry the True Fiction', eloquently equates poetry with fiction, and it kind of matches my own sense, a sense which I often attempt to deny both in practise and theoretically, that poetry is intrinsically about that which is not factual. The romanticism of the notion appals me, but I think I have found that it is in fact the basis of my own poetic realism; it implies being straight with oneself and as such the contradictions inherent in this 'unreal thing which exists' become more addictive and fascinating, not less. I also think it is to do with the unravelling of patterns, language pattern, structural shape-shifting, and one of the methods to accomplish that is narrative, or the feeling of there being a narrative, even if we are only experiencing it as a slice. Is this why *Tesserae* appeals to me so much? Here you are David, I am asking you to understand your reader.

MILLER I'm not sure if either 'factual' or 'fictional' is adequate to a process and form of writing that is more complexly concerned with exploration and disclosure. Much of my writing draws on my own experiences—to some extent, at least—yet I don't think of it as simply autobiographical. There's an uncovering, a bringing-to-light, which is basic to what I'm doing and which allies me with my mentor as a writer, Robert Lax. 'To produce is to draw forth, to invent is to find, to shape is to discover. In bodying forth I disclose.' (Martin Buber, *I and Thou*.) My reason for speaking about 'fiction' was really that I was concerned with fairly developed and sustained narratives in some works such as 'Tesserae', whereas other writings may use narrative elements but in a much more fragmentary way. At the same, 'Tesserae' is poetic in its compression, its arrangement of words, and so forth.

ALLEN The sense I get when reading nearly all your work, whatever form it takes, is essentially one of unfolding calm surprise. Mystery becomes matter-of-fact and yet gains more resonance. Places, people, things, they all become vehicles of instant alienation and illumination, as though loss and discovery were basically the same creature. How conscious are you of that?

MILLER I wouldn't have thought to put it that way, but it sounds fairly accurate. I'd certainly see loss and discovery as related to each other, in certain contexts, if not perhaps as 'the same creature'. Where there's a suspension or even dismantling of familiar relationships, an uncovering of something 'other' can occur—even if one might be working with entirely everyday material.

ALLEN Could you tell me something about the scene you are involved in in London, the reading series you've been putting on etc. Have they thrown up any interesting new-comers?

MILLER I'm not sure I'd say that I was involved in any scene. I'm friendly with certain poets, both in London and in other places, but that's about as far as it goes. I *am* involved in running a monthly reading series, Crossing the Line, at the Poetry Café in Covent Garden, as I said before. Jeff Hilson and Sean Bonney and I starting doing it three years ago, in July 2001, following a number of discussions about poetry readings in London. We bemoaned the fact that various poets whose work we respected didn't get asked to read very often. We felt that for the most part other reading series weren't all that adventurous in bringing different kinds of poetry together. We also felt that apart from one notable exception, other series at that time didn't tend to encourage more 'experimental' poetry. Lastly, we wanted to create a series that had a congenial atmosphere, where poets and poetry readers could get to know each other. We've definitely had some very good poets read for us who are either newer or not so well known, including Jules Mann, Sharon Morris, David Menzies, Richard Leigh, John Gibbens, Doug Jones, Chris McCabe, Alyson Torns and Valeria Melchioretto. But what the series has mainly done is to richly confirm my feeling that there is a diversity of exciting and singular poets working in the UK. If I mention some of the poets who have read in Crossing the Line, it will hopefully give an idea of the range involved. (This is almost at random—I realise I'm not mentioning a number of excellent poets who have appeared.) Lee Harwood, Thomas A.

Clark, Allen Fisher, Stephen Watts, John Rety, Paul Buck, Johan de Wit, Tilla Brading, Martin Anderson, Frances Presley, Alan Halsey, Alfred Celestine, Ken Edwards, Mike Weller, Andrew Duncan, Keith Jebb, Elizabeth James, Simon Smith. I'd also like to mention one poet in the series who was also very active as a magazine editor and small press publisher and who recently died: Ian Robinson. We've also had some wonderful US (or US-based) poets read, including Fanny Howe, Michael Heller, William Cirocco, and Simon Pettet.

ALLEN The only name I know in your list of 'new' poets is David Menzies, and that is healthy. Sometimes of course running a reading series is just one step away from publishing people—have you ever considered going down that road? You mentioned Ian Robinson, who of course was known for both his poetry/drawings and his publishing work with Oasis, a magazine that many of us owe a personal debt to in terms of the support it gave us.

MILLER David is one of the 'not so well known' rather than 'new' poets, really. But it's interesting that you know his work—and also that you haven't come across the others! As to running a press, I've actually been publishing Kater Murr's Press since 1998. It's a really tiny publishing venture—I guess what might be called a micro-press! I started with a series of poem cards, and in collaboration with my friend George Touloupas I moved on to folded cards of writing and visual work. We also maintain a web site (http://home.freeuk.net/katermurr). Jaime de Angulo, Robert Lax, William Cirocco, Guy Birchard, Elizabeth Robinson, David Menzies, Sharon Morris, Alyson Torns, Peter Money, Natalie d'Arbeloff, Gad Hollander, John Levy, Michael Thorp, Jeff Hilson and John Gibbens are some of the people I (or we) have published. Thinking of the dual roles of writing and editing/publishing—I should mention Gael Turnbull, who died only days ago. Gael was at his best an extraordinary poet, and his work with *Migrant* magazine and Migrant Press simply inestimable. He made American poets such as Creeley, Olson, Dorn and Duncan available in the UK when they were otherwise unknown or extremely little known. He was also responsible for bringing Basil Bunting to the attention of Stuart Montgomery (of Fulcrum Press), thus helping to make Bunting's work visible. Gael was a modest and generous person, and completely the opposite of a 'careerist'. I was talking with the poet Richard Price about Gael only today—we both agreed that he hasn't had anything like his due. I think he was an exemplary figure, both in his own poetry and (if you like) in his service to poetry.

ALLEN Yes, a lot of poets have died over the past year, but let me bring that subject of mortality into the question of transience and legacy, at least with the poetry being written now that thrills us. How do you think it compares with previous good poetry, whether of 50 years ago or 500 years ago? And do you have any ideas about what will happen to poetry over the next century? Is it important? Do you care?

MILLER There's a story about the painter Barnett Newman shifting a conversation about some of his contemporaries to a different level with the comment, I thought we were arguing with Michelangelo (or words to that effect). I certainly think it's a good thing to get a different perspective by looking at what's been done in the past rather than just referring to what's being done now. I guess my own instinct is to see what I can learn from the past, also what I can aspire to, though not in the sense of seeking to reproduce what's already been done (which strikes me as pointless). But I'm not sure how to go about making evaluative comparisons—in the sense of trying to decide if anyone writing now is on the poetic level of Donne or Keats or Hopkins. Of course I do make evaluations about my contemporaries, but at the same time I think I'm too close to some writers, and too distant from others. I do think that there are poets writing now whose work deserves to last. There are poems by Lee Harwood and Thomas A. Clark, for example, that I wouldn't hesitate about mentioning in such a context. What will happen to poetry in the future? If you mean how is it likely to develop, I wouldn't even hazard a guess. One of the things I love most about poetry is how surprising certain developments are. Who could have predicted what Sean Bonney is writing, or Jeff Hilson's work? I couldn't have. I'm not sure anyone could have. I think that poetry will continue to be written, as long as there are human beings on this planet. And yes, I do think it's important, I do care, otherwise I wouldn't be involved in writing poetry, I wouldn't be running a reading series or helping to get other poets published.

ALLEN I asked if you cared because, speaking for myself, sometimes I care and sometimes I do not; sometimes poetry seems to be a very small thing to me, hardly comparable to other marvels of life on Earth such as birds and bees. When I do care it is a strange type of care, more akin to curiosity. At a meeting once I was asked why I wrote poetry and my answer was, 'out of habit'. The others found it shocking and didn't really believe me, as I make it plainly obvious every single day that poetry is of great importance in my life and probably will go on doing so. But I have trouble transferring the 'value' of that to the world outside myself, a world that has many uses for poetry, many of which do not interest me. I suppose what I am trying to ask you is why you care about the future health of poetry. A listing of things we do that are associated with it, such as writing it and promoting it etc, does not throw light on the inner drive.

MILLER I suspect that there are times when we all wonder why we're involved with poetry. In my case, it's either when my own work isn't going well, or when I go to a poetry reading or pick up a book of poems and the work is mediocre, boring, lifeless. But there are also times when your own work is developing in ways that are exciting, surprising and rewarding. And there are the times when you've been amazed, delighted, moved or provoked by the poetry you've heard or read. I'm not speaking of poetry as mere entertainment. Rather, I'd like to speak of its capacity to embody or reveal or disclose what otherwise remains hidden. (That formulation is from Mircea Eliade, if I remember correctly, though Paul Ricœur says something very similar.)

I do think that poetry can provide a form of support, for the poet and for the person who reads poetry. The Spanish artist and poet Pepe Espaliú said, 'My work is the evidence of what makes my existence bearable, and in that sense maintains it.' I find his statement very interesting, though my own tendency is to think about writing as bringing something into existence, and I'd put the emphasis on that 'something' rather on its relation to my own life. But I'd also want to add that what I'm doing when I write is 'for the sake of what remains invisible in the showing-forth', as I say in one of the 'Spiritual Letters'. That's not being cryptic—or not intentionally so; it's just a way of referring you back to the poetry itself.

An extreme example of how poetry might be thought of as providing sustenance can be found in Anthony Rudolf's recent essay, 'Rescue Work: Memory and Text'. Tony Rudolf cites cases where prisoners in concentration camps remembered and recited poetry as a crucial part of staying alive. But we are obviously not thinking of poetry as mere aesthetic frippery or confectionery when we give an example like this.

In a recent letter, the Canadian poet Guy Birchard said that he found the writing in my book *Spiritual Letters (I–II)* 'striking, nourishing and provoking'. I especially like the conjunction of the words 'nourishing' and 'provoking'. This really brings me closer to my own experience of poetry. Poetry can enhance or open up, disrupt or overturn, what we think, feel or sense about things. It may be unfashionable to say this, but I think that poetry, like art and music, can have a very powerful effect within our lives. Unfortunately that's not true of a great deal of the poetry being written and published, I'd have to add.

Bibliography

Spiritual Letters (I–II) and other writings. (Hastings: Reality Street Editions, 2004).

The Waters of Marah: Selected Prose 1973–1995. (Philadelphia: Singing Horse Press, 2003).

Music while drowning: German Expressionist Poems, ed. with Stephen Watts (London: Tate Publishing, 2003).

Spiritual Letters (Series 2, #1–5), with artwork by Denis Mizzi. (Sydney: Nyxpress, 2001).

Dark Ground (Bray, Co. Wicklow: Wild Honey Press, 2000).

Commentaries (II). (Port Charlotte, Florida: Runaway Spoon Press, 2000).

Commentaries. (Charleston, Illinois: Tel-let, 1999).

Spiritual Letters (1–12). (San Francisco: hawkhaven press, 1999).

The ABCs of Robert Lax, ed. with Nicholas Zurbrugg. (Exeter: Stride Publications, 1999).

Art and Disclosure: Seven Essays. (Exeter: Stride Publications, 1998).

Appearance & Event (Providence: paradigm press, 1997).

Collected Poems (Salzburg: University of Salzburg Press, 1997).

A Curious Architecture: A Selection of Contemporary Prose Poems, ed.
    with Rupert Loydell (Exeter: Stride Publications, 1996).
Elegy (London: Oasis Books, 1996).
Stromata (Providence: Burning Deck Press, 1995).
Tesserae (Stride, 1993).
True Points (Peterborough: Spectacular Diseases Press, 1992).
Pictures of Mercy: Selected Poems, with artwork by Graham Gussin
    (Exeter: Stride Publications, 1991).
W. H. Hudson and the Elusive Paradise (London and New York:
    Macmillan and St. Martin's Press, 1990).
Darkness Enfolding: Eight Stories (Exeter: Stride Publications, 1989).
Losing to Compassion (Kyoto: Origin Press, 1985).
Out of this World (Peterborough: Spectacular Diseases Press, 1984).
Unity (Blue Bell, Pennsylvania: Singing Horse Press, 1981).
Primavera (Providence: Burning Deck Press, 1979).
The Story (Todmorden: Arc Publications, 1976).
Malcolm Lowry and the Voyage that Never Ends (London: Enitharmon
    Press, 1976).
South London Mix (London: Gaberbocchus Press, 1975).
The Caryatids (London: Enitharmon Press, 1975).

ERIC MOTTRAM INTERVIEWED BY STEVE PEREIRA

Egoism Vanished in the Act

PEREIRA Did you start writing poetry with a sense of an authority that had to be responded to?

MOTTRAM Not at all. But naturally a beginner unconsciously works from poetry he admires.

PEREIRA Did you respond to any educational authorities at school?

MOTTRAM I can remember teachers at school telling us to write poems about what we did on our holidays, that sort of thing; but I really was not interested in writing poetry at that time, and not whole-heartedly interested in literature. After that age—when one starts to become somebody—I became much more interested in economic and political history. At my second secondary school, from the age of fourteen, I began to learn about real political history —the history of the Trade Union movement, the Labour movement, and so forth; this really made me think. It was during the war, of course. The senior English master had in fact gone off to fight, and the sixth form had a young female teacher straight from Manchester University, and she certainly started to interest me in English literature, and such Americans as Pound and Eliot— which were in the sixth form library. By this time I was about sixteen or seventeen. Poetry could be interesting, we discovered. Up to that time I thought it was Shakespeare and such things you had to be good at. Now literature began to be intriguing—mainly because there was history and philosophy in it. I think that then, as now, there was a division in the educational system between what was easily teachable, and assimilable with the Sunday newspapers, without much training or intelligence, and what was not—that needed special training. Many people are attracted to poetry, not because it is metrical and rhymes and so on, but because it articulates anxieties and broad ideas. Teachers are not aware that you might be attracted to poetry because it is beginning to articulate things for you at your young manhood level. That's where it starts—it seems to be pointless to teach poetry before the age of fifteen or sixteen.

PEREIRA So you started to write poetry when you left school?

MOTTRAM After I left school I went into the Royal Navy for four years, and the idea of writing poems in that kind of life was impossible. Roy Fuller may have been in the RAF in South Africa and writing his major works—whatever else he was doing, he wouldn't have been preoccupied with fighting in a war! Then I went up to Cambridge at the rather late age of 22/23, and found I had a lot of catching up—a lot of living to do, after being a mine-sweeper officer with a status and a status in a job—and it did seem I didn't have the time. For various reasons I was not interested in writing poetry. What passed for poetry in the early fifties seemed to me worthless, apart from some of Dylan Thomas. The Movement did not and does not seem to be worth the paper it is printed on: the poetics are boring, the subject-matter egotistical, smug and slightly repulsive. If that was what current poetry had to be like, I wasn't interested. But since I obtained my scholarships to Cambridge largely through working at economic and social history,—and I had read Mumford's *Technics and Civilisation* at school, and Wilson's *To the Finland Station*—I had become interested in cultures, and literature, including poetry, *in* those cultures. The creative side did not yet concern me very much. But suddenly American prose and poetry entered. My first university job was at Zurich University, and the professor in charge, Heinrich Straumann, had a small department library of American literature, and his introductory lectures on American literature from the early seventeenth century onwards absolutely intrigued me—I've still got the notes. In a bookshop in the Bahnhofstrasse I discovered things like the Portable series of American writers, and so on. So when I went back to Cambridge for a year I was ready to give a talk on Paul Bowles, and also borrowed *The Portable Faulkner* from a visiting American student. While at the University of Malaya I taught American literature for the first time, and had a stab at writing poetry myself—a little; two short poems were published. I will not say where; they are appalling. At the University of Groningen I really got down to studying American writing and taught a good deal of it—in fact, I must have been the first to actually teach the new Americans associated with City Lights and the *Evergreen Review*—Ginsberg, Ferlinghetti, Corso, and so on, and used that record that came out with the San Francisco Renaissance issue of *Evergreen Review*. And also told the kids about Burroughs—Girodias had published *The Naked Lunch* in 1957. But it was not until I went to America for the first time in 1960 that I actually bought a good deal of American work—I bought Donald Allen's *The New American Poetry* actually in Ferlinghetti's City Lights shop, and met Lawrence, and through him met Ted Wilentz at the Eighth Street Bookshop in New York—and through Ted met the new American poets—it was all a continual revelation. But it was still not until after I had joined King's College here at the University of London that I went for a year to live in New York, in 1965 as a fellow of the American Council of Learned Societies—a year off with money—that I really got to know some American poets. I also wrote my part of the *Penguin Companion to American Literature* there. The American poets sort of took me up, and we went to readings—I remember intensely one night Ted Berrigan coming to my flat to take me up to hear John Ashbery reading at the Free University on 14th Street—things like that. Then there was an implication that I too was writing poetry—embarrassing at first because I wasn't. I guess the atmosphere and the encouragement must have worked, because I began.

PEREIRA So the impulse to write came from an involvement with literature?

MOTTRAM Involvement with poets. Which is a different matter. I met Paul Blackburn, Ted Berrigan, Joel Oppenheimer, Carol Berge, Muriel Rukeyser ... Ginsberg I had met already in 1960—and so forth. In the summer of 1966 I took up an appointment at State University of New York at Buffalo. Another turning point. The poet and teacher Jack Clarke who had taken over the Institute of Further Studies from Olson was appalled to hear how little I knew about his teacher. He sat me down in his office one day and played me tapes of Olson including the reading at Berkeley, and I was astounded. I had really only read *The Distances*. Then I bought *Human Universe* and so on. Once again it was a matter of: who were these poets? I was having a sense of living human beings, highly intelligent, working at their art, complex and passionate people. I had never had such a contact and so continuously. And even though Olson was dead by then, there were the tapes and photographs, and he was therefore alive to me. And my next-door neighbour, also visiting professor at Buffalo, was Bunting. I saw him thereafter every day, lunch, dinner and evening talks, hearing him give the first performance of *Briggflatts*. More learned.

PEREIRA If you hadn't become involved with these poets, would you have written?

MOTTRAM That I don't know of course. All I am saying is that they were certainly instigatory. Through Ted Berrigan calling and saying let's go up to the Free University and see Ashbery, I met Ashbery. I was learning you see. There was this sense of the presence of the poets rather than printed texts. And the poetry readings were a scene of people there, in front of us, with their voices and their bodies, their care of delivery, and the audience around them listening like hell. Just living in downtown New York—the lower West Side—and having this experience regularly was extraordinary. That seemed to do it —for better or worse!

PEREIRA Let's go to the actual process of writing. How do you come to the sources for your writing?

MOTTRAM There's a huge range. Everything—that's the quick answer.

PEREIRA Do you feel these sources are given by your culture or discovered despite it?

MOTTRAM *Interrogation Rooms* and *The Legal Poems* were written in radical opposition to what passed for culture officially in this country. The answer there would be: yes, the sources are given from the society, but I am opposing it drastically. But it may all be grist to the mill if you're honest—if you're dishonest then you write poems because you think they'll be liked by the poetry Establishment, the Arts Council toadies, the present Poetry Society, or what people like Amis and Larkin will like, and the mob of poetasters who publish each other in the capitalist publishing houses—and what the school teachers and university departments hacks will 'teach'. That's another matter altogether: for them poetry becomes a source of belonging to a sort of monstrous club in which poets do it for money and fame. Writing becomes fashionable and despicable as well as enfeebled.

PEREIRA Orwell said there are four main reasons for writing: sheer egoism, aesthetic enthusiasm, historical impulse and political purpose. Do you agree with this?

MOTTRAM It seems to me that good art does have a purpose; trying hard to be good at it is a major social function. The range of purposes included the political. As for aesthetics, my feeling is that the act of making something which is your own, and not just an imitation, you'd better learn poetics as part of your tools of trade, just as a carpenter can make a table only if he knows a chisel from a saw and knows how to use them. Egoism vanishes in the act—unless you are one of these confessional poets crazy about their own little lives, their suicidalisms, their booziness, their anxieties to come as poets. I don't think I know what 'historical impulse' means.

PEREIRA Do you recognize constant or recurring procedures in your work?

MOTTRAM Yes, and then try to stop them.

PEREIRA To what extent do your procedures make allowance for personal and chance interventions?

MOTTRAM I don't know what I'd do without them, for that's part of the excitement. Once the creative act gets going there are no accidents—to steal from statements by both Charles Ives and Charles Mingus. By chance I take it you mean random—I've never been into statistics and the kind of actions Jackson Mac Low is so brilliant with in books like *Stanzas for Iris Lezak*.

PEREIRA How aware are you before you start the creative act what the finished product is going to be?

MOTTRAM It varies quite a bit. Not very much actually, on the whole. Something very definite may begin the process, and the surprises come thick and fast. Hopefully. In one of my collections-in-progress, *Peace Projects*, the actions are partly generated from a renewed interest in Sufi recitals—I first became drawn to this, like many other people, through Olson's use of Henry Corbin's writings on Sufic procedures—in this case the idea of a religious-philosophical recital which is like a narrative of events that build towards some kind of subject—the object of the recital—of the poem, I hope. It's called a recital: they know to a certain extent what they're going to do but they don't know the completed form. There is no fixed form, but they want a space in which events can be put, as a container which does not contain too rigidly—a structure that doesn't harness too tightly. This appeals to me. The poem would be processual without being over-planned. When the poem is performed I could choose places I need off the page, so that the act of reading would be creative in itself. I tried other related methods in *Pollock Record* and *Precipice of Fishes*: to let the relatively unexpected into the performance at least. If I was better at it, and perhaps more courageous or less nervous, I would like to invent things on the spot. But I can't—so far. I admire improvisation intensely when it isn't simply, as it so often is, mere repetition by some lazy performer.

PEREIRA How concerned are you that your writing should in some way engage with non-verbal realities?

MOTTRAM Well, it always is—I'm not concerned with it: it just is. For instance, it's what I meant earlier by political. I guess what I'm often trying to do is engage in various acts of criticism of society—while also trying to find out what positives can be held to—I mean, find out scenes and people and objects to admire. To criticize oneself, and try to find things to approve of too! *The Elegies* are not poems for the dead, it speaks of celebrations—celebrations of people I admire intensely. Whereas *Interrogation Rooms*—a very difficult book to perform I'd better add —deals with matters that are repulsive or dangerous or cruel, or threatening in some way.

I'm not really the sort of poet who needs or wants to write about his private life and say 'I' all the time. I'm more concerned in me making the poem, getting the energies in control for excitement, making the social event, the poem, and of course, on rare occasions performing it. As a book is a social event, and in that way a political event. I think that anyone who has grown up since 1946 is into that in some way or another —or rather, let me be pompous and say that they *should* be! I must admit I'm not much interested in those who aren't. And in case that sounds dogmatic I'd better say that I admire Thomas A Clark's poetry immensely. Can I say that the twenty-two issues of *Poetry Review* that I edited show the biases—plural not singular. I admire those poets—I think there were something like 121 of them—for many differing reasons. Most of them were not much, if at all, published by the capitalist press mob. Most of them represented the sheer difficulty of good poetry to be published in this country other than by the so-called 'small presses'—meaning private, independent presses with not very large circulations. We do have though a community of poets: poets of intense loyalty to each other and their presses and magazines, working and publishing and performing apart from the cartel of big presses and their reviewers, for which they care little, which hardly knows of their existence, and prefers the conventional and second-rate.

PEREIRA Why do you feel the mainstream wants to exclude these poets?

MOTTRAM There are a lot of reasons —and of course it is not a matter of 'mainstream' at all, only a self-constituted preponderance. One reason may be, is a realization unconscious or not—that these alternative poets to their persistent 'mainstream' idea, know their place —their inventive imagination and the range of its productions—in relationship to twentieth-century poetics since Rimbaud, particularly French and American poetics. That is, they are not just content simply to imitate and slightly shift Victorian and Edwardian British poetics. The mainstreamers can't let go of their allegiance to the fag-end of the Victorian and Edwardian, their desperate need not to advance beyond Thomas Hardy, Edward Thomas and Robert Frost. Add a bit of Robert Lowell's borrowings from William Carlos Williams and you have the limits of the Movement poetry's poetics. They don't care to invent anything further. When you consider the range of poetics in this country, in Germany, in France, and in America, and then look at what wins prizes, gets into the *New Statesman*'s back pages, and is published by the big presses, it's clear that the boss-poets don't care to be in the twentieth century. It's like Larkin cockily believing that jazz stopped about 1925, 1930 at the latest—I guess his poetry stopped about 1915!

PEREIRA One of the arguments of the Movement was that it was a more accessible and public poetry and that the radical poets are difficult, and concerned with art for art's sake. You said in your interview with Allen Fisher ('Necessary Business', *Spanner* 25, 1985) that you are not interested in those who haven't read Pound—what do you say to someone like myself who hasn't really read Pound—am I missing out on areas of your work?

MOTTRAM No. In any case, Pound's poetry, translations and prose constitute a master-body of work which it seems to me daft to refuse. What I meant, speaking with Allen, was that not to read Pound argues a lack of interest in fundamentals of literature. As for my own work—and I certainly don't want to accept your trap of comparison or some such weakness—if people have paid for a book or paid to listen to a reading they are interested, make up their own minds, and in many cases known to me share admirations and kindred reading of poetry and much else. That community I spoke of just now extends to our readers. You write, try to get published, try to perform well to people who expect an occasion— in a word, try not to let down, and to encourage people who have an interest in your work—are prepared to talk about it—it's an open situation. No compulsions.

PEREIRA What about those people who are unable to talk with you about your work?

MOTTRAM Well, I can't know, can I? I must say I've had some pleasant surprises when reading up and down the country—encountering people who *have* the stuff—a few!

PEREIRA Do you feel there's a problem there, not only in your work but in other radical poets' work, where the public does not have available writing about the work?

MOTTRAM Yes, I think there is a bit of a problem. And to begin at the beginning much of the time the poetry is not available to even a potential readership. Booksellers won't take the books or the magazines. We take our work to readings, for sale, and hope for the best. Or rely on events like the Association of Little Presses bookfair. I suppose one ought to say that acts of deliberate suppression go on all the time — the Arts Council exerts considerable power over who reads for money and where, and whose work obtains their distribution facilities — they organise poets in residence, they hand out money, they subsidise and are answerable to none but themselves — the destruction of the twentieth-century form of the Poetry Society in 1976 is sufficiently notorious to need no comment here. And we'd better add that the smaller commercial publishers with otherwise interesting and enterprising lists are terrified of taking risks with poetry.

PEREIRA To get back to that other question: if a reader or member of the general public saw your work and hadn't read Pound and you weren't available to discuss it how difficult would —

MOTTRAM 'General public' is a phrase used to suggest mass power; and this fictional 'reader' — who is he or she? All I can say about this unknown, untrained, inexperienced fictive figure — this public reader — is: it's like going to a sports event whose rules and regulations you don't or do know. If you don't know then you don't go around abusing the event or lamenting: This isn't for me — I don't understand it — in aggressive or mournful tones. You either take the trouble of learning the procedures, or stay clear. Not to do so, and attack, is just bloody arrogance.

PEREIRA So you feel if the public want to understand your work they should come at it with the same amount of —

MOTTRAM Training: as they would to any other event or art or sport or whatever.

Whatever this public is — sounds like a Tory politician claiming that 'the public' is being attacked by the Unions! If people wish to engage in anything, want to understand something, they will — the amount of time, energy and money spent on dog-racing or the soccer racket or ocean-going yachting is enormous. But British cultural controllers and educationalists mostly do not encourage people to think of the arts as other than casual entertainment, something of little other value. And whose fault is that? but it is a disgrace for a culture to undervalue the crucial bases other than science.

PEREIRA How concerned are you that your writing may or does assume an authority that has to be responded to?

MOTTRAM By whom?

PEREIRA By the reader.

MOTTRAM That vague figure again! let's get rid of that nonsensical term for a moment. Let's think about reading processes. For millions the daily press is authority, and the mindless scansion of the crap known as the daily newspaper, *The Sun* and the rest is given endless time and energy. Voluntary brainwashing. But then some of us have been badly taught by authoritarian teachers at school; that the printed book text is sacred—their sacred precincts of literature. I expect some people would like it to be like that still, given the problems of getting kids to read books at all in some areas. But one of the things that post-structuralist writers have usefully helped us to learn is that no text is an authoritative area, a centre. You have an act of learning—kinds of acts of learning: how to read *this* book, and then *this* one. The text trains you, but you train it. When you give a poetry reading you enter a different occasion of authority—it is not The Book, not an authoritarian event, not a political tract, a philosophical dogma, a theological directive. It's not a lecture I'd better add!—but you are inviting people to listen to you and not to intervene until its conclusion. The exchange is implicit and then explicit, if you like. The difference to text or the book is that the presence of the writer is an additional control which changes the situation. You have his voice, appearance, gestures. The occasion of the Book is that no-one else reads it with you—you can put it down, throw it away—equally you can carry it with you, read it on top of a bus. And there is a third occasion through cassettes and videos. So there are different kinds of literature occasion which the poet, for example, is asking his reader-performer or hearer to lend his

attention to. It's probably more of a gift situation than a payment—
but that's a whole other matter. Now my sense is that, unless you
are still hooked on subservience to the Book these situations have
nothing to do with the authoritarian personality as such. Except,
of course, if the poet comes on as an authoritarian—which is
probably rare. We do hear of certain official poets who arrive late,
appear in a shamble, read rapidly and briefly, take the large fee
and drive off. The issue you raise is an important one therefore:
what does one expect of a poet? What you expect is a particular —
a particular occasion, perhaps, the fulfilment of a particular
expectation. And if the poet does not come on with sufficient
authority as a poet you will be disappointed. I mean he should be
presenting himself as performer of his poems in a way which is
somehow interesting and exciting. But there is no point in attend-
ing to an artist of any serious kind unless you meet his require-
ments—that's where training and engagement in the event enter.
I don't believe in some false democratization of the arts at all—
the populist notion that the artist's job is to show everything as
easily as possible to a half dumb audience. Or the attitude that
only if the poem is teachable easily is it good. That's the populist
and teacher authoritarianism, if you're going to discuss author-
ity. Any artist worth his salt will be presenting the audience with
something they've not come across before. That is the kind of
authority to respect and the most exciting authority I know. I'll
sit quiet and pay attention if that is what is going on—because I
dearly want to know. This is one of the great events in our lives —
an artist is inviting us to a creative performance; we are in the
presence of the creative — the highest human ability, potentially.
If you don't pay attention, come with the training at least, you
miss it. You've missed one of the most exciting things in human
life, and one of the main generators of value and meaning.

PEREIRA Barthes says that the real is not representable, and it's because
men ceaselessly try to represent it by words that there's a history
of literature. Are you conscious of that tension in your work?

MOTTRAM I don't think that the arts are representational: all that
Platonic and mediaeval bullshit about holding a mirror up to
nature, which you still find ignorant holding to, is pretty ludi-
crous. I mean the idea that everything you look at in art is a

reverse image of reality is nonsense. People still get irritated and worried that Schoenberg's main works don't represent a priori states of emotion and so on. But who said music is supposed to represent something you can recognise immediately—half the time, that's just arrogance—more authoritarianism. Such people just want to insist that they must be able to say: yes, I know what's going on in that work—and be comforted by that familiarity. What Harold Rosenberg called 'the tradition of the new' is what interests me—the poem may in fact be dramatising, organising with means and material which you have not experienced, or partly. The arrogance of expecting the artists to be reflections of yourself and your own limited experience seems to me—to use the word again—appalling. The next stage is refusing to read or publish anything but the authorised poem —and we have long ago reached that. The conservative let loose soon becomes fascist.

PEREIRA You don't agree that one of the poet's functions is to speak for those who are unable to articulate their views of the world?

MOTTRAM No I don't. Most people do articulate their 'views of the world', or accept the daily press's articulations, or their church's, or some politician's. The arts are the creations of those engaged in music, painting, sculpture, poetry and so on—many people are not so engaged—there shouldn't be confusions about this. During a recent exhibition of British landscape painting at the Hayward Gallery people were walking round saying: Oh look—Bognor—we were there in 1948—and so on. Dismissing with a casual glance anything not recognised. Concentrating on simple recognition acts. They missed some of the best paintings!

PEREIRA So the main difference between the mainstream and the radicals is that the mainstream deals in comforting art while the radicals are challenging?

MOTTRAM The main difference—if we can for a moment accept these terms—is very much to do with preference for variations of what people have been trained inside their own cultures—by dulling teachers of various kinds— to believe are the only parameters of poetry, of any art. The present state of the assumed primacy of pop music for millions of kids and their trainers is a case in point.

PEREIRA Last question: one of the first instincts of man is towards literature because language is power—words subdue the meaningless world to human uses —names control and own things. Do you believe that?

MOTTRAM There is no one relationship between words and other objects in reality—or one set of relationships. Words are the invention of human beings. They don't exist like leaves; they change meanings: the Oxford English Dictionary is an historical record because each word there is part of a set of datable meanings. So language itself is an historical action. Poetry is an historical action. You pick up a poem by Sir Thomas Wyatt and you read a work of Henry VIII's time—and you'd better believe it! The idea that a poem is for all time or some kind of universal is dreary nonsense—again, part of authoritarian drivel. What interests me is that idea you mentioned— that names control things— like the myth that Adam could name the animals for God but Satan could not. We have this ability of consciousness and verbal action —and for anyone involved in creative language, or language used as an art of persuasion— rhetoric—this is a crucial action. Once you restrict language to naming, though, to nominalism, you are lost. Once one is saying only 'articulation' one is lost. Because the implication there is something already there which can be and ought to be 'articulated'. Naming and articulation, merely, would be intolerably restrictive. Acknowledgement of the creativity of perception was a main turning point in our history—the sense that the perceptive act is not data gathering, and not simply followed by data naming —that the sheer act of perception itself, and then thinking itself, before and during the use of words, is creative. That the whole action of our lives is creative. There is that wonderful day to day possibility that we can move our imagination of words towards understanding our perceptibilities. And then we can make things, as the next stage. For I don't believe that the arts are simply a record of perception. They are another activity altogether. That is why we can resist representationalism and crude identifications. The arts are much more exciting, much more wonderful.

(This interview was first published in *Angel Exhaust* Six. Reprinted by permission of the Eric Mottram Collection.)

OUT TO LUNCH INTERVIEWED BY ANDREW DUNCAN

Pink Pong Punx Go Dingo

Hissed

this book propped open, almost
inviting a reader, surprise squeezed
between clenched teeth, suffering
draws red stripes on the sputum
like signal toothpaste. a conked
conceit, a do-rag pagoda head
construction, a swirl in the panic
wastepipe, an oval lake near the
love missile, in it an isle of you.
the dental clamp, the thin
stream of expectorant, the squid
decor: snotridden holidays and
painful waking. yes, these are
pages written at lunchbreak. also,
on the bus. vertical versus horizontal
until a vortex snaps residue
tension into simple pine furnished
hologram erective tissue: **hissed**
'shit' in my ear.

Heist

small lift left a sting: the slippery
udder waving above the hostile slop
pail, the glistening chapped red hands:
the goblin who whisked away the churn
of butter—*wie* **heisst** *du denn, du gelockter*
Schwanz?—the trick is on the
cards, the work is on the egg: poised
before it cracks, soldiers with raised
pikes bringing up the rear, a regular
software seesaw. haberdashery, sick
stuffed families in holiday traffic, a
head acheing from sun on aluminium
roofs. why do you pose on a column?
a thin stream of golden liquid percolates
through the expectant night air: my
crushed summer frock, my degenerate
unhealthy suetfilled existence: they
patter on the stretched membrane
of my tremulous virginal impatience.

DUNCAN How did you discover and get involved in modern poetry in the
first place?

OUT TO LUNCH Being shown a page from J.H. Prynne's *Brass* in the
Gonville and Caius Late Night Bar in Cambridge in 1975. I'd never
seen anything like it. It brought together words from contexts I'd
previously thought could have no relation—and I'd been reading
Finnegans Wake since finding it in the school library age 14. It was
the first step beyond Joyce I'd seen since Burroughs. It used quote-
marks and ampersands and colons and looked unlike any poetry
I'd seen before. It wasn't free verse, it seemed totally determined
by some hermetic principle. The print was big and black, like a
pensioner's easy-read volume from a public library, it wasn't like
the grey scatterings by e. e. cummings and Ezra Pound I'd seen at
school. It was, as they say now, 'in your face'. At the Late Night Bar
it was being passed around in an attitude of derision: I remember

my drinking companion Ted Davenport saying, 'Prynne had better watch out—a volume of his verse is loose among the undergraduates!'. But it actually succeeded in making fun of us! Extraordinary.

I knew who Prynne was. Although ostensibly studying history, I was attending his 'Language and Poetry' series. At Cambridge, you weren't confined to your subject, you went to any lectures that took your fancy. My girlfriend, who came up a year after me, was (lucky her!) studying English Literature, and in her first week she said, 'You've got to come and hear this Prynne guy's lectures, they'll make your brain burst, he's crazy.' I loved the lectures, though I didn't like the rumour that he published 'limited edition' poetry. That sounded elitist and effete: the opposite of Frank Zappa and the rock press (*NME*, *Street Life*, *Let It Rock*), my reference points for active culture. However, one glimpse, and I knew his stuff was historic. I bought *Wound Response* from Heffers, and then *High Pink On Chrome* as soon as it hit the shelves in January 1976. I was hooked.

I didn't start writing poetry myself though. I had a sceptical attitude to students who did. I bought a few things that looked like Prynne, but thought John Wilkinson was a pale wannabe, and that his boasts about playing ping-pong with a punk band were sad. I read Geoff Ward saying 'forget punk rock, Cambridge poetry is the only thing going' and decided he was a tosser. In fact, I remember reading out this statement to Andrew Blake, a sax-playing history student who'd introduced me to Albert Ayler and Pharaoh Sanders and Archie Shepp. *Feats Don't Fail Me Now* by Little Feat was on in my college room, and he jerked his thumb at the record player and said—'but what about *this*?'. Exactly. I had problems with poetry which seemed to breathe an air of privileged self-regard. I think you did too, Andrew! Why else would you have put out *Negative Reaction*, a punk fanzine, and put copies in *Remember Those Oldies* on King Street? I looked at it, admired the title, but didn't buy it. Whyever not? Stupid. We could've started a band and changed the world.

Prynne's 'poetry' wasn't self-regarding, it was all prickle and attack and shiny malevolence. It walled out collusion. It accused you. Instead of inviting you into the sad, damp atmosphere of the sensitive poet—the special pleadings of some over-educated shithead—it made you feel paranoid and panicky, a shot of adrenalin. It has an affect like pornography or alcohol or Manga animation, below the belt as it were, you can't argue with it. So I decided to wreck my academic career and change to English Literature and get tutorials from Prynne. Everyone at the college tried to dissuade me. However, I'd got a First in History Part One (by obediently regurgitating summaries of various books and articles we were told to read, the nineteenth century was a total enigma to me until I read Marx in Leeds in the 80s . . . I was also helped by being 'leaked' a question the day before one paper—it's all COMPLETELY corrupt, they give Firsts away like toffees at Cambridge). So now I could do what I wanted, which was to join the proletariat on the dole queue, engage in S&M sex with every young woman possible, drink vast quantities of homebrew, and pogo. I researched a project on Wyndham Lewis and looked at *BLAST* in the University Library. 'Ah,' I thought, 'so that's where Prynne got his mode of address from!'.

No-one ever believes this, but I never met a poet when I was a student in Cambridge! Well, I was supervised by Andrew Crozier—good poet, terrible supervisor—but I never met my 'generation'. I joined forces with some drug-obsessed rich twat from Hampstead and read sound poetry to the English Literature Society—he thought it was hilarious that they all looked horrified, but I felt hurt and rejected. I wrote *1-2-3-4* in a note-book and gave it to Prynne—he returned the volume (by this time I'd gone to Leeds) with one of his life-changing letters which compliments you and denounces you at the same time. Food for thought for years. He said 'put it out', so I printed 200 copies on the duplicator we were using for Right To Work bulletins. I remember selling one to Seething Swells on the Swansea-to-Brighton march (50p). Was it a fanzine or 'poetry'? I'm still not sure.

I was thrilled that Ian Patterson, Peter Ackroyd and Nick Totton (*A Vision Very Like Reality*), John Wilkinson (*Equofinality*), Paul Brown (*Heretic*) and Ken Edwards and Bob Cobbing (*So Much Plotted Freedom*) published my critical writing, but the poetry in these magazines didn't excite me. It didn't seem worthy of a post-*Trout Mask Replica* universe. I thought the manuscript of *Threads of Iron* you sent me was great—how did we get in touch, can you remember, it was definitely not at university?—but especially when you were writing interior political monologue, not well-turned 'poems'. I combed the shelves of Compendium in Camden Town, which the late Mike Hart was stocking with interesting things. I responded to

Bill Griffiths (the transcribed work-thoughts of *Building The New London Hospital*), Christopher Dewdney (surrealist regression to the mollusk level) and Tom Raworth (no 'poet' at home that I can see) . . . but no-one else really. Iain Sinclair, but mainly when he descended to prose.

I suppose my absolute aversion to poetry got less rigorous and principled once I'd been invited to read at CCCP2 in 1992. I gave a paper and was stunned and delighted to discover that Simon Jarvis and Drew Milne were also fusing Prynne and Adorno (shame they don't understand how the 60s put music in the forefront). I performed 1-2-3-4 and Denise Riley was nice about the slides I projected. Rod Mengham published two books of mine (*28 Sliverfish Macronix* was a thirty minute improv, no revision; *Turnpike Ruler* was written to perform with Simon H. Fell). With the publication of the *Conductors of Chaos* anthology—I know it doesn't figure in your evaluation of the politics of publishing, but it was important for me—I agreed with Sinclair that there was something crucial about disengaging consciousness to Maggie O'Sullivan's word spells: *Art, Class & Cleavage* was meant to be a manifesto for the Conductors. Shame the revolutionary cell was actually riddled with bourgeois sentimentalists, but you always hope.

DUNCAN What is the relationship between nonconformist style in art and nonconformist attitudes in politics? What is the politics of small press poetry?

OUT TO LUNCH I don't think it's possible to build a serious programme around 'nonconformity'. It's too dependent on conformity—like committing yourself to a shadow. In interviews Zappa tried to develop 'nonconformity' as a life philosophy, but he ends up with a weak kind of bourgeois individualism. Trotsky says historical materialism cares not a jot for public opinion, and I go with that. However, in my sexuality and greed for alcohol I personally try and be as conformist as possible. Only by understanding and indulging the righteous appetites of actually existing human beings can we combat fascism. Your second question? The politics of small press poetry is petit bourgeois, of course. That's why one continually trips over liberalism and fascism. But the new social movements have demonstrated what Lenin said: the petit bourgeoisie is a vacillating class, and can be fantastic. I don't think José Bové has the

whole answer but I'm on his side versus every trade union bureau-
crat and idiot stalinist sectarian.

DUNCAN We got in touch through *Equofinality*. This is historical fact—we
were in the same college, in the same year, listened to the same
music, but didn't meet until 8 years later. The other punk fanzine
in Cambridge was *Chainsaw*, and I was in a small press fair in about
1996 when Charlie Chainsaw walked in. He looked exactly the
same after 20 years. I think 8 people came into the room all day,
and he was one of them. Punk had a lot in common with small
press poetry. Did 'underground', non High Street, poetry connect
with marxist/anarchist politics, or with a libertarian and 'cool'
lifestyle, or with detachment and scepticism, or with nothing?

Maybe we can get away from 'nonconformity' and get into
molecular aversion. You dislike 'the sad, damp atmosphere of the
sensitive poet', and maybe cultural politics starts as a flight away
from those wistfully deciduous penis substitutes, the finely modu-
lated linebreaks, the passive-aggressive parish church-fancying.

That 'it'll burst your brains out' reminds me of Robert Johnson's
'stuff I got'll burst your brains out baby', and I wanted to call the
book that. We might call it 'Stop Breaking Down', another Johnson
line.

OUT TO LUNCH Only an art of complete and unbowed subjectivism and
irresponsible freedom—shaped by its own immanent energies—
can become the object of truly scientific cultural criticism, every-
thing else is prepackaged and collusive with power relations!

When you're revolting against everything and wearing a bog
chain around your neck and a flasher's mac with OUT TO LUNCH
painted on the back and bicycling off to work washing dishes at
the Cambridge School of Languages and gobbing at schoolkids on
the pavement as a gesture of pop absurdity, as I was in 1978, poetry
had better be absolutely mind-blowing or you're not going to sit
still for it, are you? Prynne deposited a few volumes of each release
in the Heffers poetry section for interested parties, but it was like
finding a can of Carlsberg Special secreted behind the works of
John Ruskin in a dusty library: it didn't get you reading the other
stuff. The other legislating influence on me at the time was the
Situationists, mediated via *Leaving the Twentieth Century*, a volume
of translations published by Christopher Gray in 1974 with graph-

ics by Jamie Reid, one of which reappeared on the back of the pic sleeve of 'Pretty Vacant'. This always made me think that Guy Debord, and hence the Marx he filched all his best phrases from, was DEEP PUNK, whatever Johnny Rotten said in *No Dogs*. Actually, what Rotten said was great [*OTL goes to his bookshelf and pulls out a hardback volume, riffles the pages*]: Ah! Here it is . . . 'As far as the music being academic, at the time very little of it seemed so. The references to the Situationists—I've only read about that in the last three years! Everybody knew about the Surrealists and dadaists, but who the hell were the Situationists? I don't know if Malcolm or Bernie ever talked to the Pistols about all of that, but I don't think it would have stuck. They would have gone down to the pub— certainly Steve would have.' Steve Jones was a deriviste without knowing it! Brilliant.

So in a context like that, what you call 'High Street' poetry held no interest whatsoever: it was *middle-class*, it was sensitive, it was about visiting churches and worrying about your bicycle clips. It was given to you to read by a teacher and then you were examined on it. It was about people who were very *English*, and I was brought up to despise the English and think France was fantastic. My parents studied Modern Languages at Cambridge before the World War II: French, German, Russian (my mother joined the Communist Party). Every Summer we'd take the ferry over to France, and everything was magical because we'd got away from the home counties, and everyone spoke French and ate garlic and pig's trotters and bread loaves were two foot long. They drank WINE with their meals! Their toilets stank and you squatted over them! Of course, Francophilia is a completely middle-class *tic* in England—but punk nevertheless invented an Englishness I could relate to because it wasn't bland, boring and conservative. In Leeds in the late 60s I talked to local punk bands like the Resistance and Abrasive Wheels and found them very impressive. They'd dissect the bass sound on an Iggy Pop record really cannily; they knew about James Brown. Not like the Mekons, who struck me as a bunch of spoiled wannabes. It confirmed what I'd learned from my Zappa guru Danny Houston, who came down from Glasgow to doss on the dole, except they made him take a job with London Underground: that the English middle classes know fuck all about music. That was the beginning of my musical materialism—not Adorno. Later, I discovered that there *is* a middle-class musical culture. I went out with a prime example! Lovely woman, nearly ruined her life. But to keep their jobs in the establishment they have to pretend to like minimalist shit, so it all goes phoney and incomprehensible. Real music is so repressed in England, it makes you want to have a revolution.

To return to the attraction of what you call the 'underground' (in the cultural rather than locomotive sense), I'd absorbed stuff from my brother Oliver—seven years older than me—who'd gone up to Durham University to learn Arabic in 1967. He used to have filthy rows with my Dad about politics, because my Dad supported Israel and Olly supported Nasser. He had piles of *Oz* magazine, which I read assiduously despite the psychedelic over-printing. I read rag mags with blue jokes, a collection of obscene stories published by Olympia, *Fanny Hill* and William Burroughs long before I could understand them. I think I've been left with a taste for the bizarre and 'incomprehensible' ever since, and expect no less of my readers. My friend I took the tube to school with, who insisted he was called Jeremiah Crispin Fitzwilliam Hall, told me he was writing 'pornography', and I was naturally fascinated. So in emulation I wrote *The Holy Boble* (pronounced 'bobble'), which was a take off of *The Bible*. I called my publishing company TAKEOF-FOBOX and 'published' handwritten books in editions of one. They swarmed with 'nudes' and 'loos', the two rudest things I could think of. Then I invented the 'nuloo' which was like a mermaid—a bare-breasted female top half and a toilet with a wriggling U bend like a fish-tail! It's quite ingenious what someone without any sisters will get up to to explore their, um, sexuality. Also my family subscribed to *Private Eye*, which I loved, and I read The Beano and Rabelais. So for me, connections between subversion, pornography and underground literature were already made when I debuted as a writer with The Holy Boble in March 1968. I'd lend my books to fellow pupils at school to read—grabbing their attention was the whole point (it depressed me no end to discover in later life that the chief way of grabbing people's attention is to be INCREDIBLY PREDICTABLE AND BORING, it seems wrong to my mind). Then someone shopped me. He said that he'd left one of my books 'somewhere' and a teacher found it, but when I think about it now, of course he shopped me. My God, it's taken me 34 years to realise that someone I knew could be that treacherous! Probably a boarder—I was a day boy and we hated the boarders, they were totally immature and nasty and fought all the time. They punched you if they found you on the school premises after 5:00pm. *The Holy Boble* was quite prescient—I played the Jesus figure, who tried to make peace between the schoolboy rebels and the school authorities and got crucified (*i.e.* expelled).

All this just to show you that the idea of rare subversive banned literature didn't come to me from poetry but from the general 60s ferment. Despite the anti-hippie rhetoric, Punk *was* a continuation of the scandalising *Oz* thing and of the *best* parts of the 60s. Both Frank Zappa and Guy Debord reviled the hippies anyway, so Punk was music to my ears. I hated progressive rock with a vengeance, which is why I'm so out of kilter with *The Wire* (Pink Floyd are back, man, and they're called Supersilent; Nucleus are called Jaga Jazzist). Punk meant I could drink cans of lager, sneer at marijuana protocol and talk a lot. Uncool was suddenly cool. All aboard for fun time! It's what I needed aged 21.

DUNCAN What were you like as a teenager?

OUT TO LUNCH In 1970, I wasn't yet ready for 'revolution', I was still very hardworking. I was bookish. It's not for nothing that my artistic icons are Schwitters and Joyce. I hate the anti-intellectualism of the anarchist *milieu*: I'm a Marxist who believes (like him) that the *geistlich* development of the self and the relation to man to woman are the two primary concerns of the species. My parents supported my occasional writings, and I wrote humorous satirical stories like *Family Day* to make them laugh, but it was really Pam Pilkington over the road who encouraged me. The Pilks were like an alternative family—they kept the door on the latch and I could go in. I watched Children's TV there (no TV at home) with the kids. There was always tea in front of the TV with things like chocolate-rice-crispie tarts and mousses and cocktail sausages I never got at home: Pam must have fed me more than my real mum! Without the Pilks, I'd never have seen *Dr Who*, I'd be a cultural zero. Pam thought it was great that I was learning rude words, and suggested that we call her husband a 'pubic louse'—and then explained what it meant. She had this great disgusting Gerald Scarfe poster of Enoch Powell as a dog returning to his vomit (this was after the 'rivers of blood' racist speech in Wolverhampton). God, my chronology's fucked—because wasn't it after Eric Clapton said

'Enoch's right innie' that Rock Against Racism was formed? Anyway, Pam was the sort of superb person who would have a poster like that on her wall, and she lent me the children's version of The Bible which provided the structure for *The Holy Boble*. I wrote *The Saga of Bannana the Farter* (Galsworthy's *Forsyte Saga* was on TV then) for the Pilkingtons (nothing to do with the glass, people always ask) named after Pam's daughter Anna, who was celebrated for her farts (and who I had this amazing erotic dream about a month ago, as you do). It was written in sections for birthdays and Christmas, it all went into a loose leaf binder I'd created for it. Then me and Jerry collaborated on a 3-volume masterpiece *The Scarlet Pimpled Hall*, which was based on *The Scarlet Pimpernel*, which had been acted as a school play (I was the imbecile Vicomte who bows a lot). I got totally megalomaniac in my contributions to the book and turned myself into Napoleon and humiliated Jerry by having his character ride through Paris in a donkey cart. That spilled over into life and I was horrible to Jerry, lost touch for years.

To return to your question: Prynne's underground poetry connected to my general idea of REVOLT before I faced any political option or lifestyle choice. This revolt centred on my disgust that I was so oppressed/repressed that I couldn't talk about sex at home. Gradually it dawned on me that you can lob *truth* into a vile social situation and everything explodes! I wanted to be the satirist of my generation. When I went to university, I thought I was an anarchist. It was the practical nature of the SWP in organising the Anti-Nazi League which impressed me—we went to shout outside the hotel where the NF were meeting, while the Communist Party went for an 'anti-racist' prayer meeting in the church. The anarchists sat around talking about acid trips. My friend Mike Laurence became an SWP member and a fervent Marxist, but I was a bit patronizing to him at first. I was reading Guy Debord and early Marx, he was an 'activist'. It took Martin Bennell in Leeds to bully me into joining the party.

Another essential source was Compendium Books in Camden Town. I felt at home there. There was tons of William Burroughs and de Sade and Furry Freak Brothers comics, which I knew about from my older brother, and I bought Raoul Vaneigem's *Revolution of Everyday Life*, the Paul Sieveking translation with the interpolated bit about Zappa and Reggae. I liked the politics and theory section downstairs too—everything apart from the hippie stuff, which I despised. I never *once* stepped into the New Age section at the back (which I recently found was the only section that actually made them any money). Mainly it was the poetry I'd buy. All hail to the late Mike Hart who had such good taste (Sugarcane Harris and J.H. Prynne, unbeatable). I pulled books out at random and opened them—if they had words that buzzed me I bought them. I looked for ice, submarines, Nazis, sled dogs, poodles, Alka Seltzer, butter on skis, BIRDLAND, huskies, Mal Waldron . . . Frank O'Hara's *Lunch Poems* blew me into the 21st Century! I discovered that practically nothing printed by a proper publisher was any good. It made me realise that official culture is about consumption and puts the seal of approval on an unjust and exploitative society—whatever it thinks it's 'saying'. Riffling through pamphlets in Compendium, that's how I found Bill Griffiths, Iain Sinclair, Denise Riley and Tom Raworth. Maggie O'Sullivan and Geraldine Monk came a bit later. I thought this literature could match up to Dada, *Finnegans Wake* and *Blast*—unlike official poetry.

To return to your question once again, I thought this poetry was libertarian and cool and detached and sceptical as well as being revolutionary . . . I don't see that being a revolutionary activist and Marxist should make you miss any of those things, they all have their place . . . but most of all it made me dizzy, alerted me to some arcane energy, which I later found was my own brain relating hitherto discrete aspects of knowledge and experience. I wasn't going to fall for any crap about 'magic', but with these writers . . . I didn't like Sinclair's infatuation with fascism in *Suicide Bridge*, that kept me away from him for years. I wrote *1–2–3–4* as a left-punk retort to Sinclair. I suppose it worked in a way, because John Wilkinson told me it was because he saw *1–2–3–4* that he got in touch with me about writing for *Equofinality*—and which finally led to my correspondence with you and our beer drinking in Jack Straw's Castle and that furious row about how many people were bumped off by the Bolsheviks.

DUNCAN What is the reasoning behind your improvised ('one take/simultaneous') poetic style?

OUT TO LUNCH I don't know, I wish someone would tell me. Actually, you got the closest . . . though come to think of it, no-one else has had a go, so that's hardly praise. But what you said in *Angel Exhaust*

No 12, ventriloquizing for the Out To Lunch of *28 Sliverfish Macronix* (Equipage 1992): 'Poetry is 'intellectual' and has low to zero affect, by the time you've achieved 'detachment and self-control' it isn't happening inside you any more ... Lunch dives straight into sexual feelings, and his face-down floundering in the fermenting kitchen waste is based on a belief that the selection process which produces civility (or the courtly lyric) out of the primary data is flawed in the same way that capitalist democracy's reflection of people's real wishes, in law or commodity, is' ... that explains me better than I can.

It's more a method than a 'style' I hope. When Rod Mengham decided to publish a pamphlet of mine for Equipage, I thought it would be cowardly and tiresome to dredge through my numerous books of 'out' language (I've found that the only way I can write poetry is to make books in the way I made *The Holy Boble*, the idea of 'writing a poem' freezes me, though I still do write single sheets when a group of words suddenly rushes at me). I spend so much of my time watching Free Improvisors create out of nothing that the idea of fidgetting about with the finished gesture seems futile— like using tippex on an ab-ex canvas. As you mentioned in your review, *28 Sliverfish* was 'written in 28 one-take improvisations; no editing. Still dripping ... '. Actually the whole thing was written in *a single performance*, not 28. I first constructed a 'blank' book with collaged illustrations and various panels of lined paper—the linage was set. I had to write in the boxes like filling in a questionnaire under pressure, or an exam. The idea came to me after Prynne wrote to me saying that the way I was writing into pages of a booklet was actually a formal restraint—as I approached the bottom of the page, the writing got more tense and dense, like the last line of a sonnet. So I had this structure I had to fill with writing. Adrenalin rushed. It *was* a performance. I was slightly sexually aroused. It felt risky and exciting. I could imagine all those Cambridge poets sneering at the results. But I'd watched Derek Bailey and Simon H. Fell and Alan Wilkinson build fantastic structures out of initial blurts and irritated ugliness, I wanted to do the same. It's what Adorno says about Beethoven (let's not beat about the bush, eh?): the theme isn't the point (Mozart and McCartney's 'genius for tunes'), it's what you do with the social situation created by the first gesture. *Dealing with it while it is happening* (to quote Zappa's *Hot Rats: Waka/Jawaka*) is the art. So it's process, not product, and proceeds as an immanent dialectic rather than as a symbol within a pre-fabricated system. I'm not sure this 'justifies' what I do entirely, or rules out other approaches like cut-up or collage, but that is the impulse behind my 'improvised' writing. As you say, if I wanted something representational or argued, I'd write prose. I'm *interested* in what comes out, so it's like automatic writing, except I hope I'm more self-critical than the Surrealists, and also hope that my reading of other poets gives me a sense of a critical audience, a *milieu*. It's not launched into eternity but at various people I imagine reading it. I don't believe in the pure Id of Artaud and Dali, I think that's sentimental and leads to radical kitsch: I think this 'thing' in you must *do battle* with the super ego. As with Free Improvisation, a certain focus—heightened attention, an audience of peers, a 'gig'—elevates the art. It's amazing how quite dull musicians will play brilliantly with Bailey. So that's why, despite Punk Rock, I still consider myself a Cambridge poet and that what I write in that direction is different from other stuff.

It's a risk for liars to improvise if people are going to ask them fundamental questions, and situational control gives all sorts of scope for manipulation. You buy a fish or a fruit, you can tell what you're getting: packaging dissembles (and what 'truths' they're forced to tell are data shaped by ludicrous anxieties about diet inculcated by the culture industry and government). Despite the phrase, *nothing* does what it says on the tin. In the 1980s boom, capitalist lies about profitability became epidemic, it actually fucked up their ability to function as capitalists! In this context, truth and immediacy become explosively subversive. I think the basic weakness in most mainstream middle-class poets is hypocritical sexuality and collusion in class society—they wouldn't dare write automatically because of what it might reveal. They fear chaos because it'll make them look uncool. My plan was always to live a life I wasn't ashamed of so that everything that comes out is vital. That's why the idea of fiddling about with the words, desperately seeking substitutes and improvements—'polishing a poem'—seems petty. I was pleased when Prynne mentioned he wrote at one blow, I'd thought his poems had that kind of gestural grace and unanswerability. I learned a lot from *The White Goddess* about mad thought, but Robert Graves says 'the writer's best friend is his paper basket', and I think that's why his poems read so bitty and keep making philosophical and political blunders.

DUNCAN We can define punk now, but at the time it was mimetic—a group feeling of solidarity drawing on expectations of what was about to happen which were intense but wholly uncertain. I can't stand the 'well-turned' poem because it's under control and therefore not out of control. But I think this might not be because it's 'commodified' but because it's self-possessed and wholly predictable—the mimetic, group feeling, thrilling, element has been snipped away.

OUT TO LUNCH I love the 'collective' nature of Punk, but in many ways I missed it. I didn't spend long enough in Cambridge to get to know the town punks well, I liked them, though they were a bit young. I only met collectivity through Rock Against Racism in Leeds, and the need for activism prevented a real aesthetic bonding. I had to work with certain people I thought were well-meaning but half-baked. But there was no choice, the NF were all over the 'F' Club, and something had to be done. By the time 2-Tone and the Specials arrived, things improved, we met some great multi-racial youth gangs. Gary Middleton, the jazz-lover from Pudsey etc. I agree that self-possession is limiting, but finally I do love poems that are compacted gems, I cannot stand Allen Ginsberg sprawl. Prynne and Hart Crane are my tops: it needs to be utterly crystalline, surrendered to the stars. I think William Burroughs managed it in *The Wild Boys*—and Christopher Dewdney. The 'self-possession' of Robert Creeley or Ric Caddel makes me feel sick: it's a request that you admire their ethic, and such 'humanity' is all about justifying private property in the end. When you get the words right, it's social and objective, not a personal plea. I want everyone to do a Goethe, take the human right down through the animal and plant to the rocks ('Oh rocks!', as Molly Bloom says when Bloom explain the transmigration of souls to her).

However, as regards Punk, I wasn't musical enough to think I could form a band, and the attempt to become a music critic dissolved solidarity. When I got pissed off with rock (gigs by Spear of Destiny and Killing Joke at the Merrion Centre in quick succession—just expensive entertainment, no-one in the audience being weird and talkable-to) I went for Free Improvisation, but I never really arrived there in the 'collective' sense. The 'being-published-as-a-critic' was a mark against me. I toured with Hession/Wilkinson/Fell, but I was still the critic. But if you're going to be a critic, be an alienated one to the max, which is why I love Adorno. No, he's not an Italian doo-wop singer from Philadelphia as you suggest, he's the 'greatest critic of the twentieth century' according to Andy Hamilton at *The Wire* (so it must be true). Actually, he's the only writer on music who manages to think cosmos, history and the low cravings of the listener's libido in every sentence.

I think Writers Forum and Bob Cobbing perhaps created a punk-style collectivity for poets in a way the 'intellectualised' atmosphere of CCCP failed to (more 'bloodstained Royston perimeter' talk?). The poets I discovered later on—Maggie O'Sullivan, Adrian Clarke, Johan de Wit and now Sean Bonney and Jeff Hilson—were all Writers Forum people. Writers Forum operated like the Free Improvisors, and the method is proved by the quality of the work. That said, I do think the Cambridge poets have things to say, and Ian Patterson and Simon Jarvis's current campaign for attention to 'prosody'—the below-rational music of writers' discourse—is spot-on, and could be a way of applying Adorno to literature. To find out who Adorno is, girls and boys, go and listen to 'Easy Meat' on Frank Zappa's *Tinseltown Rebellion* album (1981), then read my *Frank Zappa: the Negative Dialectics of Poodle Play* (1993).

DUNCAN The only question I'd actually worked out was about your programme of buying records for 99p or less.

OUT TO LUNCH It was a method for dealing with unemployment 1977–85, which entailed poverty, a lot of spare time and an extraordinary thirst for new music. It went in tandem with home-brewed beer and listening to music on home-recorded cassette-tapes, the only way to live in an expansive way when you've got no cash. A key influence was Danny Houston, my Zappa 'guru' who I mentioned earlier. He first wrote to me suggesting we get in touch after I had a letter published in *Street Life* in which I made a para-noid connection between the phrase '3 Irwin', which had turned up in a code message during an interview they'd published with an ex-CIA spy, and was also printed at the zenith of the star map on the back of Zappa's *One Size Fits All*. A Zappologist from Scotland named Stuart Lester had written in making fun of me—and making authentic factual non-paranoid zappological connections. Showing a typical disregard for methodological contradiction, Danny wrote to both of us suggesting we all meet in the Britannia, a '40s brick pub with metal-frame windows opposite the Hammersmith Odeon in London. I remember showing the bizarre letter he'd sent—a tiny square of paper with the edges singed by a match—to a bunch of other undergraduates who'd come round to drink my home-brew in Catharine Street in Romsey Town, Cambridge. Everyone I knew agreed how *extraordinary* and gauche it was for someone to get in touch without a formal introduction (they'd put 'Ben Waton, Caius Cambridge' at the foot of my letter on the *Street Life* letters page and Danny's missive had found its way to my college pigeon-hole). Now I network like that all the time (or try to, I was pissed off with Francis Wheen for not replying to me after I read his biography of Marx and wrote to him, but maybe it was his publishers not bothering to forward the letter), but Danny's notion of using modern communication systems like the mail and cassette tapes and photocopies to gratify his cultural proclivities seemed really outlandish to me then. The international tape-swapping thing got to the point where a tape would plop onto my doormat in Leeds, and it'd be Billy Bang playing violin in a Manhattan jazz club four days before. You realised your ears could roam the world! And by hearing old records, through time as well. Danny's example ensured that when cyberspace hysteria about the Internet hit the *Guardian* in 1995 I could be a bit *blasé*—if you'd been in touch with Danny you were already part of an international multi-media network. Reading Marx is a good prophylactic against capitalist boosterism, but Houstonism was crucial too: it explained that the real limit was a not technology, but people's desire for experience: [*OTL sings some lines from Zappa's 'We're Only In It For The Money'*] 'You'll be absolutely free/Only if you *want* to be'.

When I was a student I used to hitch down to London to visit Danny in his bedsit in Ealing. We'd go completely beserk with zappology and all the surreal coincidences it invokes and drink vast amounts in the Wheatsheaf—Fullers ESB 'extra-sensory bitter' was a favourite—and then stagger back to his place with armfuls of carry-outs. Danny's a few years older than me, so the 'punk' hostility to 'hippies' added a certain tension, but he regularly blew my mind with his experimental attitude towards culture and communications and sexual relations. He'd *give you things*, which no-one in my circle ever did . . . wrong actually, my fellow student and drinking companion Pete Reading went and bought me the

Doors' *LA Woman* after I admitted Jim Morrison's 'Lizard King' performance was 'not pretentious' . . . but Danny gave you things on a regular basis. He was continually dropping in on charity shops and remaindered record shops and finding stuff. If he saw a single with a crazy title and they were 10p each, he'd buy five and give you one. Later, we found that we both possessed not one copy, but *several* copies of *Breeding From Your Poodle* by Margaret Rothery Sheldon and Barbara Lockwood! We were thinking alike. It was quite frustrating sometimes. I'd be down there in his bedsit wanting to dissect the lyrics to *Apostrophe(')*, or hear *rarissimo* Zappa stuff like the GTO's or L. Shankar improvising at the Hammersmith Odeon, and he'd be playing some novelty single he'd found. However, Danny extended zappological *connectivitis* to the whole of mass produced culture, and kept making absolute trash seem like the most special thing on earth. Without him, no Poodle Play, which is why my book on Zappa was dedicated to both him and Prynne. Danny's play on value was a kind of alchemical transformation—with moments of fraudulence, exploitation and trickery as you'd expect. Fully in line with Michael Thompson's *Rubbish Theory*, though it took me years to track down a copy of that (it was from a library though, if you ever see it, snap it up). Danny once said *all* singles are good because 'everyone is worth 3 minutes of your time'. How's that for a democratic impulse? We'd have whole evenings where all he'd play was 7″ singles—he was too speedy for the album, it was too bourgeois. It was a prol aesthetic, like Tom Raworth's, what Tom calls 'low attention span', but can actually be acuter about the aesthetic material because it's not being driven by political or moral ideology. So I suppose that's where the '99p album' thing came from.

Danny created his own value system. He got me into Frank Sinatra and Jim Reeves, which was odd for someone who was attempting to triangulate the Sex Pistols, Eric Dolphy and Frank Zappa. We liked the Singing Postman from Norwich. He introduced me to going to see Iggy Pop live, who previously I'd avoided because of the self-mutilation and swastikas. I can now explain what we were doing as 'resistance to commodity fetishism', but I didn't put it like that at the time, even though I was reading György Lukács (Danny *certainly* wasn't)! To an extent it was all *NME*-reading rat-race trendier-than-thou perversity, but it broke with the idea that buying the latest full-price album by a fashionable band was a cool manœuvre—in fact, we thought that was pathetic. If you were obsessed with Zappa in 1977 and 1978, you were a complete oddity anyway, you were meant to have dumped all that in favour of the Boomtown Rats or Blondie or something equally stupid. My big musical moment in Leeds in 1979, for example, was discovering Little Richard. In May, I bought *Rock Hard, Rock Heavy*— a collection of prime Specialty stuff—for £1.95. In December I bought *All Time Hits* for £1.95 from the same shop on Roundhay Road (I was living in a back-to-back with Caroline Arscott and Paul and Gas, two Geordie Zappa freaks, in Banstead Grove, a street which has now been demolished). Prynne had told me he thought Captain Beefheart's vocal style was derived from Little Richard's (I replied, 'Surely not—isn't his main influence Howlin' Wolf?')—but it was only when I bought these records that I realised that Little Richard wasn't anything to do with Cliff Richard or Keith Richards, but that he made the most intoxicating and explosive sonic art it will ever be your chance to hear, oh poor mortals.

It's not just that there are fantastic things laid down in the reject piles of old consumerism like fossils waiting for the geologist. I mean, I built collections of Jimmy McGriff on Groove Merchant and Funkadelic on Warner Brothers and Joe Tex on Dial for next to nothing (20 cut-out copies of *One Nation Under a Groove*, shrinkwrapped with the 33rpm 7″ single 'Lunchmeatophobia (Think! It Ain't Illegal Yet!)' at 10p each from Poundstretcher on the Headrow, would you believe?), but combing the second-hand and remaindered racks is also a life principle: *fashion is a rip-off.* You get a better deal by going against the tide. When I read the Godfather of the Popsicle Academy, Prof. Simon Frith, saying he never played the B-sides of the singles he bought, I realised the strong connection between surplus wealth, conformism and fear of the unconscious. Rubbish is pertinent, the unconscious of our times, and navigating it is crucial. The famous statement of this approach is of course Walter Benjamin on the ragpicker, 'botanising on the asphalt', by which he meant a curiosity about what everyone's up to, paying attention to the litter around us, rather than simply consuming the 'good' (*i.e.* what's been directed at your particular consumer niche): 10p singles and 99p albums are refutations of what Adorno called 'identity-thinking'! Kurt Schwitters is interesting in this regard—not the onomatopoeic poet celebrated by the American conceptualists, but the actual guy who stank out a shared hotel room with a camembert wrapper he'd picked out of the garbage, and who put Hannah Höch's bra in a secret part of his *Merzbau* (behaviour utterly familiar from Danny Houston!). Buying a random selection of scratchy 45s can be so much more aurally *interesting* than listening to the White Stripes or Keiji Haino, y'know? I don't know what the equivalent practice would be today, I'm not sure a diet of Nick Hayward and Paul Young and Band Aid LPs from Oxfam shops would be a good idea—strategies today could be Internet downloads, or combing CD singles and rejected dance 12˝s in Music & Video Exchange (I notice you can still get Duke Ellington LPs for £2 from jazz shops, people think vinyl is inferior, but it's not). Of course, the provinces are much better for this kind of, um, cultural research. Personally speaking, after twenty years of professional music reviewing, my house is aswim with CDs, and I don't trawl boot sales and charity shops as much as I'd like. My thirst for musical materials has abated somewhat; it'll doubtless improve when I'm finally sacked from *Hi-Fi News* for continually trying to write about an album the Manchester improvisor T.H.F. Drenching recorded at work in his call-centre by a contact-mic concealed in his out-tray. I also buy cans of Grolsch rather than making homebrew ('sparging the wort' etc.). Ah, the decadent delights of middle-age!

[*OTL staggers over to one section of the record library which coats the walls of his flat in Crowndale Court and pulls out a bunch of LPs*] Of course I was addicted to Zappa, always bought his new record full-price—and then hated it, wrestled with it for a year before getting the point (*Thing-Fish* took me *five years!*)—then Devo were allowed in to the full-price category . . . but jazz you can always explore second-hand, the quality-quantity ratio of releases is biased towards the second-hand buyer . . . Beatles, Bob Dylan, Marvin Gaye and Elvis are tricky, everyone hangs on to their copies . . . reggae's always scratched to fuck, my collection is really dodgy, getting the right records is like scoring high-grade marijuana, expensive and dangerous, the record is a means of musical production in reggae, not a consumer item . . . unlike rock, dance music goes violently out of fashion, so you can pick up gems. For me, pursuing Free Improvisation and avantgarde poetry have run parallel to my record-buying—how to get the really great stuff for next to nothing—in-your-face, intimately, with *you* there enjoying it, not your social-reference group or cultural advice garnered from newspapers and magazines. Commodification (or 'recognition') doesn't just diminish the experience, it makes it fucking expensive. Poets and artists should be rooking the moneyed classes, not queing in line with them.

[*OTL begins riffling through his stack of LPs*] I always put the price sticker inside an LP and write down the date I bought it, so check these out from my disco section: The Trammps *Slipping Out* 75p 29/1/88; The Chequers *Check Us Out* 49p 16/7/88; The Jammers £1.99 29/12/86—they're fantastic, like everything on the Soulsoul label, have you heard 'Ex-Attack'?; Charo & the Salsoul Orchestra *Cuchi-Cuchi*—for some reason the cover's burnt, maybe a jealous girlfriend, the model on the cover, her t-shirt's wet and her nipples are erect, or maybe it once belonged to Danny £1 20/11/93; Frankie Crocker's Heart and Soul Orchestra *Presents The Disco Suite No.1 in Rhythm and Excellence* 30p 15/7/82—hardcore orchestral disco, four sides, utterly unlistenable, but weirdly impressive in the sexual sense; *Best of Barry White*, actually that was free, it came with the flat, it must have belonged to the previous occupant Mr Douglas, who shipped out to Paradise, Grenada, that was a discovery which transformed my concept of orchestration, fantastic; Giorgio *Knights In White Satin* 50p 11/4/83—much better than Moroder's Donna Summer work, one of his most amazing electro concoctions, you can see why New Order's 'Blue Monday' never impressed me, you could get this stuff from the source much cheaper!; Giorgio *From Here To Eternity* £1.50 12/9/86; Munich Machine featuring Chris Bennett *A Whiter Shade of Pale* 19p 5/1/83—superb, don't you like the cover? a pale nude woman dancing with shiny chrome-plated robots, one of the nearest visual objective-correlatives to the tingly moment of onanistic orgasm I've encountered .. . This could go on for ever, Andrew, why don't we go down the pub?

Bibliography/discography

Having grasped that post–1945 capitalism is strictly uninterested in the mind-expanding qualities of non-narrative language (*Ursonate*, *Finnegans Wake*, *The Childermass*, *transition* etc), Ben Watson resolved to produce his language-as-music as Out To Lunch, providing a marginal stain on the marginal marzipan of 'Cambridge' poetry rolled out by J.H. Prynne. Publication hasn't been the point. If no publisher is mentioned here, it's because the work has circulated as a one-off notebook, often receiving just as interesting a reception as 'published' work: *1–2–3–4* (Leeds: Leeds SWP Roneo, 1980); *Blue Book* (1980); *Green To Grey: a Book of the Past* (1986); *Pop Poems for 1987* (1987); *STACK-LOG* (1988); *Gimmee Gimmee* (1988–1993); *Vooky Aim A* (1989); *Infernel: The Sex/Work Papers* (1989); *Ideolaxl: Your Fresh Lunch on the Move* (1991); *Alan* (1991); *28 Sliverfish Macronix* (Cambridge: Equipage, 1992); *Nine To Zero* (1992); *That Doesn't Lifestyle* (1992); *L.A.* (1993); *SBD: Silent But Deadly (more hoarse hairs from the reductive asshole)* (1993); *Pop Poems for 1993* (1993); *28 Harpmesh Intermezzi* (with Karlien van den Beukel) (Leeds: FriendInParcel, 1994); *Turnpike Ruler* (Cambridge: Equipage, 1994); *Unpush Whatsit* (1994–1996); *Epicentre International* (with Esther Leslie) (London: UpForGrabs, 1995); *Benison Fence-Off* (Cambridge: Barque, 1999); *Thong Rind Songs* (2001); *Vim Plop* (2002); *Texts for Beck-Lunch Improvors* (2004); *Thanks Mick, Great Socks* (2004); *Kryatl* (2004). Some of this work has been placed on the website <*www.militantes-thetix.co.uk*>.

DISCOGRAPHY
Simon Fell/Out To Lunch *Music For 10(0)* (Leo Records, 1995, CD).
Derek Bailey/Out To Lunch *2/28 Sliverfish Macronix* (Rectangle
        Records, 1999, 7″ single).
Ian Stonehouse *Le Tombeau d'Esemplasm* (2001, CD).

ROBERT SHEPPARD INTERVIEWED BY TIM ALLEN

The Postman Below my Window

Small Voice

HUNDRED 3.7
TWENTIETH CENTURY BLUES 36

darkness drags

a headlight's irradiated cone fading to an
English print of shredded lane rheumy vapours
tickling in time the throat catches on
slices of transitory purpose lost in decline

watch a row of identical open trucks
head somewhere archaic like a Midland colliery
not singing praises it's not even singing
the sharp rasp rustles in the ear

a redundant germ that drifts this Age
of Irony now happening to be forged
it barely sustains its volume of displacement
the vandals have fled   the gate bangs

scoop phlegmy lyric from the clogging drone
from the rusted hinges' lament

bitter croak

(January 1997)

ALLEN Robert, the first time I ever read you must have been in the *new
british poetry* (Paladin 1988), and you were a new name to me then.
Tell me something about the early years of your writing. What, for
example, was the work in *The Frightened Summer* (Pig Press '81) like?
I suppose it is a rather too obvious question, but what were the
turnings and personal predilections that sent you down the road
towards the British avant garde?

SHEPPARD There are two ways of answering this one; one in terms of
reading and association, the second in terms of writing and
accomplishment. An anthology was important for me too: Michael
Horovitz' *Children of Albion*, which I bought in 1971. The presence of
Bill Butler's Unicorn Bookshop in Brighton, where I grew up, early
kindnesses from Bob Cobbing, Lee Harwood, Paul Brown and
others: all of these are formative. I knew about small presses from
an early age, and took my knowledge of the British Poetry Revival
with me to university in Norwich, as a kind of insulation against
the vibrant but mainstream literary culture there. The second way
of looking at it is slower: despite some early pamphlets and maga-
zine publications, I was actually no Barry MacSweeney, no prodigy.
My earliest poem I would preserve now is 'The Blickling Hall Poem'
(1980), which is actually a rather conservative beginning, more
Harry Guest than Bob Cobbing. It is possible to construct an alter-
native chronology by beginning with my Writers Forum booklet, a
series of experimental homages to The Soft Machine, published in
1979. But it's no good. It took time to tie up reading and writing,
association and accomplishment, if that's not too neat a way to
put it.
  Predilections? It would be easy to say that I was revolted by the
poetry of the mainstream and found a more exciting, open alter-
native, but I'm not sure that's true. That's more the cultural argu-
ment of my PhD in the early to mid eighties. In the early (school)
days it was probably more that I found a poetry consonant with

the kinds of cultural inputs one received in the 1970s as a matter of course: new Beckett plays on the radio, Stockhausen on TV, The London Contemporary Dance Theatre live, jazz-inflected rock (the Softs pre-eminently). But also an heir to the TS Eliot one studied at school: the reading of Pound and Joyce that followed, the surrealist romp of Dali posters from Athena, Burroughs (a school prize). All the more strange that the cleanest (but the dullest) of my earlier writings of the 1970s picked up on the post-Olson notational obsession: I caught it out of Harwood, Allen Fisher, even Sinclair writing about 'place'. At least by 1980 I'd found Roy Fisher who had a more rhetorical way into that 'stance toward reality'. But even this is imposing a pattern upon what was actually a quite healthy lack of direction for a young writer. I was writing fiction, too, which I only gave up once I was on Malcolm Bradbury's Creative Writing MA at UEA (1978–9).

ALLEN What you said about finding a poetry, 'consonant with the kinds of cultural inputs one received in the 1970s' is interesting, but if that was so why is it that the millions who shared those 'cultural inputs' remained immune to the exciting things happening in some poetry? Not just immune either, positively antagonistic; I lost count of the number of people I knew who had radical tastes across the cultural spectrum except where poetry was concerned. What do you think about this? Has the British avant garde been its own worst enemy or do you think that there is something particular about poetry that made this almost inevitable? And bringing that back to your personal response to such poetry, is there a 'political' aspect to it?

SHEPPARD One answer must lie in what I call the persistence of the Movement Orthodoxy. The tight lyric of personal response out of Hardy and Auden has been particularly resilient—in the public eye, through the educational system—and, without wishing to re-articulate arguments I make in my critical book, *The Poetry of Saying*—ideologically constructed, strong enough to change from a xenophobic formalism into a multicultural mélange. The effect of this—with a few exceptions—has been to ossify the determinants of the poetic in the wider culture: easy to do because poetry is a minority interest. The brief but significant hey-day of the British Poetry Revival as 'Underground Poetry' (that was the subtitle of Horovitz' anthology) was useful in raising the profile of its participants;

when I met Lee Harwood he was about 35 and famous. No young poet I know is famous like that. But the downside was that such writing became associated with the populism of the Liverpool poets, etc., something datable and dated.

I have just come back from a conference at Birkbeck College on poetics, and what struck me were the different ways British and American writers refer to the history of their work. Whereas the avant-garde has assumed a canon in the US—much to their surprise, Bruce Andrews was telling me—in Britain there hasn't been the same sense of generational progression, Oedipal conflict. Whereas the young poet Dell Olsen could play around with O'Hara's tag, 'Lana Turner has Collapsed' in one of her recent texts she read, it's impossible to imagine that level of recognition for a quote from any British poet: Harwood, Raworth, say. When Adrian Clarke quotes Allen Fisher in a poem it's a clear homage, but not one the audience can be *expected* to pick up on. The only exception is probably Prynne. In a recent poem Ken Edwards quotes Prynne and the footnote runs quite coyly, 'JHP, of course'. There's a lot in that 'of course'. However, the increased entry into the academy by some of these poets is beginning to make a difference in terms of critical reception (and I suppose I'm part of that movement).

ALLEN Yes, of course, ha, that 'entry into the academy' has been something of a concern of mine for a while because in some cases it seems to me to be a case of taking one step forward and two steps back, but sometimes the other way round too, thankfully. I do think that move has changed things though, like being given resuscitation by your worst enemy. Again, I think that situation is different in America because they do not have the same inbred cultural class attitudes of the Brits; here for example the 'entry into the academy' is seen as just a further remove for innovative poetry away from popular concerns, so is seen as even more elitist. It calls for an understanding of what is going on but such a thing is exactly what the systemic attitudes of the mainstream aim to prevent. An important question arises from all this: is there a connection between the politics of poetry and 'Politics', and if so what is it? Your work seems to me to function on the assumption that the answer is 'yes', but I think most people in this country would find that difficult to fathom.

SHEPPARD Of course we live in an age of mass higher education, so it isn't so elite any more (this, despite the fact that one of the minor points of my paper at Birkbeck was about the intimidating authority of the academy over those outside it). And the rise of creative writing as a discipline seems to me important. . . .

But politics: more important. I can't stop politics entering the poem in a brute way. I make political remarks—it's hard not to in, say, the poem I am working on at the moment concerning the 'September 12' we are all living through. But there are a number of ways in which the political can be said to inform my work, firstly as style, then as form. I've still got a little of that easy Marcusean belief in the 'aesthetic dimension' left from the early 1980s: that art offers utopic *images* of a future rationality, but it's mostly subverted into notions of radical, discontinuous *form*. That's long shaded into Adornoesque negativity: the sense that 'art's utopia is draped in black', as an act of mourning and an event of pain, a prefiguration of an almost impossible utopia. How that translates into particular structures I find impossible to say: perhaps a stylistic austerity but not, I hope, an impenetrability. It's hard to believe that my work can be funny, but there you go.

The notion of 'linking the unlinkable',—I picked up on a speculation of Derrida, much as Adrian Clarke picked up on similar formulations of Lyotard—not only links with what also links with that which links with Adorno—that is, 'Auschwitz' as a name of (in)human calamity—but it suggests the modes of 'creative linkage' that I attempted in *The Lores* and elsewhere: a kind of accelerated collage, in which the links are melted into the materials.

Are we allowed the diversions of the so-called ethical turn? My critical book, *The Poetry of Saying*, opposes an open, processual, uncaptured poetry of saying, with the ontological violence of the poetry of the said, which imposes fixity upon its products. It's all borrowed from Levinas (without the theology, of course), but the importance of this is that it doesn't involve a binary opposition. The saying can only appear in the solidity of the said, quite literally, as printed text, say. They are very suggestive categories and they haunt my sense of recent radical, defamiliarising writing— and my own writing is in there somewhere—as founded on an ethical concern, *not* to be bluntly political. Latterly, I'm rather taken by Guattari's 'The Three Ecologies' essay, in which he links the realms of the social, the processes of subjectivation, and of the environment, and the importance of the role of the aesthetic in catalysing changes in, and between, the domains.

But these are (contradictory) theories around and across which the actual poetic practice dances, betraying first one, then another, of these politico-ethical poetics, and revisiting them over time. One of my senses of the importance of poetics anyway as a discourse is that it compensates for the fact that writers can't read their own work; I've no idea how my work measures against any of this. I only know that, while on the Left, I don't use the work primarily as a political tool, which it can't be in any direct way. Do you remember at my reading in Plymouth, an American in the audience applauded the line from 'September 12': 'The fourth world war forgives itself for ever'? And I put my hand up to stop him clapping. What I meant was: it's one thing to applaud at the end of a reading, in aesthetic approval; but another to applaud the sentiment of an isolated line.

ALLEN Yes indeed, but what about applauding the apparent sentiment of the whole poem, something which leads on quite naturally to applauding the sentiment of a poet's entire œuvre, then unconsciously, or unembarrassingly I should say, looping that back into a notion of what we call the aesthetic? It's a loop I have never been able to see a way out of and what you say about the way that politics enters your work ties in with that, and yes, it is an entry that is brutal. So let's pause with the brutal for a moment—much of your work engages with the violent, and the sexually violent too, something which some readers and critics find problematic— could you say something about this, especially in relation to your comments above about 'the ontological violence of the poetry of the said'.

SHEPPARD Any violence, I would have thought, is partially glimpsed, barely enacted, merely enunciated (and sexually, I don't think I attract what Iain Sinclair calls a 'one handed readership'!). Mysterious scenarios juxtaposed with others. It's possibly the brutal entry of brutality itself: 148 million people died during war and man-made catastrophes, the quotidian extremities of the twentieth century whose blues I sing. I hope the singing, as it were, transmutes desire ensnared, thwarted, perverted, by history's narratives. So I hope I problematise a reading rather than become problematic for a reader. An encounter with a poem should be an encounter with otherness, not confirmatory—that would be the ontological violence, although its processes—of trying to see the different as the same—are inevitable. (This part of my answer is coloured by my current reading: Derek Attridge's brilliant short book *The Singularity of Literature*.) Maybe this also has to do with genre considerations. Whoever your 'readers and critics' are (I've never encountered them) I wonder whether that which they can take in Burroughs or Ballard—to name the sublime and the ridiculous—or that which they customarily view at the cinema— Cronenberg or Tarantino (which I would not)—is thought to be inappropriate in the magic medium? I don't know.

ALLEN Perhaps we are being a little too simplistic in our notion of 'reader' here, Robert. Yes, you 'problematise a reading', and those whose own reading track crosses over your own are going to enter into that problematised reading, or extend it, in the right spirit; but many will not, for a host of reasons, some of which we've already discussed—'an encounter with otherness' being exactly what many readers do not want etc, especially in 'the magic medium'. So who is your reader?

SHEPPARD Somebody who uses and operates the text creatively. The only person who isn't the reader (of my work) is me!

ALLEN Then most of your readers will automatically be creative operators of the *Twentieth Century Blues*. Where to start? Was it a project or was it a title?

SHEPPARD It was a project first, and designed with readerly potentiality in mind. (My journal for 1989, which your question has sent me back to, was full of theoretical considerations of the role of the active reader in the open work, anxieties over 'reference', things of that kind). The second half of the eighties had been quite a time for me. I'd written some very angry, clenched poems, collected in *Daylight Robbery,* a big breakthrough for me, that might be described as 'open' in their invitation to the reader, but could also be described as 'closed' in their difficulty. I often introduced my readings with the words, 'The most important influence on my work is Margaret Thatcher.' Which was true, given the ways I think we were victims of her successful campaign to change human consciousness. Adrian Clarke and I were also at this time collecting what we saw of similar new work for the anthology *Floating Capital*, so it was also a communal thing.

But I wanted to find another way to allow a reader to structure his or her responses to my work, and wanted to lighten the texture a little (which I did, years later, towards the end of *Twentieth Century Blues*, but retained textual impaction as a strategy in 'Killing Boxes' and *The Lores*, of course, where the materials got grim, when the going got tough). I'd been long fascinated by the way Yeats created textual complexity, by revisiting the same materials—the Byzantium, Coole Park, poems—and almost produced 'strands', to use my term. I was also concerned that the 'long poem' in the twentieth century tended to be prolix. I thought Allen Fisher's *Place* presented a flexible precedent. I remember I saw Gavin Selerie read his important serial poem *Roxy*—a strictly linear sequence—and realised this was the anti-model of what I wanted to build, structurally. While the 'blues'—still separate poems— would be numbered sequentially (I reached 75), the multiple strand numberings (there were 97) would suggest alternative routes between the parts of the project. Or should I say 'roots', since the Deluzoguattarian 'rhizome' was somewhere in there, the idea that the interconnections would amount to a 'net/(k)not-work(s)', in my clumsy glyph. Barrett Watten's description of Zukofsky's *A* as a mobile open work following Zukofsky's life and thought, was important too. Just look at the way war, particularly the Gulf War(s), in the 'Killing Box' strand, continue through the project and even out the other end (I wrote 8, 9, and 10, last year, history demanding it).

Somewhat later the title *Twentieth Century Blues* suggested itself. I'd rejected Beuys' *The End of the Twentieth Century* as too portentous, and this kitchy catchy bit of Noel Coward (which I vaguely remembered from an old 78) seemed just right (and seemed, but wasn't, an oblique reference to the blues music I was singing in a band at that time, which itself fed into the 'Smokestack Lightning' strand of the project). Somehow I determined that the text would complete itself at the turn of the century (nobody was then, in late 1989, using the term 'millennium'), that it would be, to use a term I probably didn't use then, a 'time-based work'. Neither did I know that it would be almost a hypertext, with its titles, interconnected titles and strands. (I say 'almost', because the strands are multiple but one-way, moving towards the time-limit, but I can see a viable use of hypertext to present the entire work eventually.) But I also believe the title helped determine the poetic focus, in many ways. The toppling of Thatcher (but not the ideology to which she gave her name), the fall of the Berlin Wall, the impending millennium (even if nobody could correctly estimate when it might end), these were important, of course . . . but I wonder whether if I would have dreamt up the conceit of *Empty Diaries* (an interrupted sequence of poems which runs from 1901 to 2000), if it were not for that.

ALLEN I'm glad you mentioned hypertext because when I was discussing *Twentieth Century Blues* with a friend a few years ago, someone who was actively into hypertext poems, I said that ideally it was probably the way your project should be approached, except that there is something about the directional quality of hypertext that still irritates me—that flashing word saying 'this way this way'. So I am much more satisfied by the multiple nature of your 'strands' and the strange mix of order and chaos induced by the numbering and sequencing. But can I ask you about the pleasurable aspect of this numerology, and the same would apply to your indexes and strands—they must be fun—if they were not fun wouldn't they be headache instead?

SHEPPARD The strands double-back on themselves, become knotted; the multiple strands suggest that any particular 'blues' belongs to several strands and you can connect them to other texts (with even a few outside of *Twentieth Century Blues*). But it is not so much a question of navigation, of links—remember the hyperlink business wasn't in existence when I thought the whole thing up—but of complexity, instability between parts of something that are parts of something else. The index is a nightmare and, I suppose, thinking of it like this for the first time, the numerology in a strange way links with the word-counts of several of the main sequences: parts of *Empty Diaries* (which I conceive of as the spine of the project, running from 'blues' 7 to the last, spanning the 'century'), and *The Lores* (which I think of as the centre of the project, though it is 'blues' 30, written in 1994–5). But the whole thing is deliberately unprogrammatic, unprogrammed, was a way of linking all of my creative output in one big sack. Though it's not *that* big. . . .

ALLEN Whose voices are those in the 'Blues'? The question arose very strongly in a debate about the *Empty Diaries*. They often seem to be women's voices and I get pictures in my head of anonymous people in old photographs of my mother's etc.

SHEPPARD To focus on *Empty Diaries*: they are precisely the voices of pictures of female people in (old) photographs, except they are very often, but not exclusively, ventriloquised by a male voice, but whether that is 'my' voice I doubt. I don't—as I am here—speak in my 'own' voice (whatever that might mean in the act of writing) in my poems. I speak in my own voice when I speak *about* the poems, rather than *in* them, which is an irony of poetics worthy of further consideration.

Empty Diaries, the first 90 in the Stride book—the 'later' ones were written in the years they pretend to belong to—were mostly written by collecting notes on 90 sheets of paper numbered year by year (1901–90), looking at photographs taken on (or about) the requisite year, and then (forgetting the images) working on the notes in various ways (sometimes the poem was scooped out from the notes, sometimes a collage of its elements, sometimes a completely different spring-boarding from, ignoring of, the notes), often with the thought of a 35 year old woman narrator (thus she would be a different narrator for each poem, though strangely similar, emphasising the constructedness, as voice). In some of the later 'Empty Diaries' (in *Tin Pan Arcadia*) I play around with this: they know they are 'made up', a usefully cosmetic pun for 'cross-gendered poetry'. Elsewhere, the voices are more or less disembodied utterances, partial enunciations of personhood, rather than personas (though I do have a cast of recurring rogues: the couple George and Pearl get re-functioned in various narratives, for example, but like moveable type in a setter's tray). There's more narrativity—the feel of narration happening—than actual narrative, although Roy Fisher warned me, when he read *Empty Diaries*, that my novelist-*manqué* was trying to get out! Remember, I 'trained' as a fiction-writer at UEA.

ALLEN Could you say more about the *Twentieth Century Blues* conception of history? Do words such as 'authentic', 'true' and 'real' have any bearing here; and if not, what kind of history is it? And another question related to this: are you conscious of other attempts at such 'histories' e.g. do you know of Giles Goodland's *A Spy in the House of Years*?

SHEPPARD Today—that's before I saw your question—I was looking over a new little pamphlet of mine, which contains reviews of five books by Iain Sinclair . . . I was checking the printing. Randomly, I noticed what I'd written about Sinclair's collaborator on *Rodinsky's Room*: 'Lichtenstein is not naïve about history and its irrecoverability,' and I thought: I'd struck a wrong note there. Who is to say that anything is 'irrecoverable'? After all, Rachel Lichtenstein's quest for David Rodinsky, the East End recluse, took her to Auschwitz. Incommensurable yes. Irrecoverable no.

On Saturday night a man in the pub showed me his holiday snaps of Auschwitz, that's what they were, touristic and grim at the same time. He meant no disrespect. 'One makes links with that which makes links with Auschwitz'—as Derrida (near enough) puts it—all over again.

Last night—this is a selective history of my last few days—I discussed with friends the complexities of actually turning up on the 'doorstep' of Auschwitz. That remark about 'daytrips from Liverpool Airport' in my text 'The Reader' was not an invention. You could actually do it at one time. Scott Thurston (who *had* visited—he lived nearby) mentioned 'secondary witnessing', so we were tertiary witnesses, in a sense.

The dangers of the Sinclair-Lichtenstein approach, of anyone's approach, are not those of history, but of myth, of speaking *for*, not *of*, the Other. (The other danger is heritage, which probably does the same, but with a guide-book.)

Oh yes, only then I read your question about all this, your mention of Goodland's book, which I know has been discussed with reference to *Empty Diaries*. . . . It seems to resemble most closely the historical year-by-year quotations of John Seed's *Transit Depots*, a work I heard John read and then found myself (unconsciously) taking the structure from (he doesn't do the obsessive word-counting of *Empty Diaries*, of course, a deliberately blunt inscription of time's measures). It seemed right to publish parts of our sequences together, which we did in 1992, the years' poems interleaved, and punctuated by Patricia Farrell's historical images. John is a professional historian, which I am not, and while my sequence was attempting to construct an 'alternative', 'fictive', twentieth century, as I've said, his was a Benjaminian book of juxtaposed quotations. OK, while I believe that history is a discursive production, I don't believe—it's the witness strain in me—that history is a fiction. Neither do I believe it's simply a re-run of reality. I don't, in any case, possess a developed theory of history.

Before I had energy to answer this question, I watched—idly, tired from work—a TV programme about an archaeological dig. They dug up a beautiful statue of a 'new' Roman goddess, Senua. Nobody had heard of her before!

Later (this is futurology), I shall return to reading Alyn Shipton's 'new history' of jazz, which is assertively revisionist. As much as I approve of his debunking of the foundational myths surrounding a figure like Buddy Bolden, that doesn't make Michael Ondaatje's brilliant novel *Coming Through Slaughter* any less affective, because it uses these myths, quite knowingly. I hope the same goes for my 'historical' writings: Elzadie and Arvella's stories, yes?

Indeed, tomorrow I am meeting somebody from the Liverpool Museums to see if I may perform my quite 'fictive' 'historical' 'guide' to Sudley House *at* Sudley House. (It's called *Sudley House!*) On my tour, there's a guide to a room that isn't there! Perhaps that's an image of what I want with history: a space that isn't there amongst those that are. Which is what Sir Philip Sidney—back there in several histories—said a long time ago in his poetics: poets 'affirmeth nothing', while history is tied to the real. But it's history that gives us Senua (today!), an innovation that is, nevertheless, not an invention. Quite miraculous! Poetry couldn't do that. . . .

ALLEN OK, so the *Twentieth Century Blues* affirms nowt, but recently Alan Munton posed the question re your work that it was a return to subject, and by that I think he meant a return from what we might call language-based work. I didn't agree because I don't think your work has ever departed from subject in that sense, but what about subject in this larger philosophical sense? I think you have partly answered this with regard to the subject as constituted in history and I take note of your saying that we should speak 'of' and not 'for' the 'other'; but a notion of subject, in the way that the twentieth century is a subject, is more problematic for me and I find it difficult to argue either way. Can you help me out?

SHEPPARD I'll try! It's not for me (as the writer) to resolve the interesting debate between Alan and Allen! I can only speak from my poetics, which probably don't address the issues in that way. I certainly felt the tension of works which operate between their materials and the materiality of the medium. In certain practices—concrete poetry, language poetry—the artifice of the medium dominates; that's its point, to critique the boundaries of artifice and signification. I have sympathy with that. In certain works, *Blatent Blather/Virulent Whoops*, my collaboration with Bob Cobbing, I take that on, but mostly I see poetry, my poetry, as the making of an artefact with materials *in* the materiality. Obviously the choice of materials matters (subject matters, we could say, punningly): in the Stride book of 'texts and commentaries', *Hymns to the God in which My Typewriter Believes*, the materials are deliberately working against the grain of my usual 'subject matters'. Or maybe not entirely: the Schlink novel, picked not because it's good but because it made me shake, Anne Sexton's drafts, Sephardic Songs. . . . Or the Sudley House text (they are going to let me perform it by the way!): a place to which I had privileged access, which gave me materials, in which I found ways to make texts (they are, of course, not messages).

The open saying of poetry dreams of a kind of content-less utterance, but its embodiment in the said, denies this. Form enters as its own poetic force, but form has to have something to form—in my work anyway. Whether that is enjambment as a device—which I've tried to apply to prose as well as 'verse', or whether it's the word-count of *The Lores* (which you could almost argue is thematic). Matter that is subject to form, we might say.

I'm not sure that the twentieth century is a 'subject' in that sense. The *Blues* treat their century as temporal material(s) to work through, to make with. It's a network that can be read in many ways, as its (near) epigraph from Coetzee suggests. It's not affirmative, no. Maybe alternative. . . .

ALLEN We haven't said anything about collaborations, of which you have done quite a few. What makes them succeed, how different are they to individual work?

SHEPPARD The longest lasting collaboration is with Patricia Farrell, mostly the booklets we've made for our Ship of Fools. What makes it interesting are the varying degrees of collaboration: from purely her providing covers for books, like *The Lores*, although even there she has treated visual materials I'd used to write the poems, and which we'd both used in a slide show that accompanied one of the performances we did, with dancer Jo Blowers, at the Writers Forum workshop. So even that one example opens out into other collaborative situations. True collaborations, like *Looking North* twenty years ago, or *Seven* ten years ago, or *The Blickensderfer Punch* recently, involved us both in processing the same photographic materials simultaneously (in two cases, images we'd taken for the purpose). These are obviously the most satisfying, but whether they are the most successful for a reader, I'm not sure. Where they work most successfully for the collaborator is where they result in something that could not have existed before (which is certainly true of the last three named). That is their aim: to take you away from your usual conceits and tricks. Then there are works where Patricia has produced visuals after the text, but we still don't think of them as illustrations because the same material has been used, almost as though we had been collaborating, as though the experience of earlier collaborations informs these pieces. *Fucking Time*—the Rochester pamphlet—is one such (a touched up (!) image from that appears on the cover of *Tin Pan Arcadia*; we shamelessly recycle). Of course, we're working in different media. Patricia—who has just agreed this description of our working methods—is writing a lot more, with increasing authority, so look out for the book of texts by Farrell and images by Sheppard. It could happen!

The first collaboration with Bob Cobbing and the one with Scott Thurston grew out of existing texts. With the Cobbing I wrote an introduction to a volume of his Collected Poems (the masterly *Processual*) as a poem, and sent the shredded fragments of the cut-up and the discarded fragments to Bob. I thought he might make a visual out of them, but no, he made an extraordinary text using every word of my poem and drafts. It ends, 'We are both!' which should be the motto of all collaborators. The Thurston collaboration is probably the most casual in history. He wrote a response to my 1980 'Blickling Hall Poem' in 1990! Later we had a spate of intense to and fro-ing, casting poems back and forth between us, until we had twelve, re-functioning the odd phrase here and there. But I think it's successful in performance, even as happened last week, when Scott read it all as part of his own reading. (We both saw Rupert Loydell doing something similar, the other month: reading both parts of a collaboration. Which reminds me that when the collaboration of this interview is over, I hope to write a collaborative piece with Rupert.[I did: it's called *Risk Assessment*.])

The second Cobbing, *Blatent Blather/Virulent Whoops*—yes, I know 'blatant' is spelt wrong—was the opposite: a frenetic to-ing and fro-ing of texts. 'You write three lines and then I'll write three lines,' Bob decided. Over one summer. I remember long-sightedly I would spy the postman below my window delivering envelopes that bore Bob's characteristically stretched handwriting, and I'd think: well, that's the morning gone; I'd try to get my response back in the post by midday. An extraordinary textual joust. The old man keeping the youngster (that's how I felt) on his toes. Bob knew he didn't have long and he wanted to do another collaboration with me (he used it to permit himself to produce semantic texts, which is why I went visual half-way through, to force it onwards). We used every technique at our disposal. We didn't so much find new techniques, but re-functioned and juxtaposed old ones, as you do in almost improvised situations. It's quite unique—that's some sort of success. Neither could have written it on his own, I think. Bob and I performed it once, and Patricia and I a number of times—in Bob's memory. Of course, the collaboration of performance is another matter. . . .

ALLEN Bob Cobbing keeps popping up in these interviews, and always with a mix of love and something else I can't pin down, fear maybe, or at least something more than respect etc—definitely a father figure for many. Could you say something about him, on any level and angle you want.

SHEPPARD Fear? No! The endearing and enduring quality about Bob was the radical consistency of his projects. Artistically he developed— more slowly than some accounts suggest—towards greater experiment. His concrete poetry was simultaneously sound poetry and visual poetry: nobody else quite did this. This meant an extension into performance (all this is documented, by cheek, Upton, me and others), but also the running of the Writers Forum Workshop, which, for nearly 50 years, was one of the unsung provisional institutions (it never lost its vital provisionality) of the alternative poetries. Non-dogmatic at the Workshop—in other contexts he could be as awkward as the rest of us!—Bob permitted all kinds of writers, artists, performers—professional and amateur, beginners and old hands—to try things out. There were no discussions, no lectures from Bob. A student of mine recently thanked me for the gentle way I'd guided his writing. That's testament to Bob: you enthuse but you don't cajole; you 'lead' by example. If he liked the work, Bob might offer to publish it. And that leads to his other 'branch' and his extraordinary dedication to the little press as a means of production. He published over a thousand booklets, a third at least of his own visual work, but the number of well-known poets' first books published by Writers Forum testifies to Bob's generosity and acuity. He took chances but he wouldn't publish work that didn't impress. He teaches us all to organise activities around our work (in the extended sense). He weathered bouts of unpopularity (and popularity too), but just kept on, knowing that these things don't matter. Work will reach those who need it, whichever way the culture leans. He was the greatest teacher, and as Adrian Clarke (himself as indebted as I to Bob) says, Bob's success was that the 'school of Cobbing' has no students, no stylistic clones.

ALLEN What about your own teaching then? How do you go about it and what is it you are aiming to do? Do you have to compromise, with regard to exams and syllabus etc, or are you in relative control? Do your own polemical directions clash with that of the students sometimes, or do they have some familiarity with your poetics before they start? How do you gauge the success of your teaching?

SHEPPARD Throughout all my teaching—the years in Further Education as well as in Higher Education—I have been lucky enough to teach interesting poetry, to arrange visiting writers, to be quite exploratory. On the other hand, it's only a job, and you have to compromise. No one possesses the moral high ground. In Higher Education, of course, I've more autonomy, am indeed expected to pursue my research interests, which are my recent critical ones— the long volume on poetry, the short Iain Sinclair guide, editing the Harwood 'Companion'—but also my own writing is classed as research, which feels rather odd. Naturally I am expected to teach out of these two, intersecting, research practices, and I think there is, as I said earlier, a general drift to the academy by linguistically innovative writers, of which I am part. I put at the centre of my pedagogy the notion of poetics as a philosophy of writing, and encourage the diverse kinds of writers who sign up for the MA in Writing Studies I lead at Edge Hill to develop their own. I introduce my own poetics as a kind of model for poetics itself, but, of course, I also introduce the kinds of poetry you'd expect me to. Out of this there has developed a small group of PhD and MA students—Scott Thurston, Cliff Yates, Alice Lenkiewicz, Angela Keaton, Andrew Taylor and Matt Fallaize and others—who have run, more or less, with a generally non-mainstream poetry. So there's quite a lively scene in West Lancashire/Liverpool, at the moment, which is a kind of unofficial success.

I guess what you are expecting me to say is that there are conspiring forces out to stop me teaching weird writing practices. I have formed a network, the wonderfully named NEWT (Network of Experimental Writing Tutors), which is lying in wait (and dormant, I admit) for predatory external examiners. But, then, you see, I am an external examiner, and fully involved in the creative writing community, have written reports on poetics, etc., so one gains an odd kind of authority, with which one can deflect negativity. Scott and I have turned some of our teaching materials into a chapter of an otherwise quite mainstream writing textbook, *The Road to Somewhere*. Hazel Smith has written a marvellous primer for teaching radical poetics. Scott and I hope to do more. Maybe a big battle lies ahead, but I don't see the dust rising.

Resistance in students takes the form of an addiction to self-expressive doggerel. No undergraduate comes up and says, 'I want to write like Andrew Motion.' If they did, I'd say, 'Go ahead!', but it would be at variance with what we do in the workshops, which, for the record, is all out of the second volume of the Rothenberg/Joris anthology, *Poems for the Millennium*.

ALLEN I know we have touched on this already, but maybe we can use this topic as a way of getting into a discussion of your theoretical mag, *Pages*, which I noticed has surfaced again as a blog. You said that your own writing is regarded as research and that this feels odd; you also say that you put at the centre of your pedagogy, 'the notion of poetics as a philosophy of writing'. Both those statements remind me of something Norman Jope once said about the difference between 'experimental' and 'mainstream' reflecting the difference between pure and applied maths. I never agreed with him because there are too many exceptions and in the end it doesn't stand up, but is it the case that in your example it could be true?

SHEPPARD No no no, poetics is not the preserve of the avant-garde! *All* writing has a poetics and all of my (MA and PhD) students are encouraged to articulate their own, as a survival and developmental discourse, even those writing crime fiction, say. Imagine the complex stylistic, environmental, political poetics of a Carl Hiaasen!

ALLEN OK, let's leave that for a moment and go back to *Pages*? Why did you stop it for so long? Wasn't it the only British magazine devoted solely to avant poetics? Funny to think now, but I remember that the first time I came across a copy I found it very difficult and not something that matched that awful term, user friendly; at the time I just didn't know enough about theory to make much sense of it even though I had read most of the poets discussed.

SHEPPARD The first series of *Pages* consisted of 2 folded sheets containing poetry mainly. You're probably thinking of the second series which wasn't user-friendly in the usual way—I knew I wasn't producing a magazine which would reach out of the small press nexus I knew already. It was a very modest venture, certainly in terms of layout and design. But I did try (in most issues) to present a generous selection of poetry by a single author (John Wilkinson —Alan Halsey—Hazel Smith, amongst others), plus an essay, a shorter response to the selection and a bibliography. I was certainly trying to present 'resources for the linguistically innovative poetries' as I put on the masthead, trying to provide readerly guidance, what Eric Mottram called 'poetry information', certainly not 'theory'. It is gratifying to see these materials taken up now and then. The last issue was the O'Sullivan, in 1997. Given the privileges and responsibilities of my job since then I haven't had the energy to get back to it, but I might, still, in a more infrequent way. [Which, as you noticed, I have recently, as a blog-zine.]

ALLEN If I can return to that earlier point; I know that poetics is not the preserve of the avant garde but I would say that from the viewpoint of the average poetry reader and the, for lack of a better word, mainstream poets themselves, and many of their critical supporters, especially those not attached to academia, poetics is something to be avoided because to entertain the very idea of 'poetics' is to entertain the idea of different choices, different ways of engaging with language. Their poetics is a given, a habit, a rule-book that you question at your peril. I would even say that in most cases it is unconscious. This is what makes mainstream 'poetics' so damn difficult to pin down and prise open.

SHEPPARD I've just flicked through the Bloodaxe volume *Strong Words* and it is clear that the contemporary 'mainstream' poets—your word, not mine—, with the exception of Sean O'Brien who only has negative things to say about the kind of poet I take myself to be (I don't understand his gesture, the readers won't know what he's on about), write a considered poetics which is speculative, reflective, and, on occasions, illuminating—but contestable. They seem to use the same discourse that you and I might: even O'Brien quotes Adorno to suggest that we are the 'culture industry'. A bit rich, I think. So I don't think it is as simple as it was, in the days before theoretical engagement, when the Movement orthodoxy was un-attenuated. Glyn Maxwell argues, as I would, that rhythm is somatic in language. What divides us is a real debate about metre and what they are pleased to call 'form'. They mean metrical pattern. Good bodies makes good metrics, he implies, while I can be found coarsely intoning, 'Writing in ancient forms shits in the mouths of the dead!' It's not that there isn't a poetics there, it's how that can be engaged with, how a debate might emerge, between poetics, beyond the level of the O'Brien put-down. The narrowness comes in how they see us. We need to avoid narrow-ness in how we see them. . . . They sell books; we smell of theory. I'm growing suspicious of all this 'us' and 'them'. There are 'exper-imental' rulebooks, too.

ALLEN I agree with much of that, you're right, there has been a shift over the past few years with people such as Maxwell and maybe I haven't paid enough attention to it. I haven't read *Strong Words* but I did read *Contemporary Poems: Some Critical Approaches* (Ed. Jeffries & Sansom. Smith/Doorstop) where I found the critics were spreading their net further in order to find intellectual backing for their opinions. It would be interesting to see how far this engagement with poetics goes, but I certainly don't see any evidence of it at the 'lower' levels, not yet. I do find my own position re this weird though because for years now I have been trying to get to the bottom of what it is that makes the difference between the main-stream poetry I like and that which irritates me to hell, and I don't think I am simply talking about quality. And I am quite aware of the tiresome 'experimental rulebook' too. One of the problems here is the blurring of the distinction between poetics and tribal loyalties, and how much you blur and how much you clarify are both down to a certain political tact. I have always been for variousness, not just ideally but because at the practical level my enthusiasms them-selves are various—it was the whole *Terrible Work* project for quite a while. Are you optimistic on this front then?

SHEPPARD No

ALLEN Why not? I have always thought that one of the mainstream's survival strengths has been its unquestioning acceptance of post-Movement poetics, to the extent that nobody had to consider the thing any more because it had become naturalised. But if what you are saying is right then that illusion is broken, which can only be good, can't it?

SHEPPARD The Movement orthodoxy—as ideological construct, it's not a club of people—has atomised, without doubt, embracing a multi-cultural, plural, democratic agenda, an inclusiveness that accom-modates institutionised marginalities of various kinds. It's tempt-ing to see the brutal exposure of Larkin's letters as the trauma that precipitated this, from which the orthodoxy has recoiled, rightly, in disgust. As it becomes ever more populist, even while it develops a poetics and openness to theory, its broad church includes every-body *but* the previously persecuted heretics, poets of the British Poetry Revival and the Linguistically Innovative Poetry and Performance Writing that followed, and whatever we might call whatever is being done now. . . .

I'm not optimistic that a genuine debate can be had between those written out of history (or inscribed negatively within it), the subalterns, and those who are culturally visible and who write the official Sunday supplement histories, the administrators of the empire. Witness Sinclair praising Prynne over Larkin on the Today programme. It doesn't work. The normative standards are so strong. Sinclair's usual tack, of walking out into the culture to discover what he encounters, a cultural *dérive,* works better (though is problematical).

Yet there is a strange irony behind O'Brien's rant, or Paterson's recent attack upon 'academic postmodernists'. Why do they continue to abuse the subalterns? Why are they not secure in their power? Why not just ignore us, if we are a coterie? Is this born of the fear that, having allowed the orthodoxy to open up to the point of dissipation, the rebels might be able to seize control—capture the radio station—using an unassailable academic authority (one in which they secretly believe?), which might reveal itself as The Judgement of History, the Test of Time, all those untheorised maskings of power to which they also appeal on their own behalves against us? But this breaking of the illusion, as you call it, leads not to a real plural debate, though it could, but to further acts of repression, however desperate. The orthodoxy is scared about what we might amount to, although it dismisses us—it used to accuse us of all being Michael Horovitz, but they can't do that anymore, he's received a gong; now it's the academic tag that condemns. What I am optimistic about is the fact that the alternative strategies—from Prynne to Cobbing, from Adrian Clarke to Sinclair, to only use names I've cited already—are more various than those found in even the currently authorised but circumscribed pluralism.

ALLEN I would agree with that Robert. Thanks.

Bibliography

CREATIVE PUBLICATIONS

FULL LENGTH COLLECTIONS
Daylight Robbery (Exeter: Stride Publications, 1990).
The Flashlight Sonata (Exeter: Stride Publications, 1993).

Transit Depots/Empty Diaries (with John Seed [text] and Patricia
      Farrell [images]) (London: Ship of Fools, 1993).
Empty Diaries (Exeter: Stride Publications, 1998).
The Lores (London: Reality Street Editions, 2003).
Tin Pan Arcadia (Cambridge: Salt Publishing, 2004).

PAMPHLETS AND FLY-SHEETS
Returns, Textures (London, 1985)
Private Number (London: Northern Lights Publishers, 1986).
Looking North (with images by Patricia Farrell) (Liverpool: Ship of
      Fools,1987).
The Cannibal Club (with Patricia Farrell) (Liverpool: Ship of Fools,
      1990).
Killing Boxes (Liverpool: Ship of Fools, 1992.)
Icarus—Having Fallen (with Patricia Farrell) (Liverpool: Ship of
      Fools, 1992).
Fucking Time (with Patricia Farrell) (Liverpool: Ship of Fools, 1994).
The Book of British Soil (with Patricia Farrell) (Liverpool: Ship of
      Fools, 1995).
Soleà for Lorca (Liverpool: Ship of Fools, 1998).
Three Poems (Liverpool: Ship of Fools, 2000).
The Blickensderfer Punch (with Patricia Farrell) (Liverpool: Ship of
      Fools, 2002).
31st April or The Age of Irony (Liverpool: Ship of Fools, 2001).
Depleted Uranium (Liverpool: Ship of Fools, 2001).
The End of the Twentieth Century (Liverpool: Ship of Fools, 2002).
Codes and Diodes (with Bob Cobbing), (London: Writers Forum,
      1991).
Free Fists (with Patricia Farrell), (London: Writers Forum, 1996).
Neutral Drums (with Patricia Farrell), (London: Writers Forum,
      1999).
Blatent Blather/Virulent Whoops (with Bob Cobbing), (London:
      Writers Forum, 2001).
Fox Spotlights (Cheltenham: The Short Run Press, 1995).
Letter from the Blackstock Road (London: Oasis Books, 1988).
Internal Exile (Southampton: Torque Press, 1988).
The Anti-Orpheus: a notebook (Exeter Shearsman Books, 2004).

CRITICAL PUBLICATIONS

Far Language : Poetics and Linguistically Innovative Poetry 1978–1997,
(Exeter: Stride Research Documents, 1999; second printing
2002).
The Poetry of Saying: British Poetry and its Discontents 1950–2000,
(Liverpool: Liverpool University Press, 2005).
Iain Sinclair, Writers and Their Work (Tavistock: Northcote House,
forthcoming).

EDITORIAL WORK

a. magazines

1983, tape cassette poetry magazine, 1–3, 1974–77.
Rock Drill, 1–5, 1980–85.
Pages, 1–46, 1987–1997 (first and second series), 447+, 2005- (third
series as a blogzine: www.robertsheppard.blogspot.com).

b. anthologies

Floating Capital: New Poets from London (with Adrian Clarke)
(Elmwood: Potes and Poets, 1991).
News for the Ear: A Homage to Roy Fisher (with Peter Robinson)
(Exeter: Stride Publications, 2000).

SIMON SMITH INTERVIEWED BY ANDREW DUNCAN

Silver Rail

Video Black

I walked to Hayley's but it could be Hades

The eyes were taking notes

Complete sense out of sight

Earplugs in this head

You can see clouds let them dissolve jump

Inside how the unmarked tallies with *lillies lillies* with stars

(Spotlights) in the firmament (ceiling)

jump inside the Sublime then jump

The eyes dart dark then gone the present goes

Crashing past the left

Ear let

It dissolve

Cream to white white to white above to China Clay what wheel
  what sparrows' reply

(Cheep cheep) as fibre-board sits one of those jump-off-

The-cliff empirical certainties to melt lettuce

The light will

Bend back its brighter peel to sublime fault fold on

Sub e f d

DUNCAN I'll begin: 'How did you start writing?'

SMITH I was a very mediocre student at school, and had no interest in
  literature or anything else very much, until the sixth form.
  Although Newport Grammar School in Essex was very conservative
  there were a number of excellent teachers who helped me along
  the way. This started with my art teachers, and once I was actually
  doing A Levels, the English Department. The Department was very
  strong, and more importantly very young. All the teachers I had
  were aged between 23 and 28, so they accepted some of us socially
  as well as professionally—probably not a state of affairs that would
  be tolerated these days. But for me, and the four or five others, it
  was extremely creative and helpful. We would go round and hang
  out at their houses at least once a week and at weekends, having
  dinner, listening to music, going to the Arts Cinema in Cambridge,
  dropping down to London to the theatres or to the galleries. I basi-
  cally had two years of University before I went to Kent. I still see
  most of these people now; they are the network of friends we all
  rely on in times of crisis.

  So that is the background, and it accelerated my development
  many times over. But there was one particular incident that set me
  off. Olive Burnside was one of these teachers, and we had to study
  Larkin's *Less Deceived* and Lowell's *Life Studies* for one question on
  the syllabus. Now I think she was getting pretty bored with the
  whole process, so she set us the task of writing a pastiche of a
  Lowell poem. I did mine and handed it in. She shared this with her

then partner John Taylor (he's the J.D. Taylor who has published poems and short stories in *Angel Exhaust* and *Stand* amongst other places); he was doing a PhD thesis at Jesus College at the time, and he was blown away. I started to go round to their place and we'd talk long into the night about writing and poetry and what was great and what wasn't. This was very big for a naïve seventeen year old—all the attention from elders who were somehow contemporaries too.

I then started to write fairly regularly, bad poetry of course, but I was doing it, and that was the important thing. It was the only activity in my life at the time that made me feel alive and connected, and I'm sure that is a very common experience for many teenagers, and why they write so many poems and pop lyrics. John and I would meet: I would look at his poems and he'd look at mine, and we'd discuss and critique. I was getting that buzz, like a drug, the one that keeps you coming back to write more and try again. These were exciting times for me and full of idealisms and enthusiasms; there was so much to learn, explore and discover.

It was many, many more years before I wrote a poem I thought worked, and there were periods when I couldn't write, mainly the times when I was studying literature.

DUNCAN Can you tell us about your self-discovery as a poet? How did you build up to that Prest Roots book (which we've probably all seen)?

Q3 The history of poetry is mostly about the readers. However, poets are also readers —and can act as witnesses. This is an age of infrastructural problems. Can you tell us how you came to find 'underground' poetry? Did you go through a phase of reading the mainstream first? When did you discover the poets of your generation?

SMITH Andrew, I think I need to answer the third question(s) first, to then answer the second. I came across the 'underground' like many people, by chance. When I was popping over to see J.D. Taylor one July evening in 1979 between school and University, he mentioned the name J.H.Prynne, a poet and don at Cambridge who by turns perplexed and annoyed him. This interested me and the name kind of lodged at the back of my memory. I went up to the University of Kent at Canterbury in October 1979, and I did a Modern Poetry course covering the stand-off between Modernism and the Georgians (nothing remarkable in that), but I also got involved with the university poetry society, quite a vibrant organization at the time, chaired by one Simon St Clair Terry. Michael Grant was a tutor in English, and his teachings and views went far beyond the lecture theatre or seminar room. The reading week that first term, I went back to my parents' house and on a trip to Cambridge found a copy of Prynne's *Down Where Changed* in Heffers. Here was a book I was completely baffled by, but I'm one of those perverse readers who feel that if there is something I don't understand that is because of me not the work, and I think I ought to engage further. This is what I did with Prynne over the years that followed. The discovery of this book was the breakthrough for me. Then I wanted to take the Modern Poetry option with Michael, but he was on Sabbatical my second year; however, in 1981–82 I was taught Chaucer to the Metaphysicals by Andrew Ross, who was working with Michael on his PhD, and that brought me back into contact. There was a kind of unwritten syllabus at UKC, and that excluded Hughes, Heaney and the rest: it seemed perfectly natural to study the line of Williams, Olson, Creeley, and then feed that back into Prynne, Peter and John Riley, Eric Mottram, Allen Fisher etc. I think the academic staff who ran the contemporary poetry courses at the time took it as read you already knew about the so-called 'mainstream'. You also have to remember the poetry society at the University was well informed by Michael Grant, and I remember Peter Riley and Eric Mottram coming to read and discuss their work. And I remember sitting spellbound as Stephen Bann, Michael, Paul Smith and Andrew Ross talked with the poet invited to read that evening. These were poets and thinkers I looked up to, they were living, there, and even offered a way one could live. Later I studied with Michael Grant, so the reading list and my awareness of the 'Underground' was quite well established by 1984: I even had had contact with Anthony Barnett by this time too, who proved to be a true friend and mentor, when most people didn't know I was writing. And nor did I want them to know, as almost all of the material was terrible rubbish: I was trying to find my way, and God knows, that has taken 20 years or more. The discovery of the poets of my generation didn't happen until much later, and started via an introduction of

Anthony Barnett to the editors of *fragmente*, Andrew Lawson and Anthony Mellors. By the late 1980s I was living in Oxford and working as a librarian in the public library service. Anthony B. suggested they contact me as a possible contributor to the first issue—at this stage I hasten to add, for reviewing. Anthony was also about to use a poem of mine in *Poetica*, and I think the appearance of that poem, psychologically, was very significant: here I had the recognition of the 'fathers' (actually I doubt many registered it, but you only learn the true impact of one's writing later on. I was so naïve.) After that, finding poets contemporary with me was a haphazard process through the 90s: Drew Milne via CCCP, Miles Champion at Subvoicive, Kelvin Corcoran at the October Gallery readings, Richard Makin via an unsolicited manuscript to my little mag *GRIIlE*. And David Rees was always a presence from 1980: we were at UKC together, and I'd like to say a few words about him later.

Night Shift, the Prest Roots book you mention, came further down the line and very suddenly. It was written in the summer and autumn of 1991, quite quickly in the end, and I think it happened in the euphoria I experienced after my appointment to the post of Assistant Librarian (Special Collections) at the Poetry Library in January of that year, and attending the first CCCP in April. At last after years of interruptions and self-doubt I was immersed in contemporary and new poetry, perhaps even drowning in it—many would probably find that environment oppressive or terribly offputting, I was buzzing and euphoric. I was also surrounded by good and helpful friends who took the work seriously; Anthony Mellors, John Taylor, Charles Bainbridge, David Rees, Harry Gilonis and you, Andrew. They were all writers themselves and kindred spirits, but most importantly of all they were honest, and often quite hard in their judgments. Good readers of one's work are absolutely vital to the realization of good poems. *Night Shift* emerged with a sense of it must have been someone else who had written it; in fact, it felt as though the text was quite alien to me personally in the end. It was a great breakthrough, as each book that followed has proved to be too, but for very different reasons.

Well, Andrew I don't want to risk telling the reader what to think or how to read the book. I think *Night Shift* was partly brought on by the change in hours I was doing at the Poetry Library, where I would work until 8pm, with only daylight for two or three months a year. Darkness and late evening became the way I experienced my free time.

As for the book's purpose? I wanted to compose something in quite a strict or regular verse form and there were quite a few sequences of fourteeners around in the late '80s and '90s, Peter Riley's 'Ospita' comes to mind, or in a very different way, Tom Raworth's *Sentenced to Death* and *Eternal Sections*. There seemed to be some sort of dialogue going on between these poetries, formally I mean, and I found myself taking part in that dialogue, or should I say the poem found its way through this kind of engagement. The poems then 'talk' to one another within the sequence. Building poems in series like this is a feature of the so-called avant garde in this country—it's a way of replacing linear narrative without losing scope, or compromising perception. Of course it's not a new idea; it simply harks back to the great flowering of the sonneteers of the 1590s. A feature common to these modern sequences is their interrogation of complexity and complex structures: they invite the reader to explore rather than present the pat answers of the short, self-contained lyric so popular presently. I mean, experience is not self-contained, so I think it's a lie if your poetry is, even if you think the reader is seeking reassurance. Poetry (for me) needs to challenge assumptions not reinforce them. That is where the whole accessibility argument starts to fall apart. The easy consumption of an Armitage poem, for example, is the core of its conservatism, its Thatcherism in fact, where it assumes we are all going to read, digest and understand (in the end) its 'meaning' as a glittering nugget of truth. Its aesthetic leaves the reader neatly trimmed of all doubts and questions about its status in the World. It is a poem for which there is no Society (to coin the great lady's phrase), because it doesn't believe in dialogue but offers transparency as dialogue's placebo. Only the individual reader, fully-formed exists, reflected in the poem's self-contained aura or mirror. Fortunately, the World isn't like this: we can't sit satisfied in the knowledge of a confirmed (and conformed) narrative about ourselves. The World is more random, complex, uncertain than that. Half the time we don't know who we really are, where we are going, or what any of it means whether it be poems, a day at work, what our friends or partners really feel and think, or what a politician is really on about. I think poems are there to challenge these easy interfaces with our culture, and that is their essential, necessary and political function. And I suppose that is a way of answering your question. *Night Shift* graphs or records a struggle to understand and offer questions of some of these issues, whilst refusing to offer pat solutions. *Night Shift* tries, I think, to keep things on the move.

DUNCAN I know you and Rees were at university together. Can we revisit your time at Canterbury? Was it a beneficial place for young poets?

SMITH As I said earlier, the syllabus was not what you'd usually expect of a University either then or now. It basically looked at High Modernism dominated by Pound, Eliot, Williams etc, and then followed that strand to Olson Black Mountain, New York and the San Francisco Renaissance and the British Modernisms of Prynne, Mottram, Roy Fisher, Bunting. There was no room for the pack of lies about the failure of Modernism from Auden onwards and the re-establishment of neo-Georgianism, Realism and all the other shit that's come since. Like we're supposed to be relieved.

Michael Grant, Andrew Ross and Simon St Clair-Terry made the experience all the more bearable and gave us a good foundation. So I think it was a pretty good place to be; but I think from what Kelvin Corcoran and Ian Davidson have told me Essex might have been better. I might have got on track sooner, but I might not have explored other by-ways as well.

But I'm not knocking Canterbury, I loved it. And I found the great Rees. We met through the minute Art Scene, and soon became a two-man band. It was at the Art Soc. opening party and we went back to his room where he had nicked a brie from High Table the previous evening. This was conveniently melted over the floor of his room, running everywhere. It was love at first sight. In the corner was an easel and in the other a black white tv, sound ALWAYS turned down. We talked (as you do at 19 or 20) till dawn then I crashed out on the floor; I lived in Whitstable at the time so the seven mile walk wasn't appealing, especially when you could rise at midday and start all over again. God knows how I got any work done, but I did. David didn't and gained a 'gentleman's degree' at the end of the year; still, it never seemed to set him back. But I learned one Hell of a lot about Norman and Gothic architecture and a love of English churches that continues to this day. David's knowledge is encyclopedic and breathtaking, as is his wit, humour and capacity for alcohol. I learnt how to drink, essential for poetry. We spent day after day around the Cathedral, St Augustine's Abbey, St Martin's Church, Reculver. Remarkable, wonderful, intelligent. It's where I learnt about aesthetics.

And then in the vacations, being both Essex boys we used to meet up in Town and do the galleries. I remember a Michael Andrews exhibition D loved and a Pissarro one he hated, both at the Hayward. Then there were the trips into what became Docklands before the Yuppies got hold of it. Mostly this was to savour industrial architecture, but also the pubs, with a different architecture and aesthetics, those of pub talk and atmosphere.

DUNCAN We've talked in the past about there being no masterpieces since *White Stones*. How do you feel about that? What's happened in poetry over the last 20 years?

SMITH I feel pretty down about it: imagine what it must have been like with 60s counter-culture and all that and great poetry too. 1969 was the last great year, and I'm no hippy. Then you get *The White Stones*, *The Small Henderson Room*, *Walking on Grass*, for High Culture too. You'd be spoilt, giddy.

The last twenty years are quite another matter; I suppose the last nail in the coffin of late British Modernism was *The Penguin Book of Contemporary British Poetry*, where the 60s and 70s are whitewashed over, erased at a stroke, and the general reading public would believe it because they were in no position to know better. There's the tragedy: British poetry set back seventy years. The products of publishers like Penguin or Faber were taken on trust, these were the brand leaders, and nowhere is there a section of the Capitalist market more ruled by brands than poetry, because of the fear of lack of authenticity. Nobody really knows if this poetry stuff is the real shit or not, that's the problem.

But all I'm seeing here are the negatives. I want to talk about the books that turned things around for me: like John Seed's *History, Labour, Night* (Pig Press, 1984); Prynne's *Oval Window* (the last volume by him I really connect with); Peter Riley's *Ospita*; Denise Riley's *Mop Mop Georgette*; John Riley's *Collected Works* (there we are all the Riley's in a row); all of Kelvin Corcoran's work; your *Knife Cuts the Water*; Raworth's *Eternal Sections* and *Tottering State* (the Paladin edition). What John Muckle was doing at Paladin was a god send; and I'd have to say the *new british poetry* did little short of change my life. I think Peter Riley's Poetical Histories series was very important through the late 8os and up to now for sampling new and unfamiliar work. Connections are made here between Prynne, Nicholas Moore, Dorian Cooke and through to Kelvin, Helen MacDonald, Peter Hughes, Geoff Ward. *Knife Cuts the Water* was the first place I made a connection with your work, Andrew. But for younger poets further afield like Helen there was also Andrew Webster and Khalid Hakim—I wish they'd publish more, quirky, funny, full of wit anger and barbs. Then there's Tim Atkins little book *Sonnets*. Great stuff. And Dave Rees's *The London,* painful in conception from the late 8os—worked over and over again. But I don't see these as masterpieces; I think the next generation needs to decide that for themselves. Masterpieces are posthumous.

But there are loads of American new poets I think are the best and most exciting: Mark Wallace is one, Chris Stroffolino another then the brilliant if flawed *Swoon* by Nada Gordon and Gary Sullivan. That was my favourite book last year. And this year it has to be John James's Collected.

Will this do, Andrew, for the last 20 years?

DUNCAN I was taken aback by John Seed's remark that Wyatt was one of his three great influences. Can you talk about your interest in Raleigh? What do you think the influence of those 16th century poets, Raleigh, Spenser, Wyatt, has been?

Those unmodernised spelling quotes lead us unto *Fifteen Exits.* Tell us the story of *Fifteen Exits.*

SMITH Well, it seems to me that any writer should be interested in excellent writing no matter how old it is. I think a sense of the history and tradition you are coming from is vital; I don't see how you could write anything any good without it. Raleigh's important to *Fifteen Exits* for the same reasons that Blaise Cendrars is or de Nerval. Journeys and travels are a strand that runs through the book. Raleigh's journeys to the Americas were all very real, whereas Cendrars and de Nerval, well, the veracity of quite what they actually did is questionable. I wanted to experiment with the journey across the page and through the imagination: it's always puzzled me quite why do people have to do all these exotic holidays to Third World countries when the real land of wonder lies between your own ears. Still, I digress. For me Raleigh is also very important because of the politics of Royal patronage and this is particularly true of the 'Ocean to Cynthia'.

That whole period was a time when poetry mattered, really mattered because it was one of the ways you got on in life and politics. They were all doing it from gentleman and nobles like Spenser, Sidney etc. to the upstart grammar school boy Shakespeare. It was one route to a place above your station. What is amusing and poignant is Raleigh's rehashing of verses for James I's wife from a fragment for the 'Ocean'—he must have been desperate. It obviously wasn't sent or didn't wash, and he ended up in the Tower for 10 years before being despatched on the suicide mission to Guyana by James I.

Fifteen Exits. It all seems a long way off now, I started it in April 1995 and it wound down in New Year 1998, really of its own accord. I set myself some arbitrary rules, like the dates (which are completely accurate), the dedications and some of the stricter verse forms. I felt I needed to ground the text at some sort of level of the real. So you can read it as a kind of poetic diary: you know exactly what I was doing between 11th September 1996 and the 15th November of the same year. But how much of a help that is for understanding the poems, well, I think it might just point up the inadequacy of chronology when dealing with texts. Early on I wanted to show I could write in so called 'traditional' verse forms: after the New Gen nonsense all the poets of that camp were very keen to show off their genuine credentials, by writing sonnets and villanelles and stuff. I thought, hold on, I can do that, but how about if I don't write about peeling wallpaper, or how screwed up my personal life is. I wanted to play around. Of course O'Hara and Ashbery and Koch and Schuyler did this in the fifties, so it's nothing new. But the two 'big' poems, 'Blue Earth' and 'Red Border' are the heart of the thing and where I developed the 'method' of the book. And this is where *Fifteen Exits* is the antithesis of *Reverdy Road.* Above the dedication is a note of the number of takes it took to get to the one you see in the book. Basically I went and sat in Gaby's Restaurant in the Charing Cross Road for nearly three years every lunch time with an hour to redraft from scratch, at each sitting, the WHOLE poem from start to finish. Later on I might tinker a bit, but each 'take' would be like a jazz take, different for that performance, but also a record of it. That's what I call 'performance' poetry! So although the book is a mere 43 pages it probably would be with its 'ghost' drafts 300–400 pages long. (Ghosts are important, I'll come back to that soon.) So the whole book is about building up a surface and tearing it down, building up and tearing down, like you might find a painter working in oils might do to give the sense of depth and texture to the flat surface. Thus the feeling of disjointing and dysfunction you experience through the text—particularly effective in the stricter verse forms as in 'Touch Wood' and 'Flowering Absent'.

'Red Border' was started on a freezing train journey to the Philip Larkin Archive in Hull on Poetry Library business, and it suddenly occurred to me I was travelling in the opposite direction to Larkin in the 'Whitsun Weddings' poem! The work is also re-working of Cendrars' 'Trans-Siberian': so Larkin and Cendrars, unlikely bedfellows, but I know who is the more modern and contemporary.

Then 'Flowering Absent'. I took the rhyming words from Shelley's 'Ode to the West Wind' and stripped out the rest of the poem, replacing it with what is there. Shelley's poem is five sonnets stuck together, but I only completed two before the Exits exited on me, and it was gone.

DUNCAN I didn't know Gaby's had this distinction. I wonder if they should have big showbiz glamour photos on their wall—D. S. Marriott and Simon Smith exchanging a celebrity embrace. Charles Bainbridge and David Rees giving celebrity smiles while eating goulash.

The School of Night took part in occult acts at Edmonton, according to a surely untrue rumour. One hears a lot, even in Edmonton, about the occult influence of a New York school. Can you confirm this? Who is in this school? What shape does its influence take?

SMITH The New York School are Frank O'Hara, John Ashbery, James Schuyler, Kenneth Koch and Barbara Guest. That's the first wave, from the 1950s. Then you have the Second Generation: Ted Berrigan, the brilliant Ron Padgett, Alice Notley, Bill Berkson, Bernadette Mayer and others.

New York has really come down to us, I'd say via poets like John James, Lee Harwood, Tom Raworth. And then there's what I take to be an interesting twist in contemporary U.S. poetry, as poets now in their 20s and 30s have revolted against the strictures and dead ends of L=A=N=G=U=A=G=E writing. I think poets like Chris Stroffolino, Mark Wallace, Gary Sullivan and Nada Gordon seem to want a line that is more immediate, fluid—a more friendly environment all in all. Most poets of the younger generations (I'm thinking of those under 45 in the main) on both sides of the Atlantic have had it with the rivalries and petty wars of the last thirty-odd years. I think we want to live in a society where people can exchange ideas and poems in a more relaxed, less loaded way. New York (and I'd suggest Jack Spicer too) offer a form of address that is less alienating, more friendly, but still exacting intellectually, and most important of all, intelligent. The re-emergence of Frank O'Hara and Ted Berrigan as leading lights has also washed over on to these shores too: Miles Champion, Tim Atkins, Ian Davidson, Kelvin Corcoran are evidently looking to poets like O'Hara and Berrigan. I think the influence of New York has freed things up both over there and over here: it's in the nature of the writing, I feel, to be open, welcoming, inclusive in a way much so-called avant-garde writing isn't. It also takes seriously the light, the flip and the humorous.

DUNCAN The environment for poets does tend to show itself concretely as little magazines, what they reject perhaps more than what they accept. It seems useful to approach this from the other side—the editor's story. Can you talk about your duties at *Grille* and *Angel Exhaust*?

SMITH Now you come on to an area of difficulty for me, Andrew. Magazines and editing. I started editing *GRIllE* in 1991 full of naïve enthusiasm. I had no ideology underpinning my strategy; I just wanted to publish poetry I valued and liked, and I was looking forward to the post each morning. But as the years went by and the post bag grew I became more and more dismayed. In two and a half years I received one publishable and exciting manuscript from an unknown writer: Richard Makin. That means virtually all the work I published was solicited, or from poets I already knew about and hadn't had a chance to invite to the party. Since my days editing I have come across one poet I really think worth reading, who has a few things now available in Jeremy Hilton's mag *Fire*, and that is Cat Simmonds, a young poet from Dorset. But all in all I found editing pretty time consuming, soul destroying and irritating. I found myself becoming ruthless and quite cynical in the end. I thought editing *Angel Exhaust* would be different, but it was actually more of the same thing. Poets and would-be contributors don't read poetry magazines and don't subscribe to them either. But I think this state of affairs is endemic to poetry, whichever school or ideology you support or peddle. There are too many poets and not enough readers. You have to be very noble I think to continue.

DUNCAN I do agree about the mail that reaches editors. The mainstream has a swollen head because the editors see thousands of junk applications which qualify them as the winners. But I wonder if we could consider the other side. Poets having a bad experience with rejections when we know, now, that they're really gifted. This sampling and rejecting is the central institution of poetry, and yet it's private and unrecorded.

A large-scale tuneful volume called *Reverdy Road* has just come out from Salt and hasn't been absorbed yet. Can you talk to us about *Reverdy Road*? Who is this Reverdy guy?

SMITH Pierre Reverdy was a French poet of the early and mid 20th Century of huge influence amongst the Dadaists and Surrealists; however, he is not the Reverdy of Reverdy Road, which does exist in London SE1, Bermondsey in fact, and would have been built by 1889, the year of the poet's birth. It wasn't until I started to translate Reverdy in the Spring of 2002 that I could see the lyrical detachment (not to say frostiness of the French poet) in the book unfolding. The disassociation of objects and perceptions in Reverdy's work started to make sense in the context of this new book. The interplay seemed quite uncanny in the classical Freudian sense. The book is a 'translation' or transmigration of Reverdy's work from a quite other place.

As I was saying earlier, *Reverdy Road* is the antithesis of *Fifteen Exits*. If *The Exits* were a layering of surfaces, the incomplete sum of innumerable 'takes', then with *Reverdy Road* I was (am) writing the poems out straight, and if they're good enough fine, if not, discard. They are very much of the moment of their composition, thus their vitality and drive forwards. I wanted to write using the vernacular as the starting point, a poetry without reference to its roots in past literatures or arcane cultural bullet points. So there are no epigraphs, no dedications or 'learned' references; there is little to weigh the poems down, instead they float off towards their own future, guided by the wind and weather. I wanted to write something that refracted light rather than reflected it. Distorting the realist narrative of Self seems to be the purpose of these poems; to challenge as creatively as I can the illusions of the descriptive anecdotal lyric, so strong and fashionable right now. I would warn the reader off a lazy interpretation, seeing these poems as a way in to the compensations of usual categories of representation. There is a chosen lexicon (although to choose sounds like a conscious decision: in fact what is going on is more a sense of what is fitting, what sounds and feels in place). Yet these poems are about the incidence of asymmetry and dissonance, and the aesthetic of chance. I like things that appear to be normal but are in reality dysfunctional, just like Life really. Things look like they happen to you for a reason, but most of the time there is no reason, unless you give that non-reason the name of God. Jack Spicer's esoteric accounts of the occult, linguistics and the Unconscious seem very relevant— I think the recent publication of his lectures a momentous event.

Reverdy Road is not a finished book: the three sections in the Salt volume I think of as being three discrete but related 'books'. I've been reading and studying Latin texts again over the last three or four years, translating Catullus, but looking at other poets too, so I see *Reverdy Road* as very much in the tradition of Martial's epigrams, although more in spirit than in intention or form particularly. In fact, the longest section, 'Xenia' (which takes its title from Martial's XIIIth book) isn't quite in the order it was originally, a good chunk of poems were taken out and are going to appear as *Mercury*—now the notional fourth book of *Reverdy Road*— from Rod Mengham's Equipage book series. Then there is more recent material in a further three sections, so even though the Salt book runs to 230-odd pages there is probably another 60 or 70 pages of poems unpublished or too new to gain a perspective on yet. The book isn't finished, but seems to unfold further and further towards the horizon.

The Salt volume starts from a far more domestic perspective (perhaps that is there in *The Exits* too, but not fore-grounded, I'm thinking of 'The Nature of Things' and 'Friday, 21st April')—in *Reverdy Road* I wanted the freshness of the now. It also gains energy, I think, from its speed of composition; all these poems have been written since March 2001, which means even excluding the translation work and essays, I've composed on average a poem every 72 hours for two years! Not that I have done, most of the work comes in groupings of four to six at a sitting, related and looped through time, ghosting, if you like. This might sound flip, but I'll sound arrogant instead: there are 20 years of thought, writing and thinking about writing pressured behind the composition and text of *Reverdy Road*.

I wanted a rough, provisional feel to the poems I'm composing now, I wanted the sense of contingency of falling forward—where? Into the next poem of course! Some people, David Rees, for instance, see the book as very much a notebook or sketchbook, and I'm happy with that view—I much prefer the sketches and drawings of Constable to the finished 'product' of the paintings.

DUNCAN Perhaps we could talk about translation now.

SMITH Translation is an activity I've come to very late, and it all happened out of a situation of complete personal despair. After two years of the best relationship I'd ever had up to then, I was left homeless, and all sense of my life rendered provisional by the break up. So everything went, except my job and the loyalty and support of a few friends. I couldn't write at all and had really hit a brick wall with the project I'd been working on, *More Ammo*. So I gave up, or rather poetry gave up on me.

Then one day I was working on a query for a client at work, on Catullus. Catullus was the first writer I'd come across called 'poet' as a 12 year old at school, and I studied him through to 'O' level Latin. Anyway, this query was all about Poem 8—one of the famous ones—and I was looking through Guy Lee's translation that he'd done for OUP. In the main it is an excellent rendering, but there were various 'flat spots', as I saw them. In the main he let the poem sing, and allowed his work to become poetry, but then he would yank it back into a kind of scholarly translatorese. I suppose he was trying to fulfil his brief: to present a version of Catullus as useful for undergrads and school children as for the general reader. I had no such restrictions, and the luxury of time. To cut the story short: I found Guy Lee's translation very frustrating, not to say, disappointing, and it was a Friday afternoon, so I started to do my own version. And suddenly there it was. This was exciting, and I wasn't in a relationship and couldn't really afford to go out, so I went up the Charing Cross Road and bought up as much criticism, background reading and translations as I could find. And then I began.

Basically, translation became a distraction behaviour from personal misery and writer's block. And it worked very well for me, I became completely immersed in the minutiae of nuance and scholarship and history and culture of the period. In fact I started to live Catullus. I think that where I stand in the translation debate over literalism and poetics ought to be another conversation, but I do feel strongly that any translation ought to be able to stand as a poem on its own, but that Catullus has been very badly served, in the main, by poets and scholars alike. He is the most translated Latin poet of our age, and there are some brilliant translations too.

I'm not sure Catullus's sensibility is very much a 20th Century one: Ginsberg said once that O'Hara was our Catullus, and I think he was only half right about that. Catullus seems to speak very directly, but that view does rather ignore the design of many of the long poems and the vitriol of the later, shorter epigrams—alien I think to our age. The more you look at the œuvre, the more distant he seems to me to be from our times: it looks, if anything, less personal and more classical, more polished and impersonal. Recent scholarship seems to see the 116 poems as a whole; three libelli (little books) published as one whole work. If we accept that view, this slim volume becomes one of the wonders of the world. For me at least.

I'd been working on these translations for seven or eight months, then I found a new love, and within weeks I was working on *Reverdy Road*. I'm certain that book would not have happened without my work on Catullus too. Translation is a way of thinking out of your own space into somewhere quite alien, quite suffused with *la différance*. To find another mindset, and work through the problems of another writer is crucial, I think now, to freshening and sharpening one's own writing. The poet/translator's agenda must be different from that of the scholar and that is where they misunderstand one another.

It is vital, I think, to review and assess one's own praxis, and launch into another direction.

So, once I'd found the title for *Reverdy Road,* quite by coincidence, I was in conversation with Charles Bainbridge, a poet and work colleague, about French poetry, and we concocted this scheme to translate some poems of Pierre Reverdy. He did some and I did some too: he then quickly found Soupault more attuned to his needs and I wound up with Reverdy and did some more— simply because I thought I ought to know about his work. Of course that objectivity and impersonality of the so-called Cubist poet is relevant to the aesthetic of *Reverdy Road*—the disassociation, not of Eliotic sensibility but of objects, the quite random juxtapositions of things within sight and sound of one another. And that's translation.

Bibliography

North Star (Cambridge: Poetical Histories, 1992).
Night Shift (Kenilworth: Prest Roots Press, 1994).
Juicy Fruit (Cheltenham: Gratton Street Irregulars, 1999).
Fifteen Exits (Brighton: Waterloo Press, 2001).
Reverdy Road (Cambridge: Salt Publishing, 2003).
Mercury (Cambridge: Salt Publishing, 2006).

POEMS AND TRANSLATIONS IN:
Poetica, fragmente, Salt, Oasis, Shearsman, Salzburg Poetry Review, Angel Exhaust, Poetry Review, PN Review.

Printed in the United Kingdom
by Lightning Source UK Ltd.
131600UK00001B/313/A